Heartland Rising

Javed Gaya is a lawyer from Mumbai, specialising in commercial arbitration law. He studied jurisprudence at the University of Oxford and has taught law at colleges affiliated to the University of Mumbai. He contributes to various publications on topics including constitutional law, history and foreign affairs, and writes book reviews. He serves as a director on the boards of several companies.

Praise for *Heartland Rising*

'Narendra Modi's Hindu Rashtra cries out for a revisionist history of modern India to account for his success. Javed Gaya's fluent, forensic account of the consolidation of a majoritarian common sense in politics and the law over the last hundred years, is that indispensable book. In a world crowded with illiberal democracies, everyone should read it.'

— **Mukul Kesavan, Essayist, Former Professor of History, Jamia Millia Islamia, and Author of *Ugliness of the Indian Male and Other Propositions***

'A detailed and fascinating analysis not only of the making of India's constitution and its law of citizenship, but of the various controversies and judgements that have come to define citizenship differently for Hindus and Muslims. An entirely unique book.'

— **Faisal Devji, Beit Professor of Global and Imperial History, University of Oxford**

'At a time of rising sectarianism and alarming hate-fuelled attacks on minority communities, it is inspiring and deeply edifying to read Javed Gaya's beautifully lucid and profoundly erudite book. His exploration of the current "architecture of hate" in contemporary India deserves a very wide audience.'

— **Jacqueline Bhabha, Professor of the Practice of Health and Human Rights, Harvard Kennedy School**

'A tour d'horizon of Indian politics with a passionate and clearly articulated argument. A very serious and learned book that will be of interest to the broader intelligentsia and to specialists on South Asia.'

— **Uday Singh Mehta, Distinguished Professor of Political Science, CUNY Graduate Center**

'A sobering read. Gaya offers a stark picture of how Partition cemented the sweeping effects of majoritarianism on almost all aspects of the social, cultural and political mechanisms of the post-colonial Indian state.'

— **Pallavi Raghavan, Assistant Professor of International Relations, Ashoka University, and Author of** ***Animosity at Bay: An Alternative History of the India-Pakistan Relationship, 1947–1952***

Heartland Rising

THE MAKING OF MAJORITARIAN INDIA

JAVED GAYA

cntxt

First published as *Majoritarianism in India: Roots and Consequences* in the United Kingdom by C. Hurst & Co. (Publishers) Ltd. in 2025

Published as *Heartland Rising: The Making of Majoritarian India* by Context, an imprint of Westland Books, a division of Nasadiya Technologies Private Limited, in 2026

No. 269/2B, First Floor, 'Irai Arul', Vimalraj Street, Nethaji Nagar, Alapakkam Main Road, Maduravoyal, Chennai 600095

Westland, the Westland logo, Context and the Context logo are the trademarks of Nasadiya Technologies Private Limited, or its affiliates.

ISBN: 9789379851383

10 9 8 7 6 5 4 3 2 1

The views and opinions expressed in this work are the author's own and the facts are as reported by him, and the publisher is in no way liable for the same.

Typeset by Mukul

Printed at Parksons Graphics Pvt. Ltd

To my wife, Farah, who has stood by me during the preparation of the book and its editing, and in memory of my late father, M.K. Gaya, Bar-at-Law, who witnessed the trauma of Partition and the division of his family.

'If, for example, we had to accept the principle of numerical superiority while selecting our national bird, our choice would have fallen not on the peacock but the common crow!'

—C.N. Annadurai, while objecting to the South adopting Hindi as the official language[1]

CONTENTS

INTRODUCTION

A skewed version of nationalism has emerged and captured the national narrative in such an extraordinary way that one cannot escape it in contemporary India. It is ubiquitous—one cannot turn on the television, read a newspaper, expose oneself to social media or indeed traverse an urban centre without seeing signs and images pullulating all over, bearing the visage of the prime minister, accompanied by some trope symbolising national pride. The obverse of such national pride is hatred of the other, and that too is unfortunately all too pervasive, with rampant Islamophobia in evidence. One sees evidence of this in cinemas where films which extol patriotism and courage in warfare score well at the box office, and on TV channels which toe a passionately Islamophobic and anti-liberal narrative to earn huge TRPs. Where did this version of nationalism arise from? What are its consequences? What is its history, and where does one locate its geography? These, I think, are relevant questions to ask.

It is useful at this point to recall an architecture of hate documented by the French philosopher, Julien Benda, who in his famous work *La Trahison des Clercs* observed, 'Our age is indeed the age of the intellectual organisation of political hatreds. It will be one of its chief claims to notice in the moral history of humanity.' Benda was writing in the 1920s and was profoundly disturbed by what he saw as a retreat from the universal values of the Enlightenment to what he considered the valorisation of various particularisms, not dissimilar to the growth of identity politics in India and the attempt to vacate a Constitution founded substantially on home-grown, liberal values similar to those of the Enlightenment. Benda's angst was directed against the intellectuals who he felt should give moral guidance, but were now instrumental in whipping up nationalist frenzies which he correctly predicted would lead to the 'greatest and most perfect war ever seen in the world.'[1] This was highly prescient as it predicted the Second World War, a war that led to the Holocaust and the explosion of the first nuclear device over Japan.

In his famous essay, *Is Hatred Essential for Nationalism?,* Gandhi repudiates the idea that hatred is essential to nationalism, stating that: 'We see that this song of hate has not benefited humanity. Let it be the privilege of India to turn a new leaf and set a lesson to the world.'[2] Indeed, the liberal nationalism of the late nineteenth century spoke of constitutional reforms, rather than spouting xenophobic rhetoric. Moderate leaders Mahadev Govind Ranade and Gopal Krishna Gokhale were keen on national regeneration through social reform. Even the nationalism of those such as Bhagat Singh, who advocated violence against the colonial rulers, was not jingoistic. According to historian S. Irfan Habib, 'It was embedded in the idea of progress where there is scope for criticism, disbelief and the capacity to question everything of the old faith.'[3] Certainly, if Bhagat Singh was alive, he would be appalled at today's toxic nationalism and Islamophobia.

It is the argument of this book that much of the hatred apparent today owes to the ideology that created the Partition and was located in the United Provinces (present-day Uttar Pradesh, also UP). As a consequence of Partition, the 'cow belt' was elevated as the political fulcrum of India, allowing it to occupy centre stage. UP redefined Indian nationalism in its image as it sought to project itself as the simulacrum of India. The 2024 elections, in some respects, altered little since the North–South fissure continues, as does the marginalisation of minorities.

The arguments for this nationalism are dependent on the most assiduous of myth-making. I say myth-making, as what is often the dynamic of the nationalisms prevalent in the subcontinent and what sustains them, is not history but, in fact, a carefully curated mythology which seeks to dignify them with the vestiges of intellectual respectability. In the words of philosopher Ernest Gellner, 'Nationalism is not the awakening of nations to self-consciousness: it invents nations where they do not exist ... it sometimes takes pre-existing cultures and turns them into nations, sometimes invents them, and often obliterates pre-existing cultures.' Nationalisms, thus, invariably predate nations, and a mythical golden age is often conjured as a fig leaf to hide an opportunistic nationalistic agenda which is self-serving for those in power.

The idée fixe of seeking to impose the idea of a homogenised, centralised nation-state in the European sense on a diverse, multi-religious, multi-ethnic and variegated society was one which seduced the first generation of politicians with the promise of equality and liberty. This schema has morphed into a virulent nationalism, an intellectual cul-de-sac, compelling the government to use all the instruments of imperial power, sedition laws, restriction on assembly and freedom of speech to impose its puissance. In this process, the idealism of the Left and the liberals has long been discarded, and the narrowness, parochialism, cultural aridity and faux religiosity of the Hindu Right have been elevated and valorised as integral to this nationalism. And yet, the cultural legacies of the past—caste divisions and communal antagonisms—persist, perhaps intensified by the territorial reconfiguration wrought by Partition, and now fuel an increasingly toxic politics.

I think it is instructive to recall an earlier expansive and heady cosmopolitanism that transcended these narrow nationalistic projects, which, as the Stoic philosopher Seneca put it, sought 'to measure the boundaries of our State by the sun.'[4] I consider that this idea of an abiding humanity and a cultural capaciousness is being diminished and lost to a nationalism insistent on denying not just history and cultural plurality, but the very essence of politics. This is a dangerous fixation, as Daniel Patrick Moynihan, former New York senator, observed, 'The central conservative truth is that it is culture, not politics, that determines the success of a society. The central liberal truth is that politics can change a culture and save it from itself.' Indian civilisation and society in 1947 were mired in a stagnant culture dominated by caste, custom and tradition, and needed reform. Freedom was seen by many as the opportunity to transform a society in decay into one aligned with modernity. The idea that transformative politics based on constitutionalism was the dynamo for social and cultural change lay at the heart of the Indian political project in the early years.

In any view, the constitution has not brought about the transformation hoped for in those early years. And its failure has had catastrophic consequences. The contagion of excessive religiosity and unreason has infected the subcontinent, displacing the liberal values, which were being embraced and enforced in terms of rights-based legislation, widening substantive entitlements through affirmative action to many who had been deprived of them, even if in a nominally liberal political matrix. I will not say 'secular' because India, from its inception, has subscribed to a peculiar compromise of a pseudo-secularism, which purported to attenuate religiosity, and has sought to privilege science and modernity. These were the values derived from the Bengali Renaissance, from Rabindranath Tagore, Raja Ram Mohan Roy and others, although the fetish for science is most identified with Nehru.

The burden of this book is to show how prejudice and ignorance on an epic scale can result in dysfunctional societies and failed states. Pakistan is a striking example of this phenomenon, a 'Muslim Zion',[5] a Frankensteinian monster, born of a confessional failure to agree on how minorities could be accommodated with meaningful autonomy and agency, with space for the practice of their cultural and religious rights. I argue that it was this reluctance to share power and afford political space to the minority—combined with the complicity of the Hindu Right as well as with the idealistic jejuneness of the Left in helping Jinnah find a solution which was unsatisfactory to all parties including himself—that led to the extreme ghettoisation of Muslims and the creation of Pakistan.

Partition resolved nothing, it only externalised the Hindu–Muslim question, but pointedly did not address its causes. It arguably wrecked a fragile communal equipoise on the subcontinent and was wholly destructive of a federal future as this book will demonstrate. Much of what is wrongly ascribed to Fabian socialism derives from a pervasive and suffocating statist culture emanating from the 'cow belt'. This was surcharged by a parochial and inward-looking mercantile class, insulated from serious taxation through the device of the Hindu Undivided Family (HUF), which was instrumental in setting an economic agenda to guarantee stagnation and deepen inequalities.

I do not propose to belabour the effects of geography, but in India, culture matters, caste matters, religion and language matter, and all this is indissolubly tied to geography. So, one cannot disregard these factors, particularly the historical role of the 'cow belt', its damaging influence in the recent past and its capacity for destabilising the national narrative by its implacable ideology, sheer size, population and political heft—factors that assume portentous significance in the current scenario. At the time of writing, the 'cow belt' has hijacked the future of India and, by the same token, the subcontinent, and has lured it into a Stygian cesspool of casteism and communalism and an unending round of grievance politics, distracting from the real issues of governance. The 2024 elections have shown the limitations of this kind of politics, but it may prove to be a false dawn. UP continues to be governed by a chief minister whose views on minorities are coloured by revanchism and the ideology itself continues to have traction.

In fact, the matter of the constitutional arrangements of the electorate comes into sharp relief when you have a large percentage of people belonging to all classes, who are susceptible to being swayed by religious sentiments leading to polarisation. This has been an issue from the very inception of the Indian constitution, regardless of whether equality or freedom prevailed. It has been pointed out incisively by Faisal Devji, professor of imperial history, that whether you have the freedom to practise your religion or you proceed on the principle of equality, where the State seeks to stipulate the equal treatment of religious and racial communities, the concepts of freedom and equality are mutually antagonistic. As he argues, there arose a

> disagreement between those Indians who thought that political liberty should precede social equality and bring it about, and others who feared that such a liberty would only perpetuate inequality by empowering majorities and the powerful at

> the expense of minorities and the powerless. This difference characterised not only the relations between religious communities, primarily Hindus and Muslims, who had been the primary addressees of the Queen's Proclamation, but also came to define those between higher and lower castes as well.[6]

The point that Professor Devji is making is of seminal importance, that political representation in a multi-religious and multi-ethnic people's territory need not be based on the 'One man, one vote' mantra, but rather on one that recognises communities—religious, ethnic and linguistic—and seeks their empowerment by ensuring representation and opportunity. That may be through separate electorates, federalism, proportional representation, reserved seats and any number of other devices to subserve the larger purpose of guaranteeing equality and diversity. At any rate, the purpose would, in the words of supreme court lawyer Saurabh Kirpal, mean 'equality of outcome as opposed to equality of opportunity.'[7]

The quest for equality between communities has been displaced by the sedulous consolidation of the majority community through preferential expansion in reservations in government jobs and educational institutions for Other Backward Classes (OBCs). This is particularly evident in UP, where there is an audacious experiment afoot to replicate the caste system in reservations. It has the dual advantage of excluding minorities altogether as well as devaluing the worth of reservations for the Scheduled Castes/Tribes. This has been accompanied by the erosion and evisceration of independent institutions and individual rights, given that some problematical issues—such as preventive detention, sedition, blasphemy and the power to declare emergencies during which constitutional rights can be suspended—were built into the Constitution at the outset.

But constitutional principles matter far less than political expediency. The fact that India adopted a constitutional democracy with fundamental rights and judicial review was remarkable. At the time, minorities bartered away their special rights and privileges, such as separate electorates and reservation, on the basis that certain fundamental rights would be protected by the Constitution and by the courts in the event that legislatures attempted to infringe upon them. What has happened, however, as will be seen in the course of this book, is that their hopes have been belied and their constitutional safeguards have foundered.

As I will show in the pages that follow, the Brahmin lobby in the erstwhile United Provinces was unwavering in its desire to largely eradicate the region's composite culture, even if that meant the denial of constitutional rights to minorities, relating to language, diet and employment. The insistence on these matters upends the notion of a pluralistic society. Russian-British philosopher Isaiah Berlin, in his famous lectures on 'Two Concepts of Liberty',[8] controversially condemns a positive State agenda for social and economic liberties for being a potential road to totalitarianism, but lauds the negative liberty of being left alone, of the State not intruding on matters which are judged to be personal, such as what we eat or what we wear. Even this limited notion of liberty has been brutally eviscerated.

Unfortunately, from the earliest period, the Indian government has shown an incorrigible disregard for people's autonomy to conduct their own lives, treating an ambulatory notion of hurting the sentiments of other people, which is invariably the majority sentiment, as being the litmus test of acceptability. In a way, this is far more detrimental to civil liberties than even a theocracy, wherein at least you know when you have transgressed the limits. The notion of people's sentiments being hurt is so vague and amorphous that books, opinions and films can suddenly instigate people to violence, causing public disorder for the flimsiest and most facile of reasons.

So, it is not obvious that constitutional safeguards can be treated as sacrosanct within the current political matrix. A study of the Indian supreme court addressing controversial issues such as cow slaughter, the right to convert, and the role of religion in electioneering, as well as the attempt to distinguish what is the essence of religion in determining social practices, gives little hope to minorities in India. In most cases, the views of the court invariably align with the majority sentiment.

Political scientist Francis Fukuyama has argued that national identities can 'be built around liberal and democratic values and the common experiences that provide the connective tissue around which diverse communities can thrive. India, France, Canada and the United States are examples of countries that have tried to do this.'[9]

One of the objectives of politics is to create consensus and unity, but in the pursuit of what was described as 'nation building', that goal has been abandoned. As Fukuyama maintains, 'national identity is built around the legitimacy of this contract; if citizens do not believe they are part of the same polity, the system will not function.'[10] He also draws a parallel between America during the Civil War and present-day Modi's India, stating that the shifting of the national identity to one based on Hinduism invites communal violence.[11] According to political scientist Amrita Basu, there is a clear correlation between incidents of communal violence and the ability of Hindu nationalist organisations to flourish.[12]

It is not as though India has not already contained and ghettoised certain regions, or stigmatised people as outsiders in areas seen as lying beyond the perceived mainstream, such as Kashmir and the Northeast. But this may be only a harbinger of what is to come. A triumphalist Hindu, Hindi-speaking majority with the political heft to push through a unifying project to reshape India in the simulacrum of UP and Bihar will encounter opposition from states in the south and the east, which have shown unwillingness to cooperate in this schema, and trigger cultural flashpoints which the Nehruvian settlement contained, causing cultural wars similar to those in the US to erupt.

It is curious to note that in one of the most salient and protracted of international conflicts that continues to plague international relations, that is the Israel–Palestine dispute, the Indian position in 1949 as expressed in the United Nations was that there should be a federal solution with the explicit and legal protection of minority rights within an undivided Palestine—the so-called 'Nehru plan'.[13] Pluralism would have trumped the nationalist obsession. It is regrettable that this attitude was not adopted by the Congress in the 1930s, as we would not now have to live within the South Asian reality of a three-state solution.

Federalism is a nomenclature without substance as the centre has misused constitutional devices to undermine the autonomy of the states, and we appear to be trapped in a colonial stranglehold, which is obsessed with power for power's sake and not with the development of an architecture that enables improving the quality of governance and the distribution of public goods. In many respects, there is much we can learn from China and the autonomy it gives to local authorities. Instead, the last decade has shown a consistent appropriation of powers from the states to the Centre in an unprecedented fashion. In this respect, the 2024 election is a pushback to this insidious centralisation, with the voters of West Bengal, Tamil Nadu and Karnataka rejecting the discriminatory treatment meted out by the Centre and, in general, regional parties have emerged as winners at the cost of the National Democratic Alliance (NDA). This is one silver lining in the recent polls.

The bizarre apathy apparent in political discourse is profoundly worrisome given the fact that the subcontinent is facing serious existential challenges on many fronts, not least in terms of the ravages of climate change, water scarcity, poverty (in some cases below that of Sub-Saharan Africa), unequal access to education and health, gender discrimination, the unravelling of rule of law and the choking of media. Instead of staring at the coming abyss, the people of the subcontinent appear to be transfixed by issues of staggering banality. Ironically, the democratic model we have adopted only serves to accentuate this nationalism, as there are no serious checks and balances on executive power.

For one, if we look at the subcontinent, including Bangladesh and Nepal, by 2030 it will house nearly one-third of the world's population. Both India and Pakistan are nuclear powers, and it is entirely plausible that we may see an apocalyptic presentiment if these two countries, armed with the latest nuclear technology and wedded to a politics derived from tribalism and medieval constructs, engage in conflict. While this in itself is hugely disturbing, there is a further feature which needs to be considered—the struggle between India and China, another nuclear-armed country, over a serious and seemingly intractable border dispute which has festered for years without any obvious resolution.

The constitutional arrangements arrived at post Partition are largely responsible for this predicament that has overtaken the republic. There was too much faith in constitutional expedients and centralisation of power to effect social reforms without consideration for the possibility that such centralisation could stifle democracy. The

Constitution may have paid lip service to the idea of federalism, but it is in effect unitary in its form and effect. This was, in part, because of Ambedkar's legerdemain in creating 'the flexible Constitution'. The geographical landscape of the country after Partition privileged the 'cow belt', particularly UP, which has given India the maximum number of prime ministers. There are few constitutional safeguards; the Rajya Sabha is only a mirror image of the size of the states, unlike in the US, where each state has equal representation. The judiciary has been ineffectual in placing any serious check on the executive. We also have a first-past-the-post system of electoral democracy which favours the party that gets the most number of votes at the cost of minority representation. All these factors surcharge an increasingly centralised and authoritarian government and induce a political culture which takes its lead from states such as UP, a process that will only be turbocharged by delimitation if that happens in 2026, in which case UP will almost double its representation in parliament by reason of the size of its population.

So, India is in danger of being consumed by the past, by the banshees of Partition, by unresolved matters for which only history has the answers, by an indomitable refusal to revisit choices made in the 1940s for which we are paying the price today. The Cabinet Mission Plan was the last opportunity to retain a unified India, one that was properly federal. It was repudiated by the Congress with the support of many on the Left. But it is perplexing that public intellectuals do not revisit these decisions with the same vigour that pseudo-intellectuals of the new nationalism do, curating a mythology aligned with the political narrative. Theirs is unfailingly a threnody of humiliation, of manufactured grievances—an elaborate stratagem to deflect from the reality of a society which is grotesque in its social and economic inequalities, where historic vestiges of a sclerotic and suffocating casteism overlap a burgeoning crony plutocracy. The brutal fact is that the richest 1 per cent of Indians are in 2025 as rich, if not richer, than they were in colonial times.

PART I

THE ROAD TO PARTITION

1

THE MYTH OF ETERNAL INDIA

The attempt to impose a civilisational basis on a territorial state is always fraught with difficulties, and unfortunately, there has been an insistence both by Nehruvian thinkers and the protagonists of Hindutva to assume a civilisational basis for the existence of the Indian state—the former with inclusivity, the latter with a desire on the basis of religion. To sustain this fantasy, myths have to be created and history re-written. In this process of seeking to replicate the Western paragon of a nation-state, aspects of what one can call the Indic civilisation get lost, such as the huge and enduring impact it had on Southeast Asia where many overtly Hindu festivals and ceremonies still have relevance in countries like Thailand and Indonesia.

Political scientist Partha Chatterjee makes a seminal distinction between States and nations. He argues that the Mauryas, the Guptas and the Mughals were States, as they were 'held together by military force and tribute-paying arrangements', whereas a nation exists and is developed by its people. It is the very notion of sovereignty of the people that defines the nation. This does not necessarily mean that only democracies can be nations, but rather that the locus of validation and legitimacy must indubitably be popular consent. Chatterjee puts it succinctly, 'Without the claim to popular sovereignty, there can be no nation-state or Rashtra. Therefore, all nations are modern.'[1] This argument confronts the one about a civilisational state, making the point that it is superfluous to nationhood.

British India was, in fact, a colonial project involving a certain level of arbitrariness, with no obvious cultural or civilisational cohesion in its delineation of boundaries as there is in the case of the nation-states of Europe, such as England, France and Spain. There had been large concessions to the princely states of India, with some 562 states[2] constituting nearly one-third of the geographical area of India. These states remained outside of British India but still accepted the paramountcy of the Crown. It was not obvious that such disparate areas would necessarily want to join the nationalist project or that the rulers of such princely states would be willing to concede their sovereignty to the popular will and merge with the constitutional democracy that was to become India.

So, if this desire for nationhood eclipsed any close approximation of a distinct civilisation or territory, then the very idea of India—which nationalists wrote about in the most sentimental and roseate language—remained inchoate. In *A Nation Calling for a Home*,[3] Dr B.R. Ambedkar opens a paragraph meditating on the shame the Hindu would feel if India was not a nation. He states,

> In a world where nationality and nationalism were deemed to be special virtues in a people, it is quite natural for the Hindu to feel … that it would be [as] improper for India to be without a nationality as it would be for a man to be without clothes in a crowded assembly.

He elegantly points out that nationalism predates nations and how the former was a necessary construct of the twentieth century. Writer Salman Rushdie, in his Booker prize-winning book *Midnight's Children*, described the India of 1947 as the new myth of the year of Independence, 'a mythical land, a country which will never exist except by the efforts of a phenomenal collective will—except in a dream we all agreed to dream.' This may sound extravagantly whimsical, but in the light of Ambedkar's insightful pronouncement, it is very apposite. Self-determination was the prevailing credo and such self-determination was confused with cultural nationalism.

The problem really arises when there is an attempt to give substance and credence to the idea of the existence of an ancient eternal India as a nation-state. The very term 'India' derives from the Arabic term 'Hind', which in turn derives from the narrower term 'Sindh', which in Sanskrit means 'frontier'. But, in fact, there were no clear delineations as to the territorial limits of 'Hind'. Indian historian Sanjay Subrahmanyam identifies the argument that most nationalists seem to peddle, calling it 'the notion that at some distant point in the past, say about AD 500, the concept of "Indian civilisation" had already been perfected. Everything of any importance was in place: social structure, philosophy, the major literary works.'[4] So, if a civilisation was well in place, it was a small step to suggest that Indian civilisation amounted to a nation-state. This, at least, is what the nationalists subscribe to, including Nehru in his book *The Discovery of India*.[5]

The Borders of a 'Bharatvarsha'

The idea of an ancient India, 'Bharatvarsha', and its inhabitants have come under scrutiny from B.D. Chattopadhyaya, a serious historian who has examined many of the ancient texts and inscriptions only to extirpate this fallacy of an eternal India. In *The Concept of Bharatavarsha,*[6] he deconstructs the idea of a 'bharatvarsha' with references to ancient texts and inscriptions as well as to rudimentary geographical concepts. Chattopadhyaya concludes that the terms 'swadesa' (one's own country) or 'videsa' (a foreign country) would be of no relevance in the context of 'bharatvarsha'. The notions of a border or a frontier were absent, as, historically, there was no serious distinction between outsiders and local inhabitants. Chattopadhyaya concludes 'that the major divide in Indian society was perceived through the angle of "varna" (caste) which made the all-important difference between those within it and those without it.' It is all too easy to superimpose Western geographical and political concepts retrospectively, and, for the sake of convenience, ignore what was relevant to the people of the time. The renowned historian of Indian nationalism, Sir Christopher Bayly, understood the Hindu conceptualisation of geography to mean that 'bharatvarsha' was a 'sacred space'; it was emphatically not a territorial region with defined borders as is now widely assumed.

These assumptions persisted well into the nineteenth century. One of the signal signs of a sense of robust nationhood is the attitude towards foreigners or towards people not of the territory, which was never the case until relatively recently. Faisal Devji, writing on the Great Uprising of 1857, stated that:

> The English therefore do not seem to have been disliked for being foreigners at all, but only for breaking the moral compact that defined India as an empire of distinctions.[7]

The point being that the imperial push for proselytism was seen as objectionable by the Hindus and Muslims alike, and in doing so the English had crossed a line.

The true value of Chattopadhyaya's book, however, is how he interrogates the issue which forms the bedrock of much nationalist thinking: that ancient India approximated to a civilisational state. This was clearly the understanding of both Gandhi and Nehru. This was a convenient argument. It had the virtue of neatly sidestepping the controversial fact of medieval India and its Muslim conquests, as what was sought to be represented was a historic continuum which had been etiolated by the ravages of the Middle Ages and colonialism, but had now the opportunity to regenerate itself in the sunlight of freedom.

Chattopadhyaya is, however, dismissive of this single political construct of India and presents an analysis of regional cultures and how they came about. As he puts it, 'Modern regions like Bengal, Maharashtra or Rajasthan would not have existed throughout Indian history. Historical evidence and perspective therefore demand that we look for processes that went into the making of regions and the particular characteristics associated with them.'[8] He manifestly repudiates the construct of a superstructure and remarks that 'the perspective of looking at Indian civilisational entity from above will be turned upside down, and the effort should be made to look for the historical processes involved in making of the large entity rather than widely distributed sites of diversity as all derived from one tradition.'[9] Sanjay Subrahmanyam further explicates this and talks of a new homogeneity being founded in the early nineteenth century, attributing it largely to Western orientalists. In this context, the work of orientalists William Jones and H.T. Colebrooke is also relevant, as they sought to establish an overarching common origin of civilisations. As historian Dilip Menon remarks, 'It was in the Sanskrit texts that the real genius of India's Hindu past was looked for and not in the multitude of Hindu religious practices.'[10] To this extent, other popular Indian cultures which had strong roots in regions such as Bengal and Andhra Pradesh were discarded in favour of this fetish with high Brahminical culture. As Savarkar put it, there was a 'process of assimilation, elimination and consolidation,'[11] adumbrating what we call Hinduism.

It would not be incorrect to assume that many of these territories, which are now West Bengal, Orissa, Rajasthan and Andhra Pradesh, had distinct languages, histories and cultural traditions divergent from each other and would have had the basis to be regarded as independent sovereign entities, but for the colonial intervention. These facts sustain the argument that the normative position for a loose federal structure was very much in place post Mughal rule and the perception of eternal India as a single political construct, in the same way as imperial China becoming one under the Qing dynasty, is baseless and illusory.

2

THE COLONIAL STATE AND THE SACRED SPACE

It is thus necessary to question the paradigm of eternal India; at least as a territorial state in the Weberian sense prior to British rule. It is true that the Mughals left behind a compelling legacy of cultural and institutional cohesion, which historian Richard Eaton describes as being a result of co-opting the political authority of the Caliph, embracing the principle of universal justice and accommodating cultural diversity.[1] But it was the British who built on that foundation and located political authority within the matrix of a sovereign centralised structure, and significantly, within territorial boundaries. This process of drawing territorial boundaries was, as geographer Matthew Edney states,[2] an indubitably British exercise, placing their imperial interests in a position of paramount concern without any regard to Indian culture or religious sensibilities.

The notion of having a border in these colonial territories was very different from what it was back home in England. That arch imperialist and viceroy, Lord Curzon, was dismissive of the notion that India had any natural frontiers, and that was consistent with his dismissal of an Indian nationality. In his Romanes Lecture, *Frontiers*, at University of Oxford in 1907, he delineated the imperial frontiers as consisting of three layers. The first was administrative in nature. The second was the frontier of active protection. The third was an outer or strategic frontier. It was only within the administrative layer that the normative activities of a modern State occurred, such as the granting of property rights, their registration and protection, and the existence of legal and administrative paraphernalia that is associated with the infrastructure of the State.

The drawing of borders represented the grudging recognition of tribal rights by the colonial powers who would treat these areas as zones of native protection, occasionally enforcing its own sovereignty through random military expeditions, but largely leaving the tribals to themselves. This was certainly the case in the tribal areas of Assam as well as the area between Baluchistan and Kashmir called the North-West Frontier Province (now known as Khyber Pakhtunkhwa).

If one were to go back in history, there are, of course, rulers and dynasties which had dominion over large parts of North India (which would include Pakistan). The Mauryans, the Guptas and the Mughals had conquered the South up to the Deccan and the East to the extent of a border with Siam. But it was the British who exercised the widest sovereignty and legislated this in 1899, by sedulously transforming what had been a mere cultural adjective into a bounded territory. This putative nation's borders approximated pre-Partition India in large measure. For instance, the British annexed Assam in 1826 by defeating Burma and forcing the Treaty of Yandabo on the defeated Burmese.

Much of what we now call Arunachal Pradesh, including Tawang, is contested territory because of British incursions into Tibet and the claim that, at the time, Tibet was ruled by China under the Qing Dynasty, which is as plausible an argument as that India can claim Afghanistan because it was once ruled by Maharaja Ranjit Singh.

In the case of territories, which became part of independent India and Pakistan, the immediate concern of both governments was to stamp the imprimatur of sovereignty on these lands.

Atul Mishra, associate professor at Shiv Nadar University, writing on the fruits of Partition and the creation of the two States —both seemingly fixated on the chimera of sovereignty, a pursuit that can never be fully satisfied—argues that the quest for sovereignty becomes 'an end in itself.'[3] Sovereignty is not sought to be justified or validated by reference to the common good, in terms of better governance or more public goods. It is something which deprioritises the people, making them irrelevant to what is essentially and avowedly a statist trajectory that demands unquestioning loyalty and obeisance. In doing so, by removing people and their quotidian needs from the equation of governance, the requirement for accountability is also done away with. The fetish of territory disregards the people. We have already seen an example of this in Kashmir where, for the sake of a largely symbolic gesture—the abolition of Article 370 of the Indian constitution—a whole population living in the Valley had been incarcerated and denied the benefits of the internet, amongst other facilities, for over a year, without any persuasive reason.

In the other nation, Pakistan, the sovereignty argument is easy to spin as the threat to it from India is routinely trumpeted by the military and the media, even when the recent past has only shown the Pakistani army and its surrogates to be the aggressors. The Pakistani army has become the biggest beneficiary of this pervasive siege mentality, cornering power and land and controlling the narrative on foreign and defence policies. We also see the validatory role of religious zealots and entrepreneurs seeking to confer divine sanction on this Deep State. No lessons have been learnt from the policy towards East Pakistan, which resulted in the third partition of Bengal, as presently the Pakistan army appears to be imposing its writ in the most brutal manner in Baluchistan. Meanwhile, vast resources needed for public welfare, health and education are diverted to feed this obsessive fetish of protecting territory.

The apogee of the territorialisation argument of India's sacred space is, according to Atul Mishra,

> The iconography of '*Bharat Mata* or Mother India' produced through the divinisation and feminisation of the modern cartographic depiction of India. Superimposed on a modern map of India, the feminine and divine figure encompasses the entirety of India's expansive space ... it is the ultimate statement of a unified and organic sacred geography that needs to be jealously guarded by the children of the divine figure, who naturally belong to the majority religion.[4]

The logical consequence of this is that minorities are pointedly excluded from what is evoked as a sacred geographical configuration. The use of the figure of a goddess as emblematic of the territory is adroit as it summons a primeval symbolism redolent of sacrality, making the protection of such territory the sacred duty of the sons of the soil, treating any interloper with the same brutality one would a hapless perpetrator of 'love jihad'.

This disturbing iconography is confronted by the studied ambiguity of the nature of the Pakistani state which is at once a political entity as well as a religious one, reflecting the tension between those who envisaged Pakistan as the homeland for the Muslims of India and those who audaciously saw it as an ideological beacon for the ummah (the faithful), a Muslim Zion which is not constrained by borders. Territory is seen as addressing that most existential question of the State: its identity, an issue which emerged in sharp relief after 1971 with the collapse of the two-nation ideology. Mohammed Ayoob, professor of International Relations at the Michigan State University, puts it succinctly: 'Pakistan's inability to shed its Indian geopolitical, cultural and Islamic identity has forced it to adopt anti-Indian postures in order to differentiate itself from the mother country. It is its inability to define itself without reference to India that lies at the base of Pakistan's hostility to India.'[5] Simply put, a nation which has existential crises of identity will not just suffer perennial domestic instability, but this will inevitably spill over to its foreign policy, making it a rogue State, unpredictable even for its principals such as the United States and, now, China.

The notion of sovereignty carries a further burden in the Indian context and that is the sense of the 'sacred spaces' which the Hindus traditionally regard as forming part of this sacred geographical configuration. Although there is little in terms of Hindu 'sacred spaces' in the Northeast, the very principle of territorial integrity trumps everything. Political scientist Christophe Jaffrelot draws an eerie parallel between Israel's notion of the sacred land of the Jews with the idea of India being the punyabhumi of the Hindus.[6] Historian Sam Dalrymple, too, in his recent book *Shattered Lands: Five Partitions and the Making of Modern Asia*, directs attention to the reality of British India in the 1930s, which included within its territories not just Burma, but Aden and the Persian Gulf states as well, which were only ceded in April 1947. He makes the point that 'by separating the largely non-Hindu parts of the Indian empire and at the same time making India resemble Bharat of Hindu legend, the British had given credence to the Hindu nationalist claim that India belongs primarily to the Hindus.'

The Chinese have expressed displeasure at India's attempt to present itself as the legatee of the British to these 'sacred spaces' on what they conceive of as imposed boundaries and patently colonial constructs.

What the Indians do not quite appreciate is the distaste with which the Middle Kingdom—a term the Chinese like to use to describe their country—views this fusion of the colonial past (the icy hauteur of Lord Curzon) with the Indian present (the dissembling oleaginous charm of Narendra Modi). For the Chinese, the colonial period was one of unalloyed shame, and for the Indian state to treat these colonial borders that they see as imposed on them by the 'White devils' as sacrosanct and inviolable is itself deeply provocative. The basis of this provocation is historical. It has to be seen in the context of the opium wars, the role of the Indian mercantile communities as facilitators in this squalid trade and, what was more of an affront, the brutal actions of Indian soldiers under the command of British officers in the appalling sacking of the Forbidden City, something indelibly etched in the collective memory of Chinese society.[7]

From what I understand from one of the last surviving members to attend the meetings held between the then defence minister of India, V.K. Krishna Menon, and the then Chinese premier, Zhou Enlai, India was practically on the cusp of a border settlement with China in 1959. According to retired Indian diplomat Shivshankar Menon, 'Zhou said that if India would recognise the line up to which Chinese administration had reached, China would recognise the Indian administrative line in the eastern sector.'[8] This would have been the most practical resolution of this border dispute, but Nehru was opposed by some of his cabinet members, including the minister of Home Affairs, G.B. Pant. When the matter of Nehru's China Policy came up for debate in Parliament, to his surprise, perfectly rational people like Chakravarti Rajagopalachari and Minoo Masani, along with the Leftists like Ashok Mehta and Ram Manohar Lohia, excoriated any peace plan with China which involved giving up territory.[9] As Mohammed Ayoob stated, 'The 1962 war was forced upon Nehru by an ill-informed and jingoistic opposition and public opinion posed a major challenge to his foreign policy.' No one could see the utter folly in the strategy, which has worked against India in many ways, not in the least by driving China into the arms of Pakistan and vice versa. Apart from a disastrous Indo-China war in 1962, there have been continuous skirmishes at the border, with India now facing two enemies at two different borders, making it logistically harder to defend territory.

As a matter of priorities, there is little point in asking whether it makes sense to scale up hostilities in an area which Nehru famously described as a place where 'not a blade of grass grows'.[10] For China, it is a no-brainer to tie down its largest potential Asian rival in pointless hostility, diverting important resources from productive use to inflate the defence budget. This fetish with physical borders and their protection is a rather quaint conceit in an era of AI, drones, etc., where an enemy can degrade its opponent virtually by bringing down their power systems, without the need for any physical intrusion.

In this context, it is pertinent to cite Robert Kaplan, American author on foreign affairs, when he describes the historical context of the current China-India predicament,

> The subcontinent is a blunt geographical fact, but defining its borders will go on indefinitely … whereas Chinese dynasties of old almost completely fall within the current borders of China. The dynasty to which India is heir to, as we have seen, does not. Thus, India looks to Afghanistan and its other shadow zones with less serenity than does China to its shadow zones. India is a regional power to the degree that it is entrapped by this geography. It is a potential great power to the degree that it can move beyond it.[11]

This correctly summarises India's dilemma. My point, thus, is that a new nationalism subsumes and appropriates the terms and tropes of a 'sacred space' and extrapolates it into a nineteenth-century European construct of the nation-state to give legitimacy to arbitrary colonial boundaries, which have and will continue to be persisting sources of argument, angst and conflict.

3

THE COLONIAL STATE AND MINORITY RIGHTS

One of the consequences of appropriating colonial borders and applying them to a modern nation-state is that a significant part of the population that comes within these borders does not belong to the same racial stock, speak the same language or share the same religion as the majority of the population. The colonial rulers recognised this and sought to retain traditional structures of governance and customary law in these territories.

It is in this context that group rights come into focus, particularly the rights of religious and ethnic minorities, as a democratic polity would view such rights differently from a colonial ruler. It is this paradox, the mythology of a civilisational State imposed upon an imperial territory, that has led to such confusion as to the nature of minority rights and goes to the heart of what constitutes national identity.

There were many minorities in colonial India, but I make no apologies for focusing on Muslims as being a substantial minority—25 per cent of the population—and one which represented the most complex and intractable of problems to the nationalist movement. The Muslims of North India, looked with the most foreboding to their future in a democratic India as was evident from the politics of Sir Syed Ahmed Khan and the growth of the Aligarh Movement.

To understand minority rights in India now, it is important to consider the issue of representation in colonial times and the manner in which minority rights were protected through various stratagems and devices. This included reservations, such as having a fixed number of seats in legislatures, having separate electorates whereby the electorates were demarcated on a religious or community basis and giving the religious minority's vote higher weightage in legislative bodies than their numbers warranted. For example, in the Bombay Legislative Council, Muslims had 29.6 per cent of the seats when their population was only around 20 per cent.[1] These were undoubtedly controversial policies, such as having separate electorates where only Muslims could vote for Muslim candidates. The colonial government was minded to extend this policy to what were termed the 'depressed classes'. In 1927, the Simon Commission was established to explore the extension of separate electorates to other communities. Although boycotted by the Congress, Dr Ambedkar participated in its deliberations, arguing that there was merit in reserving government jobs for the depressed classes.

Whilst it is fashionable to cite the expansionist intentions of colonial rulers as the reason for their much-vilified 'divide and rule' policy, author Abhinav Chandrachud, in his book *Republic of Religion*,[2] suggests that secularism was a factor too. There was always the concern of the majority trampling on the rights of the minority, particularly with the growth of religious evangelicalism amongst Hindus and Muslims at the time. The origin of these representation policies, particularly that of having separate electorates, was introduced by the India Councils Act, 1909. It is at this point that the hoary 'divide and rule' argument is often raised, but as H.M. Seervai sagely observed, 'There was an element of truth in this; but a legislative provision may be desirable, or necessary, independently of the motive which originally led to its enactment.'[3]

Separate Electorates

It was putative nationalism that led the Hindu Right to view separate electorates as a source of future antagonism and disaffection. This was certainly the view of Sardar Patel and echoed in a report published in 1937, written by Rajendra Prasad and Govind Ballabh Pant.[4] The reason these gentlemen rejected the idea of separate electorates was much more mundane. It was because it presented difficulties for the Congress party in Muslim constituencies. It never seemed to occur to these worthies that perhaps a more inclusive agenda would have helped win over the Muslims, but the Congress in UP and Bihar were unfortunately held hostage to the majoritarian thinking of Pant, Madan Mohan Malviya and others. This was the crux of the problem.

Dr Ambedkar, however, was able to provide a much-needed corrective to this nationalistic prejudice and bigotry. He gave the example of Sikhs, who despite enjoying separate electorates, could not be accused of being 'anti-national'.[5] He even went as far as furnishing the example of Mohammad Ali Jinnah, who was a product of separate electorates, but which did not prevent him in his earlier avatar from espousing a formidable nationalistic ethos. Therefore, he argued, it was neither obvious nor inevitable that the device of separate electorates would lead to anti-nationalism or disaffection.[6]

The Nehru Report and the Pakistan Resolution

Mohammad Ali Jinnah had raised various issues as a means of opening a dialogue with the Congress with a view to strengthen the nationalist effort. In 1927, with great effort, he managed to persuade the Muslim League to jettison the idea of separate electorates in exchange for a fixed one-third share of seats in the Central Legislative Assembly for Muslims. He also sought to propose the separation of Sindh from the erstwhile Bombay Presidency in order to establish a new Muslim-majority province.

In 1928, there was an attempt to resolve party differences on the question of minority representation, in what was termed the Nehru Report, authored by Motilal Nehru, Jawaharlal's father. The Nehru Report made several important proposals in relation to the Hindu–Muslim question. It essentially substituted the controversial matter of separate electorates with reserved seats for Muslims which were to be given in proportion to their numbers and not on the basis of a principle of representation such as the one-third share, which is what Jinnah insisted on. This represented a setback to the Muslims and was a marked departure from the conviviality of the Lucknow Pact of 1916. As professor of South Asian history Joya Chatterji puts it, 'Demos was the way the Congress was going, with no safeguards for minorities, it seemed. Jawaharlal's fingerprints were all over the Nehru Report—indeed, Nehru Senior acknowledged his son's contribution to the proceedings.'[7] This was one of the first signs of Congress showing its fangs in relation to the position of Muslim representation, and it led to a rift in the relationship between Jawaharlal Nehru and Jinnah. Jinnah responded with fourteen points[8] under which an agreement could be devised, which included effective representation for minorities and one-third representation for Muslims in all cabinets, but was fundamentally predicated on a federal structure with residuary powers with the states. The Congress did not accept this, and Jinnah described it as a parting of the ways for India's Hindus and Muslims. His exact words were 'If you cannot agree, let us at any rate agree to differ, but let us part as friends. Believe me there is no progress of India until the Musalmans and Hindus are united, and let no logic, philosophy or squabble stand in the way of coming to a compromise and nothing will make me more happy than to see a Hindu–Muslim union.'[9]

Nehru's inability to comprehend the cultural underpinnings of nationalism had a major influence on his dialogue with Jinnah. Jawaharlal repeatedly brought up the class angle, and given Jinnah's friendship and support from the Muslim aristocracy and the business community who funded the League, as well as his predilection for Savile Row suits and his signature monocle, this charge struck home. Having said that, Jinnah had every right to view Nehru's invocation of class politics as hugely hypocritical given the nature of the composition of the Congress Party, which, at least in its heartland, UP, had a Brahmin and upper-caste hegemony. The Congress was funded by an avowedly Hindu business class who, whilst paying lip service to national unity, had an overweening desire to diminish, if not eradicate, much of the Muslim cultural legacy in North India and substitute it with a confessionally Hindu Brahmanical paradigm,[10] involving the prohibition of cow slaughter and mandating the use of Devanagari script and what is called 'shudh Hindi'. This position was no secret and was fairly acknowledged by Gandhi in the 1931

Karachi Congress session in which he drew a distinction between Aryan Hindu culture and Persianate Muslim culture, which both deserved space in India, according to him. However, most of the Congress leadership, particularly from UP, were opposed to this.

In contrast, the British under the Government of India Act of 1935 vested the colonial governments with what was termed a special responsibility towards ensuring that the 'legitimate interests of minorities'[11] were protected in public employment, that is Muslims enjoyed 25 per cent of the seats in government jobs, approximating to their population aligning with Queen Victoria's Proclamation of 1858.

The Congress did exceedingly well in the 1937 elections, with the League winning only 109 out of the possible 482 seats and only 5 per cent of the Muslim vote. These results laid bare the weakness of the League as a force for mobilising Muslims. The Congress used that miserable performance to treat the League as scarcely relevant, Nehru even suggesting that the Muslim League of UP be dissolved and made a part of Congress. The reason for raising this issue is to draw attention to the deplorable and unwise post-election treatment of Muslim minorities particularly in UP, which has been adduced as one of the more compelling reasons behind the passing of the Lahore Resolution, commonly known as the Pakistan Resolution of 1940, by the Muslim League at the Lahore Session.

It is commonly argued that the conduct of the Congress government, which acted in a triumphalist fashion, exacerbated Hindu–Muslim tensions. Author Ian Copland points out that:

> Muslims were justly angered by the additional emphasis on the Hindi language and on Hindu culture and history in Congress-run state schools. Soon anti-Congress sentiment (inflamed, to be sure, by clever League propaganda) was running high among aggrieved Muslim parents, among Muslim professionals who felt that their employment prospects had suffered, and among Muslim businessmen who had watched lucrative government contracts go to Hindu firms with Congress party connections.[12]

This perception is contested by historian B.R. Nanda, who argues that there was 'hardly any evidence in the records of the Home Department of the Government of India to support the theory of a

Hindu Raj in Congress-governed provinces.'[13] It is material that much of what Copland claims was antagonistic would not be recorded by the Home Department. Whatever may be the case, there may well have been triumphalism and arrogance shown by provincial Congress leaders, which were seen as provocative by the minorities.

One aspect which was particularly offensive to the Muslim minority in UP was the education policy. Dr Sampurnanand, who was the minister concerned with education in the Congress government, according to columnist William Gould, 'made no bones in his writing about linking educational ideals to the philosophy of Vedanta and Indian traditions.'[14] So, at a practical level, he encouraged the adoption of what was known as the Wardha scheme of education. This education scheme, it was argued by Muslim League politicians, presented a one-sided view of history, and included religious education, which emphatically did not address Muslim needs. Around 1,300 primary schools were converted into this Wardha scheme after 1938 and for many Muslims, it was a presentiment of what was to come. Even right wing secular leaders like Minoo Masani excoriated it.

This perception of a Hindu Raj in the guise of Congress-run governments provided grist to the mill for those few Islamist ideologues who sought separation from India. The Lahore Resolution itself needs to be quoted:

> No Constitutional plan will be workable in the country or acceptable to the Muslims unless it is designed on the following basic principles, viz., that geographically contiguous units are demarcated into regions which should be so constituted, with such territorial readjustments as may be necessary, that the areas in which the Muslims are numerically in the majority as the north-western and eastern zones of India should be grouped to constitute 'Independent States' in which the constituent assemblies are autonomous and sovereign.

B.R. Nanda states that the 'Pakistan resolution, as it came to be known, gave a new twist to the communal problem. All the solutions hitherto thought of—separate electorates, composite cabinets, reservation of posts—suddenly became out of date.'[15] In fact, I think the contrary was the case; it compelled those seriously concerned with the impending partition of the country, to consider introducing constitutional safeguards to protect the interests of the minorities. It must be stated that the resolution did not mention Pakistan or, indeed, the word partition, save and except laying an emphasis on territoriality. There is a teasing ambiguity in the wording to give the intimation that this was intended to be a bargaining counter for future discussions for which Jinnah was to be the sole spokesman for his community. Perhaps it gave a new dimension to the Hindu–Muslim question as it raised the spectre of a divided India and caused a rethink amongst many as to whether there could be any other constitutional device that could provide a measure of security to Muslim minorities rather than risk the partition of the country, since the Congress had retreated into a reverie of complacency after winning the 1937 elections.

Many observers believe that the failure to address some of the League's demands post the 1937 elections and the insistence, particularly by Sardar Patel, that the League merge with the Congress in UP, was the cause of future problems. This was the view of economist H.V. Hodson[16] and writer Sir Penderel Moon.[17] If the Congress had treated the League with more respect and agreed to some of their terms, including on the controversial matter of a substantive role for Urdu as a second language, perhaps the Partition could have been forestalled.

UP figures significantly in this episode. The Congress party was deeply split in UP and if Nehru and Sapru represented the liberal wing of the Congress, open to preservation of the existing composite culture, politicians like Govind Ballabh Pant, Purushottam Das Tandon and Sarvasi Sampurnanand were insistent on marginalising what they saw as the composite or Muslim culture of UP. However, for the freedom struggle, UP was pivotal, and the unity of the Congress trumped everything, even if it was at the cost of the minorities. Nehru tried to justify his indifference to cultural rights by reference to the impetus of modernity, of future differences arising out of economics rather than caste and religion.[18] This quixotic belief in the momentum of modernity, banishing differences of religion and caste in favour of economic and class issues, ignored the ground realities of UP politics, which was only fixated on cultural issues. But it was a convenient stratagem to avoid controversy and a potential schism within the Congress in a state in which it held hegemony—a factor that became the basis for Congress rule for at least three decades after Independence. In fact, what Nehru plainly stated was that 'by virtue of numbers and in other ways, [the majority community] is the dominant community and it is its responsibility not to use its position in any way which may prejudice our secular ideals.'[19] So his notion of minority rights was confined only to the security of their culture and their lives. He saw no role for the minorities in government, nor did he assure them of any representation in jobs.

Dr Ambedkar put the point well in his book *States and Minorities*:

> Unfortunately for the minorities in India, Indian nationalism has developed a new doctrine which may be called the Divine Right of the Majority to rule the minorities according to the wish of the majority. Any claim in the sharing of power by the minority is called communalism while the monopolising of the whole power is called Nationalism.[20]

It is fair to say that this perception of nationalism was also shared by Tagore, who excoriated the 'organising selfishness of nationalism'. Their point is well taken.

Desai-Liaquat Pact

There were several efforts in the 1940s to try to work out an arrangement whereby Muslim rights were protected. One of the first of such attempts was the Desai-Liaquat Pact. This was a pact between Bhulabhai Desai, the president of the Bombay Provincial Congress Committee, and Liaquat Ali Khan, the general secretary of the Muslim League. The pact attempted to provide a basis for Hindus and Muslims to form a coalition ministry at the Centre. The principle which animated this pact was the notion of parity between the Congress and the League as well as the representation of other minorities, including the Scheduled Castes and the Sikhs.

This pact was signed in November 1945 but foundered when provincial governments could not be formed after the governor general of India imposed governor's rule under section 93 of the Government of India Act, 1935 (a power analogous to the President's

Rule under article 356 of the Indian constitution) on areas where provincial governments were to be formed. Some have sought to sow doubt as to whether Gandhi was complicit in this pact. However, Sir Motilal Setalvad establishes beyond doubt Gandhi's knowledge and concurrence to the pact.[21]

Sapru Committee Report

There was another important report issued at the time known as the Sapru Committee Report. Headed by leading lawyer Sir Tej Bahadur Sapru, the committee was composed of eminent men who had no affiliation with either the Congress or the Muslim League, and who were directed to find a solution to this impasse. The thirty-member committee came to a finding that in the constitution-making body there should be parity between Hindus (other than Scheduled Castes) and Muslims, and that elections to the Central legislature would be conducted on joint and not separate electorates.

Much to the annoyance of the Muslim League, the report rejected Pakistan as a solution, as it stated that the division of India would 'endanger the peace and progress of the entire country.' It had the foresight to also suggest the setting up of a Minorities Commission. Whilst these recommendations did not have any discernible impact on the political class, it is relevant that the notion of parity between the communities was once more asserted by the commission and this point was repeated by Sapru before the Cabinet Commission in April 1946.

Seervai observed that:

> The Desai-Liaquat Ali Pact and the Report of the Sapru Committee showed that the fear of the Muslims for their future in a united India was genuine, and required to be allayed. And both the Pact and the Report had found 'parity' at the Centre an effective means of allaying those fears.[22]

Seervai also refers by analogy to the constitution-making process in the US subsequent to their War of Independence, where certain compromises were made to ensure unity between the then thirteen states willing to join the Union, including entrenching certain rights and, critically, creating some constitutional fictions for the purpose of giving a semblance of equality between the larger and smaller states. For example, every US state, whether big or small, was given the right to send two representatives to the senate, and that right could not be revoked without the consent of that state. This, in my view, is a fair and apposite analogy.

Even Ivor Jennings, the great apostle of constitutionalism, who had engaged in drafting the constitution of both Ceylon and Pakistan, was wary when it came to the suitability of having a system of universal suffrage in a post-colonial society. He strongly believed that constitutions should be adapted to local conditions and was not averse to considering devices such as a limited franchise, indirect elections and community representations. Author and constitutional scholar Madhav Khosla puts it with brisk economy—'Implicit in Jennings's advice was the idea that national sovereignty could be severed from the question of suffrage. A country could be free even if all its citizens did not have the right to vote.'[23] This is perhaps a more extreme solution, but whichever way you cut it, there had to be some kind of protection for minority communities from the dangers of rampant majoritarianism.

When we discuss minority rights, we often forget the political and historical climate of the time, and it is fair to say that the matter of protection of minority rights had received much attention post the signing of the Treaty of Versailles between Germany and the allied powers after the First World War, which effectively led to self-determination amongst the territories formerly ruled by the Austro-Hungarian Empire and the Ottomans. Author Neera Chandhoke points out that, 'after the Paris Peace Treaty, the leadership of the International Committee recognised that ... the rights of the Minorities especially [ought to be] protected and guaranteed under a system of international law.'[24] So much so that such minority rights were guaranteed in five separate peace treaties between the allied countries and Poland, Czechoslovakia, Romania, Greece and Yugoslavia. In fact, the admission of the Eastern European countries into the League of Nations was made conditional on the grant of such minority rights. The League of Nations was made the custodian of ensuring the implementation of such rights, the legal body for such recourse being the International Court of Justice. In this context, it is relevant that the two countries that pointedly did not want to give any protection to their minorities were Germany and Italy.

Matters of cultural plurality and minority rights are much embedded in the discourse of human rights. In a united India, such rights would have had universal application to all minority communities, including Hindus in Muslim-majority provinces. The dismissal of such rights as being too contemporary and woke, is manifestly a transgression of history. The issue always was the idiom to be used in the mêlée of mass politics, which is inextricably linked to the nature of the franchise. It is here that the debate between the proponents of political liberty who talk of a mass franchise, collides with those who believe that political liberty in terms of the franchise was always contingent on social equality. As Faisal Devji puts it, 'disagreement [exists] between those Indians who thought that political liberty should proceed social equality and others who fear that such a liberty would well perpetuate inequality by empowering majorities and the powerful at the expense of the minorities and powerless.'[25] Ultimately, the Constitution ended up entrenching both the dominance of caste and majoritarianism, devaluing citizenship and diminishing social equality. In fact, Isaiah Berlin in his seminal work, *Two Concepts of Liberty,* directed this lecture at the post-colonial world, warning national liberation movements that the fight against colonialism could not necessarily be identified as fighting for liberty. It was indubitably a fight for recognition as a people and for the status of nationhood. To believe otherwise would be to guarantee disillusionment.[26]

I believe that had such concessions to minority rights been made, it would have had a domino effect in the provinces where there were Muslim majorities such as Punjab and Bengal, creating space for a new language and idiom for such political discourse, as bestowing such rights on Muslims in Hindu-majority provinces would have instigated similar demands from the Sikhs and Hindus in Punjab, Bengal and Sindh. By doing so, the matter of minority rights would not be seen as confined to a particular religion: it would have been secularised. This new paradigm would substantially have mitigated much of the communal poison that talks of minority rights provoked and continue to provoke. Of course, this is all counterfactual as we do not know what the contents of such rights would be, but it would have undoubtedly acted against majoritarianism and its inevitable consequence in India—'Sanskritisation', a policy to consolidate the Hindu vote in its existential struggle against Islam.

One of the deficiencies in the Muslim League agenda was defining the contents of the rights it sought to protect, as author Maya Tudor put it, 'as pan-Islamism receded ... the Muslim League would be reincarnated to promote the interests of the entrenched Muslim landed aristocracy in the United Provinces.'[27] The complexities of pan-Muslim politics defied any clear manifesto, so the League was content to peddle religious catechisms with the intent to thwart Hindu hegemony. It must be recalled that the Unionist party in Punjab was a party of landlords, whilst the Krishak Sramik party in Bengal was anti-feudal, both were Muslim-majority provinces and the League had to sedulously manoeuvre such antinomies.

It is safe to conclude that it was largely the unwillingness of the Congress to share power that led to the call for Pakistan, which has now become a lightning rod for the virulent new nationalism consuming India. It also had a consequential impact on the Muslims of Pakistan, bringing to the fore a new breed of Muslim clerics, such as Maulana Maududi, who were determined to create a millenarian Islamic state. With the founding of Pakistan, he had a ready-made experimental laboratory to do so. We have seen the grotesque denouement of such a misguided policy.

Given the history of constitutional arrangements in the colonial period, it is evident that there was much concern for minority rights and various devices were created to protect these rights at the cost of adhering to the shibboleth of 'one man, one vote'. I believe it is important for these facts to be recorded because they show, demonstrably so, that the argument for parity between the communities was not some Pollyannaish pipedream that came from nowhere, but was very much part of the political discourse for decades, before the Cabinet Mission Plan came to be proposed and enjoyed a degree of consensus amongst an influential group of Indian intellectuals and lawyers.

The issue, fundamentally, is between those people who want to live with one another as equal citizens and those who sought a relationship of dominance over a minority.

4

THE PARTITION

The perplexing issues of nationhood, federalism and the treatment of religious and ethnic minorities and their rights, juxtaposed with an audacious vision of modernity and economic progress, were very much at odds. If one argued for colonial secularism, you were accused of being regressive. But all these issues boiled down to the future contours of the nation-state, and it is the gravamen of this book that the possibility of a united India was presented in the form of the Cabinet Mission Plan in 1946 which was rejected by the Congress. It is often and, in my view, wrongly argued that the creation of Pakistan was the ultimate act of Muslim appeasement; this is far from the case. There is little or no evidence that the majority of Muslims wanted Partition. When references are made to the results of the voting done under the Government of India Act of 1935, the electorate comprised only 14 per cent of the total population of British India and to assume that the enfranchised Muslims who voted for Pakistan represented the majority of Muslim opinion is patently wrong. In any event, there was an evident reluctance on the part of the states that formed the core of present-day Pakistan to follow the Muslim League, and even Bengal's desire to join Pakistan was problematic.

But what gets lost in this debate is the fact that the demands of minorities for cultural and religious rights were not exceptional, and it was for the majority to cede such demands if the country was to be kept intact. The majority was not prepared to cede such rights to the minority and preferred the solution of Partition. This was made amply clear when British statesman Sir Stafford Cripps told Syama Prasad Mookerjee that '[t]he Hindus were in an overall majority in India and must be prepared to make the maximum concessions. The principle of majority rule, which the Mahasabha invoked in their Memorandum, could not be applied in an unmodified form where there was a perpetual majority and a perpetual minority.'[1] It must be remembered that Cripps was a well-wisher, a socialist and someone who had a strong belief in Indian independence, apart from being a lawyer of some eminence. At any rate, the Partition was not possible without the tacit support of many of the Hindu Right. In this context, the Left and political centralisers also played a significant role, as both Nehru and Ambedkar were anxious to create a unitarian structure, although one which was nominally styled as federal, to push through an ambitious social and economic agenda.

I think it apposite to view the Partition through the lens of 'the hospitality of narratives',[2] as it invites one to consider that many different, informed perspectives on the same set of events can and do exist—this liberates us from finding or subscribing to a single unifying narrative of the past. An analysis of the partition would be a book in itself, but it is essential to analyse this singular event after Independence, without which one cannot understand our present predicament. It was uniquely transformative in both its scale and the searing impact it had and continues to have on our collective memory. It was and is our very own Holocaust.

Historian Yasmin Khan does not assume that the Partition was inevitable, and dwells on what she states: 'Partition set in motion a train of events unforeseen by every single person who advocated and argued for the division.'[3] She attributes much blame to the British for the shoddy way in which the Partition Plan was implemented, but ultimately it is instructive to analyse what the principal actors at that time thought of the future and what were their expectations and hopes.

What animated the key players at that time and their vision of the future Indian state is relevant and I will deal with each of the main actors in this fascinating dramatis personae later in the book, but some events around the time must first be highlighted to provide context.

The Cabinet Mission Plan and the Partition

An interrogation of the historiography of the Partition shows the controversies over federalism as pivotal in deciding whether British India was to remain a unified structure. The opportunity for the discussion on this was the Cabinet Mission Plan in 1946, which set out a political structure allowing a degree of federalism to forestall the matter of Pakistan as a sovereign State. Broadly speaking, the Plan involved devolution of power to Muslims within the body of a united India.

The proposed federation was to be organised in three layers, with a central government controlling the portfolios of defence and foreign affairs. The next layer envisaged provinces with autonomy in certain matters, but with the option of grouping together to address other questions of their choice. This gave the Muslim blocs a certain veto right, contingent on whether the issue warranted its exercise. In this regard, it provided a degree of parity between Hindus and Muslims, which is what the League desperately wanted. I believe it was ingeniously drafted.

An important aspect of the plan was that it preserved the right for a province to secede if it was dissatisfied with the status quo for a period of ten years. Author and journalist Zareer Masani describes this as well-intentioned, in 'that this cooling-off period might enable politics to coalesce around non-sectarian lines, with time healing both sectarian divisions.'[4] To my mind, at the time of the Cabinet Mission Plan, whilst some divisions existed, there had been no obvious communal incident that would have animated this primeval barbarism. But certainly, it gave impetus to a federal structure to develop and safeguard the interests of the minorities and, crucially, retain the glittering prize of a united India.

The Muslim League had in principle agreed to the Plan, but it was rejected by Congress. While it may not be entirely accurate to state that Congress rejected the Cabinet Mission Plan entirely, it did not accept the groupings of states that were critical to the Muslim League's acceptance of the plan, principally the position of the North-West Frontier Province, a Muslim-majority province that voted for the Congress. The crux of the issue was the matter of parity. Jinnah sought the views of Sardar Patel on the vexed issue of majoritarianism and Patel plainly stated that he would never consider parity in the Central government.[5] All of this led H.M. Seervai to conclude that '[t]he relevant documents published in The Transfer of Power, 1942–47 show beyond any doubt that it was the Congress leaders who insisted on partition. The Congress refused to accept the Cabinet Mission Plan, which would have preserved the unity of India, because it was not prepared to allow the Muslim League to form the Government at the Centre or to recognise the principle of parity between the Congress and the League. Jinnah, on the other hand, did not want a truncated and 'moth-eaten' Pakistan, which was what Mountbatten and the Congress insisted upon.'[6]

Ultimately, it was Nehru who torpedoed the whole plan with a remark at a press conference in Bombay in July 1946 after the All India Congress Committee meeting that the groupings of states were only transitional arrangements pending the drafting of a popular constitution.[7] This caused the League to withdraw its consent to the plan and unfortunately led to bloodletting, consequent to Jinnah's call for direct action. There is much ambiguity about what 'direct action' exactly meant. What Jinnah seemed to mean was what Congress had been pursuing all along; not being constrained by constitutional methods and taking to the streets to express their feelings. Unfortunately, this was followed up by a call by Jinnah to observe 16 August 1946 as Direct Action Day, and in Bengal, the prime minister of Bengal and senior League member, H.S. Suhrawardy, declared a public holiday, causing communal violence to erupt. Calcutta was the epicentre of this violence, leading to over 6,000 deaths, and most of the victims were, ironically, Muslims. Jinnah had never anticipated such an occurrence, but having unleased such violence, it was difficult to contain.

Nehru's recalcitrance may be traced to core differences in the political and economic ideologies of the Congress and the League. While some indulge in the quixotically fanciful binary between Nehru, 'being a committed socialist' and wanting a strong government at the Centre, and Jinnah with his commitment to 'free markets', the position was more nuanced. Nehru was undoubtedly left-leaning, but the Congress was not committed to a socialist ideology. Mahatma Gandhi, Sardar Patel and others could not, by any description, be described as socialists. In fact, Congress was very dependent on financing from businessmen such as the Birlas and the Bajajs. G.D. Birla's shadowy role and influence on Gandhi is rarely talked about, but some of his interventions were extraordinary, such as writing to Gandhi to torpedo the prospect of a Hindu–Muslim coalition in Calcutta in 1942 as something that would prejudice Marwari business interests.[8] On the other hand, there is a perception of Jinnah's commitment to free markets. He was ever the political opportunist. This was demonstrated in the 1947 budget, which was presented by Jinnah's protégé Liaquat Ali Khan, which was so radical that it shocked Congress. In fact, Congress opposed the imposition of a wealth tax on the grounds that it discriminated against the Hindu merchant class.

This budget in February 1947 more or less sealed the issue of Partition for Sardar Patel and V.P. Menon. It was extraordinarily redistributive, abolishing the Salt Act, removing the bottom layer of society from income tax, imposing 25 per cent corporation tax on companies with a profit of more than INR 1,00,000 and imposing a capital gains tax. Much of the detailed work had been undertaken with the assistance of H.M. Patel, then an Indian Civil Service (ICS) officer, who later became Finance Minister in the Janata Government. Sardar Patel was shocked by the budget and Nehru embarrassed, given his much-vaunted socialist predilections and, perhaps, that was the intention.

So, the real reason that prompted the Congress to reject the Cabinet Mission Plan was indubitably the desire for power at the earliest, one untrammelled by the necessities of having to deal with the pesky complexities of the Muslims, the Dalits and the princely states. Therefore, the visions and meanings of statehood and the Partition for different principal actors of that time are an essential study to gain meaningful insight into the Partition and the events leading up to it.

Nehru

Jawaharlal Nehru was dismissive of any clear-cut definition of what a 'nation' consists of. He refused to believe that it could be sought from historical or cultural factors or even racial or linguistic ones.[9] What he viewed as essential was a consciousness of unity and so, if a number of communities aspired to work together and form a political construct, they could be regarded as a nation. However, the nationalists' position was that the Indian nation would only include those who lived in the territorial entity known as India and acknowledged they were Indians belonging to one nation. As Maulana Azad put it, 'Religion is for God and the Homeland is for everyone.'[10]

Nehru had little time for the Hindu–Muslim problem, and according to Madhav Khosla, he saw 'the challenges that modernity posed were economic and political rather than religious ...'[11] With this view, it was difficult for him to even comprehend the fears of the minorities; he just assumed that such protections that will be provided within the constitutional framework would be sufficient. He characterised Jinnah's politics of mingling religion with politics as belonging to the Dark Ages. This proved to be a major disadvantage during negotiations with the League.

I believe that Nehru's outlook on nationalism was colonised by a nineteenth-century liberal modernist understanding of history which assumed a linear and progressive view of human development; what historian Herbert Butterfield has cuttingly called the 'Whig view of history'.[12] Political scientist Sudipta Kaviraj analyses this with acuity when he observes that, 'this [view] often implied an irreversible historical motion from traditional identities like religion to modern ones like the nation, and simply assumed that once a modern "nationalist" identity was formed, social groups could not "regress" into traditional identity again.'[13] This belief in the inevitable shedding of identities meant that he did not believe that minorities deserved any special entitlements. Historian Sunil Purushotham argues that:

> Nehru was a majoritarian in the sense that he did not believe in the necessity or the absolute rights of the minority to participate in state power. Rather, he thought that the majority should

> wield power in a responsible manner that acknowledged the vulnerability of the minority, essentially adapting Gandhian notions of trusteeship to a statist order.[14]

Economist H.V. Hodson[15] characterised the sabotage of the Cabinet Mission Plan by the Congress as a blunder of the first order. This statement is based on the assumption that the Congress saw the preservation of a United India as its primary objective over independence at any cost. On the contrary, I believe that the Congress was more interested in acquiring power at any cost, even if it meant a partitioned country. One could argue that independence per se was not an issue any more, as the British under the Attlee government had agreed to give India independence, and post-1945, the Congress was effectively pushing at an open door. As Attlee put it in the British parliament, 'The British Commonwealth Empire are not bound together by chains of external compulsions ... and so if India elects for independence she has every right to do so.'[16]

The critical issue that remained was what kind of India was to be envisaged. It is at this juncture that the issue becomes complicated, not just because of the League's forceful advocacy for Pakistan, but also for powerful constituencies and interest groups within the Congress which went along with the partition narrative for their own reasons. Author Neeti Nair cites a leading Punjabi Hindu leader Dr Gokul Chand Narang, who some twenty years after Partition, commented that Jinnah was, in a way, wrong in asking for parity. 'You know he wanted parity. If parity was there, Hindus would have been absolutely nowhere. I was chairman of a public meeting. I said that I would agree to Pakistan, but never to parity. Pakistan was a much lesser evil than parity.' Nair concluded that some Punjabi Hindus preferred Partition to a united India.[17]

This aspect of the Partition debate is rarely commented on as it is much more convenient, I believe, to heap the blame on Jinnah and the Muslim League. As journalist Aakar Patel puts it,

> It is incorrect and cruel therefore to say that Muslims partitioned India when their every attempt under Jinnah was to try and preserve the Union. It is equally wrong to assume that a weak Congress capitulated. It is the strength and backing received

from over 90 per cent of the Hindus, that gave Congress the arrogance to go it alone and dismiss the legitimate demands of India's Muslims.[18]

Dr Ambedkar

While Dr Ambedkar's views on centralisation are well known, his views on the Partition and the Muslims are less so. His book *Thoughts on Pakistan* is often referred to as a powerful argument by Ambedkar for Pakistan. It is essentially a performative exercise in dissembling impartiality, as it gives the impression that he thought that Pakistan would be a satisfactory solution for the Hindu–Muslim issue. However, whilst he feigns at being fair and making an even-handed assessment of the demand for Pakistan, the actual thrust of his argument is that an undivided India was a far worse alternative than Pakistan. In support of this proposition, he referred to the Muslim League's litany of demands which he claimed would weaken the Indian state, reducing it, in his words, to the 'sick man of Asia'. He was also dismissive of the sentimentality of the composite culture which those Congressmen anxious to preserve a united India referred to, describing it as 'a result of a dead past that had no present and no future.'

Ambedkar also expressed concerns about the large Muslim presence in the army, as he identified that a political army would pose the greatest danger to India's liberty. The Muslim presence in the Indian army was around 40 per cent, disproportionate to its population, a fact that troubled Ambedkar as he believed that if there was ever a clash between the communities, the feelings of disaffection could percolate down to the armed forces and could lead to civil war.[19]

This fear of violence was pervasive and historian Shruti Kapila has captured his thinking very well by placing his vision in the praxis of an 'institutional design in which the subject—national and Dalit—was embedded in popular sovereignty. Agonism, or the recognition of hostile distinctions as opposed to their violent eradication or wilful neglect, in effect, became the nonviolent condition for the life of the Indian nation and democracy.'[20]

He was aware that the creation of Pakistan made Partition and population transfers necessary, but did not feel that these would be very substantial. I also think Ambedkar was conscious and insecure about the proselytising tendency of Islam, as many Dalit and Adivasis were likely to be targeted, reducing his constituency and potential power base.

Both Nehru and Ambedkar were anxious to have in place a strong central government in a substantially unitary state, though which was federal in name. I believe that they thought this was to promote central planning, as is often stated, but, critically, also for legislating wide-ranging social reforms, particularly in relation to Hindu society and to address centuries of oppression and discrimination meted out to the Dalits and lower castes. As Madhav Khosla puts it, 'As far as they were concerned, India needed democracy and it needed modernity—and democracy and modernity needed one another.'[21]

Sardar Vallabhbhai Patel

Sardar Patel is a prodigiously significant figure in the run-up to the Partition and thereafter. If Nehru represented the Left or liberal wing of the Congress Party, Patel represented that traditional Gandhian element, a politician who shared Gandhi's emblematic frugality and abstinence but not any of his redeeming qualities such as empathy for the weak and the minorities. What he did have was a sharp and deep understanding of the Hindu psyche, as he was not only a devout and religious Hindu but one who harboured a deep-seated animosity towards Muslims and syncretic culture,[22] which he regarded as an abomination.

Patel, contrary to current mythology, was content to let Nehru project himself as the progressive face of the Congress, whilst he was the backroom boy, exercising the real levers of power in conjunction with the more traditional elements of the party, the local Congress provincial leaders and the princely states. This even extended to elements outside the party, reaching shadowy organisations such as the Mahasabha and the Rashtriya Swayamsevak Sangh (RSS), for example. His close relationship with N.B. Khare, the prime minister of the princely state of Alwar, was emblematic of this. It would be fair to say that even if he did not openly subscribe to the two-nation theory, his politics were explicitly majoritarian and wherever possible, he would seek division and was not averse to instigating violence where he deemed it necessary. According to Shruti Kapila,

> Throughout 1947 and 1948, Patel steadfastly maintained that the potential means and ends of violence rested with the people ... Both at the height of violence and in peaceful pauses, he continued to pursue the logic of division or Partition as the necessary condition for the attainment of national sovereign power.[23]

If there is a scintilla of doubt regarding Sardar Patel's views on Muslims and the future of Pakistan, Leonard Mosely, the British journalist who covered the independence period, disabuses one of any illusions.[24] He discloses that when Jinnah left Delhi in 1947, after delivering a conciliatory message in which he appealed to both Hindus and Muslims to bury their past and wished India success and prosperity, on the following day, Patel, in response, said that:

> The poison has been removed from the body of India. We are now one and indivisible. You cannot divide the sea or the waters of the river. As for the Muslims, they have their centres here. I do not know what they can possibly do in Pakistan. It will not be long before they return to us.

His contempt for Muslims was well known, as was his contempt for their culture. He famously remarked that 'Muslims do not like to work hard. They want to wear fine clothes and sing ghazals. Who will do the hard work in Pakistan?'[25]

In line with the current political temperament, where ideological differences ineluctably lead to hatred and alienation, the propaganda is that Patel and Nehru's differences spilled over into personality clashes. The new revisionism about Patel paints an unbridgeable divide between him and Nehru, in the belief that Patel lusted for the position that Gandhi ultimately bestowed on Nehru.

In a recent book by author Narayani Basu on Patel's great protégé, V.P. Menon,[26] it is alleged that Nehru was so upset and alienated from Patel that he did not want him to be in his first Cabinet.[27] However, historian Srinath Raghavan has shown this to be patently untrue on the basis of contemporaneous correspondence, including a letter from Nehru to Patel dated 1 August 1947 inviting him to join the Cabinet and describing him as 'the strongest pillar of the cabinet'.[28]

It is also important to understand that while the population exchange was the lightning rod for the violence of the Partition, it was not obvious to many at the time that Partition would necessarily involve such exchanges. Historian Gyanendra Pandey observes that 'until almost the end of August 1947, Jinnah and Jawaharlal Nehru, along with a host of other leaders and officials, expressed their opposition to any large-scale transfer of populations. Yet by the beginning of September, several lakhs of Punjabi refugees were on the move, under official coordination.'[29] Even as late as May 1948, the prime minister of Bengal, H.S. Suhrawardy was still urging the minorities to return to Sindh and East Bengal. Patel, however, played a double game.

He encouraged Hindus in Muslim-majority provinces (which would become Pakistan) to migrate to India and even went as far as to suggest to Nehru that if the migration of Hindus from Pakistan persisted, India would be constrained to expel Muslims in equal numbers from West Bengal. Nehru ignored this advice, but it shows demonstrably so that, as far as Patel was concerned, his goal was that of a majoritarian state and the fewer Muslims he had to deal with, the better. Together with Syama Prasad Mookerjee, he was also a passionate advocate of the division of Bengal along communal lines, claiming that this was the true desire of Bengali Hindus, a proposition strongly contested by Sarat Bose who had the foresight to see the extraordinary disaster the partition of Bengal would cause, both economically and politically.[30] In fact, according to bureaucrat M.K. Kriplani, the exodus of Hindu Bengalis was accelerated by the deteriorating economic conditions in East Pakistan due to 'India's strangulation'.[31]

It must be understood that in April 1947, H.S. Suhrawardy had been requesting that the British and Jinnah consider the possibility of an independent Bengal. What Suhrawardy proposed was an independent, undivided and sovereign Bengal as a separate dominion of a divided India. Jinnah did not have an issue with this and told Lord Louis Mountbatten, viceroy of India, that he 'should be delighted, what is the use of Bengal without Calcutta; they had much better remained united and independent; I am sure they would be on much friendly terms with us.'[32] Almost as a presentiment of the future, the president of the Bengal Muslim League, Abul Mansur, stated in 1944 that:

> Religion and culture are not the same thing. Religion transgresses the geographical boundary but *tamaddun* (culture) cannot go beyond the geographical boundary [...] For this reason, the people of Purba [Eastern] Pakistan are a different nation from the people of the other provinces of India and from the 'religious brothers' of Pakistan.[33]

This is crucial to understand that there was an all-embracing recognition of the power of a common culture and linguistic identity as being critical to the creation of a nation-state, with religion coming a poor second.

It was Sardar Patel who insisted on the division of Bengal on communal lines[34] and to that extent, accentuated the damage wrought by Partition, as this division was entirely egregious and could have been avoided. People were unnecessarily displaced, with many flooding into Calcutta and Assam, creating issues that still persist to this day. Now we have the reality of Bangladesh, an independent sovereign state, but one born out of a horrendous bloodbath, which could have been avoided along with the serious economic disruption caused by the Partition, particularly to Calcutta. The Partition cut it from its hinterland and condemned it to rapid decline from its position as the great entrepôt and cultural cynosure of Bengal, and what, as Geoffrey Moorhouse described, 'the second city of the Empire'.[35] The reality was that a united Bengal would have had similarly sized Hindu–Muslim populations, with the Muslims having a slight majority. I believe that the possibility of continuous strife and possible bloodshed was remote and, with the benefit of hindsight, perhaps an independent Bengal would have created the basis for a new Indian federation, independent of the straitjacket of the Government of India Act of 1935. A large, culturally and linguistically homogenous state comprising both Hindus and Muslims would have been a new paradigm and would have compelled the consideration of a more decentralised federation.

If there was a desire to see India as a composite state, which is identified with Nehru, the distinction Purushotham draws between Patel and Nehru is that Patel 'thought that it was primarily the responsibility of minorities to behave appropriately. For Nehru, however, the legitimacy of Indian democracy would be measured in terms of the effectiveness of state protection of Muslim life and property.'[36] These contrasting views were evident in a phenomenon not much remarked upon: the return of disillusioned Muslim migrants from Pakistan to India between 1947 and 1948. At this stage, the Indian government had promulgated the Emergency Permit System in July 1948 to distinguish and almost certainly discriminate between the two migrations into India—a permit system for a permanent resettlement for Hindus and Sikhs and a permit for permanent return for Muhajirs (Muslims returning from Pakistan). There were different procedures which distinguished these two channels of migration, one designed to welcome Hindu and Sikh migrants, the other to discourage the Muslims who sought to return to their former homes. This was very much the brainchild of Sardar Patel as the Home Minister and is consistent with his mindset.

It is also alleged that those Muslims who left for Pakistan in 1947 were somehow disloyal to the idea of secularism and had repudiated India. Patel stated that 'those who are disloyal will have to go to Pakistan.' [37] This is patently unfair, as in many cases the reason behind the migration had little to do with ideology, and more to do with fear of how they would be treated as minorities in India. Yet Sardar Patel, who was anxious to encourage the migration of Hindus and Sikhs from Pakistan, did not see that those who chose to migrate to Pakistan did so for much the same reason that Hindus and Sikhs were fleeing Pakistan. Some of the grisliest massacres of Muslims occurred in the princely states of Jammu and Kashmir, particularly Jammu (over 200,000 dead) and on the Meo Muslims of Alwar and Bharatpur (82,400 killed and 44,000 converted). These happened in advance of the Partition to create a sense of panic amongst Muslims. They were used by N.B. Khare (the prime minister of Alwar) and Patel to expel the Meo Muslims from Alwar to Pakistan, even before the terrible massacre of Sikhs in Rawalpindi had begun, which triggered the Punjab bloodshed. The Jammu massacre, amounting to ethnic cleansing, is a matter that does not feature much in the public discourse and it is to the credit of journalist Swaminathan Anklesaria Aiyar that he brings up this long-forgotten massacre and draws an eerie parallel with the expulsion of Kashmiri Pandits post the eruption of terrorism in Kashmir in 1989.[38] Even Gandhi commented on the 1947 massacres, saying, 'The Hindus and Sikhs of Jammu and those who had gone there from outside killed Muslims. The Maharaja of Kashmir is responsible for what is happening there ... Muslim women have been dishonoured.'[39]

One of the myriad tragedies of Partition was the fate of the Hyderabad state, the grandest and most opulent of all the princely states. The egregious massacre of Hyderabadi Muslims was almost entirely initiated by Sardar Patel, deceptively described as 'police action'.[40] The term 'police action' seeks to burnish, with a patina of legality, a brutal and savage pogrom against the Muslims, which in today's argot would be described as 'ethnic cleansing'. It is estimated that anywhere between 30,000 to 40,000 Hyderabadi Muslims were killed in this shameful episode. It was also an attempt at vandalising a rich and vibrant syncretic culture and civilisation that had developed over centuries, culminating in a delicate and sophisticated sensibility. One finds the vestigial remnants of this prodigiously evolved culture in Hyderabad even today, in the cuisine, the Dakhani language and the architecture.

Much has been commented on the implacable obduracy and intransigence of the Nizam to any sensible solution. He had a delusional sense that if the state had access to a coastline such as the Goa corridor, he could seek independence and autonomy. The harsh realities of geography made Hyderabad a state surrounded by India and militarily indefensible. This fact, coupled with the demographics of 90 per cent of the population being Hindu, made the secession of the Hyderabad state to India more or less inevitable. It was only a question of what privileges the Nizam could salvage from this and what safeguards could be put in place for the preservation of the old Hyderabadi culture, which politicians like Patel viewed as 'an ulcer in the heart of India.'[41]

Yet this grotesque obstinacy on the part of the Nizam in refusing a settlement which was offered at the time, cannot justify the degree of savagery unleashed on Hyderabad and its Muslim population by Sardar Patel and the Indian army, as a form of collective punishment for the earlier depredations by the Razakars[42] in rural areas. Patel's culpability in initiating such massacres is indubitable. The Sundarlal Committee, set up by Nehru, issued a report in 1949 which directly implicates the Indian state in the massacre of people who had surrendered. This report was never released, and as such, no government has an interest in releasing such a record of infamy. The Indian government still refuses to officially release the report, although somehow it is available on the internet.

If there was any doubt about the scale and viciousness of the violence inflicted on the minority community during the police action in Hyderabad state, I will quote from the Sundarlal Committee. The committee reported that:

> We can say at a very conservative estimate that in the whole state at least 27,000 to 40,000 people lost their lives during and after the police action ... in the town of Latur the home of Kasim Rizvi—which had been a big business centre with rich Kucchi Muslim merchants, the killings continued for over 20 days. Out of a population of about 10,000 Muslims, they were found to be barely 3,000 still in the town. Over a 1000 had been killed and the rest have run away with little else besides their lives and were completely ruined financially.

They went on to report that 'rape, abduction of women ... loot, arson, desecration of mosques, forcible conversions, seizure of houses and land, accompanied the killings ... the sufferers were Muslims who formed a hopeless minority in the rural areas.'[43] Sunil Purushotham remarks that much of the silence on the part of the Muslims in relation to this violence and depredations suffered by them was in contrast to the violence in Punjab 'which was not necessarily about pushing them out but rather about pushing them down. Violence forged, at once, a relationship of association and submission.'

It is relevant that at the Cabinet meeting after the police action, Nehru was so disturbed that he walked out, and so, to his credit, did Rajagopalachari, but this did not prevent Sardar Patel from continuing with the Cabinet meeting as if nothing had happened.

It is evident from his speeches that he remained 'convinced that our having agreed to Partition has been for the good of the country.'[44] He even said that '[n]ow that Pakistan has been established, there can be no quarrel between Hindus and Muslims.'[45] For Sardar Patel to even imagine that with the creation of Pakistan, the Hindu–Muslim question had now ceased to have any traction was absurdly myopic, to say the least. His strategy in encouraging the Hindus and Sikhs to migrate to India from Pakistan only assisted the cause of the 'confused fantasists'[46] and Sharia ideologues in their project to create an Islamic state, leading inexorably to conflict with India and its eventual alignment with an unfriendly power such as China. Given its size and capabilities, Pakistan was always going to be a client state. The only question that remained was whose client state it would be. The Congress foolishly succeeded in externalising what was an internal conflict into an international one, and Patel is the prime culprit in all the steps taken in this regard. One explanation for this could be that Patel assumed that the whole edifice of Pakistan would collapse overnight,[47] and that Partition was going to be a brief albeit horrible interlude between division and a subsequent forced reunification of India, in which the Hindu Right would be at liberty to impose their terms on the inevitable return of Muslims.

However, to Patel's credit, his most lasting achievement was the incorporation of the princely states into the construct of modern India together with V.P. Menon. The singularity of his achievement can be demonstrated by the comparative failure of the Muslim League, which had fourteen princely states, either within Pakistan or contiguous to it, and by 14 August 1956, only one princely state, Swat, had acceded to Pakistan. In contrast, on the 15 August, India's Independence Day, all but six of the 548 princely states had been incorporated into the Indian union.

Gandhi

Gandhi was more realistic than Nehru in that he understood the menace communalism posed and, in his lifetime, sought to establish a sense of trust between the two communities he viewed as brothers. In such roles, he believed, there was a duty cast on the brothers to practice unity, to help each other, and to relinquish matters of value if such matters offended the other. One such issue that Gandhi wanted the Muslims to voluntarily concede to was the prohibition of cow slaughter, but he also sincerely believed that it was the duty of Hindus to protect Muslims, the latter being a minority.[48] He never saw the issue in terms of rights-based solutions, but one based on the principle of universalism and trust. As philosopher Martha Nussbaum puts it, 'Gandhi reinterpreted the Hindu tradition in a more egalitarian manner than was conventional.'[49]

This position was consistent with his conception of the state in contrast to Nehru's, and in many ways, his horror at what a centralised state may lead to was very prescient. In his principal work, *Hind Swaraj,* he envisaged an India of villages, where the village was pivotal in defining society, power relationships and economics. He belonged to the pluralist tradition where the locus of power is dispersed and fragmented amongst various groups and associations. So, he saw the dangers of nationalism arising particularly from a centralised political structure and for that reason, was deprecating of the Western model. He argued that it would lead inevitably to coercion and that, in effect, India would be substituting one kind of oppression for another.

Gandhi's view on future constitutional arrangements was at best inchoate. It was clear that he didn't warm to the idea of Western civilisation which he termed 'The Kingdom of Satan' dominated by the 'God of War'.[50] In sharp contrast, he described Indian civilisation as dominated by the 'God of Love'. He saw freedom as an opportunity for Indians to 'revert to their own glorious civilisation.'[51] He was characteristically opaque as to what parts of this civilisational patrimony were required to be retained and what were to be excised; in that he was as ever the master of exquisite equivocation.

Social theorist Ashis Nandy tries to explicate this argument in the context of religion and secularism by arguing that the Gandhian position was that the intoxicating power of religious belief should be harnessed to practise tolerance and that these principles of tolerance and co-existence were best defined by society rather than through state mandate.[52] This thinking is consistent with Gandhi's belief in a duty-based system rather than a right-based one; under which people had an a priori duty, for example, to protect minorities and to not disrespect Dalits and Adivasis. The difficulty with this argument was that the momentum and impetus of modern democratic politics lay stress on identities, religion and caste as mobilising forces. This has led to a political cul-de-sac of an illiberal democracy that energises community sentiment for political favour, jobs and benefits, and these trump all the civilities that Gandhi considered central to his project. This also has to be coupled with the momentum of territorial nationalism, which views the retention of every inch of territory as being part of the government's principal duty to maintain sovereignty at any cost.

Gandhi's first important intervention in Hindu–Muslim politics was supporting the Khilafat Movement, to consolidate the Muslims of India against British rule by their common opposition to the war against Ottoman Turkey led by the British Empire. It was argued that the Muslims of India owed a sense of loyalty to the Ottoman Caliph who, at that time, was the guardian of the holy sites of Mecca and Medina. This movement was avowedly religious in character, and gave Gandhi the opportunity to sideline the more secular and westernised Mohammed Ali Jinnah amongst the Muslim masses, with the evocative cry of 'Islam is in danger'. Many saw this as opportunistic, and it is indeed remarkable in that one of the last mainstream politicians to take up the cause of the Caliphate before ISIS was Gandhi, the father of non-violence.

The jury is still out as to the far-reaching consequences of the Khilafat Movement, as it was clearly a controversial move. As a political tactic, it was truly inspired and had the undoubted effect of galvanising the common Muslim behind the nationalist movement in a way that no elite Muslim leader had managed. But the strategy was fraught with risk, as it brought to the surface the most atavistic and regressive forces and, unfortunately, fed into the majoritarian narrative of Muslims being a people who looked to Mecca and the Middle East as the source of their redemption, not to India.

During the period leading up to Partition, Gandhi's role was more symbolic than political, much of his thinking in *Hind Swaraj* for example was ignored by both Nehru and Ambedkar, as were his views on cultural plurality by many on the Hindu Right, including his protégé Sardar Patel. His decision not to support the British in their war effort proved costly for the Congress in that it allowed the League to assume control of provincial governments with the support of the Hindu Mahasabha. His attempts at preventing the partition of India, including the Gandhi-Cripps Pact, were doomed, as was his effort to secure the support of Congress in favour of the Cabinet Mission Plan.

Many would argue that the manner of his death, the brutal assassination by Nathuram Godse, a self-proclaimed Hindu nationalist, set back the cause of Hindu nationalism and paved the path for the adoption of a nominally inclusive and secular India, at least in the 1950s and 1960s, the high noon of the Nehruvian consensus. If nothing else, the manner of his death brought together otherwise dissonant voices in the Congress party on the same platform, albeit for a brief period. As political scientist Pratap Bhanu Mehta puts it, if not for Gandhi's assassination, '[t]he new State would not have been able to delegitimise Hindu Nationalism to the extent it did.'[53] Perhaps that remains his most enduring and signal contribution to the cause of the people he so loved.

Jinnah

At the time, Jinnah was working closely with Hindu secular leaders like Gokhale to keep religion out of politics and had successfully engineered the Lucknow Pact of 1916, which provided a basis for future Hindu–Muslim cooperation. He saw the Khilafat Movement, with all its religious symbolism and the emotional fervour it inspired, as undoing his work as a secular liberal Muslim working in the nationalist interest. He never forgave Gandhi for his support of the movement. When Jinnah resigned at the 1920 Congress session held in Nagpur, he stated: 'I will have nothing to do with this pseudo-religious approach to politics. I do not believe in working up mob hysteria, politics is a gentleman's game.'

The most compelling description of Jinnah's metamorphosis from an apostle of secularism to a champion of the Muslim interest is found in H.V. Hodson's book *The Great Divide*. It is worth quoting at length—'Jinnah's estrangement from the Congress and his emergence as a purely communal champion were evidently due both to personal causes and to political conviction. His Muslim nationalism had become paramount above his Indian nationalism. His pride had been wounded by the disdain with which the Congress and Liberal leaders of the late 1920s had treated him. Jinnah never submitted to a slight: anecdote after anecdote tells of his cutting rejoinders to anyone who snubbed him intentionally or unintentionally, whoever he or she might be—a Judge, a Governor-General, a Secretary of State, a noble lady. Neglect was a slight rebuff of an insult. The grievance of his rejection by the Congress leaders would not be assuaged until he had finally frustrated their purpose, twenty years later. Mahomed Ali Jinnah was always a man of principle, but he was supremely a man of pride.'[54] I think this sums up the man exquisitely, particularly his exaggerated sense of amour propre.

Jinnah was compelled to argue for an Islamic state, which he thought was necessary to mobilise the Muslim community and to secure the rights of Muslims, particularly that of Muslim minorities in UP and Bihar, in a quest for parity. Author Farzana Shaikh shrewdly observes that,

> Jinnah himself contributed to this process by appealing to the language and rhetoric of Islamic universalism as a means of defeating the tribal, racial and linguistic affiliations that threatened to ruin his Muslim nationalist project. Unfortunately for Jinnah, much of the discourse of Islamic universalism upon which he had been forced to rely to realise his political project had been shaped by the ulama and their version of a Sharia-based Islam.[55]

Journalist Khaled Ahmed remarks that Jinnah had no idea that allowing the Sharia the upper hand would involve the introduction of barbaric criminal punishments, such as stoning and hands being cut off, and that is the prospect many of the conservative Ulema were salivating at. In fact, Allama Iqbal in his book *The Reconstruction of Religious Thought in Islam* in the 1920s dismissed the idea that rules relating to the penalties of crime should be introduced, arguing that they were only specific to the Prophet's time.[56] In fact, Allama Iqbal's son, Javed, clarified that '[t]he Jinnah-Iqbal correspondence, discussing Shariah, points to the establishment of a state based on Islam's welfare legislation; it does not propose that in the new state any laws pertaining to cutting of the hands (for theft) and stoning to death (for fornication) would be enforced.'[57] This was highly controversial at that time, as Iqbal was declared a kafir (a non-believer) for saying this.[58]

However, Jinnah did what he was told to do by the Ulema and his campaign and speeches are replete with fundamentalist tropes, as documented by author Venkat Dhupalia.[59] Dhupalia's book was well received, particularly in post-9/11 United States, as it dealt with revanchist Islamic thinking and the desire amongst some Muslims for a Caliphate as a political construct, and fed into the 'Clash of Civilisations' narrative perfectly. Transposing these farragoes of fundamentalist fictions as the reason for the creation of a despised and discredited ally was most convenient for the United States, particularly when presented in the guise of history, one which the Pakistani establishment could not sensibly counter. It also chimes well with the revival of the two-nation theory now espoused by the Hindu Right.

In his study, Dhupalia downplays the role of the Hindu Right as the key facilitator of the Partition; however, the fact was that Savarkar had accepted the two-nation theory before Jinnah. If one leaves Savarkar's views aside, the reality was that there were three provinces where the Hindu Mahasabha aligned with the Muslim League in 1941 to form governments and remained emphatically agnostic to the Partition.

Clearly, there were numerous writers and propagandists who urged for an Islamic state, but it is not certain to me that Jinnah subscribed to these thoughts. Even if the argument that there was widespread desire for an Islamic state is considered as the gravitational force for the creation of Pakistan, the argument is plainly deficient in that it ignores the economic dimension, which was the trepidation of getting employment for young Muslims, who had been less able to secure education than their Hindu counterparts, which explains the eventual large-scale migration of young and educated Muslims to Pakistan. Neither does the argument really deal with the growth of Hindu extremism as an existential factor in fuelling the Muslim fear of living under Hindu raj. Dhupalia concentrates almost entirely on religious dogma and millenarianism as being the driving force for Pakistan, a clever conceit to distract from the reality of an intransigent Hindu Right. As politician-diplomat Mani Shankar Aiyar puts it, the idea of Pakistan originated 'with such a tiny handful of confused fantasists that to even suggest that the demand began with the Muslims of India would be a transgression of history and a violation of fact.'[60] Yet these confused fantasists and assorted obscure clerics and ideologues are valorised and given undue prominence in relation to the creation of Pakistan, as it conveniently diverts attention from the real culprits: the Hindu Right, the centralisers as well as the Left.

Jinnah's implicit vision was that of a federal India with a degree of parity between Hindus and Muslims at the union level, a position where he believed the rights of Muslim minorities in Hindu-majority provinces could be protected. As historian Ayesha Jalal perceptively pointed out,[61] the Achilles heel in his strategy was his failure to persuade the minorities in the Muslim-majority provinces, particularly Punjab and Bengal which were ultimately partitioned, that they would be protected and have full citizenship rights in the new state as minorities.

According to author Barney White-Spunner, Jinnah manifestly had no vision for Pakistan for the simple reason that he had never intended for it to be a separate state outside a federal structure. 'The appeal to the British to stay longer, the insistence on the division of the army, which he and Liaquat both thought would be unacceptable, even if it was accepted would take several years, reemphasise that Jinnah was, as Wavell had pointed out, using the idea of Partition as a threat to get what he wanted. But Jinnah did not actually say what he wanted.'[62] His chemistry with Mountbatten was a disaster, as Mountbatten took him at his word and condemned him as a psychopathic case.

Ultimately, Jinnah ended up with what he described as a 'maimed, moth eaten, mutilated Pakistan',[63] with two wings, the North-West Frontier Province, Baluchistan, Sindh and Punjab in the West and East Bengal, by far the numerically largest province, in the East with over 1000 miles of India in between and hardly any tangible protection for the Muslim minorities that remained in India. In this regard, Jinnah's project was an abject failure. Khosla captures his achievements and failures in the most incisive way, stating, 'Mohammad Ali Jinnah's achievement lay in posing the problem of representation at a time when few others were willing to address this issue. His failure lay in an intransigent commitment to an earlier form of politics. He tried to place an old model of representation onto a new system, which unsurprisingly territorialised the question at hand.'[64] I think Khosla gives greater agency to Jinnah than he actually had. The reality was that the Muslims of undivided India were only spatially concentrated in the areas which became Pakistan, leaving the more intractable issue of the fate of the Muslims who remained behind unaddressed. These were issues which could only have been dealt with within the context of a federation as was envisaged in the Cabinet Mission Plan, with some form of parity between Hindus and Muslims, but that was contingent on the Congress' acceptance.

Jinnah's endeavours to preserve the unity of Punjab and Bengal, even going to the extent of agreeing to an independent Bengal, completely failed. Jinnah's dalliance with some of the Rajput royals such as the maharaja of Jodhpur who almost joined Pakistan, indubitably demonstrates his desire to have a substantial Hindu population within Pakistan, as that, in his view would have entrenched a powerful constituency for secularism along the lines of his 11 August 1947 speech in Karachi.

In this context, I think that the two Kathiawadis were on the same wavelength. As Faisal Devji has observed 'Jinnah, of course, had also resisted the Partition of these provinces [Bengal and Punjab] and was perhaps unfairly interpreted as doing so in order to gain more territory for Pakistan, while retaining the large Hindu and Sikh minorities in it as "hostages" to guarantee India's good behaviour towards her Muslim minority. But just as the division had been forced upon Jinnah by the same argument he used for the Partition of colonial India, so too did the Mahatma reject sectioning the provinces on the same grounds that he refused to countenance the country's division, saying that "one kind of Partition did not justify another". And while this could have meant handing Punjab and Bengal to Pakistan in their entirety, it would also have resulted in that country being deprived of an absolute Muslim majority, which might well have been Jinnah's desire as well.'[65]

As per Ayesha Jalal's path-breaking scholarship, Jinnah was using Pakistan as a bargaining counter for getting a federal India, with the states deciding the nature of the constitution on the principle of parity between Hindus and Muslims., Pakistan was not his real goal. Many books have attempted to challenge this scholarship. Ishtiaq Ahmed is a leading Pakistani political scientist who relies on Jinnah's speeches to show that Pakistan was what he really wanted.[66] However, relying only on his speeches literally does a disservice to understanding the quicksands of the politics of that time and the intriguing complexity of the man.

I believe that Jinnah used the demand for Pakistan as a bargaining counter for obtaining entrenched rights in a federal configuration. From the time of the Lucknow Pact, he was overly anxious to protect the rights of Muslims in Muslim-majority Hindu provinces, even at the cost of Muslims in majority provinces such as Punjab and Bengal. He also considered Delhi and Uttar Pradesh important as they were the epicentres of North Indian Muslim culture and felt that for political reasons, Bombay was important.

It beggars belief that the Muslims living in these areas would be attracted to the prospect of uprooting themselves to exist as exiles in an alien land or to live on sufferance as second-class citizens in India. Both prospects were unappealing, and the only plausible construction one could put on his strategy is that he was bargaining to acquire a modicum of parity at the Centre, which is what the Cabinet Mission Plan promised, to ensure some leverage for Muslims against the Hindu Right.

In discussing Jinnah and the Partition, one is also forced to consider the colonial role in this matter. The fact that Congress did not support the war effort and adopted the Quit India Movement in 1942 allowed Jinnah to momentarily emerge as an ally of the British. Ishtiaq Ahmed, a Pakistani political scientist, has advanced claims that the British supported Muhammad Ali Jinnah—including the alleged existence of a secret pact in 1940 under which Winston Churchill is said to have promised Jinnah the creation of Pakistan in exchange for backing the British war effort. However, there is absolutely no evidence to support these claims other than rumours.[67]

With regard to this, there is a deliberate effort to conflate the interests of the West, particularly in connection with Soviet-controlled Central Asia and an acute suspicion of Nehru's left-leaning sympathies with the alleged British support for Partition. Whilst it may have suited the interests of the West to have a pliable ally in Pakistan as a buffer state on the Soviet border with Karachi as a significant port in the Indian Ocean, where air bases and troops could be based whenever required, it is a bit of a stretch to assume that the British were central in bringing about such a deliverance. This also absolves the Congress and the Hindu Right of the blame they so richly deserve.

Mountbatten

Mountbatten, a man singularly ill-suited to be the viceroy, was tasked with a highly complex situation in relation to a subcontinent of which he had very little knowledge. This ignorance, compounded by an acute distrust of experts and governors of prominent provinces and Imperial Civil Service officers, along with his desire to impose his own intuition and gut feeling, was the source of many problems which persist to this day. He was in a hurry and felt the need to get the job done within an impossible timeline, regardless of the consequences. He was also extraordinarily indiscreet and never hid his visceral repugnance for Jinnah, whom he described as 'most frigid, haughty and disdainful.'[68] This prejudice has been brilliantly articulated by historian Andrew Roberts, who pinpoints how Mountbatten's partiality for Nehru and his dislike for Jinnah affected the terms of the final settlement.[69] The fact that V.P. Menon, in his capacity as Mountbatten's constitutional advisor and attached to the Congress and attended all the staff meetings with no Muslims present, was indubitably partial. As Robert puts it, 'Time and again carrots were dangled for Nehru, whereas Jinnah only experienced its stick.'[70] As an aside, this is a factor the Hindu Right find difficult to digest, that it was Nehru's relationship with Mountbatten and, certainly with Edwina Mountbatten, that smoothed the path for the creation of India in its present form, which included the prize of Jammu and Kashmir, something that would have not been possible without the covert support of the viceroy. This is a point that Andrew Roberts remarks on, stating that 'Mountbatten's bias in favour of India seems all the more extraordinary in view of his wife's love affair with Nehru.'

The main charge against Mountbatten was his manic desire to speed up the process of handing over power, and he himself confessed that a sense of urgency took hold of him at once and never left.[71] This intent was epitomised in his 3 June decision to forward the date of transfer of power, originally envisaged by Attlee as no later than the end of June 1948 to August 1947. The timing of the transfer—the midnight of 14/15 August—was chosen by Mountbatten as it was the second anniversary of the Japanese surrender in the Second World War. It has been suggested by Richard Hough in his biography of Mountbatten[72], that the viceroy had timed the handing over of power in a manner that he could get back to London in time to attend the royal wedding between his nephew Philip and the then Princess Elizabeth, who would later go on to become Queen Elizabeth II.

It was widely commented upon that the timescale involved had the effect of aggravating the Punjab disturbances. This was certainly the view of Sir George Cunningham, the former governor of the North-West Frontier Province and the private secretary to the viceroy.[73] In his words, the violence in the Punjab was directly attributable to Mountbatten's unwisdom in accelerating the date of Partition so suddenly.

One area where the British must bear the blame, and one which has not been adequately commented on, is their role in not mitigating the excesses of the Partition-related violence. In this context, the role of Mountbatten assumes importance. The British exit from India was deliberately hurried as they had become aware of the impending violence and wanted to avoid responsibility and blame. The British governor of the Punjab, Evan Jenkins, had been sending urgent messages to London warning of the coming conflagration, violence and turmoil, so they were fully apprised of the situation.[74] Hodson seeks to contextualise this by emphasising the general breakdown of civil government in Punjab, which he ascribed to the growing communalisation amongst Indians both in the armed forces and in the government.[75] This may be true, but it does not quite explain the extraordinary haste in the passing of the final act of Parliament which, in the words of Yasmin Khan, 'unhooked India from its Imperial master.' She observes that 'it is difficult to avoid the damning conclusion that, in the minds of British policy-makers, the duty to protect the lives of South Asians had already ended.'[76]

Another important factor, which is rarely remarked upon but is well articulated in historian Alex von Tunzelmann's analysis[77] is the matter of the wherewithal. Apart from the perfidies of Mountbatten, the real constraint on Imperial policy was the lack of resources. The British public had voted for the Labour Party in 1945 by a landslide, indubitably demonstrating a desire to put domestic British interests first and to firmly repudiate the imperialist ambitions and delusions of Churchill. As Tunzelmann puts it 'the British government was in the middle of its worst financial crisis since the Great Depression … hundreds of thousands had been killed and millions expended [in the Second World War]. Their normal industries had been battered, their towns destroyed, and their families broken up and stuck back together. Still, they languished under the strictures of rationing, which were getting tighter, not looser. To these ordinary people, the Empire was a superfluous accoutrement.'[78] This is a pragmatic assessment of the position, but one distinctly at odds with Mountbatten's extravagantly grandiose representations and assurances regarding the matter of security the British imperium offered in the event of the violent dislocation of society predicted by the colonial governors at the time. Mountbatten's solution to mitigate British culpability was to deliberately delay announcing the Punjab Award[79] partitioning Punjab and Bengal until after 15 August 1947, so that the blame for the inevitable bloodshed would be borne by the incoming government.

I think it is appropriate to quote Ayesha Jalal's conclusion about Mountbatten's triumphalism. She states, 'While Punjab writhed and turned under the impact of decisions taken in distant places, Mountbatten boldly claimed credit for having accomplished, in less than two and a half months, one of the "greatest administrative operations in history". On behalf of the Hindus, Sikhs and Muslims who were slaughtered in their hundreds of thousands, and the refugees who in their millions stumbled fearfully across the frontiers of the two States, the historian has a duty to challenge Mountbatten's contention and ask whether this "great operation" was not in fact an ignominious scuttle enabling the British to extricate themselves from the awkward responsibility of presiding over India's communal madness.'[80]

I believe that the most perceptive and balanced judgement on the Partition and its responsibility was given by one of the greatest Indian jurists of the time, Sir Chimanlal Harilal Setalvad.[81] He stated:

> In 1947, it's futile to attempt to hide the naked truth by saying that force of circumstances has compelled the Congress to accept the Partition of India and they had to submit to the inevitable. The circumstances were of their own creation, and what had once been warded off was made inevitable by their own deeds. The cherished boon of a united India had fallen into their lap, but they by their own want of political wisdom threw it out and made it beyond their reach ... What has happened is indeed a great personal triumph for Mr Jinnah. Within seven years after the Lahore Pakistan resolution of 1940, he has succeeded in defeating a great political organisation of sixty years' standing with the backing of the large majority of the Indian people. But has he succeeded in doing good to the Muslims themselves and to his country? ... this division of India has laid the foundations of interminable quarrels and chaos which will bring untold suffering to generations yet unborn.

This is a very prescient observation as to how the future would unfold; Jinnah had indeed won a Pyrrhic victory. His high-risk gamble in a bid to secure parity and federalism had failed, and he was left to confront the solution he had pleaded for but had never imagined would come true. He became the prisoner of his own stratagem, at the tragic and enduring cost of his co-religionists.

The toxic and malign politics emanating from the United Provinces, as well as a history of bitter and unresolved confrontations between Hindus and Muslims, in the context of a society which, notwithstanding the Muslim's numerical minority, exercised cultural hegemony over the state, deeply provoked the Brahmin elite. This desire to eradicate a syncretic culture spilled over, poisoning Hindu–Muslim relations in North India, eventually transcending into a grudging coexistence to ignite disaffection, violence and bitterness which persist to this day between the Hindu and the Muslim and the Indian and the Pakistani.

PART II

THE POLITICAL AND CULTURAL CONSEQUENCES OF PARTITION

5

THE RISE OF THE COW BELT

Partition changed not only the borders of India, but the character of the new State as it increased the political heft of and privileged the cow belt. It was in UP that the Hindu–Muslim struggles were the most salient prior to Partition and where caste competitiveness was most compelling in determining the contours and the idiom of future political discourse.

The politics of UP during that period was a decisive factor in the creation of Pakistan, as many of the issues which formed the fault lines and fissures between Hindu and Muslim communities in North India were found in the cow belt as early as the nineteenth century—the ban on cow slaughter, the Ayodhya dispute over the Ram temple, the allegations of mosques being built over temples and the Urdu-Hindi confrontation. Incidents of music being played outside mosques to disturb namaz were persistent irritants between the two communities even in the nineteenth century. This has been remarked upon by historian Francis Robinson in his study of Muslim separatism and, more recently, by professor of Indian history William Gould in his seminal work, *Hindu Nationalism and the Language of Politics in Late Colonial India*.[1]

UP and Bihar were peculiar, in the words of author Jim Masselos, as there was 'a synthesis of Islamic and Hindu cultures … in such cities such as Allahabad and Banaras [known as Varanasi], it was the Muslims who constituted the dominant elite. Here, where the language of government offices and law courts was Urdu ... the Muslims were at an advantage.'[2] It was this cultural hegemony that Hindu society, led by Brahmins belonging to the Congress party, sought to challenge and displace, and which laid the foundation for the demonisation of the Muslims. Even in pre-Independence times, the intent of the Hindu Right was to consolidate Hindus against Muslims.

The primacy of this politics arose from the importance which the cow belt enjoyed in independent India. The structure of the caste-system and the position of Muslims were different in the other two large states which were divided by reason of Partition, Punjab and Bengal. After Partition, even though East Punjab and West Bengal became part of India, they did not enjoy the same influence that they did in pre-Partition undivided India.

The partition of Punjab and Bengal had huge implications for the future of India, in ways that were unintended. These large, rich and intellectually significant states were greatly diminished by the Partition. Lahore was once called the 'Paris of the East' and was a great centre of education and culture, theatre, music and even had a fledgling film industry; it reigned as one of the pre-eminent cities in India. Punjab's tribal configurations trumped religion, as sociologist Roger Ballard puts it, 'all religious practices in Punjab, whether Sikhism, Hinduism or Islam, shared common beliefs, traditions and lived experiences. The 1881 census, for instance, revealed that a majority of jat or birdaris (caste or kinship or, in the words of British colonialists, tribal groups) included Hindu, Sikh and Muslim members.'[3] This view of the notion of 'biradari' was encapsulated in the remarks of Malik Khizar Hayat Tiwana, former prime minister of Punjab and leader of the Unionist party, who virulently opposed the partition of the Punjab province. He told Jinnah, 'There are Hindu and Sikh Tiwanas who are my relatives. I go to their weddings and other ceremonies. How can I possibly regard them as coming from another country?'[4]

Calcutta was the birthplace of the Bengali Renaissance and the administrative capital of British India until 1911. Apart from being a hub for frenetic intellectual vibrancy, it was a significant port and commercial centre for colonial India. It was also the birthplace of several important reform movements in relation to the Hindu religion, including the Brahmo Samaj.

The 'bhadralok' or the bourgeoisie of Bengal, in a sense, defined early nationalism and made the important distinction between the material and the spiritual, something unknown in the rest of India. This was part of the Bengali renaissance which questioned religious traditions and adopted, with great alacrity, modern science, history, literature and Western education, the leading figures of which were Ram Mohan Roy, Rabindranath Tagore and Vidyasagar. The notion of the private self being central to the identity of the modern individual was truly remarkable in that it quarantined religious practices and rituals into a private domestic space within the family. The only time that this demarcation would be violated was at the time of the Durga puja ceremonies once a year. The Bengali outlook, both in terms of caste and religion, but particularly on religion in public life, was altogether different from that of upper-caste Hindus in the United Provinces, where religion impinged on all elements of public life.

By a conservative estimate, today the population of an undivided Punjab roughly would be around 168 million people, and the population of an undivided Bengal would roughly be over 200 million people. These states could have become a huge buffer against the malign politics which originated from UP. They would certainly have had linguistic and cultural autonomy and character, which would have assisted in the emergence of a more federal system. It is also relevant that these states were not obvious Congress states. They had powerful regional parties, like the Unionist Party in Punjab; and particularly in East Bengal, there was the Krishak Praja Party (KPP) led by the charismatic A.K. Fazlul Haq, who played an enormous role in pushing through reforms in land ownership and education. Many have suggested that the social reforms that have taken place in independent Bangladesh were a result of the reforms put in place by Haq in the 1940s. The Congress did have a presence in Bengal through the Bose brothers (Sarat Chandra and Subhash Chandra), but it didn't enjoy the kind of brute hegemony it enjoyed in the cow belt. Perhaps this influenced the Congress leadership on the question of partitioning Bengal and Punjab, since it substantially guaranteed the continuance of the Congress as a political force in India post-Independence.

Once Punjab and Bengal were divided by the Partition, the contours of the Indian republic and its politics became apparent; they largely mirrored the ideology and prejudices of the Indo-Gangetic plain, which had an inexorable predilection towards communal and caste politics and cultural revanchism. We see this in the unending desire to reclaim temples and find the source of the mythical river Saraswati and other such fetishes.

It is critical to understand that the new nationalism, whilst paying lip service to V.D. Savarkar, deviates from his thinking. Savarkar was not interested in elevating the cow, this being very much the fetish of the cow belt. It is not an accident that the lightning rod which propelled the Bharatiya Janata Party (BJP) to its current hegemony started with the Ayodhya movement, and it is hugely symbolic of this journey that we see the prime minister of a soi-disant secular state inaugurating a new Ram Temple at Ayodhya and a new temple corridor in Varanasi with great pomp and ceremony, as if they were national events of seminal importance. According to Pratap Bhanu Mehta, 'UP has been critical to the public staging of the Hindutva Project in a way that is not true of other states. The project of communalising all of India is central to the BJP, but the symbolic significances of Ayodhya, Kashi, and Mathura as performances of Hindu unity and as a wedge around which to consolidate a communal consciousness cannot be underestimated.'[5]

The United Provinces

The United Provinces have been described as 'an artifact [that] was formed gradually by conquest and annexation'.[6] Starting in 1775 when Lord Wellesley acquired the lower Doab region (Doab being the land between the Ganga and Jamuna rivers), Rohilkhand and Gorakhpur. There were further conquests and annexations until the British imposed their sovereignty in forty-nine districts.

The United Provinces could boast of many of the past glories of Muslim rule: Jaunpur, the capital of the Sharqi rulers; Fatehpur Sikri, founded by Akbar; Agra, the city associated with Shah Jahan and the Taj Mahal; Bareilly, the seat of the Rohilla kingdom; Faizabad and Lucknow, under the rule of the Nawabs of Oudh. With these royal courts and the Mughal court in nearby Delhi, there grew a cornucopia of culture and high art, music, poetry and architecture in the United Provinces, which formed the very essence of Islamic civilisation in India. On the other hand, UP also housed some of the most consequential centres of Hinduism: Prayag (Allahabad), where the confluence of the sacred Ganga meets with the Jamuna; Ayodhya, the birthplace of Lord Ram; Haridwar, the site of the Kumbh Mela and Mathura, the birthplace of Lord Krishna. In light of such history, it is easy to see how fissures arose between the cultural heartlands of the Muslims and the sacred spaces of the Hindus in the United Provinces.

It was not just the cultural factors but also religious tropes that endowed and suffused the Indo-Gangetic plain with a divine, sacrilegious quality for the Muslims. As Christophe Jaffrelot puts it, 'Traditionally, Hindus claimed that the territory below the Himalayan arch was their holy land. Muslims could now feel the same because the Indian sites where Sufi saints were buried were endowed with sacredness too.' Muslim kings patronised these shrines, promoting pilgrimages to theses sacred spots (ziyarets). Royal visits to such sites involved big donations and grants made to local Sufi orders (silsilas). This is a factor many people miss, transfixed by Savarkar's observation that Indian Muslims only genuflect before Mecca. They pointedly ignore the existence of popular shrines like Ajmer Sharif in Rajasthan, Hazrat Nizamuddin in Delhi, and myriad other holy places spread throughout UP and Bihar. Similarly, two of South Asia's most vaunted institutions of Islamic learning—the Darul Uloom of Deoband and the Darul Uloom Nadwatul Ulama of Lucknow, are both located in UP and both these institutions have flourished in recent times in spite of their profoundly regressive agendas.

UP was distinguished by its peculiar caste configurations. Upper castes, such as Brahmins, Kshatriyas and Baniyas, amounted to around 20 per cent of the population, many of whom had a traditional antagonism to Muslims, who comprised around 25 per cent of the population. This antagonism has manifested in several forms, including on the matter of cow slaughter. If the religious argument for banning cow slaughter is at best dubious, the political impetus for this policy was the means to consolidate the lower castes against Muslims. A factor pointed out by political scientists, Sudha Pai and Sajjan Kumar, is what they describe as 'the delayed development of Dalit consciousness among the large mass of persons described as untouchables', which distinguished UP from the western and southern parts of India and enabled upper castes to co-opt what we now describe as Dalits into an expansive Hindu identity.[7]

Historian Francis Robinson traces the roots of the disputes between Muslims and Hindus in UP to the development of urban administration and the process of elections to these bodies in the late nineteenth century. Traditionally, Kotwals, who were almost always Muslim, oversaw urban administration and exercised considerable influence through systems of patronage. Kotwals were replaced by municipal boards, and the locus of patronage shifted accordingly. The chairman of a municipal board, for instance, now held significant authority over various aspects of urban life, including sanitation and public works. This position could easily be used to advance personal religious or cultural agendas. As Robinson remarks, 'So, under the guise of hygienic management of slaughter houses and kabab shops, Hindus could defend the cow and impose their standards on Muslims, while, for the Muslims, the maintenance of their right to slaughter cows and eat them could become a symbol of their ability to protect their religion and culture.'[8] He also highlights the growth of 'Nagari' (the Devanagari script), which was widely adopted in the late nineteenth century in UP, much to the chagrin of Muslims and some upper-caste Hindus, as another example of discord. These were presentiments of future conflicts and were the consequence of growing Hindu assertiveness and increasing Muslim defensiveness and fear for the future.

There were also economic forces at work, many of the poorer Muslims were weavers by trade (Julahas), something they took great pride in. They were readily distinguishable, and what we find in colonial records and gazettes of the middle to late nineteenth century is a curated image of bigoted and aggressive Julahas instigating communal riots. The economic catalyst was the loss of status of the Julahas, partly because of the rise in cotton prices, the introduction of the factory system, and the loss of patronage from aristocratic courts that were replaced by shopkeepers and merchants. According to historian Gyanendra Pandey,

> This stereotype as we know it appears to have been forged in UP. This fact is surely not unrelated to the recurrent conflicts over religious practice and ritual precedence in this region that we have noticed earlier, and the fact that exclusively Muslim political organisations of a modern kind found their earliest roots here.[9]

The economic dislocation and immiseration of the Julahas was compounded by cultural wars which had been simmering from the nineteenth century; it did not take much to spark a communal conflagration. In 1931, Kanpur witnessed a most bloody and vicious riot, which was occasioned by what the Muslims complained of as being the activities of Hindu preachers. As Gould puts it, 'Most of this evidence related to the late 1920s and the Arya Samaj campaign of shuddhi, or purification. But the continual use of religious rhetoric to propagate Congress ideas in the early 1930s must have created more immediate associations.'[10]

The shock of the Kanpur riots was instrumental in the drafting of the then Karachi Resolution of fundamental rights in 1931. The new rights included the right to cultural autonomy and the right to equal educational facilities. This was of particular relevance in UP, as that was the very cauldron of these cultural wars. Gandhi himself moved the resolution and made a distinction between the Aryan and Islamic cultures, pleading for tolerance. He pinned his banner to the notion of 'religious neutrality', which meant that State neutrality was to be adopted in religious affairs.

UP played a central role in the partition of India as well, as there was a failure to find accommodation between the two communities. The assertiveness of Brahmin Congress leaders such as Madan Mohan Malviya and Govind Ballabh Pant, as well as Dr Sampurnanand (a Kayasth), expressed an implacable desire to remove all vestiges of

Muslim culture, and forced many nationalist Muslims onto the back foot. This is rarely discussed. The narrative is focused on the alleged separatist tendencies of the Muslims, but little thought is given to why such separatism arose in the first place. If some accommodation had been given to Urdu, much of the constituency on which the League relied in UP would have vanished.

What is fascinating is much of the work done by political scientist Paul Brass which makes the point that, contrary to the stereotypical image of the sleepy, backward Muslim community, the Muslims of UP were urbanising much faster than Hindus in the half-century until 1931, thus making it easier for the Muslim League to recruit young urban Muslims which they did in substantial numbers. They were able to win over half of the Muslim votes in 1937 and 71 per cent in 1946. According to author Pratinav Anil, 'The Muslims were mobilising faster than Hindus were assimilating them. Put differently, nationalist Muslims were very rapidly being put out of business by separatist Muslims.' This is an interesting point based on solid data. For example, Anil refers to the case of 1,00,000 Urdu-speaking Muslim students emigrating from the countryside to cities where there existed only 20,000 places in Hindi-medium institutions, which 'meant that the balance 80,000 students would create Urdu ones [Urdu-medium institutions].'[11] These factors—urbanisation, literacy and employment—metamorphosed a community into a putative nation.

The History of Uttar Pradesh

It is perplexing that the state of Uttar Pradesh has retained the acronym UP from the old United Provinces and difficult to understand why it was not divided to ensure better representation of the different linguistic traditions. It has sixty districts which address the needs of over 241 million people. The old British creation of the United Provinces included, in the Northwest, a large part of what we now know as Haryana, which became the PEPSU states before Punjab was further divided to create the new state of Haryana. The hill areas now comprising the state of Uttarakhand were also taken away from UP in recent times. But barring these divisions, the original state remains largely intact, although it includes distinct areas which have different demographics and subcultures, such as the Bundelkhand which extends up to Madhya Pradesh, western UP which has much in common with Haryana, eastern UP where the local dialects including Bhojpuri are very pronounced and Awadh, which is the central part of UP. It is a testament to UP's political importance that this further subdivision has not occurred. It also speaks to the desire of the Hindi-speaking belt to retain some degree of hegemony in the North, through the imposition of a Brahminical Sanskrit culture at the cost of many other subcultures and languages.

Within the States Reorganisation Committee (SRC) constituted in the 1950s, there were disagreements as to what should be done with UP, given its humongous size and dominance. K.M. Panikkar, one of the members of the committee, was of the view that UP was so large and densely populated that it posed a challenge to the political equipoise of the federation. In fact, he plainly stated that it was 'likely to undermine the federal structure itself and thereby be a danger to the unity of the country.'[12] Panikkar had proposed partitioning the state into five separate regions. Dr Ambedkar was also troubled by the size and dominance of UP and suggested that it be divided into three parts—the western area with its capital in Meerut, the central area having its capital in Kanpur and the eastern part with its capital in Allahabad. The reasons he gave for proposing the division were very prescient: that it was necessary to counter the 'consolidation of the north and Balkanisation of south' and to provide a 'safeguard to the minorities.'[13]

Despite these dissenting voices, the then chief minister of UP, G.B. Pant, was of the view that the state represented an unbreakable culture and religious integrity that was the heart of India, and championed the preservation of the state along colonial lines. He played a signal role in preserving UP as a state post-Independence. He became the Union home minister in 1955 and was responsible for implementing the States Reorganisation Act, 1956. He ensured that there was no division of UP, as other members had suggested.

Therefore, apart from some minor changes in the Northwest and in the hill areas that later became Uttarakhand, the British demarcations remained largely intact, augmented only by the accession of three princely states of Tehri Garhwal, Banaras and Rampur. This territory comprises at least four different linguistic areas, namely: Awadhi, Braj Bhasha, Kannauji and Bhojpuri. The fact that this state has not been further divided is also a testament to upper-caste hegemony and the overweening desire of the new nationalism to privilege Hindi, as evidenced by the demand that Hindi be made the national language. Whilst this fetish with the imposition of Hindi was largely aimed at eradicating or marginalising Urdu, it instead resulted in diminishing the usage and value of these subaltern languages, literary traditions, and the rich subcultures associated with them.

The issues that we see in evidence today as being central to the new nationalism, derive from the homogenising ideology of the cow belt, which proclaims the centrality of being Hindu and of speaking Hindi to the configuration of a pan-Indian identity, while sustaining entrenched caste allegiances. A warped view of secularism, coupled with a diluted and hollowed-out federal structure, has created a brand of politics which is both toxic and damaging for the Indian state. It proclaims an ideology which is insistently revanchist in that it looks back to a mythical past for the recovery of lost status and dignity, but one which offers no solutions to any of our myriad contemporary problems.

The price paid by the people of UP for this artificial construct has been ruinous. It has been argued that it is too big a state to be properly administered, and certain areas such as Bundelkhand, for example, have suffered greatly for being part of the state. This region, which runs along the southwest of UP, is mired in backwardness and has been insulated from whatever minimal development that has occurred in the rest of UP. According to journalist Abhigyan Prakash,

> The argument that UP needs to be split into many states—following the formation of Uttarakhand—arises from the lack of holistic development in the state. Better employment opportunities and better grassroots economics will ensure that the people of the state are not forced to leave it in such large numbers as they do now to look for work in other parts of India.[14]

What is missed here is a point that G.B. Pant iterated when the SRC was in discussions in the mid-1950s, that the survival of UP in its present configuration was needed to reify its 'cultural and religious integrity'. It is seminal to note that this integrity encompassed the national integrity, which meant that if Hindi became the state language of UP, it is axiomatic that it would also become the national language of India. According to Neera Chandhoke, this was 'a narrow construction of nationalism based on an authoritative canon created as texts within the Vedic and Upanishad traditions.'[15] That was indubitably a Brahmanical construct, one which destroyed and obliterated not just Urdu but other regional and subaltern languages and dialects in the process of creating the simulacrum of a national identity: the Hindu, Hindi-speaking paradigm.

The Congress in UP

The Congress rule in UP for the first several decades of Independence was marked by a succession of Brahmin chief ministers who enjoyed the loyal support of Muslims, the Scheduled Castes and Dalits. Through this montage, they presented an image of an Indian identity, seeking to present a multi-faceted and inclusive face. Admittedly, the challenge in the 1960s, at least in UP, was from the well-to-do farmers, the peasant parties and the Lohiaite Socialists, who did not pose a threat in cultural terms, save for their fetish for Hindi and their desire to impose it as the national language. With the advent of Indira Gandhi and the splitting of the Congress Party, the centralisation of power concomitant with the cult of personality inexorably enfeebled the party organisation, causing, in the words of author Sunil Khilnani, 'The crisis of the Indian state ... is also a crisis of the idea of India.'[16]

The conservative nature of the representation of Congress in North India, particularly the over-representation of the upper castes in its ranks, influenced its politics. According to Christophe Jaffrelot, 'the massive presence of conservative upper caste notables and the intelligentsia among the party's leaders reinforced its opposition to the social reform programme of progressive elements in the leadership.'[17] The Brahminic hegemony was formidable, and whilst this did not necessarily mean that every Brahmin was a reactionary, but as Jaffrelot has put it, 'for one Nehru, there were many Malaviyas'. This conservatism was buttressed by the need for money to fight elections. The Congress from its earliest days had the support of Hindu business magnates, such as the Birlas and Bajajs.

Oddly enough, according to author Joya Chatterji, the 'hard right within the Congress party was bolstered by Gandhi's death, even as its reputation was damaged among the population at large. This was made clear by the victory of Purushottam Das Tandon (1882–1962) in the 1950 election to the Congress Presidency, winning by an increased share of the vote. A darling of the Hindu Right, Tandon was an orthodox Hindu from Uttar Pradesh, with powerful anti-Muslim views.' As per Chatterji, the Congress in UP was more or less autonomous:

> [i]gnoring Nehru's attempts to force it to follow the 'national' line. Full of Hindu Right-Wingers like Tandon and Charan Singh, India's new largest province promoted Hindi in the Devanagari script in schools, denied support to Urdu and took active measures to make sure that Muslims in government service, particularly policemen, were driven out of their jobs.[18]

The social conservatism prevalent in post-Independence UP and the cow belt in general shaped the politics and the future of India and, sadly, continues to do so. For example, the fact that UP was largely agricultural could not but be a factor in the state's refusal to tax agricultural income and place no cap on such an exemption. The UP land reform laws, which imposed a forty-acre ceiling on individuals in order to provide land for the landless, were designed to fail as there was only going to be 1.3 per cent of surplus land. With a wealthy agricultural class remaining untaxed and tax benefits being afforded to HUFs, the government was exempting the Hindu mercantile class from serious taxation, leaving the tax base of the country limited and narrow. In this context, the lazy arguments about Fabian socialism being the bane of the Indian economy should be seen as nothing but a deflection from the truth that no serious redistributive programme could have been implemented without substantial fiscal support which could hardly have come from the fledgling corporate sector. The Hindu mercantile and landed classes wanted to insulate themselves from serious taxation, and the Congress obliged.

The economist Ashoka Mody meditates on what could have been, drawing the parallel of post-independent India having a development strategy similar to that of Japan after the Meiji Restoration,[19] which had transformed an impoverished agrarian country to an industrial powerhouse with in the span of fifty years. In fact, this development model had been discussed and had found a place in India's first five-year plan. However, land reforms, which were critical to accelerating agricultural productivity, were stymied by wealthy farmers who replaced the zamindars, leaving small farmers, agricultural labourers and the landless in the lurch. If land reforms were not implemented, the absence of any serious attention to basic primary education in the early years had grave implications, in that the workforce was unable to acquire much-needed skills and increase productivity even in subsistence agriculture. East Asia is remarkable for the success with which it achieved universal primary education in Japan, for example, universal primary education for girls was achieved by the 1920s. Nothing like this was replicated in North India, and even today the situation is dire. India as a nation has a literacy rate of around 80 per cent in 2025 and needless to say there is great divergence across states: UP clocks in at 78.2 per cent compared to 95.3 per cent scored by Kerala.

The issue of education is seminal. Nehru is often blamed for not encouraging primary education and concentrating more on tertiary education, on setting up the IITs and IIMs, for example. However, primary education was a state subject, and the real issue was the need to have an economic incentive for improving education, which would only have come through land reform. Educational institutions were either colonial or, if funded by Indian businesses, philanthropic: not investments for economic productivity. Landlords in nations where land holdings are concentrated and unequal have a vested interest in a continuous flow of cheap unskilled labour, and thus care little about promoting the cause of education. In UP and much of North India, because of the failure to implement land reforms, the incentive to create a technically proficient workforce was non-existent.

A lack of interest in investing in people transcends the Left-Right divide. This was apparent in the 1950s when the matter of prioritising primary education was a policy which even Milton Friedman, the Nobel prize-winning economist was in favour of and no one can accuse him of having left-wing sympathies. In a memorandum to Nehru in 1955, he strongly advocated huge public investment in education. In his words, he argued that:

> The present writer is convinced that the fundamental problem for India is the improvement of the physical and technical quality of her people, the awakening of a sense of hope, the weakening of rigid social and economic arrangements, the introduction of flexibility in institutions and mobility of people, the opening up of the social and economic ladder for people of all kinds and classes.[20]

The reluctance to encourage education was compounded immeasurably by the parochial proclivities of the commercial class and the suffocating existence of the caste system. To draw a parallel, one can look to a study of Italy in the 1950s done by the American political scientist Edward Banfield, who sought to explain why the south of Italy was so much poorer in comparison to the north.[21] He attributed this difference to the intense family ties present in the south which, he argued, diminished trust outside of one one's kinship group and weakened cooperation towards furtherance of common public goals which resulted in lower regional prosperity. To some extent, this sums up the North Indian business class which as an institution is embedded in the HUF, growing prosperity within the family at the cost of society.

In *Why Nations Fail,* economists Daron Acemoglu and James A. Robinson argue that:

> Economic institutions shape economic incentives: the incentives to become educated, to save and invest, to innovate and adopt new technologies, and so on. It is the political process that determines what economic institutions people live under, and it is the political institutions that determine how this process works ... For example, it is the political institutions of a nation that determine the ability of citizens to control politicians and influence how they behave.[22]

It is these political institutions that are at fault. They have been so compromised that citizens of such countries are unable to influence politicians in the way citizens in successful nations are able to. The authors go on to show that getting it wrong is not by mistake; rather, 'it is mostly because those in power make choices that create poverty.'[23] This is an important point, and it has widespread ramifications on the North-South debate, as states like UP have little in terms of institutional frameworks, both economic and political, and appear to have no interest in developing them, as the mainspring of the political agenda in such states is the 'other'ing of minorities.

So, we see a reprise in Muslim baiting—which was all too prevalent in the late nineteenth century and the first half of the twentieth century—as the engine for the new nationalism. In India, the force that animates this nationalism appears to be hatred and demonisation of minorities, particularly Muslims, as a political strategy to unify what is termed as Hindu society, which is then encouraged to consolidate and vote for one party en bloc. An example of this was the choice of a most divisive and polarising figure, Yogi Adityanath, as the chief minister of UP in 2017, when the BJP won the state election by a landslide.

Yogi Adityanath was a controversial figure well before he became the chief minister. He had a number of criminal cases registered against him, including those for murder and rioting. He conveniently got the state government (which he then ran) to drop these cases and now rules over a state which comprises 16 per cent of India's population but boasts of more than 25 per cent of the national crimes against women and girls. He is infamous for his rabid communal speeches proclaiming, 'If they kill one Hindu, then we will kill 100 Muslims.' In order to sustain his brand of politics, he set up something known as the 'Hindu Yuva Vahini' as a vigilante force aimed against Muslims in Gorakhpur and its surrounding districts. His politics are unashamedly communal, prescribing vigorous action against slaughterhouses and alleged cow slaughter. In the demonstrations against the Citizenship (Amendment) Act, he went to the extent of passing laws to confiscate the property of protesters, a step which the Supreme Court rightly nullified.[24] He also has the dubious record of presiding over the highest percentage of extrajudicial killings in India. In a period of three years, there have been 179 alleged criminals killed in over 10,000 encounters.[25]

UP's economic trajectory is sliding downwards under Adityanath's stewardship. His signature, and seemingly most significant, reforms relate to changing the names of cities. Allahabad has now become Prayagraj, Faizabad district has been renamed Ayodhya, and Agra, once a Mughal capital, is waiting to be renamed. Sudha Pai and Sajjan Kumar remark on the gravitational pull the BJP has over many of the Dalit sub-castes in UP, despite the atrocities committed against their women, by reason of the growth of the 'Labharthi' (beneficiary culture), largely piloted by Modi with his development, cultural inclusion and hyper-nationalism agenda.[26] This is the much-lauded UP model of governance.

This model of governance along with UP's version of Hindutva majoritarianism is radiating outwards and changing the idiom and character of political discourse, such that other states are metamorphosing into the larger UP. Harsh Mandar, the political activist, has remarked that 'when Uttar Pradesh's combative Chief Minister Adityanath first weaponised the bulldozer to destroy, in a loop, the properties and the morale of Muslim citizens, other Bharatiya Janata Party chief ministers, in Madhya Pradesh, Uttarakhand and Assam, emulated him.'[27]

The question which arises then is whether the results of the 2024 Lok Sabha elections, which showed BJP suffering substantial losses in UP, including in the constituency of Faizabad (location of the Ayodhya temple), undermine the argument posited in this book? Whilst the BJP suffered a setback in UP, most of the seats in the election came from what we know as the cow belt—states like Madhya Pradesh, for example, gave full support to BJP's agenda. It can be argued that in UP there were local issues at work which undermined BJP's strategy. In the run-up to the election, the temple agenda was posited as a game changer for the BJP, on the basis that agitations in relation to both the Gyanvapi mosque in Varanasi and Mathura's Shahi Idgah would likely harvest the same electoral returns as Ayodhya had in the past. The 2024 election results, however, cruelly laid bare the limitations of a Hindutva agenda bereft of any serious attempt to engineer economic and social development. The BJP's dog-whistle messaging directed towards the minority community compelled the consolidation of the Muslim and some of the Dalit vote, leading to their wholesale evacuation from the Bahujan Samaj Party (BSP) to Akhilesh Yadav's Samajwadi Party (SP). In the past, BJP had relied on BSP in UP to split the Muslim and Dalit votes, however BSP succeeded in polling less than 10 per cent of votes, down from almost 20 per cent in 2019.[28] In addition to the BSP debacle, there were disagreements within the BJP over candidate selection, with Yogi Adityanath at odds with Amit Shah, and this sabotaged the election effort. Another factor which led to many hardened BJP supporters not voting for the party was the cynical fielding of political turncoats in many seats, a disproportionate number of whom lost. However, the chemistry between the Congress and the Samajwadi Party (SP) proved to be a winning formula, with the alliance bagging forty-three seats compared to thirty-three for the BJP. These factors, in my view, played a role in the election result, but do not undermine the argument about the centrality of UP and the cow belt in India's elections. BJP's performance in UP undermined its Hindutva plank, but the caste and community factors remained relevant.

OBC Votes in UP

In the 1960s, a mysterious caste category known as the OBCs emerged in India. These are the castes that enjoy hegemony in political terms in contemporary India and dominate UP and Bihar politically; a category to which Narendra Modi owes his prime ministership. The OBC factor is seminal in UP politics.

The first attempt at defining an OBC was undertaken by the First Backward Caste Commission in 1953. The criteria adopted to define 'backwardness' revolved around matters such as trade, occupation, educational achievement and representation in government. These criteria themselves have context in a caste-based society, where certain occupations were invariably undertaken by people of lower castes. The commission drew up a list of 2,299 groups, which roughly approximated to 32 per cent of the entire Indian population. The hesitancy over the propriety of this entire exercise was epitomised by the chairman of the commission who, at the last minute, in frustration, castigated the report on the grounds that such a project was at odds with the paradigm of a casteless society.[29] This blatant act of renunciation by the chairman itself questioned the very foundation of what was being sought to be achieved, the caste-centric schema being at variance with social justice.

Given the social and economic benefits that were conferred on an OBC status, the exercise has become increasingly political, with communities being offered reservations in educational institutions and government jobs in exchange for their political fealty to the party promising such advancement. In fact, the history of UP politics can be seen as a graveyard of opportunistic alliances between communities and castes, like the decades-long Congress alliance of Brahmins, Dalits and Muslims, and Mayawati's Dalit and Brahmin alliance of 2007. A politically momentous turning point came in the 1970s with the alliance of the Lohia socialists with Charan Singh—who represented Jat farmers, including lower castes involved in agriculture—under the rubric of 'Kisan'. It was this consequential coalition that was the catalyst in bringing the first Janata Party government into power at the Centre from 1977 to 1979. It was this government that set up a commission to look into the matter of OBC quotas: the controversial Mandal Commission.

The second Janata Party government, under the prime ministership of V.P. Singh, sought to implement the Mandal Commission Report. If implemented, the report would have greatly reshaped Indian society, as it identified 3,743 groups in India as backward classes, constituting 52 per cent of the population. For OBCs, the V.P. Singh government proposed a reservation quota of 27 per cent in addition to the 22.5 per cent SC/ST quota. The ensuing conflagration between the upper castes and the OBCs resulted in the decimation of the largely upper-caste Congress in the cow belt and its substitution with OBC leaders such as the Yadavs in UP and Bihar, Mulayam Singh Yadav and Lalu Prasad Yadav being prominent faces of this new hegemony.

What is remarkable has been the success of the BJP in garnering the OBC and Dalit vote, which, to a large extent, has been the contribution of Narendra Modi along with the introduction of well-directed welfare schemes and cultural inclusion policies. He is the second OBC prime minister after H.D. Deve Gowda, and he flaunts his caste origins to show that he is one of the masses, the proverbial chaiwalla (tea seller). This political trajectory is a consequence of the Sanskritisation of the OBCs, whereby upper castes seek to offer positional change to OBCs in the caste dynamics by behaving in a culturally inclusive way, a factor which has been prevalent in the history of UP starting from the nineteenth century.

Sanskritisation has been discredited in certain circles as being ineffective in creating social transformation. As sociologist M.S. Srinivas states, 'The mobility associated with Sanskritization results only in positional changes in the system and does not lead to any structural change. A caste moves up, above its neighbors, and another comes down, but all this takes place in an essentially stable hierarchical order. The system itself does not change.'[30] So, this process actually reifies the existing power structure and the values that sustain traditional Hinduism. Christophe Jaffrelot draws a valid distinction between the lower castes of North India who in his words 'tend to remain imbued with the ethos of Sanskritisation or with that of spiritual, other worldly equality' and this he contrasts with those in the southern and western parts of India who have been able to 'emancipate themselves through collective mobilisation, using primarily the idiom of ethnicity.'[31]

Under Narendra Modi, BJP has been far more politically adroit at managing the antinomy of being, on the one hand, an upper caste, pro-business party while assiduously promoting an image of also being a party for the masses that pushes an ambitious social justice agenda. To this extent, BJP's political machinations represent the acute political insight of both Modi and Shah. Surveying the post-Mandal political scenario—the entrenchment of Yadavs both in UP and Bihar as well as the emergence of Mayawati as a Dalit leader, who became UP's chief minister from 2007 to 2012—Modi and Shah realised that this identity leadership, after decades in power, had become corrupt, despotic and complacent. Modi and Shah encouraged the political aspirations of other marginalised OBC and Dalit sub-castes such as the Pasis and the Balmikis, whose causes they championed. They managed to do this through a stratagem which aligned with their politics: the complete exclusion of Muslims from social mobility projects. Not that there were any such programmes in place, but with parties like the All India Majlis-e-Ittehadul Muslimeen demanding reservations for Muslims, it suited the BJP to conjure this communal binary. This strategy energised the social justice platform, and coupled with various well-directed welfare programs which had a disproportionate impact on the OBCs, morphed social justice politics into the fulcrum of Hindu unity.

Whilst ostensibly privileging its OBC base, the BJP was not indifferent to the claims of its upper caste constituency; it passed further legislation to address what it termed 'economic backwardness': a category detached from caste, offering 10 per cent quotas for Economically Weaker Sections (EWS), thus entitling non-OBCs to the benefit of quotas. The significance of the 103rd constitutional amendment introduced by Prime Minister Modi has been commented upon by writer Abhinav Chandrachud, who called it 'a substantial departure from the scheme of the Constitution.' He further states, 'the Government has excluded Scheduled Castes, Scheduled Tribes, and Other Backward Classes from the ambit of the EWS reservation', essentially implying that this is only an upper-caste reservation.[32]

However, the real shame of this allegedly social justice agenda is the manner in which it deflects the narrative from the real issues of social mobility and opportunity. The beneficiary culture is no substitute for education and skilling, and it demonstrates that the political class is wholly indifferent to outcomes. Political scientist Pratap Bhanu Mehta puts it incisively: 'In my years of dealing with higher education, it was rare to come across a social justice party that shed a single tear for the decimation of public education or the destruction of universities. But all their social justice outrage was focused on the one single point of reservations.'[33] If this thinking is regressive, the new nationalist agenda is far worse, in that it continues with the indifference to quality in education, but seeks to impose the straitjacket of Hindutva ideology on the curricula. It further expands political oversight by assessing the ideological acceptability of academics, a trend strengthened by the Centre's ability to now appoint vice-chancellors to state universities.

It must be noted that the social justice agenda occurs at a time when the Union government has been promoting neo-liberal economic policies of privatisation and disestablishing the public sector. These are precisely the activities which would attenuate jobs in the public sector. The real issue for those ostensibly keen on caste quotas is how to extend them to the private sector. This is opposed by many on the plea of merit. However, studies have shown that in the case of Indian Railways, for example, productivity had improved with a higher proportion of SC/ST employees in senior positions,[34] thus making this merit argument problematic.

Demographics and the Primacy of the 'Cow Belt'

The cornerstone of this political strategy is to focus on the demographics of North Indian states such as UP, Bihar and Madhya Pradesh, which have bought into Hindutva-driven, toxic narratives in ways most South Indian states have not—Karnataka being the possible exception. The reasons for this are not hard to see; these Northern states are trailing behind by all applicable developmental criteria. The actual states of UP and Bihar are the most salient manifestation of poor to non-existent governance is clear when one makes international comparisons as if they were independent countries. Journalist Shekhar Gupta states:

> If Bihar was a nation, it would likely rank at 184 of 195. Just above Niger, Eritrea, Afghanistan, Sierra Leone, Somalia and a couple others ... If Uttar Pradesh was a nation, it would rank around 172, competing with Mali. Tanzania and Togo will be above it ... India might have more people in extreme poverty than all of sub-Saharan Africa together. And on most social indicators. It is a lot of poor, and poorly governed people.[35]

Whilst this depressing litany of statistics captures only some of the parameters of deprivation, poverty and inequality, they cannot truly convey the granular, all-pervasive despair and sense of hopelessness.

The disparities in population growth are also remarkable. For example, in 1951, Tamil Nadu's population was marginally higher than Bihar's; but sixty years later Bihar's population is one and a half times Tamil Nadu's population. In fact, the population increase in the cow belt has reached a stage where UP and Bihar constitute 23 per cent of India's population and are expected to grow by 12 per cent and 20 per cent respectively in the next fifteen years. It is relevant that most states in India have stabilised their Total Fertility Rate (TFR) and have attained below replacement figures. For example, states like West Bengal, Andhra Pradesh and Tamil Nadu have reached a TFR of 1.6 in 2017 whilst the cow belt states have a higher than replacement TFR: UP had a TFR of 3.0 and Bihar of 3.2.[36]

This factor of the high rate of population growth in the northern states and the declining population growth in the southern states is likely to be addressed in political terms by an increase in the representation of the northern states in the Parliament commensurate with their populations. This exercise has been held in abeyance and has been termed delimitation. In 1976, the parliamentary seats were frozen in accordance with the 1971 census by way of a constitutional amendment, and that was to extend till 2000. The reason for these indefinite postponements in the delimitation process relates to the very tangible concern of the need to prioritise family planning and to not reward states which have not properly implemented such policies. However, delimitation was further postponed to 2026, so currently the parliamentary seat representation is determined by a population census taken over fifty years ago.

It is to be expected that this government will insist on delimitation for entrenching its brand of politics, which has greater purchase in the cow belt. If delimitation comes about, there is a projected increase in the number of Lok Sabha seats to 850 as compared to 543 today, and if the Union government chooses to allot seats on the basis of current population figures, we could be looking at UP increasing its allocation from the current 80 seats to 143 seats. In contrast, Kerala would continue to have 20 seats in the Lok Sabha.[37] So one can see that the voice of the South is being diminished and that of the North increased. Unfortunately, this is the mandate of Article 82 of the Indian constitution.

For many Lok Sabha constituencies in the cow belt, the current situation seems unfair, as their populations have grown but their representation in Parliament has not. In UP, there are around 2.5

million people per parliamentary seat; in Bihar it increases to 2.6 million; in Tamil Nadu it is only 1.8 million and in Kerala, it is barely 1.7 million.

Former diplomat Gopalkrishna Gandhi states that such a radical change in the character of Parliament warrants serious consideration. He makes the point that the South has contributed much to the parliamentary discourse and to diminish that contribution would be to demean the Parliament. He further suggests that there are two alternatives before the government. The first would be to continue to freeze the electorates at the 1971 levels until all states have achieved population stabilisation. The other would be to devise a mathematical formula, like the 'Cambridge Compromise', a sophisticated mathematically equitable formula which was used for the apportionment of seats between member states in the EU parliament. Gandhi accepts that the formula used there was bespoke, and we would need to devise our own formula. He concludes that 'we need to limit population, not representation'.[38]

This matter of representation is further complicated by the fact that there is an asymmetry in the matter of financial contribution as the southern states have been complaining that they contribute far more to the Union finances per capita than the cow belt states, but receive far less in terms of funding from the Centre.[39]

The Fifteenth Finance Commission has been complicit in ensuring that UP and Bihar receive more in financial assistance than their entitlement in earlier determinations. Finance commissions, traditionally, have adopted particular parameters such as population, fiscal discipline and improved infrastructure in calculating disbursements. It is pertinent to note that in the Fifteenth Finance Commission, the population numbers were based on the 2011 census and not the 1971 one. UP, with its highest population of 241 million, therefore receives higher financial benefits, leaving it without any incentive to seriously implement family planning.

In addition to demographic factors, the single biggest factor to decide weightage is what is known as 'income distance', which amounts to 45 per cent. It is the distance of a state's income from the state with the highest income. The income of a state is computed as an average per capita gross state domestic product (GSDP) over a three-year period. A state with lower per capita income will have a higher share to maintain equity among states.[40] The problem with this assessment is that it is calculated using the 2011 population at each stage. As author Nilakantan R.S. concludes, 'About 72.5 per cent of the overall weightage in the horizontal devolution criteria either explicitly favours the high-population states or is a proxy favouring high–population states. Worse, all of it is based on the 2011 population data.' This, of course, has had a highly prejudicial effect on the southern states which have been successful in keeping their population figures down: so, for instance, the allocation for Tamil Nadu has fallen by 23.1 per cent from the Twelfth to the Fifteenth Finance Commissions.[41]

It is relevant that UP and Bihar have consistently been privileged, that their chronic failure to develop is concealed under a carapace of opacity, hiding important aspects of state development in order to enhance the weightage it would receive under the Finance Commission. The Union government has deliberately manipulated and diluted the data for this purpose. To take one example, there is the matter of literacy rates. In UP, the literacy rate appears to have increased substantially from 1951 to 2011, from around 12 per cent to 68 per cent. However, one must be wary of such figures, as the definition India employs to define a literate person is an outlier. To be considered literate in India, one only has to be able to read and write their own name; this requires a very limited notion of the alphabet. If your name is Shiv, for example, you only need to know four letters. The Annual Status of Education Report (ASER) released in January 2024 shows that more than 50 per cent of fourteen to eighteen-year-old children in rural India are unable to solve a simple three-digit division problem that is taught in class III. Literacy skills are not much better, as from the same sample over 25 per cent were unable to read class II level textbooks and just shy of 50 per cent could not read sentences in English. Of those who could read, 26.5 per cent did not understand what they were reading.[42] These are very damning statistics and point to population growth being an impending disaster rather than the much-vaunted demographic dividend envisaged by economists and politicians.

In this context, the priorities of state governments, and particularly that of UP, are relevant. In 2022, a new session commenced in UP, but school children had no books as the government alleged it had insufficient funds to float a tender. School teachers complained that in the absence of new books, they had to collect books distributed to children in the previous school session. However, the UP Government seems to have ample funds for spending on religious affairs. The Department of Religious Affairs had forwarded a budget of 1,100 crores for FY 2022–23. This is to be contrasted with the more parsimonious allocations of previous years—a paltry 32.5 crores was spent in 2017–18, which rose to 604.88 crores in 2021–22.[43]

These priorities have to be seen in light of the vainglorious narrative that the Union government seeks to project regarding the incipient digital and knowledge economy. This seems rather fanciful given the absence of any desire to impart basic skills of literacy and numeracy; post-COVID, some 51,000 government schools have shut down without there being any express intention of replacing them.[44] There is much excitement about digital learning, but this disregards the fact that only around 50 per cent of Indian households have access to the internet, and that figure is only 37 per cent in rural India.[45] So, it is evident that education is not a priority and whatever resources the UP Government has are directed towards promoting greater religiosity, a fact that portends the future of the cow belt. With the grandiose consecration of the Ram temple at Ayodhya, the theme of religious tourism is being projected as the 'desideratum' for UP in terms of business and employment generation, but it is something that even the electorate of Faizabad roundly rejected in 2024.

This is the preparatory ground for the emergence of a significant politician from the cow belt, a national leader who would lead post the present prime minister, someone like Yogi Adityanath who has shown great fidelity to the principles of Hindutva. Post the 2024 general elections and, with rumours of there having been a falling out between Yogi and the Centre, this trajectory does not seem as self-evident as it once was, and much will hinge on the UP elections in 2027.

With the emergence of the cow belt as the cynosure for the new nationalism, and with the prospect of delimitation looming, one discerns a new and unsettling diffidence amongst public intellectuals as well as politicians from the South, on the inviolability of the formula of 'One Man, One Vote', the signature tune of majoritarianism. In fact, what Gopalkrishna Gandhi has urged is postponing delimitation until the cow belt's population growth comes under control (which may never happen). Clever contrivances suggested by him, such as the 'Cambridge Compromise', look suspiciously like the concerns Ivor Jennings, the constitutional lawyer had alluded to in the 1950s, that in a post-colonial society, 'a narrow franchise, indirect elections, tribal representations may all be [seen as] quite sensible.'[46]

But this is the very essence of the new nationalism, which projects an overriding belief in majoritarianism, as if the majority outcome of a vote on any issue, no matter how absurd or discriminatory, should be upheld. In this context, it is worthwhile to ponder the words of former UK supreme court judge Lord Sumption,[47] when he meditates on the meaning of majority rule. He concedes that:

> Majority rule is the basic principle of democracy. But that only means that a majority is enough to authorise the State's acts. It is not enough to make them legitimate. This is because majority rule is no more than a rule of decision. It does nothing to accommodate our differences. It just restates them in numerical terms. Democracies cannot operate on the basis that a bare majority takes one hundred percent of the political spoils. If it did, it would harbour large and permanently disaffected groups in their midst, who had no common bonds to transcend their differences with the majority. A state based on that principle would quickly cease to be a political community.

This is a chilling reminder of what will happen if we continue to go down this road of majoritarian politics. Politics necessarily involves a discourse between people whose views differ; it is forever the art of the possible. Philosopher Isaiah Berlin spoke of 'temporising compromises' over political experimentation, which means having some compromise with a party who you may disagree with.

Given the prevalence of caste-based politics, we now enter what writer Nivedita Menon characterises as the era of birth-based majorities. She comments that:

> A permanent birth-based majority is the very antithesis of democracy, for it is based on two problematic assumptions—that a small group claiming to represent that majority can permanently direct public policy, and that the birth-based group is homogeneous in its interests. Majoritarian politics is entirely directed towards shoring up both these assumptions and attempting to silence any questioning of them.[48]

This can be tested by the fact that, barring recently, the cow belt in the last forty years since Independence has enjoyed the political hegemony of one party, and the BJP appears to have substituted the Congress in that position today. This prospect may be upended by the 2027 UP election results, provided the opposition remains united.

In this process, the wider notion of the public good is lost, as Ambedkar put it pithily, 'fraternity is the root of democracy'[49] and as such, the basis of a political society.

6

LANGUAGE AND CULTURE

TOWARDS PURITY

Language is more vital and organic to people than inanimate objects, and is a source of great culture in terms of prose, poetry and drama. It is essentially a liberating force in that it allows for the fullest expression of feelings, moods and thoughts. As literary critic George Steiner puts it, 'No two languages, no two dialects or local idioms within a language, identify, designate, map their worlds in the same way. The memories stored, the empirical surroundings inventoried, the social relations which the language organises and mirrors (kinship, for example), the colours distinguished in its vocabulary of perceptions, differ, often radically, from tongue to tongue.'[1] Language was a seminal part of the cultural fabric of India—to protect language is to protect plurality and cultural diversity.

When the Constitution was being drafted, the notion of cultural rights, particularly special cultural rights of minorities, was admittedly inchoate. The question was whether minorities ought to be guaranteed freedom in the matter of religion, language and culture and be protected from discrimination and interference by the State. The Congress had supported a policy of preservation of minority culture, script and language as early as in the Karachi Resolution of 1931.

However, Dr Ambedkar, the chairman of the Drafting Committee, saw a limited role for the State in the preservation of culture. Author Rochana Bajpai sums it up by stating, 'The form in which cultural safeguards were eventually incorporated in the Constitution was that minorities were free to promote their culture with the possibility, but not an entitlement, to assistance from the state.'[2] So the role of the State was negligible. It was to play no active hand in assisting the minority to preserve its culture and linguistic heritage.

This insouciance for the preservation of minority culture is disturbing in a society which ostensibly strove for pluralism, since in most cases assimilation is tantamount to annihilation. Contemporary thinking has privileged the notion of cultural preservation in a multicultural society. For the Muslims of UP and Bihar, Urdu's importance was seminal. Yet successive Congress governments in power in UP in the 1950s and 1960s were actively negating minority linguistic culture and heritage, despite the existence of legislation which was to be used to assist the cause of Urdu. This point will be substantiated later in the book, but the matter of the right to cultural preservation is vital.

This policy should be looked at in a historical backdrop where Persian was the primary language of the North Indian elite and Urdu was most definitely an Indian language. Francesca Orsini, an eminent scholar of South Asian literature, traces the development of Urdu to the nineteenth century, when 'Urdu took over the mantle from Persian.'[3] At that time, it was certainly not identified with Muslims, although it was identified with the upper classes. In UP, apart from the Muslims, it was widely spoken by the Kayasths, the Khatris and, of course, the Kashmiri Pandits.[4] Nehru, for example, continued to write in Urdu through the 1950s and only towards the early sixties did he switch to Devnagari.

In 1900 North India, Urdu was overwhelmingly the language of public discourse. In fact, columnist Santosh Kumar Khare writes that 'the notion of Hindi and Urdu as two distinct languages crystallised at Fort William College in the first half of the nineteenth century.'[5] He further suggests that 'their linguistic and literary repertoires were built up accordingly, Urdu borrowing from Persian/Arabic and Hindi from Sanskrit.' However, the crux of his argument—

something that would disturb most proponents of Hindi—is that 'modern Hindi (or Khari Boli) was an artificial construct of the East India Company which, while preserving the grammar and diction of Urdu, cleansed it of "foreign and rustic" words and substituted them with Sanskrit synonyms.' It is paradoxical that it is now the RSS, the foremost protagonist of Hindi today, that takes the most pleasure in deriding English speakers in India, calling them 'Macaulay's children'. At any rate, the RSS position on Urdu is hostile; it ridicules the idea that Urdu is the language of a minority in UP should be privileged in any way.

But, in a way, the position of UP's Urdu speakers now mirrors the plight of the 'Bhadralok' of Bengal at the time when the Communal Award of 1932 was announced that created separate electorates for communities. The award reduced the position of Bengali 'Bhadralok' to a minority presence in the Legislative Assembly. A memorial in protest was sent to Lord Zetland (former governor of Bengal) by the 'Bhadralok' community claiming that 'your memorialists belong to the Hindu Community of Bengal which constitutes a Minority Community and, as such, is entitled to the same protection that is guaranteed to the Minorities of the other Provinces ... the Hindu minority of Bengal claim their due weightage of representation as a recognised Minority right.'[6] It is interesting to note that in the name of 'culture', which anyway was an amorphous term as it did not include language, the Bhadralok spoke about federalism and then Partition when the issue of a United Bengal was proposed in 1946.

The Muslims of UP or, at least the 'Ashrafs'(upper classes), have been vilified for insisting on the retention of Urdu, as it was considered unreasonable for a small elite to privilege high culture and also insist on Partition as the solution. There was no reason why there could not have been a compromise and Urdu could not have been retained as the second language in UP instead of Sanskrit which hardly anyone spoke. Yet no one draws parallels with the Bhadralok of Bengal who succeeded in dividing the province because of their paranoia about cultural subjugation. Why was it unreasonable for the Ashrafs to insist on Urdu and not unreasonable for the Bhadralok to demand Partition on the grounds of cultural subjugation by people who they considered inferior?

We do not appreciate sufficiently how systematically Urdu has been erased from daily life in North India. As historian Mushirul Hasan states, 'The Pro-Hindi lobby, which was vocal in the Constituent Assembly, had its way.'[7] Seth Govind Das, a member of Parliament from the First to the Fifth Lok Sabha, stated, 'The Hindi-Hindustani controversy has come to an end simply because Article 99 of the Constitution refers to "Hindi or English" alone in relation to the transaction of business in our Parliament. Thus, the question of Hindustani exists no more.' The UP Board of High School and Intermediate Education decided on Hindi as the sole medium for writing in high school examinations from 1953 onwards. In order to make it even more difficult for Urdu speakers to transmit their patrimony to their children, the UP and Bihar governments suspended aid to Urdu medium schools. Hasan conceded that Nehru was deeply disturbed by this virulently anti-Urdu policy, but there was little he could do, once even confessing that '[i]f my colleagues do not agree, I cannot help it.'[8]

The real death knell for Urdu was the three-language formula adopted by schools. In UP, this consisted first of the national language, Hindi, with Sanskrit being the second language and the third being a choice between English and Urdu. For those who wished to forge ahead in the new India, learning English as a language was critical, and it would be wrong to blame the few Muslims or those from Urdu-speaking backgrounds who chose English over Urdu. But manifestly the three-language formula was skewed in favour of Hindi and Sanskrit with a clear intent to consign Urdu to the dustbin of history.

Urdu did have its votaries amongst upper-class Hindus such as Sir Tej Bahadur Sapru, who, as stated above, favoured the continuance of Urdu as the official language of North India. He was acutely suspicious of Hindi, considering it merely a ploy to Sanskritise Hindustani by removing from it the many Urdu words and usages. It must be said that there were many Hindu writers of eminence who wrote in Urdu, such as Munshi Premchand, Firaq Gorakhpuri, Pandit Harichand 'Akhtar' and Anand Narain 'Mulla', amongst others. It was a secular bridge between the communities, apart from being the source of great art and high culture.

It is not as if Urdu was being replaced by something popular and vibrant. Hindi was and is dead and bureaucratic. As Octavio Paz, Nobel laureate and former Mexican ambassador to India wrote, 'The Hindi that has been imposed on present-day India has yet a further disadvantage: it is a language that has suppressed foreign voices, whether English, Persian or Arabic; in their place it has inserted Sanskrit neologisms. It is as though the English were to purge their language of all words of French origin because they are relics of the Norman invasion. The truth is that very few people fully understand official Hindi, which has become an affected and bureaucratic dialect. In order for "High Hindi" (as some call it, sarcastically) to become a living language, it must submerge itself in popular speech and accept the voices of outsiders, no matter what their origin. Living languages are hybrids and impure.'[9] The intent behind the emphasis on Hindi was clear—erase Urdu to prejudice Muslims and attack the composite culture, nothing else.

Retaining Urdu as the second language of UP would have been in keeping with the mandate of Article 29 of the Constitution, which explicitly protected the right of any group to nurture their language and culture. In UP, which was Urdu's birthplace, the language was a marker of civilisation, literature and culture, deserving not just of protection but of pride. It was also the mother tongue of 20 per cent or more of the population. Academic Faizan Mustafa has pointed out that under article 350(A), the state government was mandated to provide facilities for instruction in the mother tongue of linguistic minorities at a primary stage, and under article 350(B) there was a requirement for the appointment of a special officer for linguistic minorities. Yet in UP, none of this was done, as Urdu was dishonestly identified as the language of a religious minority—rather than a linguistic minority—whose culture was required to be marginalised, if not eradicated. In fact, UP went further and banned Urdu medium schooling altogether, something which was not even done in states like Maharashtra. The famous Urdu writer, Shamsur Rahman Faruqi, was quite blunt about this, saying that there was an effort to extirpate Urdu in UP post-Independence.[10]

There have been attempts to say that the Hindu Right was not being unreasonable in its desire to rid UP of Urdu.[11] It was said that the Urdu script was not easy and despite centuries of being in use in the North by Muslims and Hindus alike, Devanagari was a more practical language and easier to write. This may sound plausible and divest the debate of anti-Muslim animus, except for one thing: the acrimonious debate over numerals. The Hindi supporters pointedly refused to accept Western Arabic numerals (0,1,2,3,4 ...), which are in use today and insisted that Devanagari numerals be adopted. The reason, although it has not been stated as such, was, according to historian Gyanesh Kudaisya, 'their Islamic provenance'.[12] If the West had no difficulty in adopting the Arabic numerals, it is difficult to see a reason for their rejection by Hindi supporters, other than a visceral hatred for and a desire to vaporise the Islamic patrimony. India came very close to officially adopting Devanagari numerals in 1949, after a tied vote in the Constituent Assembly. Nehru's intervention prevented this, who stated that Devanagari numerals should not be forced on the country by such a slim margin.[13] I stress this example as it epitomises the attitudes of many members of the Hindu Right towards Muslim heritage. This was particularly apparent in UP, a point that underwrites the argument that there was little or no appetite on their part to come to any sensible arrangement on cultural matters with a large and entrenched minority.

This implacable insistence on removing Urdu carries significant implications, because with a language comes its literature, and with that literature comes a rich cultural heritage—what George Steiner referred to as a cultural patrimony.[14] There have been attempts to translate Urdu poetry into Devanagari as well as into the Roman script, notably by Professor K.C. Kandy and other gifted translators, but it is not easy, and invariably a language and its literature disappear with the degradation or diminution of its script.

This is clearly apparent in the case of another Indic language which is spoken by over thirty-five million people worldwide and particularly by a community which, despite its small number in India, has played a disproportionate role at the forefront of enterprise, wealth creation and philanthropy: the Sindhi community. Sindhi language is written in several scripts, including Perso-Arabic. Some of the greatest poets and writers of Sindhi literature, such as Shah

Abdul Latif Bhittai, have written in this script, adumbrating Sindhi folklore and traditions. It is a profound tragedy that many young Sindhis today are denied the opportunity of imbibing the grandeur of their literature and syncretic heritage because of a bigoted desire to eradicate its traditional script and replace it with a script in which there is little Sindhi literature to speak of.

The curious aspect of this is the fact that when India attained independence, Hindi was made the official language of governance, with English being given an interim status. However, the victory of the 'Hindiwalas' was, in the words of Francesca Orsini, 'pyrrhic' since it could never substitute English, as can be seen from the popularity of English in primary and secondary school education, even in the Hindi-speaking states. Many, if not all, votaries of Hindi have sent and continue to send their children to English-speaking schools.

Paradoxically, notwithstanding the clear desire of the Hindu Right to eradicate Urdu, columnist Shoaib Daniyal states that, 'demotic Urdu along with a substantial part of its Persian loans still lives on in India. Its 19th-century status as a register of elite society means North Indians still look to Urdu in their cultural consumption.'[15] This is in large part the influence of Bollywood. In fact, it is this Hindustani that bridges the gulf between the North and the South much more efficaciously than an arid bureaucratic Hindi does.

Towards a Pure Culture

Since 2014, the desire to rid Indian culture of what is considered foreign has proceeded apace. Narendra Modi's references to 800 years of slavery, the obsession with renaming cities and the rewriting of history books point to the reality that the discredited two-nation theory has been resurrected.

Although changing the names of cities, for instance, has been a recurrent feature of governments in the subcontinent, it was done largely to replace colonial names with names that resonated locally. So, in Pakistan, Lyallpur became Faisalabad, whereas in India, Calcutta became Kolkata, Bombay became Mumbai, and Madras became Chennai. However, until recently, Mughals were generally considered Indian and were left alone. Now, particularly in UP, there has been a spree of renaming, so Allahabad has become Prayagraj and Faizabad district has become Ayodhya district, which shows the unalloyed intent of the government to depict Mughal rule to be as colonial and foreign as British rule.

This aligns with treating the artificial constructs of India and Pakistan as civilisational entities with their distinct histories and traditions, which have little to do with each other. To go down this road is to become a 'Hindu Pakistan'.

There has been a whole rash of books which have sought to provide some intellectual credibility to the Hindutva narrative, the two-nation theory and the need for cultural purification. The book *A New Idea of India*,[16] written by Harsh Madhusudan and Rajeev Mantri, presents an argument for the adoption of a new concept of nationalism, one that is closely aligned to religion and to what is described as a 'civilisational ethos'. In this book, there is an attempt to change the discourse, to shift the narrative from the originalist thinking of the Constitution makers such as Nehru and Ambedkar, which was based on the Western principles of liberty, fraternity and equality towards using the nativist idiom of '*dharma*' as being the schema of government. The writers argue that there should be a shift of focus from the Gujarat model to the UP model, which is much lauded as being the future path of India, with fulsome praise and accolades being showered on Yogi Adityanath. There is also an audacious attempt to depict the Mughals and other Muslim rulers as colonists, by persons such as Sai Deepak, an engineer turned lawyer, who has been prolific in his publications and has argued that Islam imposed colonialism on India. We have another engineer and banker, Vikram Sampath, who has completed a biography of V.D. Savarkar. He has also been critical of historical methodology. There is also Sanjeev Sanyal, an ex-banker and now an advisor to the Union government, who has been writing on Indian history through the prism of Hindutva.

All authors are interesting in that they claim to set out a serious and informed case for the new nationalism and its cultural agenda. Yet, the trajectory of this nationalism reveals something different:

while it celebrates a civilisational ethos, it does so for reasons that are ultimately misplaced. This is apparent in one of the most evocative sentences in *A New Idea of India*, where it is stated that 'of all the modern states in existence today, India represents the pinnacle of syncretic polytheism and Pakistan probably the most unrestrained instincts of proselytising monotheism. All the Urdu shayari, music and tasty kebabs and all the Gods of our pantheon cannot change that reality any time.' This statement is a giveaway in its crass, reductive caricature of culture and what constitutes a civilisation. The disciplines of history and cultural studies evade the authors, with their crudely communal slant; unfortunately, much of this is camouflaged by reference to decolonisation.

As Pratap Bhanu Mehta says, the term 'decolonisation' has become 'the ideological flavour of the moment.' It has become the imperative behind a variety of actions such as, in his words, 'calls to restructure education, to re-write laws, reconceptualise history, reimagine public spaces.' This language aligns with modernity and trendy post-colonialism jargon, and detracts from what is really an attempt at cultural purification, something which the Left accuses fascists of doing. But if you remove this despised colonial heritage, what do you replace it with? Pratap Bhanu Mehta responds incisively, 'The purpose of the invocation is not a real diagnosis of Indic knowledge or even a programme for its regeneration. It is to mark the boundaries of exclusion and inclusion.'[17]

Coming to which, we have to go to the maestro of this cultural laundromat, one of the greatest ideologues of Hindutva, Savarkar, whom the authors quote liberally and with much approval. He drew a crucial distinction between Hindus and the other inhabitants of the territory, the Muslims in particular. In his tract *Hindutva: Who is a Hindu?*[18] he defines a Hindu to mean a person who regards this land of Bharatvarsha, from the Indus to the seas as his 'fatherland' as well as his 'holy land'. This is plainly an exclusionary definition, as Muslims were seen as persons who regarded Mecca and Medina to be their holy lands, whereas Christians considered Jerusalem or Rome to be so. This is not dissimilar to European fascism of the 1920s and 1930s that singled out Jews for harbouring international or, at least, extraterritorial loyalties, leaving them open to the charge that they could never be truly patriotic to their home country.

Savarkar believed that the purpose of nationhood for Hindus was to create a state for the development of a specifically Hindu identity. He recognised that Muslims constituted another nation and used the term 'two nations' liberally. His seminal book *Hindutva* was published in 1923, at a time when Jinnah was identified as a secular hero and lauded for his nationalism. In his book, Savarkar, with his strait-jacketed notion of nationalism and Hindu identity, foreshadowed much of Jinnah's later rhetoric. Years later, Savarkar, in a press conference in Nagpur in 1943, stated plainly: 'I have no quarrel with Mr Jinnah's two nation theory. We Hindus are a nation by ourselves and it is a historic fact that Hindus and Muslims are two nations.' This may come as a surprise to those who subscribe to the view that it was only Jinnah and the Muslim League who were votaries of the two-nation theory.

Curiously, Savarkar was not a devout Hindu; he was an atheist but had the genius to see the infinite possibilities in building a nation on the basis of a specifically Hindu identity. This identity rested much on a shared culture, one that was necessarily based on Sanskrit and what he described as 'common laws and rites'. These factors would exclude more than half of pre-Partition India: Muslims, Scheduled Castes, the tribal population, Sikhs and Christians. The obvious question is how minorities would be treated within this manifestly majoritarian construct. Whilst Savarkar does not properly articulate his vision for minorities in any of his writings, in an interview he gave to an American journalist, Tom Treanor, in 1944, during his tenure as the head of the Hindu Mahasabha, he revealed that 'the Muslims will have the position of negroes in your country.'[19] Given the quasi-apartheid conditions that were pervasive in the US in the 1940s, that could not have been a very appealing prospect for Muslims.

Savarkar was not being flippant when he recognised that whilst there may be two nations on one soil, the only solution was homogeneity. He was not interested in any attempt at power-sharing or in minority rights: only brute majoritarianism. There would have to be uniform laws governing all the inhabitants of the territory without difference, and they would be based on Hindu culture and religion. This was where Savarkar departed from the Congress consensus at the time, which at least paid lip service to plurality and unity in diversity. It is interesting to note what Dr Ambedkar had to say about this:

> The scheme of Swaraj formulated by Mr Savarkar will give the Hindus an empire over the Muslims and thereby satisfy their vanity ... But it can never ensure a stable and peaceful future for the Hindus, for the simple reason that the Muslims will never yield willing obedience to so dreadful an alternative.[20]

The intent of this nationalism was to divest Indian civilisation of Islamic influence, whether it be in terms of language, art, architecture, music, apparel, textiles or food. This toxic nationalism then takes on the trajectory of a cultural war, one that serves very little purpose.

The India of the 2020s is a very different place from when *Hindutva* was written by Savarkar over 100 years ago. It is far richer and more cosmopolitan, with a growing middle class that has an unquenchable appetite for the best the world has to offer. The desire to set up a cultural construct which is purportedly free of all foreign influences is a fool's errand, an impossible task. In the age of the internet, with a large non-resident Indian (NRI) population, increasing access to international culture such as art, music, literature, cinema, streaming channels, food, social media and myriad apps all make for a multitude of cultural interactions, from which people derive pleasure and which are integral to their daily quotidian existence. This is the reality cultural warriors of Hindutva have to address.

The unstated aim of this culture war is not just to diminish and marginalise the Islamic past, but to glorify a conveniently unknown past as 'bharatvarsha'—the ancient India which all nationalists privilege as the real India, one about which very little is known other than some inscriptions, architecture and, of course, the great epics. This can be usefully contrasted with ancient China, which has a rich historical archive in terms of manuscripts and records. This 'Bharatvarsha' is a blank canvas on which there have been attempts at inscribing a past; a kind of palimpsest on which anything can be written or embellished, including carefully curated mythologies.

The documented medieval period—which has far more relevance to our daily lives than a distant mythological chimera—is sought to be denigrated and erased for not being truly Indian, or rather not being truly 'Hindu'. The authors of *A New Idea of India* dismissively refer to 'tasty kebabs' as a foreign import. But if foreign origins are the measure, what about the humble samosa (from the Uzbek samsa) or the jalebi (from the Iranian jallebi)—both widely seen as Indian today? Even pulao and biryani, now among the country's most beloved dishes, are products of the Mughal culinary legacy.

In fact, this notion of repudiating a culture only because it is associated with a political context such as invasion and that which you consider humiliation, is a rather perverse way of looking at things. The primary issue should be the extent to which such a culture has enriched your life. Literary critic Martin Puchner puts it very persuasively,

> None of the ancient works or their creators discussed here are without blemish. The cultures that shaped them had values and practices different from our own; they were products of societies few of us would like to live in. Like the societies that produced them, these works carry the values and injustices of their eras. Considering them worth preserving, and accepting them as part of our common cultural heritage, does not require that we agree with the values of their era or single them out as moral examples to be emulated in the here and now.[21]

This exposes an oddly woke argument that these ostensibly right-wing nationalist pseudo-historians seek to invoke.

I believe that India is a vessel of what American philosopher and writer Kwame Anthony Appiah calls 'cultural contamination'. He cites Salman Rushdie, who said about his controversial novel, *The Satanic Verses*, that it,

> ... celebrates hybridity, impurity, intermingling, the transformation that comes of new and unexpected combinations of human beings, cultures, ideas, politics, movies, songs. It

> rejoices in mongrelization and fears the absolutism of the Pure. Mélange, hotchpotch, a bit of this and a bit of that is how newness enters the world. It is the great possibility that mass migration gives the world, and I have tried to embrace it.[22]

Behind this desire to reclaim what is considered to be their Hindu patrimony is the belief in ownership. This matter of cultural patrimony raises a whole set of new issues and should be addressed. Kwame Anthony Appiah says that 'a great deal of what people wish to protect as "cultural patrimony" was made up before the modern system of nations came into being, by members of societies that no longer exist. People die when their bodies die. Cultures, by contrast, can die without physical extinction.'[23] If that is so, how can we privilege the descendants of a particular people for having a greater claim on such a patrimony?

This is a seminal point, as the location of artefacts may remain constant, but the people change. The ruins of Ephesus, situated in modern Turkey, are an example of this. They are clearly Greek in provenance, but they are located near Izmir in Turkey, and the people who live there now are largely of Central Asian origin. Who has a claim on these ruins, the Greeks or the Turks? It may be best to view these structures and artefacts as belonging to our universal patrimony, making it difficult to nationalise such cultural artefacts in the way the Hindu Right has. In simple terms, if you can't claim ownership, on what basis can you allege a wrong?

In fact, as a persuasive rebuttal to the argument of cultural appropriation, Martin Puchner argues that 'culture is not a possession, but something we hand down so that others may use it in their own way; culture is a vast recycling project in which small fragments from the past are retrieved to generate new and surprising ways of meaning-making'.[24] Puchner concedes that such cultural interactions were invariably accompanied by violence but cultures under assault developed astonishing strategies of resistance and resilience; he argues that cultural transmission has led to the creation of new forms of culture and the world has benefitted from that.

The force that animates and powers the Hindutva project is a desire to expunge all traces of Muslim patrimony, a period extending over 800 years and one embedded in the North Indian psyche, language, lifestyle and sensibilities. In this process lies the effort to unify Hindu society. As Nivedita Menon notes, 'There is no single majority religious community in India. Hindutva is the latest stage in the millennia-old attempt to produce one.'[25]

7

THE WEAPONISATION OF HISTORY TO UNDERPIN NATIONALISM

According to political scientist Francis Fukuyama, the teaching of history together with residency laws and immigration is one of the building blocks of citizenship; what children learn about the past is important to the kind of society a nation aspires to build. The centrality of history to citizenship and identity assumes much greater signification than one would normally assign, particularly in contemporary times. American professor Jason Stanley argues that 'authoritarian regimes find history profoundly threatening ... these regimes find ways of erasing or concealing history in order to consolidate their power.' He draws a comparison with democracy which requires,

> [t]he recognition of a shared reality that consists of multiple perspectives. Through exposure to multiple perspectives, citizens learn to regard one another as equal contributors to a national narrative. And they learn, we learn, to accept that this narrative is open to continued reflection and reimagination, constantly taking into account new ideas, new evidence, new perspectives and theoretical framings. History in a democracy is not static, not mythic, but dynamic and critical.

This he contrasts with authoritarians who mispresent history 'as a single story, a single perspective,'[1] which in India means Hindu victimhood and Muslim barbarism.

Post-Independence governments have largely removed vestiges of the colonial past. The NDA government wants to extend this policy of removing symbols of what they term as 'tyranny' and 'enslavement' to Islamic monuments and cultural artefacts as well, with an intent to serve an openly political agenda, to marginalise and ultimately eradicate the Muslim contribution to Indian culture. It has sought to identify and target the Muslim legacy as a colonial legacy, a departure from the earlier kind of nationalism which saw Muslim contribution to Indian culture as an integral part of it.

In India, it is easier to push this desire for a pure imagined culture for several reasons. History is not treated with gravitas as an intellectual discipline, so when state governments interfere in the writing of school textbooks with impunity, the bogey of the left-wing historian is paraded to justify their actions. Since there are no established historical works that predate the Muslim conquests other than chronologies and inscriptions, history can be written as a palimpsest, with the distant past recast in the image of the present, dominated by a Hindu/Muslim binary. In such a framework, it becomes easier to demonise and caricature history, to correct alleged wrongs and to pursue a purified version of the past.

Ancient Indian Culture and Its Understanding of History

Often, an argument is made that Hindus had no historians and thus were at a disadvantage when narrating their own history. This is too simplistic an understanding, as there is serious doubt whether ancient Indian culture had a historical sense at all. A number of Orientalists and even votaries of the Hindu Right, such as V.S. Naipaul, have wondered whether Hindu thought and philosophy had any proper understanding of history as an intellectual discipline, in the manner understood by Western and Islamic thinkers. Author Richard Lannoy remarks that:

> This very marked and (deeply felt) indifference to the Western concept of history and of man's incapacity to change is far more consistent than in most other civilizations, including the Chinese and the Islamic. The durability of the cyclical-time concept at the most advanced levels of Hindu metaphysical thought makes this indifference to what we would call history one of the distinguishing traits of the Indian cultural tradition.[2]

Still, a cyclical conception of time does not preclude the appeal of returning to one's roots or invoking a mythical golden age. In fact, Lannoy argues that this mythical golden age is 'built into the very fabric of religious belief, as they once were in Christian Europe.'[3]

The Hindutva Version of the Role of History

This issue of whether Hindus ever had a historical sense has immediate contemporary resonance, as one of the principal projects of the new nationalism is to endow and suffuse Indians with an elevated sense of pride in themselves as a people and banish what they characterise as the shame of defeat and, even slavery, at the hands of Muslim conquerors. Much blame is attributed to Marxist historians who are alleged to have distorted Indian history.

The reality is that with the greater vernacularisation of Indian education from the late 1970s, a historian like V.D. Mahajan was more popular and had a much greater influence on the study of history in most schools and colleges than any of the left-wing panjandrums. The only exceptions were elite institutions like JNU, which, in any case, preach to the converted.

In a valid criticism of left-wing historians, William Dalrymple complains that they depopulated history of personalities and made it distinctly reader-unfriendly by concentrating on economic movements and data in a depressingly turgid style rather than dwelling on the character and foibles of kings, queens and generals, the charming tapestry of life.[4] They made history boring with state backing from Congress nationalists. He may be correct, but even in the West, many academic historians were heavy going, and only historians with a flair for writing well, such as G.M. Trevelyan and A.J.P. Taylor, made the reading of history pleasurable and popular.

It is not as if Hindutva thinkers have an issue with state patronage of historians. Their idea of the role history plays is for it to serve as a handmaiden for political ends, and as such making it very state-centric. This is confirmed by historian Rudrangshu Mukherjee when he observes,

> Another kind of objection has come from the Sangh Parivar, which has no reservations to either the state being involved in history-writing or to using history for nation-building. They also have no objections to projecting the nation in heroic terms. They only want the secular nation to become a Hindu nation, secular heroes to be replaced by Hindu heroes.[5]

Whilst every age may choose to put a different interpretation on events, these interpretations arise from new facts, sources, archives and materials. Many fresh interpretations emerge because historians uncover evidence their predecessors never had. That's why one cannot be cavalier about corroborated facts and assume that interpretation is everything.

In 2022, the Union government attempted to make serious changes in the drafting of a National Curriculum Framework which would govern state education boards. This exercise is to rewrite school textbooks and, given the predilections of BJP/RSS, rewriting history is high on the agenda. The intent is plain, to remove, 'unhistorical facts and distortions about national heroes.' What it really attempts to do is far more insidious and regressive as it seeks to change the historical discourse, valorising ancient history and addressing the controversial medieval period, not in terms of how history has evolved, but to hark back to violence, invasions and warfare. An example of this is the attempt to excise from history book, the well-documented work done by the Mughals in translating texts such as the Mahabharata and the Ramayana into Persian, since this suggests the existence of composite cultural traditions. The intent is to deliberately hollow out history of any contemporary relevance it may have, such as to help students understand how the modern world has evolved in terms of culture, language, economics, architecture and apparel, and to reduce it to a militaristic binary—such as the history of kings and queens as taught to my generation—but now filtered through the narrow prism of nationalism and Hindutva.

It is not as if historians preferred by the Hindu Right are unique in this worldview. Pakistan also has an appalling reputation of having rewritten history textbooks to subserve an Islamic ideology. Pakistani textbooks do not, for example, even cover the existence of East Pakistan until 1971. The extraordinary and egregious significance given to Muhammad ibn al-Qasim's raid into Sindh in the ninth century is emblematic of a desire to Arabise the history of Muslims in India and to emphasise the military achievements of Muslim historical figures. Instead of lauding the Mughals for their diplomacy, trade, consensus-building and co-option of local rulers and notables into their government, there is an attempt to fetishise only the military accomplishments of the Mughals.[6] It is for this reason that Mughals other than Aurangzeb are not valorised in Pakistani history. Mughals are now likely to be erased from the annals of Indian history because they were not Hindu but also from Pakistani history because they were not Muslim enough.

The Out of India Theory

I believe that the most reliable way to test the honesty of persons who subscribe to the Hindutva narrative is by gauging the way they address the controversy of Aryan migration.

It is here that not only does one encounter more than a tinge of racial superiority, not dissimilar to Nazi Germany, but an egregious case of cultural appropriation, as per which the Indus Valley civilisation is claimed to be integral to the Aryan-Hindu culture. M.S. Golwalkar, the second RSS chief, claimed, 'We—Hindus—have been in undisputed and undisturbed possession of this land for over 8,000, or even 10,000 years before the land was invaded by any foreign race.'[7] He goes on further to identify Hindus with Aryans, confusing ethnicity with religion. This runs contrary to the school of thought which has proved conclusively that the modern human race, Homo sapiens, came from Africa and then spread and populated different parts of the world. The race theory propagated by Hindutva has been discredited all over the world. However, it is the reigning doctrine as well as the basis of official historiography in India, as reflected in the syllabus of the University Grants Commission (UGC).

This most egregious refusal to accept the Aryan invasion as a historical fact is central to the Hindutva argument, as it reduces Hindus to the status of invaders or, at least, of migrants—not very different from the Muslims they so abhor. Author Tony Joseph relies on DNA studies amongst other data to demonstrate India to be what he calls 'a multi-source civilisation not a single source one',[8] the Aryan migration being the last of the significant migrations. He concludes his work with the line, 'We are all Indians; we are all migrants.' Much of his work is derived from a major genetic study titled 'Genetic Evidence for Recent Population Mixture in India'. The report is based on genome data from seventy-three population groups that resided on the Indian subcontinent from 2200 BCE to 100 CE.

Notwithstanding this formidable research and, perhaps as a reaction to it, in 2017 Prime Minister Narendra Modi set up a committee to go into this issue, with the stated purpose of identifying Hindus as being the original inhabitants of India. Of course, that is the last we heard of it, but it demonstrates how important history is to validate this new nationalism and portray Muslims as invaders.

Colonial Historiography

The matter of historiography is also important, as many of the great textbooks on Indian history produced in the late nineteenth and early twentieth centuries had a seminal influence on perceptions of the medieval period. Peter Hardy, an Indo-Persian historiography expert, was dismissive of a number of popular Orientalists such as Vincent Smith, Sir Wolseley Haig and Sir Jadunath Sarkar, accusing them of uniformly 'narrating the history of medieval times as a succession of battles, rebellions and of depositions of one Muslim soldier of fortune by another.'[9] These were, in Hardy's eyes, old-fashioned approaches:

> The working hypotheses of most modern historians—that a society must be studied in its own terms and that all aspects of the life of a people, a society or a civilisation are to be assumed to be interconnected and interdependent—seem not have greatly influenced the study of medieval Indian history.[10]

One of the great developments in modern historiography ushered in by the twentieth century is that the compass of history became much wider and started to deal with society at large, moving away from the quaint conceit that history is only to be confined to stories of kings and queens. It is this solipsistic obsession with personalities in a world foreign to us that distorts our view of history and the past.

Herodotus was one of the first to advance the view that geographical location was the most important determinant of a nation or people's fate, having ramifications on their culture and economics. This concern with geography has resurfaced from time to time, and French historian Ferdinand Braudel has treated this as a great tool in understanding world history. Napoleon famously said, 'To know a nation's geography is to know its foreign policy.'[11] North India was perennially hostage to invasions from Central Asia because of its location. These invaders and plunderers were drawn to the North Indian plains, the lush fields of Punjab, and the wealth concentrated in many of the temples and urban dwellings. The problem is that these invaders are now equated with Muslims, an idea that introduces an insidious religious dimension to history. We must ask why historical narratives exclude the pre-Islamic period, which saw waves of invaders from Central Asia and Greece, who also engaged in plunder.

The notion of geographic location does not figure as a tool of analysis in Hindutva historiography. I believe that it is essential, as one cannot understand North Indian history without it.

Colonial historians were minded to segregate the past through the prism of religion. Historian James Mill segregated Indian history into three periods: the Hindu, the Mohammedan and the British. British historians framed Indian history as unfolding through 'two great ruptures' in time. The first, which defined the transition to the medieval period, was portrayed as a descent from an earlier 'Hindu golden age' to one of 'Mohammedan tyranny'. As per Richard Eaton this gave the British the opportunity 'to imagine India's second great historical rupture—the transition from "medieval" times (i.e. Muslim rule) to modernity (i.e. British rule)—as having validated the coming of European governance as a blessing for a benighted land.'[12] Thus the British, in one fell stroke 'liberated India from eight centuries of "Muhammadan" stagnation.'[13] Eaton examines how Indian society changed during this period of so-called 'Muhammadan' stagnation, stressing the buoyant economy, the cultural efflorescence that arose from the interaction of Sanskrit and Persian worlds, the emergence of the Bhakti Movement and Sikhism. In other words, it reveals what a dynamic society India was in this medieval period in contrast to what colonial historians like to portray it as—a society that was depressingly static, eagerly awaiting colonial redemption.

Viewed through this prism, the British cast themselves as saviours who rid India of the Mohammedan yoke, portraying eight centuries of Mohammedan rule in North India as a period of unremitting oppression and unprecedented barbarity.

The British East India Company, now seen for good reason as the reviled exploiter and looter of India, was privileged and given benediction by the Hindu Right, largely because they relied so uncritically on colonial historiography to create and embellish the anti-Muslim narrative. There was a quartet of British military scholars or scribes who were largely responsible for the creation of this new perspective: Lieutenant Colonel Alexander Dow, Lieutenant Anderson, Captain Scott and the redoubtable Lieutenant Colonel Briggs. This quartet sang the same song, as Manan Ahmed Asif put it, 'extensive essays and exegeses on the origins of Muslim fanaticism and temple destruction, the character of the Hindu people and those who had been forcibly converted, as well as the ways in which the current Mughal polity was oppressing the population of British India.'[14]

It is this malign outlook, which, unfortunately, skewed the common perception of life during medieval India. It even influenced sympathetic readers such as Jawaharlal Nehru, whose book *Glimpses of World History*, struggles with the artifice of this simplistic binary between Akbar and Aurangzeb as the only way of looking at Mughal rule. It is only in the post-Independence era that historians started to question these colonial verities and stereotypes, and were able to interrogate this historiography to show it for the sham much of it was.

There is a trend in postmodernist theory which denies there is any such thing as historical truth or objectivity, the view being that language cannot relate to anything except itself, which must entail the dissolution of history. However, what we are confronting in India is not any sophisticated post-modernist theory, but prejudice, a bankrupt ideology, and an uncritical reliance on colonial texts.

The realities of Muslim rule were much more nuanced than these simplistic, reductive binaries. For example, if one were to examine the story of the Gorakhnath Math—the current mahant being none other than Yogi Adityanath, whose main political agenda is to extirpate the Mughal legacy from India—one would see a very different perspective. The Nath yogis, who comprise the Gorakhnath Math, had powerful historical connections to several Mughal emperors from Babar, Akbar to Aurangzeb. Even the temple land of Gorakhnath in Gorakhpur was endowed by Nawab Asaf-ud-Daula of Awadh in the eighteenth century for the construction of the present temple complex.[15] According to historian Christine Marrewa-Karwoski, '[t]he Nath yogis are a heterogeneous community of ascetics that dates back to around 13th century and whose beliefs overlapped with Jain, Tantric, Muslim and Sikh communities.'[16] Karwoski argues that the inclusivity of their message allowed for both Hindu and Muslim rituals which were attractive to many Mughal emperors. This is part of the rich tapestry of Indian history and a luminous example of many cases of such munificence which require to be acknowledged and appreciated. This is not to question cases of Muslim barbarity and intolerance, only that matters should be seen in perspective.

What about the South?

We invariably look at Hindu–Muslim history in India solely through the prism of North India and the incursions it suffered from Central Asian and Persian invaders; but South India, where Hindu–Muslim relations had a very different trajectory, is largely ignored.

If one looks at the South, the relationship between Hindus and Muslims was very different. For example, the oldest mosque in India was allegedly built in 629 CE at Cheraman in Kerala. The history of Hindu–Muslim relations, as well as that of Christians in Kerala, was largely influenced by trade and commerce and did not lead to colonialism—unlike in the case of the Portuguese, the English and the Dutch.

South India had a number of great dynasties, such as the Cholas, Pallavas and the Pandyas, who were not only significant and iconic builders but also great conquerors. All these dynasties conquered lands in Southeast Asia. The Cholas controlled territories from the Bay of Bengal to Sumatra in present-day Indonesia. Their capital was Tanjore, and they built the grand Brihadeshwara Temple in Tanjore in 10 CE.[17] The Pallavas were responsible for the construction of the grand Mahabalipuram temple complex in the seventh and eighth centuries. Chalukyas, who ruled over Karnataka and southern Maharashtra, were responsible for the construction of the exquisite temple complex at Badami. These dynasties reigned for many centuries—the Cholas for 1500 years and the Chalukyas for over 600 years.

Perhaps the reason that these empires are not discussed as avidly as the dynasties of North India is that, at least in the case of the Chola dynasty, it is inconsistent with one of the verities of Hindutva—that Hindus never invaded any country or sought to impose their religion on anyone or, for that matter, destroyed any temples or engaged in pillage. The colonial aspect of Hindu rule is remarked upon by a historian of ancient India, Dr Upinder Singh, who, in her magisterial series on ancient and early medieval India, writes that:

> One of my major dissatisfactions with ancient Indian history writing—perhaps its greatest one—is the fact that most of it is incredibly India-centric and ignores the rest of Asia ... Scholars such as R.C. Majumdar and K.A.N. Sastri talked of Hindu political and cultural colonization of the lands of Southeast Asia, although they differed to some extent in the details, for instance on whether the significant Indian influences emanated from Bengal or South India.[18]

It is pertinent that Dr Singh refers explicitly to 'Hindu political and cultural colonization', something Hindutva thinkers would be aghast at. Even nationalists, such as the great Swami Vivekananda and Mahatma Gandhi, did not refer to this history. Vivekananda solemnly pronounced in Colombo in 1897 that 'India has for thousands of years peacefully existed ... We of all nations of the world have never been a conquering race and that blessing is on our heads.'[19] However, this prelapsarian view of Indian history can be contested.

Ordinarily, these views should not be an issue unless one subscribes to this curious amalgam of victimhood and exceptionalism that seems to be integral to the Hindutva discourse of Hindus never having invaded and subjugated people. In fact, according to some nationalist thinkers, including Gandhi and Nehru, the ancient Hindus never took recourse to violence, an assertion which is wholly unsupported. American Indologist Wendy Doniger puts it rather well, stating that, 'Nonviolence became a cultural ideal for Hindus precisely because it holds out the last hope of a cure, all the more desirable since unattainable, for a civilization that has, like most, always suffered from chronic and terminal violence.'[20] Dr Singh supports this view and states,

> Although there were many different ideas of ancient India, it was the idealized Nehruvian model of the ancient Indian past—one in which Buddhism, Ashoka, nonviolence, and cosmopolitanism had pride of place—that were reflected in the national flag and more so, in the national emblem. This model affirmed the nonviolent ideology of Gandhian nationalism and projected a set of aspirations for India's future.

Dr Singh has found such an understanding deficient for being 'based on a very selective reading of India's ancient history.'[21] These scholarly works make it amply clear that the mythology of the non-violent Indian is precisely that; it has no basis in history.

Here, a discussion on issues such as the colonisation of areas and religious conversions becomes relevant since, by not confronting this aspect of history, Hindutva thinkers actively conceal some of the true glories of Hinduism. In this process of conquest of Southeast Asia, kingdoms were created, trade flourished, and temples were erected to Hindu gods on a grandiloquent scale. One of the most resplendent cities of its time was Angkor, located in present-day Cambodia. It included the Angkor Wat temple complex, which was originally built as a Hindu temple. Despite receiving the UNESCO accolade of their the most important archaeological site in Southeast Asia, it hardly figures in the public imagination today.

Buddhism is the other major soft cultural export of ancient India that has been forgotten. It had a seismic civilisational impact on China during the reign of the Han dynasty, over two millennia ago. One imagines that this is something that India is proud of, as it projects an important part of India's soft culture in a particularly consequential part of the world, but that would be a mistake. Shaped by Brahmanical prejudices, Buddhism is commonly viewed as an apostasy, with the Hindu Right remaining oddly reticent on this very critical contribution to India's engagement with China, Japan and South East Asia, as though it were something to be ashamed of.

It is relevant that many on the Hindu Right speak of converting India into a civilisational state, a state which owes its legitimacy to a civilisational core, one indubitably embedded in religion as opposed to civic citizenship which forms the basis of the Indian constitution, as if such a transition would be a panacea for all our problems. Such a state may correspond to the borders of contemporary India, but would pointedly fail to recognise that the Indic civilisation had a pervasive influence in Southeast Asia in such territories as present-day Myanmar, Cambodia, Thailand, Sri Lanka, Java and Bali. In fact, the great Sanskrit scholar Sheldon Pollock referred to this culture as the 'Sanskrit Cosmopolis'.[22] Accepting the position that Indic civilisation encompasses much more than the nation-state of India undermines the civilisational construct posited by proponents of Hindutva. Therefore, they prefer to diminish the Indic civilisation by fetishising Hindu dharma and purity, turning their backs on an illustrious past which has been enriched by its interactions with the Persianate world. Shashi Tharoor has questioned this idea by asking, 'What today is Indic civilisation? Some have argued that India is a "civilisation-state" rather than a "nation-state", but they anchor the idea of Indian civilisation solely in the Hindu dharma, with no regard for the multiple non-Hindu influences that have undoubtedly helped shape contemporary Indian civilisations.'[23] The more important question to ask them would be what prompts their deep animosity towards Muslims, particularly the Mughals, that fuels this ideology?

Were the Mughals a force for the good?

Whilst the history of southern India is a useful corrective to the lugubrious threnody of defeat and shame in which Hindutva thinkers revel, there is no sensible explanation for their attitude towards the Mughals, whom they have sought to excise from history. The Mughal dynasty is considered one of the most significant dynasties of world history, rivalling the Ottomans and the Hapsburgs in their imperial significance, wealth and cultural legacies. It is for this reason they cannot be consigned to oblivion; they were just too consequential a force on the world stage to be ignored. The question is, whilst no one can seriously deny their cultural achievements, as a dynasty were they a force for good, or should they be just looked through the prism of invaders who stayed and enslaved the Indian masses, as is now being peddled? What, in effect, are the charges levelled against them?

The first charge is that they were foreigners and invaders. This argument needs to be understood in the context among the Aryan invasion. If we accept the consensus among the new breed of Indian historians and public intellectuals, who use multi-disciplinary tools such as DNA testing and linguistics to show that Aryans were not indigenous to India but migrated from Central Asia around 1500 BCE, it is evident that this 'foreigner' allegation is contrary to contemporary academic understanding.

Even Sir Jadunath Sarkar,[24] one of the historians most identified with the Hindu Right for indubitably subscribing to the narrative that saw the Mughals as foreigners, was constrained to observe that 'the Mughal Emperors united many provinces of India into one political unit, with uniformity of official language, administrative machinery, coinage and public service, and indeed a common type of civilization for the higher classes. They also recognized it as a duty to preserve peace and the reign of law throughout their dominions.'[25] This is high praise indeed from someone who, until the 1950s, was commonly regarded as the foremost historian of medieval India.

The Mughals have often been accused of plundering and looting India. However, this assumes that the Mughals were a foreign colonial power. This is contentious. According to John F Richards, '... the dynasty and the empire itself became indisputably Indian. The interests and futures of all concerned were in India, not in ancestral homelands in the Middle East or Central Asia.'[26] Their governance was emphatically not colonial. The Mughals, who from the beginning, had severed their ties with the Fergana Valley, of which Babar writes so achingly in his autobiography, *The Baburnama*. It is fair to conclude, as does Parvati Sharma in her biography of Jahangir,[27] that the Mughals have been labelled foreigners not because of their place of origin, but rather for their Muslim identity.

What Hindutva writers ignore is the fact that if the Mughals were not a colonial power, then any prosperity enjoyed by them would have to be a shared prosperity. India during the Mughal rule saw massive economic growth and prosperity. One way of measuring this extraordinary financial efflorescence is to look at the state of silver imports at the time. Sixteenth-century Indian economy was largely self-sufficient, barring silver and horses, which had to be imported. The horse trade boomed, bringing great affluence along the horse-trading routes from Central Asia to India, as horses were shipped to Europe from Indian ports as well as bought by Indian rulers. Peter Frankopan has observed that 'with European silver pouring in to buy goods from the east, much was spent buying the best steeds ... rather as money that has flowed more recently into oil-rich states has been spent on the best rides: Ferraris, Lamborghinis and other fine cars.'[28]

In sharp contrast, the East India Company collected taxes in India, and a third of the monies collected was used to fund the purchase of Indian goods to be exported.[29] As a result, there was a reduction not only in the amount of silver flowing into India as payment for exports but also in India's capacity to import silver. This has been described as a huge scam, theft on a grandiose scale where the British deployed tax revenues collected in India to acquire Indian goods for re-export, thereby generating the resources needed to import strategic materials vital to Britain's Industrial Revolution, including iron, tar, and timber. India in the nineteenth century saw the steady de-industrialisation of the economy at the behest of the British.

Richard Eaton further observes,

> American silver arriving in India was immediately minted into silver rupees, which became the Mughals' principal currency medium from about 1580. In 1615, one observer estimated the Mughals' annual revenue at 120 million silver coins, compared to forty-five million for the Ottoman empire and just fifteen million for neighbouring Iran.[30]

So, the Mughals were by far the most opulent rulers of the three Islamic gunpowder empires. He further observes that between 1600 and 1800 CE, India absorbed about 20 per cent of the precious metals produced throughout the world. This is really quite an achievement, as this growth was on the back of the exponential rise in exports of Indian textiles, which had effectively displaced rice and spices as the most significant item of trade in the Indian Ocean.

To finance the import of silver, large areas of North India were brought under more intensive land use in order to generate more revenue. Even more significant was the imperial emphasis on the collection of revenue in cash, which 'fostered monetisation, forcing producers to go in for cash, crops which had demand amongst consuming elites and markets in India and overseas.'[31] This greater circulation of cash in terms of silver coins increased merchant wealth and created new markets and new interdependencies. As Eaton puts it, 'Bengal depended on yarn from Gujarat, Coromandel acquired its cotton from the Deccan, and Gujarat relied on raw silk transported from Bengal.' These developments presaged the growth of a pan-Indian integrated economy, involving the hinterland more directly than just the coastal areas, in some ways outpacing the political entity that would eventually become India.

This growth in the textile industry was remarkable, even by historical standards. India had been exporting textiles since Roman times, but never on this scale. The key factor was the design, much of which emanated from Central Asia and Persia. For example, the paisley print, which is so often identified as the cynosure of Indian prints, actually originated in Yazd, Persia, and is named after the town of Paisley in Scotland. Even until 2019, the textile industry in India employed over forty-five million workers, many in the informal sector. So, it cannot be said that the impact of the Mughals on the Indian economy was transient and fleeting. According to economist Angus Maddison, India saw the highest economic growth at over 20 per cent under the Mughals, and in the eighteenth century, India overtook China as the largest economy in the world.[32]

The subsequent mercantilism the British imposed on India was horrendous, monopolistic and impoverishing, leaving Indian merchants without the protection they had enjoyed under Mughal rule until the end of the eighteenth century. Economist Adam Smith called these 'the mean and malignant expedients of the mercantile system,'[33] as it was based on a palpably rapacious policy, one which even the most protean thinker on political economy excoriated. Yet, the pseudo-historians of Hindutva shamefully insist that British rule was preferable to the Mughals. In addition to this, it is not as if this wealth was not shared with the Hindu Baniya class, who benefitted commensurately—evident from the resplendent havelis and temples Jain merchants built in Shahjahanabad at the time that exist to this day.

This perversity sits very oddly with much of the recent historical research and writing, which shows the extent to which the British, through the East India Company and then the Crown, plundered India financially. Economist Utsa Patnaik, drawing on nearly two centuries of data on tax and trade has calculated that Britain enriched itself by a total figure of USD 45 trillion in the period between 1765 to 1938,[34] which is around seventeen times UK's GDP in 2018. This figure became higher in a recent study conducted by Oxfam showing that the theft was around USD 64 trillion.

It is relevant to note that this rapacious attitude was not just confined to the East India Company but extended to the British government and persisted well into the twentieth century. India post-Independence was Britain's most substantial creditor, having the maximum sterling balances amounting to GBP 120 million in 1945 (GBP 5.2 billion today). Even this figure was reached only after the most acrimonious negotiations, where the British tried to reduce their liability through some very questionable tactics. Later, these balances were reduced by the British through the insidious stratagem of sterling devaluation in 1949, something which the Bank of England, according to B.K. Nehru, the then High Commissioner to the UK, had assured would not take place.[35] The rapacity displayed by the British in nearly 200 years of their rule is evident from the state of human development indices in 1947. For example, Indian life expectancy at the time was around thirty-two years, which is now nearly seventy years.[36] At the same time, life expectancy in the UK in 1947 was in excess of sixty years. This indicates the flawed legacy left by the British at the time of Independence.

Destruction of Places of Worship

The other charge levelled against the Mughals is the matter of destruction of places of worship, the Ram temple in Ayodhya being the most sensational example of this. To be fair, the charge does not relate just to the Mughals, but to all Islamic invaders who came from the ninth century onwards.

I believe that India is not unique in experiencing the destruction or desecration of places of worship, given that the destruction of iconic temples, mosques and churches is a peculiarly secular activity and is invariably guided by considerations of realpolitik. The most infamous examples of this from the ancient world include the destruction of the famed city of Persepolis by Alexander the Great and the obliteration of the great Temple of Solomon in Jerusalem by the Romans in 70 CE. In Spain, the Great Mosque of Cordoba was converted into a cathedral after the city was conquered by Christians. Whilst none of these acts can be condoned on any grounds, to associate the destruction of holy places with just one religion and to relate it to monotheism is a transgression of history and facts.

At this stage, it is necessary to understand why, historically, rulers, including Hindu ones, have felt the need to desecrate places of worship. The practice of Hindu rulers destroying Buddhist temples is well documented. Even Swami Vivekananda remarked 'that the Temple of Jagannath at Puri was once an ancient Buddhist shrine. We Hindus have turned that and many other Buddhist shrines into temples.'[37] According to Hiuen Tsang, the seventh-century Chinese

Buddhist monk, Mihirakula, a sixth-century Huna ruler and devotee of Shiva, destroyed 1600 Buddhist stupas and monasteries and killed thousands of Buddhist monks and laity. Notably, this vandalism also included the destruction of Hindu temples by Hindu rulers. When the Cholas defeated Mahipala, the maharaja of the Pala Empire in 1025 CE, they carried off the bronze image of Shiva from the royal temple along with many precious gems. They also raided Orissa and appropriated images of Bhairav, Bhairavi and Kali.

Richard Eaton explains that 'in order to sever the links between a defeated king and the visible manifestation of his divine patron, it was necessary to carry off images or in other ways desecrate his royal temples.'[38] This point is hugely important when the Sangh Parivar targets Muslim rulers for causing destruction because of iconoclasm and not for mundane political considerations.

The Vishwa Hindu Parishad (VHP) argues that around 160,000 temples were destroyed by Muslim invaders, with no evidence to back this fact. In this context, Richard Eaton has only documented eighty instances of temples being destroyed by Muslim conquerors in 800 years, a far cry from the huge number of demolitions claimed by the VHP.[39] Other than alluding to iconoclasm as the reason behind the destruction of temples—even though there is no evidence to support this argument—Hindutva thinkers are not able to provide any other motive. In my view, the only way to connect the actions of Muslim invaders with the present-day Muslim community is through religion.

The momentum of politics forces ideological parties to thrive and exaggerate victimhood to continue to burnish and vivify such alleged wrongs. This is the unfortunate consequence of grievance politics; it has no interest in closure or healing. Post the demolition of the Babri Masjid, the UPA government passed a legislation known as the Places of Worship Act, which purported to freeze the status of places of worship as they were on 15 August 1947. Five judges of the constitutional bench of the Supreme Court gave the imprimatur of approval to this legislation[40] as it was meant to prevent the recurrence of disputes over places of worship such as the Ram Temple in Ayodhya. Notwithstanding the approval of this law by the Supreme Court, fresh challenges have been launched against the constitutionality of this legislation in relation to the Gyanvapi Mosque at Varanasi and the Shahi Idgah Masjid in Mathura. A politician by the name of Ashwini Upadhyay is aiming at recovering around 900 lost temples, all presumably now housing medieval mosques which require demolition. That seems to be the agenda for the 'New India'.

Even apart from this statute, there exist limitations on the usurpation of sites of Muslim heritage. Most of such sites are actually governed by a separate law, the Ancient Monuments and Archaeological Sites and Remains Act of 1958. Under the act, the Archaeological Survey of India (ASI) is empowered to protect and maintain such properties. For example, the Taj Mahal is covered under this statute as it is a dead historical monument, in that there is no active worship there. However, a combination of politicisation and criminal underfunding of the ASI[41] has created a situation of neglect of such sites and, in the case of Muslim monuments, complete disregard. An instance of this was the demolition of the glorious Mubarak Manzil in Agra by a builder, with the ASI failing to intervene until it was too late.

I believe that the true test of commitment to cultural heritage and patrimony lies in the priorities set for their care, renovation and maintenance. Despite the considerable clamour by proponents of Hindutva about their concern for Hindu culture, there exist exquisite temples which have fallen into complete disrepair. In Varanasi, the Prime Minister's own parliamentary constituency, there are about 2000 temples in dire need of repair. And yet, there is hardly any serious attempt to address these issues in contemporary India unless there is a political angle to be exploited.

PART III

SECULARISM

8

THE INDIAN VERSION OF SECULARISM

Secularism is a term that has been much misunderstood. It suits the interests of a particular constituency for this term to be as vague and stigmatised as possible, as it is often associated with Nehru, minority appeasement and Western thinking.

There are many definitions of secularism, but the one which I find most compelling is that of Romila Thapar—'Secularism involves questioning the control that religious organisations have over social institutions. It does not deny the presence of religion in society but demarcates the social institutions over which religion can or cannot exercise control. This distinction is important.'[1]

Indian secularism is, however, sui generis. Despite the best efforts of liberals such as Ambedkar and K.T. Shah, there was never a clear demarcation between the public and private spaces as exists in most States that call themselves secular. Mahatma Gandhi, who no one could accuse of being irreligious, conceived Indian secularism as one that treated all religions on an equal footing. However, India doesn't make any pretence of treating all religions equally; as I have already established, Hinduism and Hindu sentiments have been privileged from the very beginning in public policy, laws and seminal Supreme Court judgements. These facts are undeniable, but the Hindu Right needs to manufacture a sense of grievance that a wrong has been done to them by way of the imposition of secularism. Much is made of Indian secularism changing after 2014, but the term 'secularism' was compromised from the very beginning. The only difference since 2014 has been that the State has taken on the characteristics of an ethnocracy. This has implications for public policy and ultimately renders the term secularism vacuous and nothing more than a charade.

One of the factors which has had a malign influence on the debate about secularism is the view espoused by many members of the Congress party, since the 1960s, and one which seems to have much currency today, that the best guarantee for secularism is, as political scientist Sumantra Bose described it, a 'romanticised notion of Hindu tolerance.'[2] This can be seen in the 1999 resolution of the Congress party in which it asserted what appears to be an eternal verity 'that Hinduism is the most effective guarantor of secularism in India.'[3] This is a somewhat problematical notion, as religions cannot be stereotyped in such a manner. As Bose concludes 'all religions have both tolerant and intolerant characteristics, and that all religions can assume either a tolerant or intolerant form depending on context and circumstance.'[4] An example of this would be Buddhism, which is widely perceived as being a peaceful religion, yet in the last few decades the most violent and brutal cases of ethnic cleansing and expulsions in South Asia have been associated with confessionally Buddhist countries like Sri Lanka and Myanmar.

The sequitur of this discussion would be whether India needs to be a secular state at all, as the assumption is that given Hinduism's extraordinary tolerance, minorities will always be secure. However, as one examines the nature of the Indian state, it becomes clear that the idea of universalism and tolerance is a chimera and that many religious freedoms which are taken for granted in democracies are either lost or are being trespassed upon by the Indian state. In any event, it is important to note that equating tolerance with policies that foster diversity, equality, co-existence and multiculturalism, which most modern states with ethnic or cultural minorities enforce, is an outmoded conceit. As historian Marc David Baer puts it,

> To tolerate means to suffer, endure, or put up with something objectionable. The tolerating party considers its own religion to be true and the tolerated groups' religious claims to be false. John Locke famously refused to include Catholics in his conception of tolerance. Tolerance is in fact the expression of a power relationship.[5]

This notion of tolerance being the panacea that can help navigate the complexities of the Indian state post-Independence fails to address seminal cultural and economic diversities.

While these observations may trouble those who saw 2014 as a disturbing and seismic shift in public policy, it is the burden of my argument to show that this concern is exaggerated. From the very beginning, the Hindu Right, that is, persons who seek to privilege what they conceive as their religious practices at the cost of minorities and public welfare, have had a disproportionate say in public policy. If Gandhi's understanding of secularism—the equal treatment of all religions—was a non-starter, then what was the basic understanding of secularism that informed much of the discourse and public policy in the early years of Independence? Secularism was sold as a homogenising force consistent with nationalism and one which was profoundly antithetical to any notions of pluralism.[6] The only exception relates to the caste system, whose historic injustices towards Dalits and Scheduled Castes were sought to be addressed through the creation of affirmative action programmes.

Secularism has been used as a device to deny minorities cultural rights as well as the benefits of affirmative action programmes on the ground that Article 15 of the Constitution prohibits the privileging of any religion; but such considerations do not apply to Hindu society, where reservations for Other Backward Classes (OBCs), introduced in the name of addressing backwardness, have turbocharged political discourse and have now been extended to even upper castes.

A recent example is the attitude of the UP Government in relation to the Uttar Pradesh Board of Madarsa Education Act of 2004, which had basically sought to streamline Muslim education, but was held unconstitutional by the Allahabad High Court for violating principles of secularism. The court also objected to the madarsas being managed by the minority welfare department rather than the education department. Subsequent to the Supreme Court staying the Allahabad high court's ruling, the UP government decided to accept the high court's order. In 2024, Supreme Court quashed the ruling, stating that the high court had misconstrued the objective of the act which was to regulate madarsas in the state of UP. The court accepted the argument that madarsas provided education in secular subjects like maths, science, English and Hindi and not merely religious education. Allowing the high court's ruling to stand would have affected some 17,000 students and a system of education that had existed for 120 years. Senior advocate Abhishek Manu Singhvi also raised the contrast with 'gurukuls' being run in Haridwar and Rishikesh which provided Hindu religious education but were not being targeted by anyone.[7] In some ways, it is outrageous that the UP Government seeks cynically to uphold secularism at the cost of denying education to poor Muslims.

The Role of Religion in Public Life

The promise of secularisation articulated by sociologist M.S. Srinivasan 'implies that what was previously regarded as religious is now ceasing to be such, and it also implies a process of differentiation which results in the various aspects of society—economic, political, legal and moral—becoming increasingly discrete in relation to each other.'[8] This seems to be a mirage; secularism is in tatters, and what is apparent is that obscurantism is on the rise, challenging modernity. Nehru strongly believed in the centrality of rationalism and the importance of a scientific temper. Even though there is much in postmodernist thinking to harbour doubts about the unqualified efficacy of Western science and medicine and the neglect of our own indigenous traditions, such traditions also have to be proved by recourse to established methods of reasoning and evidence. What is sought to be introduced by the Hindu Right is blind faith. As a consequence of this, there is a prejudice against modern science and learning which is evident in certain policies of the State.

It is important to point out that in spite of the lack of any Hindu religious injunction against evolutionary sciences, as exists amongst

American evangelicals, for example, the Indian government has deleted evolution from Class X's NCERT science textbooks. As Nitin Pai, director of the Takshashila Institution, points out,

> Darwin has not been totally expunged from the CBSE curriculum. Even so, given that only a small fraction of CBSE students take biology in Class XII, the vast majority of CBSE students will leave school without being taught one of the most important principles of science. Understanding natural selection is important for everyone—not just biology students—for everything from learning how to deal with pandemics, take care of one's health, improve agricultural productivity and care for our environment.[9]

In a recent pronouncement by a panel of scientist citizens, it was alleged that India is facing 'a systematic threat to its scientific and educational foundation', as a result of institutional promotion of pseudoscience, declining funds and changes in school curricula.[10]

Often when discussing how Indians view religion and tolerance, culinary metaphors have traction. We are to believe that there are two paradigms: one being the 'thali' paradigm (where there are many small dishes or katoris, each separate and discrete on a common thali or platter, like different communities residing in segregated spaces). Pratap Bhanu Mehta states that 'India is committed to an ideology of toleration but practices what I elsewhere called segmented toleration: each community has its place so long as each stays in its place. The drawing of boundaries is quite sharp.'[11]

According to a 2021 PEW India Religious Segregation Study, inter-religious marriages have become the lightning rod that provokes the greatest controversy and discord. Oddly, Hindus and Muslims are united on this view, with about the same percentage (70 per cent) viewing such marriages with disfavour. It is obviously this unease which propels the 'love jihad' narrative, as in the case of Hindus, it also feeds into the ludicrous paranoia that Muslims will overtake Hindus in population, a statistical impossibility.

These attitudes lead to physical segregation. This desire for physical segregation between religions is evident in the 'Gujarat Model'—cities like Ahmedabad, which were never cosmopolitan, have now transformed from claustrophobically parochial cities into segregated ones. This segregation is obliquely enforced by law. Journalist Aakar Patel points out that successive BJP governments in Gujarat imposed legislations called the 'Gujarat Disturbed Areas Act' which became an instrument to monitor and control property purchases in areas where 'the balance in the Majority Hindu/ Minority Muslim strength' might get affected.[12] This legislation has serious ramifications on minority communities who face great difficulties in buying property in predominantly Hindu areas.

The danger is that for many minorities in urban India, segregation, in practical terms, means ghettoisation. It also means that in the distribution of public goods, governments who are so inclined can discriminate with ease, denying benefits to certain areas which are seen to be minority areas, residents of which, in all likelihood, may not vote for the ruling party.

We have seen graphic evidence of this in Ahmedabad's Juhapura, a slum which houses over 50 per cent of Ahmedabad's Muslims, that is around 500,000 people. It has grown exponentially since the 2002 riots, as many middle-class Muslims have gravitated there for safety considerations. The area has an acute deficiency of 'public infrastructure' which, in small part, has been mitigated by the active involvement of certain Muslim NGOs. This development has come with worrying consequences as these foundations are sponsored by the Deoband Movement—conservative and anti-Western in its ideology but perforce enveloping the education space where, in the words of Christophe Jaffrelot, local schools merge seamlessly with madarsas 'instilling conservative and intolerant values into the students'.[13] Many on the Hindu Right have difficulties with the increase in Muslim fundamentalism in Kabul but seem indifferent to its increase in Ahmedabad, on account of policies that drive the minority community towards ghettoisation and fundamentalism, and yet any action which seeks to mitigate these outcomes is labelled 'minority appeasement'.

Secularism and Its Discontents

In this analysis of secularism, I wish to address the main objections raised by those who assert that the secularism that was sponsored and promised by the Constitution has either failed or is inherently unworkable. These objections are well summarised by political theorist Rajeev Bhargava, who identifies three separate objections to 'constitutional secularism'.[14] The first is that it is an imported and foreign concept; it has nothing to do with India and infringes upon traditions of co-existence and harmony between the communities which were pre-modern. Secondly, and this argument in part derives from the first objection, that this type of secularism is somehow irreligious or anti-religion, part of a desire to banish religious belief from the public space and create a Western secular or a godless society, which is the paradigm for deracinated thinkers and atheists.

The third and most popular objection is that even if one assumes that secularism implies equal respect for all religious practices and beliefs, because of electoral politics there is an inherent bias towards minorities at the cost of the majority, which in effect makes Indian secularism inherently anti-Hindu. In this context, the continued application of Muslim personal law is often alluded to. Bhargava puts this objection very well: 'Hindu people are saddled with an anti-Hindu state.'[15] This discontent was projected famously by BJP politician L.K. Advani, who likened Congress secularism to 'pseudo-secularism which was founded on appeasement of minorities.'[16] In the words of social activist Asghar Ali Engineer, 'he came out with a strange theory that the Hindus have been "besieged" in their own country due to the politics of appeasement pursued by the Congress.'[17] I will now examine all three of these objections in greater detail.

The Foreignness of Secularism

Andre Malraux, the great French novelist and thinker, asked Nehru in his autumn years, what had been his most 'difficult task'? Nehru responded that it was 'creating a secular state in a religious country'.[18] His admission was not a rejection of faith, but the desire to place reason and the scientific temper at the centre of the State's ideology and thinking.[19]

But the subtext of his answer is the plain acknowledgement that India is a religious country and has not ceased to be so, regardless of what the Constitution has provided. The fashionable notion that Nehru was irreligious, perhaps even an atheist, forms part of the charge sheet prepared against him by the current dispensation. Such people ignore the fact that the author of *Hindutva,* Savarkar, was also an atheist, but that had not precluded him from becoming the head of the Hindu Mahasabha. As former American president Richard Nixon has put it, 'A man's religion is of no concern in politics provided he has a religion.'[20]

In the original draft of the Constitution, there is no reference to secularism. K.T. Shah, a member of the Constituent Assembly, sought to insert it in the Preamble, without success. The word was inserted several decades later by Indira Gandhi in 1976, as part of the controversial Forty-Second Constitutional Amendment. Shah's unsuccessful attempt was in fact opposed by both Nehru and Ambedkar, and for good reason. Whilst both subscribed to the principles of secularism, they were aware that secularism in the European sense—the separation between Church and State—could not be applied in the Indian context. India had to chart its own form of secularism, one that would have a specific Indian meaning. Historian Sanjay Subramanyam detaches the European understanding of secularism from our own by observing that '[i]n reality, the term has a political weight in India that it has never had in the West, and it has acquired a deep meaning and significance in India that many Europeans simply don't understand. Thus, secularism has become almost as Indian a word as "preponed" or "denting" (for removing a dent in a car).'[21]

There are countless references to the term 'secular' in the Constituent Assembly debates. It is apparent that apart from a few members such as Ambedkar and Rajkumari Amrit Kaur, who were concerned about the discriminatory nature of many religious practices, for many members of the Constituent Assembly, as Shefali Jha puts it, 'secularism meant a more expansive role for religion'.[22] She refers to the speeches of K.M. Munshi, who is often identified with the politics of Sardar Patel, where he has said that as per Indian secularism 'the state could not possibly have a state religion, nor could a rigid line be drawn between the religion and church like in the US.'[23] This is an argument that favoured the Hindu Right, as it gave impetus to those who sought to enlarge the role of religion in public life. Ambedkar recognised this when he stated, 'What should be the policy of the State, how the Society should be organised in its social and economic side are matters which must be decided by the people themselves according to time and circumstances.' He wisely saw the potential collision that this rigid notion of secularism could have had with the impetus of democracy.

This argument may come as a surprise to many who are fixated on the notion that secularism is essentially something foreign and externally imposed, and in any case, so compromised for the sake of electoral politics as to be irrelevant to the needs of contemporary India. It is to be noted that the meaning of secularism has been deliberately perverted to mean irreligiousness and to portray it as an unevenly applied principle that privileges minorities over the majority.

Gandhi also subscribed to the notion of universalism and was deeply averse to the idea of State-supported religion since he thought of religion as something entirely spiritual in character. He raised the question, 'What conflict of interest can there be between Hindus and Muslims in the matter of revenue, sanitation, police, justice, or the use of public conveniences? The difference can only be in religious usage and observances with which a secular state has no concern.'[24]

Secularism was considered fashionable amongst many in the heady early years of the republic when it was regarded as integral to nationalism; as an instrument to obliterate what were seen as sources of disunity, tribalism, language differences and other aspects of what we now recognise as pluralism, but previously was referred to as colonial secularism. The confusion resided in the common perception that secularism was to be contrasted with communalism. It was for these reasons that national unity and integration were seen as pivotal to 'nation building'. Group rights other than those groups that were considered backward, such as the Scheduled Castes and Tribes, were disregarded with great alacrity, and there was consensus on this across the political spectrum. This insouciance had particular application to religious minorities, particularly to their cultural rights, as will be seen in relation to the Muslims. The malefic shadow of Pakistan loomed over this discourse.

The existential struggle between Hindutva and modernity is something I will come to, but the objection of foreignness is clearly anti-modernist. The same objection should then apply with equal force to nationalism, which is also a nineteenth-century European construct, as is the very notion of culture, as pointed out by philosopher Kwame Anthony Appiah.[25]

The Irreligiosity of Secularism

I believe that contrary to the supposition that constitutional secularism sought to banish religion from the mainstream of society and political discourse, it actually privileged religious thinking, practices, customs and culture to an extent not even found in some theocracies. The reason for this is that most of the legislations and judgements dealing with public funding of pilgrimages, temples and shrines, prohibition on cow slaughter, prevention of conversions, allowing religious symbolism as a means of garnering votes in a democratic election, have been passed or pronounced post-Independence. Almost all these laws and judgements favour the majority community, and there is hardly any criticism of this, except from hard secularists, who are a dwindling tribe.

Culture covers much more than religion and rather than being static, it is dynamic and pervasive. As the journalist Aakar Patel remarks, 'The concept of Hindu Rashtra was not a mere bundle of political and economic rights. It was essentially cultural, and not political or legal. It revealed itself through the urge for the realisation of God: a "living" god and not an idol or immaterial form.'[26] He is referring to the ideology of M.S. Golwalkar, the second head of the RSS, and this is a point that is critical to the discourse as it is manifest that neither the legislatures nor the courts appear to be restrained by the concept of constitutional secularism.

Whenever a discussion about Hindu culture is undertaken, the aspect which exercises a prodigious centrality to the discourse is the practice of pilgrimage to various shrines on festive occasions. Historian Radha Kumud Mukherjee has argued that this practice forms the very core of the geographical unity of India, as, according to him, it cultivates the love of the motherland.[27] Today, religious tourism is the pre-eminent kind of tourism in India, and state governments play a critical role in encouraging this by developing infrastructure to access important temples and providing grants to pilgrims. There are few countries in the world which claim to be secular, but also provide such generous financial assistance to people to undertake religious pilgrimages. India is one of them, and the range and extent of financial assistance it provides has expanded exponentially, particularly in BJP-run states. That for the organisation of the Maha Kumbh Mela in 2025, INR 7500 crores was allocated by the UP Government, is an example of this.[28]

Any discussion on state patronage of pilgrimages ought to be done in the context of the appalling tragedy of the second wave of the COVID-19 pandemic and the obtuse insistence of the Uttarakhand state government to host the Kumbh Mela in 2021 in the midst of the greatest public health catastrophe that India had witnessed since 1918. There is historical evidence that connects the spread of infections and Kumbh Melas, which has been particularly noted by colonial administrators in the nineteenth century. As economist Chinmay Tumbe says, 'Puri and many other pilgrimage sites were perceived by Europeans in the nineteenth century in the same way many see Chinese wet markets of meat in 2020, that is, as places that generate pandemics …'[29]

Few incidents demonstrate more clearly that when Hindu cultural traditions conflict with modernity and science, it is tradition that triumphs, as was the case of the Kumbh Mela in 2021. In that case, nine million pilgrims converged at Haridwar over a period of six weeks, participating in various 'shahi snans' (holy dips in the Ganga), which took place on 1 April 2021. Pilgrims travelled from different states where they returned after the pilgrimage. Journalist Barkha Dutt describes the effect as carnage, with people falling dead in villages from a mysterious fever, many of them with no access to any health infrastructure.

It is not as if the Uttarakhand government was unmindful of the risks posed by holding the Kumbh Mela at this time. The incumbent chief minister of the state who had opposed hosting the Kumbh Mela in the state was sacked by the Union government and replaced by a more pliant chief minister, Tirath Singh Rawat, who was in favour of holding the festival in all its glory and claimed that 'with Goddess Ganga's blessings, faith will triumph over disease'.[30] He expressed the view that the waters of the river Ganga were holy and could kill any virus.

It must be further understood that to host over nine million people involved great logistical planning as well as funding; the government had set aside INR 35 crores and retained twenty-five trains to bring pilgrims to Haridwar, a privilege that millions of migrant labourers fleeing cities by reason of the abrupt lockdown in March 2020 had been denied. It was only after the figures of infections and deaths began to spiral out of control and India came under the international spotlight, that the prime minister suggested to the heads of 'akharas' (centres of spiritual learning) that the last holy dip taking place in the middle of May ought to be made symbolic.

The extent of the spread of the virus during the Kumbh Mela in 2021 will never be known. Thousands of people could have contracted COVID-19 there and spread it throughout India, thus accelerating the impact and footprint of the second wave in rural areas and small towns. As per the *New York Times*, the number of deaths during the second wave ranged from 1.6 million to 4 million, which was at sharp variance with the official government figures. This massive death toll has been validated by credible bodies such as the WHO,[31] which has, in particular, excoriated the modest government figures of 50,000 deaths, exposing the obscene denouement of the decision to hold the Kumbh Mela.

This decision, even more than holding massive election rallies, stands out for the triumph of 'Hindu culture' and the quest for political hegemony in the cow belt. The real issue is not how the government upholds the right of a person practising his or her religion, but the extent to which such a practice should be upheld when it conflicts with other people's fundamental rights. That the government encouraged the Kumbh Mela to be held in the midst of a pandemic infringes on the very right to life of Hindus and Muslims alike.

The transformation of religion in the twentieth century has to be taken into account. We have seen how many of the small, localised traditions of religious worship and practice have slowly been subsumed within the larger notion of Hindutva. This leads to public displays of religiosity which has its uses. As author Hilal Ahmed reminds us, 'the crucial distinction between religion as a spiritual-moral force and religion as an expression of identity is gradually disappearing. Religions are primarily observed as competing ideologies.'[32] This, coupled with Hindutva-driven nationalism, leads to all manner of public displays of religiosity supported by the State, some designed to antagonise and punish the minority community. During last year's Kanwar Yatra procession in UP, the state government insisted that all eateries en route display the names of their owners so that the pilgrims did not eat at a restaurant owned by a Muslim by mistake, creating communal fractures in an already fraught environment.

With religions becoming consolidated, there is a rise in the number of 'godmen' who have a pan-India reach, and their chemistry with politics and politicians has become positively toxic. The role these godmen or religious leaders play in validating and endorsing political figures has acquired a disturbing prominence in current times. The 'godman' has metamorphosed into a businessman, akin to the US televangelist who has political patronage and endorses political parties. One example of this is Gurmeet Ram Rahim Singh, who attracted low caste Dalit Sikhs to his fold under his group 'Dera Sacha Sauda'. He was instrumental in BJP defeating the Congress party in Haryana in successive elections, with the former even giving him timely paroles from prison post-conviction. Rahim's Dera is notorious for being the hotbed of a number of criminal activities, including rape, alleged castrations and murders.

But the most striking example of religious branding converting into stellar financial branding is 'Patanjali', a company which deals in a variety of Ayurvedic cures, oils, cosmetics and foodstuffs, under leading godman and yoga teacher, Baba Ramdev. His company appears to be fully backed by the political establishment, which, in one instance, even involved itself very overtly by securing lines of credit for the company from public sector banks to acquire for a pittance another company called Ruchi Soya, amongst myriad other benefits.

Secularism Is Compromised Because of Vote Bank Politics

That India as a secular state would not have an anti-religious outlook was clear from the discussions in the Constituent Assembly. K.M. Munshi drew a contrast between a secular state and a theocratic or religious state. Given the formation of Pakistan, this principle offered a convenient counterpoint: 'citizenship is irrespective of religious belief, that every citizen, to whatever religion he may belong, is equal before the law, that he has equal civil rights, and equal opportunities to derive benefits from the State ...'[33] All this is unobjectionable as it merely provides procedural equality. Author Rochana Bajpai points out that the stipulation of the State's neutrality in matters relating to religion, a point taken up by K.T. Shah in the Constituent Assembly, as necessary to give substantive character to secularism did not carry much favour.

The matter of minority appeasement is really only directed at Muslims, the largest minority, and has been articulated by leading RSS intellectual Balraj Madhok, who refers to the Constitution to point out the issues which he alleges discriminate against Hindus.[34] If one were to unpack these issues, they relate to Articles 21, 30 and 370, which are alleged by him to be discriminatory. Article 21 relates to 'protection of life and personal liberty', and it is not clear how this discriminates against Hindus and is in favour of minorities. In relation to Article 30, which relates to the freedom of minorities to establish and administer educational institutions, it is not clear how this discriminates against Hindus, particularly as some of the minorities included are predominantly Hindu, such as some of the Sindhi community, since the definition of a minority is not confined to religion, but extends to linguistic groups. Surprisingly, the Arya Samaj, which ostensibly escapes the definition of a religious minority, has institutions in Punjab which fall within the definition of minority institutions as their medium of instruction is Hindi, so the term minority is all-encompassing.[35] Regarding Article 370, the provision has become a matter of history, given its revocation in August 2019, but even before that, it was not discriminatory. It aligned with the concept of 'asymmetrical federalism', under which even non-Muslim states like Uttarakhand and Himachal Pradesh enjoy special privileges, including restrictions on outsiders purchasing land within the state. Additionally, there is the issue of Muslim personal law, which will be addressed later in the book.

Of course, there are other, relatively minor issues, such as promises of financial assistance, quotas within educational institutions, subsidised Haj travel, and public holidays for Muslim religious festivals like Eid Milad-un-Nabi, the Prophet's birthday, which was declared a holiday by V. P. Singh during his tenure as the prime minister. But the important question is that how is this any different from the vote bank politics practised by the BJP governments directed towards garnering the OBC vote, by making assurances regarding reservations in jobs and education, etc. It is not clear that these assurances to the Muslim community, even if implemented, which they rarely are, infringe on any notion of secularism or equality. Some special treatment meted out to minorities is common to modern electoral politics, and there is nothing sinister in that. In fact, as the Sachar Committee Report[36] has made clear, in all established criteria, the Muslim community is indubitably backward and discriminated against, so where is the pampering? In fact, in a bizarre reaction to the report, the RSS has argued that the making of this report itself is an example of Muslim appeasement. This allegation is bizarre, according to author Hilal Ahmad, who argues that 'Muslim appeasement has found a new political life in post-2014 India. The BJP has successfully established the fact that addressing *Muslims as Muslims* is an act of appeasement.'[37] This, of course, assumes that there is no discrimination and, significantly, that the Muslim community is one and undifferentiated. Neither of these assumptions is true.

9

SECULARISM AND CASTE

I think the larger issue with the secular narrative that the Hindu Right has developed is that it takes a very selective view of group rights. It must be recalled that in the Constituent Assembly debates, except for SCs and STs—who it was widely agreed had suffered great historic injustice and continued to be marginalised—and Anglo Indians—whose numbers were vanishingly small, there was an insistence on denying group rights to others, and this included not just religious groups but caste groups. The impetus for secularism can fairly be said to lie in eliminating religious groups as well as caste groups 'as categories of public policy'. As professor of law Marc Galanter has put it, 'Proponents of such a transformation were not always clear whether they meant the disestablishment of social hierarchy or the actual dissolution of caste units. But at the minimum what was referred to was a severe reduction in the salience of caste in all spheres of life.'[1]

This point was emphasised in an important Supreme Court judgement in the 1951 *Champakam Dorairajan* case[2], in 1951 which struck down reservations on the basis that they seemed to be communal quotas, not devised on the principle of backwardness, but as with colonial secularism, with the intent to maintain a balance of power between different communities. However, all that the judgement succeeded in achieving, as per constitutional law expert Mohan Gopal, was the restoration of 'a Brahmin monopoly over admission for medical and engineering colleges in the then Madras Presidency'.[3]

What is manifest today is that the politics of caste is writ large. Pandit Nehru himself entertained reservations about caste, writing that 'a caste ridden society is not properly secular'.[4] This is a point which Romila Thapar also takes up, arguing that the main problem of secularism is rooted in caste. Secular, in her view, is that which is worldly and distinct from religion, as stated earlier. To discuss secularism without discussing caste is to ignore the elephant in the room.

Many communities, whether real or imagined minorities, are seeking an even larger share of a diminishing pie. This demand is increasingly determined by political exigencies and divorced from any sense of economic justice or the principles of diversity that are embraced by most modern economies in their quest for societal transformation. For example, most modern economies seek to assist and provide quotas for persons such as women, disabled people and communities subject to discrimination, LGBTQIA+ people and others with the aim of ensuring diversity and equality in society. This is not the case in India where economic justice has been substituted for social justice and that, too, is restricted to the majority religion, within the configuration of the caste system.

The logic of the OBC category becomes sorely tested if we take into account the creamy layer exception from the 2008 Supreme Court case of *Ashoka Thakur v. Union of India*.[5] In this seminal judgement, the court recognises implicitly that the growth of this OBC culture appears to be motivated by dynamics of political patronage and of vote bank politics of the most opportunistic kind. The creamy layer exception, which was downplayed by the court, is sensible in itself but undoubtedly exposes the intellectual speciousness of this argument for caste-based reservations. As constitutional law scholar Sujit Chaudhary puts it, '[i]f the creamy layer doctrine makes sense—because it emphasises the link between special treatment and backward status—then one would ask why caste is used to identify beneficiaries in the first place.'[6]

It is a complex subject, particularly for those who have never had exposure to discrimination and ostracisation associated with caste. Former chief justice of India, D.Y. Chandrachud, famously remarked that those who proclaim the virtue of castelessness are those privileged people who can afford to do so as their caste privilege has 'already translated into social, political and economic capital'. This is a valuable corrective to those who deny affirmative action on the grounds of caste. However, there must be data regarding the extent of backwardness and deprivation to back any argument for reservations. This point was echoed by the Supreme Court in the *Indra Sawhney* case[7] where it was directed that the backwardness criteria had to be properly evaluated and proved before a provision for reservation was made for any community. But this exercise is probably embarrassing for politicians who seek votes in the name of caste, and that is why it is not carried out.

So this argument that secularism is compromised because of vote bank politics as practised by 'pseudo-secular' parties is, in my view, a brilliant way to distract attention from a much larger problem which, unfortunately, is making itself evident in all manner of ways: Hindu majoritarianism and its grotesque intrusion in our day-to-day lives. This impact has the widest reach on people's quotidian existence in terms of what they eat, who they marry, which faith they choose to observe, where they live, and what they wear. It is, in a fundamental sense, changing the society we once were, to one which is overly regulated and intolerant of any difference, that is parochial and claustrophobic in the extreme.

The Road to Theocracy

The Hindu Right have always attempted to distinguish their thinking from what they label as the one that a theocracy, saying that Hindutva will not lead to a theocracy such as the one that exists in Pakistan, where religious laws are implemented and Sharia is the foundation of all laws. In practical terms, it is very difficult to distinguish between the two, as they both share an acute antipathy towards religious minorities. For example, Pakistani courts have turned a blind eye to thousands of cases of forced marriages and conversions of both

Hindu and Christian underage girls to Islam. This is not dissimilar to the discriminatory principles that apply to Hindus converting to Christianity or Islam, and what is known as 'Ghar Wapsi' or homecoming for when minorities convert to Hinduism.

The truth is that India had and continues to have a secular constitution, but one that is being undermined by aggressive Hindutva back to Hinduism.

This brings us to the seminal question that scholar Sudipta Kaviraj has posed: How can a secular state succeed in a society that is still deeply religious? This is an issue which keeps recurring, particularly in the judicial sphere, where now the Hindu Right insists that judges who refer to secularism as a foundational principle of the Constitution are acting against democracy. In this respect, thinkers like T.N. Madan and Ashis Nandy have long argued that the problem lies not in secularism as an ideal, but in the attempt to impose a dream of a small intellectual minority on the wider electorate—an act that is inherently undemocratic in a majoritarian polity.

10

SECULARISM, PERSONAL LAWS AND THE UNIFORM CIVIL CODE

The issue of personal laws—laws that relate to marriage, divorce, inheritance, etc.—has been politically surcharged by the Hindu Right to show how minorities are privileged. However, it is useful to understand the logic of colonial secularism. In general, the British avoided controversy by restricting the reform of personal laws, which, according to constitutional law scholar Abhinav Chandrachud, would have infringed upon the principle of privacy. This was a response to what Hindus and Muslims were asserting was not 'a right to the free exercise of religion but a right to freedom from interference in family matters.'[1]

Hindu Law Before the Hindu Marriage Act

Matters regarding pre-Independence Hindu law should be put in perspective. Hindu law, largely based on custom, was a system of byzantine complexity; there were numerous schools such as the 'Mitakshara' and the 'Dāyabhāga', as well as matrilineal schools of thought from southern India which had limited territorial application. There were multiple, often contradictory texts, and the pervasive influence of caste and custom played a central role in the application of law—frequently overriding textual authorities themselves. It must be remembered that in many of the princely states, Hindu customary law was applied with full vigour; Brahmins were even given immunity from some criminal acts. Even more complicated was the role that the colonial judiciary and the Privy Council played in interpreting the law. The British preferred to rely on textual authorities rather than on customary law, leading to many controversies which, according to professor of Oriental law J. Duncan M. Derrett, had the effect of ossifying the law,[2] despite the fact that it was, in essence, customary. Author Manu Pillai calls the culmination of the British attempt to clarify Hindu law 'a muddle, the damage scarring generations.'[3]

There was no limit to the number of wives a Hindu man could have and there was no obvious means for a Hindu woman to seek a divorce—since a Hindu marriage was considered a sacrament—unless she lived in a Presidency town like Bombay or in South India where different customary laws applied. This point was made lucidly by Lok Sabha member N.C. Chatterjee during debates about the proposed Hindu Marriage Bill. He was opposed to it and held the view that imposing monogamy and providing a right to divorce violated the very sacrament of marriage. He quoted from Manu's *Manava Dharma Shastra*, in which chapter 9 (verse 46) stipulates 'that there shall be no dissolution of the marital tie. If you try to desert your wife, if you sell your wife even then the marital tie can never be disrupted.'

Ambedkar had tried and failed to push through a composite Hindu reform legislation in 1951 in the provisional parliament that included giving equal rights to women in coparcenary property, but the Hindu Right had been unwilling to concede that. He was distraught at this setback, and this served as a moment of epiphany for him and his politics. Subjected to the most vicious taunts and insults from the Hindu Right, he beseeched his followers to convert to Buddhism and lamented that his Hindu Code Bill 'was killed and died unwept and unsung.'[4] Ambedkar's bitterness towards the Congress and what he characterised as Nehru's hypocrisy and betrayal, when it came to indulging the Hindu Right in their reactionary attitudes towards the rights of Hindu women, has not been afforded the attention it should have received. In his speech on 10 October 1951, resigning as the law minister, he pulled no punches and caustically remarked: 'To leave inequality between class and class, between sex and sex, which is the soul of the Hindu society untouched and to go on passing legislation relating to economic problems is to make a farce of our Constitution and to build a palace on a dung heap.'[5]

H.V. Pataskar, a member of the first Lok Sabha and the union minister for legal affairs, who had opposed Ambedkar's consolidated Hindu Bill, managed to guide the reforms later in separate legislative packages, but in the face of fierce opposition from the Hindu Right, who were largely members of the Congress party. The path-breaking dimensions of this legislative effort were, as remarked by Marc Galanter, that it 'creates the hitherto unknown capacity to marry and adopt across *varna* lines and, with a few minor exceptions, eliminates all of the distinctions along *varna* lines embodied in the old law.'[6] Prior to the passing of the Hindu Marriage Act in 1956, Hindu women, with some exceptions, had no right to a divorce, and it was only after the passing of this act that they became entitled to seek a divorce albeit on limited grounds, with divorce by mutual consent not being a recognised at that time. Hindu women (and even men) belonging to the Dalit or Scheduled Caste category too suffered great disability under the old law inasmuch as that, barring those residing in Presidency cities, they were not allowed to marry outside their caste, making it clear that traditional caste-based discrimination was at the heart of these restrictions. As far as women's inheritance is concerned, historian Tanika Sarkar clarifies, 'In the Dayabhaga system of Hindu law that prevailed in Bengal, women neither inherited their father's land nor had a definite right to the land of their husbands. At most, they had usufruct rights on behalf of minor sons if they were widows.'[7]

So, under the old customary laws, Hindu women were in a very dire position as they had limited choice in terms of who they could marry. They had no right to secure a divorce and, fundamentally, they had no rights in family property other than their 'stridhan' which was what they received at the time of marriage. To give women the vote, yet deny them the most basic of human rights connected with gender equality was something which few societies would countenance, and still, that is what prevailed in India post-Independence.

Nehru, I think, is wrongly blamed for not using the opportunity he had in the 1950s to roll out a uniform civil code (UCC) which would apply to all religious communities. At the time, he had been primarily focused on the reform of Hindu customary law, as there were urgent issues that had been adumbrated, issues that did not affect Muslims. Muslim women had the right to seek divorce by virtue not only of customary law but also the Dissolution of Muslim Marriages Act enacted in 1939. There were no obvious caste prohibitions in the Sharia as regards marriage. Neither was there an issue regarding ownership of property, as Muslim women could own and dispose of property in their name. In any case, UCC would have been opposed in the Constituent Assembly (and later the provisional parliament) by both the Hindu Right and the minorities, so no reform would have been possible.

In 1937, the Shariat Act was passed, which directed that Muslims would be governed by Sharia rather than by customary laws. This was the first example of reform of personal laws, an instance of the law made by legislators overriding customary law which is based on community consensus. This set the ground rules for the reform of Hindu law, which happened in the 1950s. The common principle was to codify the law on statutory principles and discard customs and traditions.

Problems with Hindu Law Post-Reform

It is important to remember that reforms to Hindu personal laws happened in the 1950s and that the world has moved on quite a bit since then. Much of the legislation was modelled on English laws of that time, which is why the legal framework looks increasingly outdated, given the huge transformation of Indian society since the 1950s. There are many problems with Hindu law in its current form which invites reform and, to that extent, the fetish with a UCC is an attempt to provide a diversion from this.

Given that Hindu marriage is considered a sacrament, the Hindu Marriage Act of 1955 was a compromise as it incorporated the 'fault principle', relying on which either party could seek a divorce. This was not dissimilar to the English law at that time, where grounds for a fault-based divorce were adultery, cruelty, desertion, etc., since Christianity held the same view that marriage is a sacrament. It is for this reason that Catholics, even today, view divorce with great disfavour. In contrast, Islam looks at marriage as a contractual relationship, the dissolution of which can be done extra-judicially, that is, by way of pronouncing 'talaq'.

It is pertinent to note that by virtue of the Matrimonial Causes Act of 1971, irretrievable breakdown of marriage was made a ground for divorce under English law. This is far more practical for a modern society, provided that financial arrangements on the dissolution of marriage are equitable. However, a provision for irretrievable breakdown of marriage still does not exist in the Hindu Marriage Act in spite of strong recommendations made by the Law Commission in its 71st Report published in 1978 as well as several remarks over the years from various high courts and indeed the Supreme Court[8] that state that once a marriage has irretrievably broken down, it should be dissolved.

Under Hindu personal law, there is also the problem that divorce can be obtained only through the court system. Given the broken-down state of the lower judiciary, it often takes years and the payment of substantial legal fees to obtain a divorce, keeping unhappy (even acrimonious) spouses tied to each other for years on end.

Inheritance: Differences in Principles

There is an asymmetry in the law related to inheritance that governs Hindus and Muslims. A Hindu man or woman, post reforms, can will away his or her assets in their entirety, subject to coparcenary laws. Testamentary succession, or succession through the testamentary instrument of a 'will', is a colonial concept unknown to Hindu customary law. The provision for testamentary succession under the Hindu Succession Act has the potential for reinforcing patriarchy by providing a means to vitiate the gender equality enshrined in the act.

It is a method that can be used to deny female heirs any share in the deceased's property. Under Sharia, the principle of forced heirship prevails, as per which the estate is divided amongst the family in certain pre-determined shares. In India, Sunni Muslims can will only up to one-third of their property, while the balance is distributed as per Sharia, under which the widow takes 25 per cent and the children inherit the balance, with the son taking a double share to that of the daughter. The restriction on the amount that can be willed away allows for the protection of vulnerable family members. Many Western countries have sought to adopt the principles of forced heirship through legislation. Thus, there shouldn't be a visceral dismissal of forced heirship principles on the ground that they arise from primitive thinking. In the context of a post-colonial society with gender disparity in many fields, forced heirship can be a useful tool to strengthen female rights, as is apparent from the English legislation, Inheritance and Trustees Powers Act of 2014, which provides for the widow to be given a substantial financial share before enforcing the stipulations of a will.

Historian Maria Misra observes that 'critics pointed out the inequity of insisting that Hindus should reform their customary law in accordance to what was "modern" and "rational", while Muslims should be left to carry on their traditional practices'.[9] She remarks that this analysis is 'uncomfortably true,' but in my view, it would not be correct to draw this unflattering binary between the two faiths, privileging one for its modernity and rationality and disparaging the other for being traditional. Admittedly, they are different systems, but as a lawyer, I am not persuaded that one can be labelled as rational and the other irrational, merely because the latter is traditional. It is not self-evident that a marriage premised on a holy sacrament is more rational than one based on contract.

The Wife as Chattel

There is much in the codified Hindu personal laws that goes contrary to the principle of gender equality. First, the view that a man's wife is his chattel and nothing more, is epitomised in his right to demand restitution of conjugal rights under section 9 of the Hindu

Marriage Act. Even though this is a remedy that both the husband and the wife can take recourse to, most reported cases show that it is invariably the husband who seeks to enforce this remedy. Restitution of conjugal rights is a legacy of colonial law and is premised on the assumption that one spouse is entitled to the society and comfort of the other. The continued existence of such a provision in an Indian statute is particularly anachronistic, since it was done away with in England in the 1880s.

An even more disturbing feature of the current law is the non-recognition of marital rape as a crime or as a ground for divorce. The matter of marital rape is based on the fiction that all sexual intercourse conducted within marriage is consensual. But it is relevant to note that the exemption given to marital rape has no parallel in other cases of serious misconduct—a husband indulging in sexual molestation, voyeurism and forcible disrobing of his wife is treated as any other man would be under the criminal law.

The provisions for restitution of conjugal rights and the exemption for marital rape are colonial vestiges that are an affront to the principle of individual autonomy as set out in Articles 14 and 21 of the Constitution. This position was reinforced in the landmark judgement of *Joseph Shine v. Union of India*[10], where the Supreme Court struck down the provision that made adultery a criminal offence on the ground that it treated a married woman as the property of her husband and offended her right to equality, dignity and autonomy. However, this is not a stand that the Union government has accepted easily. In this very case, it filed an affidavit saying that diluting adultery in any form would impact the 'sanctity of marriage'. Later in the Marriage Equality case, the government took a stand before the Supreme Court that restricting marriages to only couples of opposite sex was a matter of 'legitimate State interest'.[11]

When the UPA-II government presented a bill to radically reform the Hindu Marriage Act on demonstrably gender-neutral lines, particularly in connection with the reform of divorce law, it was violently opposed. It had sought to bring in irretrievable breakdown as a ground for dissolution of marriage and to enhance the financial rights of the wife in connection with matrimonial property, particularly the family residence, which would be divided equally between the couple. The latter is based on the principle of community or co-ownership of family assets, which has been the norm in Europe and the US. This bill was opposed by BJP on the grounds that it was anti-Hindu, and accordingly, the bill had lapsed. This serves as a presentiment of what lies in store for any avowedly secular legislation seeking to detach family law from religious scripture or custom.

The Persistence of Hindu Customary Law

It is often overlooked that Hindu customary law was not completely abolished in 1955. The key area of property ownership and inheritance within the Hindu family continued to be governed by the customary law principles of Hindu Undivided Family under the stewardship of the family elder, the 'Karta', where partition of ancestral properties was done by metes and bounds. These principles have been grafted onto successive income tax statutes. The HUF was generally governed by the Mitakshara school, which was widespread in Rajputana and UP. Bengal and Assam were governed by the Dāyabhāga school. In Punjab, the HUF was unknown until after the Partition when it was introduced as an import from the cow belt. According to the Mitakshara school, the family's ancestral properties and any accretions thereto were required to be held jointly by the father and the sons, with the quantification of the distinct shares of each son crystallised at the time of his birth rather than at the father's death. The HUF property would be distributed in those shares at the time of a formal partition. Daughters and wives were given a right to maintenance from the HUF, and daughters were also entitled to dower (stridhan) at the time of their marriage; however they were otherwise excluded from a share in coparcenary property. The karta was the manager of the HUF property. Except for self-acquired property, which could be alienated, Hindu personal law treated HUF (or joint family) property as inalienable. The HUF itself was called a coparcenary—a legal unit that was also recognised as a taxable entity under the Income Tax Act. Fortunately, in 2005, reforms were introduced to the HUF granting women parity with male members of the HUF. This much-lauded intervention was something Ambedkar had pushed for in 1951, but at that time, it had become the reason for the entire legislation to get scuppered.

The concept of the HUF had come under greater scrutiny in the latter half of the 1940s during the discussions on the Hindu Code Bill in the Constituent Assembly. Many legislators were of the view that the HUF was the perfect foil to prevent family wealth from fragmenting. The then Law Minister, H.V. Pataskar, stated,

> 'The joint family system is a peculiar institution of Hindu law, not known to other systems of law which are more or less based on individuals. Till only a generation or two back, the joint family system worked well. It has maintained the continuity and stability of our social structure for centuries past. That is why there is objection to the throwing open of inheritance to the daughter. That objection is not for political or social reasons but because if you open the inheritance to a daughter the result is that the whole social structure based on the joint family system will be broken.'[12]

This assertion has to be seen in the context of traditional society. Author Sudhir Kakar sums it up well when he observes that '[m]ore than any other factor... it is the family and the role family obligations that play in the life of an Indian which is the glue that holds Indian society together.' He further points out a downside that 'this focus on the family as the exclusive source of satisfaction of all of one's needs also reflects a continuing lack of faith in almost every other institution of society'. Indeed, a man's worth is 'inextricable from his family's reputation'.[13]

The cinematic apogee of this social construct was best seen in the Bollywood movie *Hum Aapke Hain Koun..!* Rachel Dwyer, SOAS professor of Indian culture and cinema, observes that the movie's 'celebration of the family—the hero's jeep even bears the graffiti declaration, "I love my family"—shows all the life rituals and celebrations from birth through marriage to death, with its songs and costumes imitated in real life, establishing the film's depictions as definitive'.[14] This shows the joint family or the HUF as being the true unit of society, which demands loyalty and sacrifice as well as provides love and support. This is a valuable cultural insight as to the centrality of the HUF, probably why the Hindu family is economically empowered to hold property as a collective. Elsewhere, taxation is applied on individual wealth and income, and in a secular fashion without reference to religion. As such, allowing the HUF to be taxed as a single unit repudiates the notion of religious neutrality in an area which, in most societies, falls indubitably within the secular domain. Author Eleanor Newbigin points out that the 'historic relationship between the HUF and the democratic government does little to encourage Indian legislators to establish a uniform civil code in place of personal law.' She argues that to do so would 'disturb the complex networks through which different aspects of Indian economic production operate and intersect.'[15]

It must be remembered that the coparcenary system ran afoul of gender equality, a fact which was only corrected in 2005 when a married daughter was given a share in her natal family's coparcenary property. This anomaly was justified by Pataskar during the parliamentary debates on the proposed Hindu Succession Bill in 1954, who stated that to 'put the daughter on the same footing as a son with respect to the right by birth, right of survivorship and the right to claim partition at any time, will be to provide for a joint family unknown to the law and unworkable in practice.'[16]

When one looks at the role of the HUF, one cannot detach it from the rise of Marwari hegemony in business and commerce in post-Independence India. This community was active in providing electoral funding to the Congress party, so its political influence outweighed its numbers. According to historian Ritu Birla,

> By the 1920s, Marwari commercial and industrial interests protected kinship-based organization not by promoting the validity of an indigenous mercantile law and the model of the family firm, but rather by rallying for the joint family as an absolute limit not to be transgressed by the law. Social reform and cultural protectionism, both of which sought persistently to legitimize the Hindu joint family, were central to Marwari strategies for commercial and industrial dominance.[17]

The key to understanding this Marwari hegemony is to see the role of the HUF as a means of accumulating capital in the most tax-effective way possible. This device also buttressed the grip of families on businesses, a fact of Indian business life which is problematical. We face the fact that persons of Indian origin are CEOs of international corporations such as Google and Microsoft amongst many, but there are few Indian CEOs in Indian companies who are in the same league. Journalist Kanika Datta gives the reason behind this: 'It's not that we lack dynamic, even top-class managers. But organisations with reporting structures that proportionately weigh in favour of the boss's son, daughter, spouse etc ... have a discouraging effect on managerial innovation.'[18]

It is also pertinent to note that ever since the HUF was recognised as a taxpayer under the Income Tax Act of 1922, it has been a source of much controversy, principally as it was seen as a tax exemption for the Hindu mercantile class. In fact, the Justice Wanchoo Committee Report published in 1971 expressly concluded that the HUF was a means of avoiding paying tax.[19] Even a Law Commission paper announced that 'it is high time that it is understood that justifying this institution on the ground of deep-rooted sentiments at the cost of the country's revenues may not be judicious.'[20] Without going into the details of how tax is avoided, suffice it to say that this is a huge pecuniary benefit enjoyed by the majority community which is not available to other minorities, and it is a discrimination which is hardly commented on.

Reform of Muslim Personal Law

Muslim personal law, or Sharia, has been much misunderstood, partly because of what can be considered the Muslim Right, which includes the 'Ulema' and self-serving Muslim politicians. I must confess that to describe them as fundamentalists would amount to doing violence to the language, as it assumes that what they believe in is fundamental to the religion. The All India Muslim Personal Law Board (AIMPLB) propagates the view that divine law cannot be interfered with, but it is a controversial view. There are Quranic verses which stipulate conduct, that are reinforced by the sayings of the Prophet (the Hadiths) which take matters further. There are also schools of jurisprudence, of which there are four significant ones in Sunni Islam, which largely flesh out the law. But these schools were formed centuries after the Prophet's death. If we are to believe that there is only one law given by the Prophet which is inviolable, then why are there four schools?

What would be relevant for this discussion is the work of one of the greatest Islamic thinkers, Nasir al-Din al-Tusi, who sets out the temporal nature of Islamic jurisprudence. As per him, the government is given the duty to bring about a state of affairs in which each person obtains and is content with his/her rights, i.e. a state of justice, and that law has to be particularised as to what is needed for the welfare of the people at all times and circumstances. This is contrary to the belief of many that Sharia is one and immutable, and is insulated from any government interference. In practice, this was never the case, and in the twentieth century, we have witnessed many Muslim countries amending the law to subserve essentially secular concerns and demands, such as the need to address gender inequalities. The Tunisian Civil Code is an example of this; it abolished polygamy and introduced gender equality in a Muslim-majority country as early as 1957. In any event, the practice of Sharia, insofar as it relates to criminal punishments such as stoning and cutting off hands, has become rare, and many Islamic jurisdictions have completely abolished the practice. No one talks anymore about the many Islamic laws and rules requiring the keeping of slaves—a practice that was rampant in the Islamic Middle East and Africa in the eighteenth and nineteenth centuries. So this notion of an eternal law written in stone is something which has been conveniently concocted by the Muslim Right to enforce an unjust patriarchy on women and should be viewed as such.

It is material to this discussion that Nehru was alive to the many injustices which Muslim women were subjected to, and in his last years in office even attempted to redress the problem. He appointed a committee to review the most controversial aspects of Muslim law, particularly the practice of denying a Muslim woman the right to a divorce under Muslim law if she left her faith. Unfortunately, according to author Pratinav Anil, the then vice president, Zakir

Husain's discomfiture with the committee and the pervasive unease expressed by Aligarh-based luminaries killed off a promising initiative.[21]

There are problems peculiar to Indian Muslim women which need to be addressed, but suffice it to say the situation is not as dire as it once was. The condition of Muslim women has marginally improved because of pragmatic judicial interventions and the enactment of important secular legislations such as the Protection of Women from Domestic Violence Act of 2005.

Polygamy

Polygamy, unfortunately, is one of those distractions that refuses to go away. The practice of polygamy had a context at the time of the Prophet—with continual warfare, there were many women with deceased husbands, and the purpose of allowing a man to take another wife was to provide support to widows and their children. In the present day and age, with many women working, they don't need support after being divorced or widowed. For those who are not or cannot, there should be family support and state help. In fact, a point which is not so well known is that an indigent Muslim woman is even entitled to approach the Waqf Board of the state where she resides for financial assistance. The Waqf Boards, being the third largest land owner in India after the Army and Railways, are hugely wealthy.

In any event, in India there is acute gender imbalance, that is, there are more men than women in the population, therefore there is no reason for polygamy as a practice to continue to exist. In fact, if polygamy was practised at any serious level, it would have the consequence of depriving many of the men the chance of becoming fathers, given the poor gender ratio. This has to be seen as the path to decontextualise many laws and practices which have no relevance to present-day circumstances and are discriminatory. But it continues to perplex me as to why polygamy, which excites so much Hindu and liberal opprobrium, continues to be treated as something sacred and inviolable by the Ulema in India when many Muslim societies have done away with this regressive practice.

Whilst it is true that the Indian Muslim husband is legally entitled to have more than one wife, this is not a common practice. In fact, statistics show that Hindus remain more polygamous than Muslims.[22] There has been talk that through the device of polygamy, that if it is allowed to continue, Muslim population would exponentially increase and outnumber the Hindus one day. This canard is also pushed by authors of the Hindu Right,[23] who have suggested that the population of Muslims is increasing by reason of polygamy and is growing faster than that of the Hindus. However, this is not apparent from the most recent statistics released in 2022, which show that Hindu and Muslim birth rates indicate a small difference between the number of children on average, with the Muslim birth rate being 2.6 compared to 1.94 for Hindus.[24]

On the vexed question of Hindu–Muslim demographics, former chief election commissioner of India, S.Y. Quraishi,[25] demolishes this whole argument as absurd and specious. The key question is whether Muslims have a higher birth rate because of their religion or whether there are other factors at play in what demographers call Total Fertility Rate (TFR). These factors include age of marriage, literacy levels, access to contraception, income levels and infant mortality rates. India has great regional variations in TFR. Religion is not the key factor, as Muslims in Tamil Nadu and Kerala have considerably lower TFRs than Muslims in Bihar and UP. If one were to take these variables into account, the differences between the communities would disappear. For this reason, there may be a North-South imbalance, with Kerala having a TFR of 1.56 (below replacement) and Bihar having a TFR of 3.4 (in excess of replacement), but that is because of other factors, not religion. The National Family Health Survey 2019-21 shows that the Muslim birth rate has fallen further to 2.3 during the period of 2019 to 2021, from 2.6 recorded in 2015.[26] The fertility rate among Hindus is currently at 1.94, which is slightly lower but which still makes the presentiment, which the Hindu Right constantly projects with fevered paranoia of the Muslims overtaking the Hindus in terms of population, absurd and wildly fantastical.

In a latest move, the Assam state government plans to criminalise polygamy by enacting, the Assam Prohibition of Polygamy Bill

2025, making it punishable by imprisonment of up to seven years and, in the case of concealment of the first marriage, to up to 10 years imprisonment. It appears this seems to be the latest attempt by the BJP-led state government to specifically target the Muslim community, since the act excludes from its ambit scheduled tribes who comprise nearly 13 per cent of the population.

Triple Talaq

For Muslim men, if the ability to take more than one wife is considered a great boon, so is the practice of easy divorce with hardly any financial implications. It is true that Sharia as practised allows for a non-judicial divorce. However, the matter of the triple talaq as it exists even in the Sharia is highly problematical, as it does not allow the man any time to reflect on his actions.

The triple talaq issue is undoubtedly controversial. The Quranic injunction on this issue is to give a period of time between each talaq or pronouncement of divorce. The customary practice of pronouncing talaq three times at the same time, without a gap between the pronouncements—a practice fairly unique to India—got legal sanction by virtue of the Muslim Personal Law (Shariat) Application Act of 1937. The Muslim Women (Protection of Rights on Marriage) Bill, colloquially known as the Triple Talaq Bill, was enacted into law in 2019, making instant triple talaq a criminal offence. It was made a cognizable offence, which meant that a policeman could arrest the accused without a warrant. The offence was also made punishable with imprisonment for up to three years together with a fine.

There is no doubt that the practice of triple talaq was not only legally problematical, it was also highly unpopular with Muslim women, 92 per cent of whom expressed disapproval of the practice of verbal triple talaq.[27] When it was challenged by one Shayara Bano in the Supreme Court,[28] the court ruled it to be unconstitutional but at the same time failed to give much direction, save to say that this is a legislative matter and the role of the judiciary in this was limited. In this case there was a proxy battle between the All India Muslim Personal Law Board and the Union government, which was trying to burnish its reputation as a crusader for women's rights by identifying this odious practice and projecting it as a prime example of Muslim backwardness. Unfortunately, the AIMPLB took the bait, never missing an opportunity to make the Muslims look their antediluvian best. The affidavit filed in the proceedings by the AIMPLB asserted that matters related to personal laws came under the ambit of legislative policy and could not be challenged for being violative of fundamental rights, nor could they be rewritten by reason of social reform. It also asserted that Muslim personal law was based on holy scriptures and got its legal validity from the 1937 Sharia Act, which is why it would not be not amenable to any reform.

Thus, it came to pass that the AIMPLB scored an own goal and brought the government to enact the Muslim Women (Protection of Rights on Marriage) Act. The act's provisions hardly paid any consideration to the effect of the criminalisation of triple talaq on the wife, if the husband, who was still obliged to support her, was imprisoned. It almost guaranteed destitution for her and her children, especially if the woman was dependent on a husband who was a daily wage earner. For the sake of form, the act has a provision that entitles the wife to claim a subsistence allowance from her husband for herself and dependent children. But given the fact that many Muslim men work in casual jobs, this is more of a paper concession. Even more absurd is the very basis of this crime. As author Hilal Ahmed puts it, 'if the marriage, as a civic contract, cannot be broken by the husband even though he says 'talaq' three times, how could this act be treated as a non-bailable crime strictly in legal terms?'[29] This argument makes sense. If the pronouncement of talaq three times in one sitting is legally void, then no divorce has actually taken place. In that case, it is difficult to justify imprisoning a man for attempting a divorce that, in the eyes of the law, never occurred—quite apart from the consequences such action would have for the wife.

Maintenance

Another lightning rod that animates a lot of the liberal opprobrium is the vexed issue of maintenance from her husband post-marriage. The

Shah Bano case[30] in 1985 dealt with the issue of whether a divorced Muslim woman was entitled to maintenance from her husband beyond the period of 'iddat' (four months from the date of the divorce). The Supreme Court in *Mohd. Ahmed Khan v. Shah Bano Begum*[31] ruled that section 125 of the Code of Criminal Procedure applied to all divorced wives irrespective of their religion, distinguishing the case from the ostensible impediment posed in Section 127(3)(b) which carved out an exception for cases where maintenance as prescribed by customary or personal law had already been paid. This was hailed as a radical judgement by the women's rights movement, but upset conservative Muslims.

The Supreme Court had examined Muslim personal law to establish that under the Quran, maintenance was required to be paid however, merely payment of 'meher' (the bride price) would not suffice as maintenance. The court had also made certain ancillary observations about the need for introducing UCC. This judgement was controversial, and various members of the Congress party advised the then prime minister, Rajiv Gandhi, to assuage the concerns of Muslim conservatives. This led to the enactment of the Muslim Women's (Protection of Rights on Divorce) Act 1986, which, in effect, legislatively overruled the Supreme Court judgement.

This step regrettably hastened the growth of the BJP and provided fodder for it to make claims that the Congress party was interested only in appeasement politics. Contrary to the mythology around this much denigrated legislation, it did not intend to leave the Muslim woman in poor financial straits after her divorce. Under the act, the ex-husband remained liable for the continued welfare of the divorced wife during the iddat period, with no limits placed on the amount of maintenance liable to be paid, unlike section 125 of the criminal procedure code. Only after the iddat period was over did the liability fall on her family or on the state Waqf Board as a tertiary support system. A subsequent Supreme Court decision in *Noor Saba Khatoon v. Mohd. Quasim* has clarified that minor children are entitled to claim maintenance both under section 3(1)(b) of the Muslim Women (Protection of Rights on Divorce) Act and section 125 of the Criminal Procedure Code, since nothing in section 125 exempted a Muslim father from his obligation to maintain his children.[32] Fortunately, in 2024, subsequent to the Supreme Court decision in *Mohd. Abdul Samad v. State of Telangana*, Muslim women, by and large, enjoy the same rights to maintenance under section 125 as their Hindu sisters. In this case, the court clarified that the right to claim maintenance under section 125 is not excluded by the 1986 Act and as such, while deciding the amount of maintenance under section 125, courts should take into account the sum already paid under the 1986 Act.

Waqfs

Waqf is a religious endowment peculiar to Muslims. It is property that is permanently donated for religious or charitable purposes. Once property is declared as Waqf, it cannot be sold or used for any other purpose. Broadly speaking, there are three kinds of Waqfs—the 'Public Waqf' supporting educational institutions and hospitals; the 'Family Waqf' which is for the benefit of the descendants of the donor; and the 'Waqf for mixed purposes'.

Waqf properties in India exceed one million acres and as such are not inconsiderable. It is for this reason that the BJP-led Union government could be looking to exercise greater control over such endowments through the passing of the Waqf (Amendment) Bill, 2025. One of the provisions of this statute was the removal of the category of 'Waqf by user'. As per the amendment, a person could declare only such property as Waqf property that he or she owned, even if the property had been in use as Waqf property for a matter of years. This would affect all Waqf properties that are five or six hundred years old, many of which have little or no documentation to establish title, and some of which are already under litigation. In cases of uncertainty of ownership, if the collector of the area deemed a property to be government property, then it would lose its status of Waqf property. The amendment even went as far as to deny Waqf bodies the right to initiate proceedings against encroachments, even though there exist some 58,929 cases of encroachment on Waqf properties according to government data.

The political context of this purported reform was the prime minister's remark that there is no place for Waqf in the constitution, oblivious of the fact that under Article 26 of the Constitution, minorities have the right to establish religious/charitable institutions and manage them.

The main grouse is the entirely false narrative that in the past, the management of Waqfs has been riddled with corruption, and the failure to regulate Waqfs is another instance of Muslim appeasement. Corruption, unfortunately, is a common feature of many Indian institutions, and corruption cannot be made the ground for interference with minority institutions. Even the argument of a lack of regulation of Waqfs is incorrect. The first legislation regulating Waqfs was enacted in 1913, which was followed by the Waqf Act of 1923. Post-Independence, the Central Waqf Act of 1954 was introduced to protect property and ensure accountability from the Muttawalis (trustees). This was followed by the Waqf Act of 1995, with amendments in 2013 introducing penalties such as imprisonment for encroachers and an express prohibition of legal transfer of any Waqf property. It also included within the definition of Waqf properties any property donated by a non-Muslim, something which the 2025 amendment proposes to reverse. In fact, Waqf boards remain amenable to writ jurisdiction under Article 12 of the Constitution, so it is not as if there was no supervision of Waqf activities prior to the amendment. There are many issues with Waqfs, including the law against perpetuities which ties up properties indefinitely, but amendment is of a very statist nature and has not sought the voice of the Muslim community in framing these alleged reforms.

The Uniform Civil Code

One of the main arguments in favour of promulgating UCC is that Article 44 of the Constitution, which is a part of the Directive Principles of State Policy, enjoins the State to strive to secure a Uniform Civil Code (UCC) for all citizens throughout India.

Professor Faizan Mustafa, however, has a slightly different perspective on this. He examines the wording of Article 44 to say, 'While Article 44 uses the words "state shall endeavour", other Articles in the "Directive Principles" chapter use words such as "in particular strive"; "shall in particular direct its policy"; "shall be the obligation of the state" etc. … All this implies that the duty of the state is greater in other directive principles than in Article 44.' For instance, Article 43 specifically notes that the State 'shall endeavour by suitable legislation', however, this vital verbiage is absent in Article 44. He also notes that 'uniform' is not the same as 'common': 'common' would mean one and the same in all circumstances, while 'uniform' means 'the same in similar conditions'.[33] Different people belonging to different groups may have different laws, but the law within a particular group ought to be uniform. Even Article 14, which gives the right to equality, requires that 'like be treated alike' and allows for reasonable classification between the 'unlike'.

Unfortunately, nothing in the majoritarian narrative suggests any degree of genuine interest in reforming family law in a gender-sensitive manner, or in engaging seriously with alternative legal frameworks to achieve such reform. An example of this is the UCC introduced by the Uttarakhand government, which does not inspire any hope about a gender-sensitive approach; on the contrary, it appears deeply regressive. For instance, it still retains the atavistic restitution of conjugal rights and the coparcenary system of holding property for Hindus.

One aspect of this debate which is often ignored is that personal laws, covering marriage, divorce, inheritance, and adoption, fall under the Concurrent List of the Constitution, for which both the Union government and the state governments can make laws. This speaks to the fact that the drafters of the Constitution envisaged diversity of laws in such matters, contrary to the standard mantra of 'one law, one people'. It is incorrect to assume that wanting a diversity in personal laws is a function of minority appeasement when it arises from a constitutional mandate. This was the position before the first general election and the intent, according to Faizan Mustafa, was to indubitably entrench such legal diversity. The fact that Uttarakhand has legislated its own UCC only supports this argument.

It is relevant to note that there does not exist complete uniformity even within Hinduism, as is sought to be projected. For instance, Goa was annexed by India in 1961, and thus the reformed Hindu laws of 1955-56 are not applicable to the Hindus of Goa. In fact, Goan Hindu men are entitled to polygamy. Similarly, there is a difference between marriage laws in the northern and southern parts of India; while in the former, marriage amongst close relatives (sapindas) is prohibited but it is accepted in the latter.

Swapan Dasgupta floats the canard that,

> The Constituent Assembly had recognized that all Indians should be governed by common laws relating to marriage and inheritance. However, at the urging of the leadership, which felt that the time was not yet ripe to expose a Muslim community still suffering the trauma of Partition to such radical change, the issue—along with the Gandhian pipedream of prohibition and Nehru's quest for a 'scientific temper'—was listed as one of the Directive Principles of state policy.[34]

This is part of the Hindutva mythology; it is counterfactual and what, even charitably, can only be described as an alternative truth. There is no evidence of any such desire other than the views of the sub-committee on fundamental rights, under the chairmanship of Minoo Masani, who was atypical in his social attitudes and whose demands on the timelines were explicitly rejected by the Constituent Assembly. It is rather ironic that Sardar Patel, the darling of the Hindu Right, was the chairperson of the Advisory Committee on Fundamental Rights, Minorities, and Tribal and Excluded Areas that declined to advise the Constituent Assembly to include UCC under the chapter of fundamental rights, leaving it to be a mere directive principle, something Dasgupta omits to mention.

To my understanding, the imposition of UCC in this climate is not the most sensible project for India to embark upon—a greater reform of personal laws which may involve the government playing a decisive role would be a more practical approach, if the desire is to detach justice from politics. This view is shared by Marc Galanter who wrote:

> Supposedly a common civil law will provide provisions of superior justice and utility and will be more uniform and certain, and finally it will reduce communal divisions and promote

> emotional integration; the first of these arguments does not argue for a civil code any more than a reform of personal law, especially where practice and utility are measured by the feelings of those affected. The real arguments, it seems, are those of national integration and modernisation of the State. There is reason to doubt that enforced conformity would reduce rather than intensify difference and communal antagonism.[35]

This correctly identifies the tensions that may surface with this obsession for uniformity in a nation which otherwise, albeit grudgingly, tolerates linguistic and cultural plurality. Then why not have diversity in religious practices, provided they do not fall foul of the constitutional mandate?

One of the most disturbing examples of this new thinking, indissolubly linked with the nationalist ethos, is the 'love jihad' laws. These undeniably undermine and compromise the agency of a woman to marry whom she pleases. In UP, the anti-conversion ordinance of 2020 seeks to control inter-religious marriages. The UCC legislation of Uttarakhand does not even address this issue. In fact, this legislation is even more regressive as it seeks to register even live-in relations, which as per constitutional scholar Gautam Bhatia, amounts to outsourcing 'the work of coercion to society', that is facilitating social pressure, bullying and intimidation through the requirement for registration.[36]

Thus, regressive patriarchal practices are not the monopoly of one religion, and the panacea for them is not UCC. Those who urge such a deliverance need to ponder these issues. A more practical project, almost the lowest-hanging fruit, is to simply reform existing legislation—the Sharia Act, the Hindu Marriage Act, etc.—and align it with the mandate of gender equality. This would be a more effective initiative rather than embarking on a project that is egregiously polarising and one that is likely to be based on regressive principles, going by the Uttarakhand example.

I believe it is critical to transcend and explicate the traditional binaries and narratives about the foreignness and unsuitability of constitutional secularism. So much attention is devoted to the continued application of personal laws and the inability to promulgate

UCC, when the condition of Muslim women is only one of the many myriad examples of oppression by custom, patriarchy and revanchist ideas pervasive in Indian society. There is far less public outrage against regressive practices such as child marriage, sex selection and discrimination against the girl child—issues that affect women across all communities—than there is about practices that impact destitute Muslim wives.

What is also often overlooked in debates on UCC is that it does not mean extending Hindu personal law to all communities. Rather, it implies creating a genuinely common set of personal laws applicable to all citizens, regardless of religion. That would necessarily require reforming certain practices currently accepted under Hindu law—such as the coparcenary system of joint family property and the remedy of restitution of conjugal rights. Any serious move toward a UCC would therefore demand changes across communities, and such reforms may well encounter resistance within the Hindu community too.

PART IV

FEDERALISM, ASYMMETRICAL FEDERALISM, CITIZENSHIP AND THE INDIAN DIASPORA

11

FEDERALISM, HISTORY AND THE ORIGINAL SIN

Federalism has long been a site of serious disagreement, with the debates shaping the course of politics and development in India. The central question concerns the nature of the State—whether it is fundamentally unitary or federal in recognising the autonomy of the provinces. Before turning to colonial constitutional arrangements, it is important to consider the character of the Indian state, which is geographically the seventh largest country in the world. Demographically, at the time of writing, India has pipped China in terms of population, becoming the most populous nation in the world at over 1.4 billion people. In environmental terms, India is extraordinarily diverse, with ten biogeographic zones compared to twelve in the United States, a country three times its size. India has around 780 spoken languages and a multitude of indigenous and ethnic communities, religious groups, castes, classes and other stratifications. This vast cornucopia of diversity is administratively bounded into twenty-eight States, eight union territories, nearly 8,000 cities and towns, and anywhere between 600,000 to a million villages. This is the complexity and plurality of the Indian state, and federalism should be considered only in this context.

I say this because it is not obvious to me that a unitary and centralised structure is to be regarded as the normative configuration for a State of such diversity and complexity. The argument is that the collapse of the Cabinet Mission Plan in 1946, followed by Partition, led to what Ambedkar described as a 'dual polity' in India, with a constitution that could be 'both unitary as well as federal according to the requirements of time and circumstances.'[1] This original sin has led to an unprecedented concentration of political power at the Centre which has had serious ramifications on politics and development. We will return to this point later, but it is important to understand how we got here.

History of Modern Indian Federalism

It is common knowledge that the East India Company ruled parts of India through a system of subsidiary alliances with princely states, under a Governor-General who enjoyed supreme powers vested in him by Pitt's India Act of 1784. By the enactment of the Charter Act of 1833, the company's trading functions were abolished and its role as the putative Government of India was validated. This machinery of government was presided over by Lord Dalhousie and undertook a considerable expansion of British territory in India, including the annexation of Oudh in 1856—an event that became one of the catalysts for the Indian Revolt of 1857. The critical year, however, which marks the beginning of modern India, is 1858, when Queen Victoria became the Empress of India, displacing both the Mughal dynasty and the East India Company as the effective 'de jure' ruler of British India. According to Faisal Devji, the Queen's Proclamation of 1858 'stopped British reprisals against the rebels and promised a policy of toleration and non-interference in India's religions, establishing a secular order in the subcontinent that did not yet exist in the British Isles'. In some respects, the proclamation can be regarded as India's 'Magna Carta'.

This period continued until the coming into force of the Government of India Act of 1919; the Montague-Chelmsford reforms gradually introduced self-governing institutions to British India, even as the position at the Centre remained largely unaltered. In relation to provincial governments, a system known as 'dyarchy' was introduced that divided powers between British officials and Indian ministers. 'Transferred' subjects, such as education, public health, agriculture and local self-government, were administered by Indian ministers, while 'reserved' subjects—finance, law enforcement and land revenue—remained under the control of British governors, who retained wide powers, including veto and ordinance-making authority. For Indians, this was a highly unsatisfactory state of affairs. However, it was very much within the common British tradition of extending promises and illusions of reform and agency without ceding much power.

Thereafter, the Government of India Act of 1935, which grew out of the Simon Commission of 1927–28 and the Round Table Conferences beginning in 1930, which proposed an all-India federation. The four principles which were accepted and enshrined in the act were: provincial autonomy, an all India federation, central responsibility and safeguards relating to the security and stability of the various governments. Interestingly, one of the reasons for introducing this legislation was articulated by Sir Samuel Hoare, who said that 'Indian questions, such as the question of child marriage, of temple entry and of the depressed classes, have been thrusting themselves more and more upon public attention, and more and more it became clear that these questions could be dealt with effectively by responsible Indian politicians.'[2]

This act was clearly a precursor to some form of 'dominion' status and was driven in part by the coming into power of the Labour government in Britain under the leadership of Ramsay MacDonald, who was keen to prepare grounds for a responsible government for India. Reactionaries like Churchill were highly critical of it, calling it 'a gigantic quilt of jumbled crochet work, a monstrous monument of shame built by pygmies'.[3]

Sir Tej Bahadur Sapru, lawyer and politician, had been advocating a federal system of government and sought the support of the rulers of the princely states for a union with the rest of the country. The 1935 Act, therefore, was an important development in the creation of a fledgling democracy as it extended the franchise to around thirty-five million people and vested the eleven British-Indian provinces with a fair measure of self-government. It also classified legislative powers into separate lists: federal, provincial and concurrent.

Powers not enumerated in the legislative lists were vested in the Governor-General, who retained overriding authority to allow either the federal or provincial legislatures to legislate on subjects in any of the three lists. Subject to these powers, the provinces were to acquire substantial autonomy on elections being held. However, for the federation to come into existence, half the princely states had to voluntarily agree to accede to the federation by way of separate instruments of accession. Understandably, many of the princely states were reluctant to enter the federation, apprehensive of the Congress and its demand for a democratic government. So, absent the participation of the princely states, the federal dream stood compromised. This, I think, was unfortunate since it retarded the growth of powerful regional sentiments and political equations which could have acted as a counterpoint to extreme nationalist sentiment.

Historian Ayesha Jalal references the 1935 act and states, 'The debate on the relationship between the federal centre and the federating units could assume real significance only when the British were ready for the transfer of power. At the time, this was not likely to happen. The Act had been designed to safeguard British rule in India, not to weaken it.'[4] This analysis is sound and further buttressed by the very design of the legislature in which princely states and minorities were privileged with the intention to dilute the power and impact of the nationalists. Yet, this experiment had the impact of greatly increasing the popular entrancement with democracy even though the franchise was limited; just over 14 per cent of the population were enfranchised. The elections under the 1935 Act had a dramatic impact, greatly popularising the Congress party. Its membership rose exponentially, increasing from about 500,000 to 4.5 million by 1938.[5]

Between 1935 and 1946, the prospect of imminent popular sovereignty generated intense political contestation among parties and the colonial state. The Cripps Mission of 1942 was significant in that it buttressed the principle of provincial autonomy, including the right of the provinces to refrain from joining the union. As historian Arvind Elangovan puts it, 'Cripp's declaration for the establishment of the Constituent Assembly was made subordinate to the right of the provinces to secede, thereby giving primacy to the question of communal differences rather than to the stated task of framing a constitution for a united India.'[6]

The next most significant step came with the Simla Conference in 1945, presided over by Viceroy Wavell, who was anxious to devolve much of the powers of the government onto a new executive council which, in keeping with colonial policy, would provide parity between Hindus and Muslims while also including representation for Sikhs and the Scheduled Castes. This arrangement was intended to be temporary, with the Viceroy remaining accountable to the British Parliament and responsible for maintaining the British presence in India. It was conceived as a transitional step towards the eventual grant of dominion status. Unfortunately, the conference served as a catalyst to excite latent differences; for example, the Unionist government of Punjab, which ruled a Muslim-majority province, posed a challenge to Jinnah's claim to be the sole spokesman for the Muslim community. The issue of parity also upset a number of Hindus. The Simla Conference ultimately failed for various reasons, but the question of representation proved to be the central issue.

The formation of a constituent assembly was central to Congress's argument, which wanted that a body be instituted that would decide the Union constitution and frame the parameters for provincial constitutions. Nehru articulated his views on provincial autonomy clearly, stating that 'while the Congress contemplated autonomy for the provinces that meant internal autonomy; it was quite another thing for autonomy to be used to create the new piece of constitutional machinery going beyond the boundaries of the province.'[7] This was diametrically opposite to Jinnah's views, who argued for provincial autonomy by suggesting that provinces and groups of provinces needed to meet separately to determine their own constitutions and work in tandem with other provinces for the purpose of framing the Union constitution. Thus, the federalism envisaged by Jinnah was one in which the states would decisively determine which powers they retained and which they chose to cede to the Union government. But since it was the Congress party that both encapsulated and appropriated the freedom movement and was most interested in shaping the contours of nationhood, its insistence on a powerful unitary structure prevailed, even at the cost of a united India. Accordingly, one of the seminal constitutional precepts that was upended by Independence was federalism, which cannot be divorced from the events of Partition. To govern such a diverse and plural society through a largely unitary structure is fairly unique and one fraught with the dangers of incipient homogenisation and consequent strife or blowback. The only comparable states in the twentieth century one can think of that have attempted this ambitious goal were the USSR and Yugoslavia, neither of which exist today.

Nehru and Federalism

Many of Nehru's ideas on federalism were shaped not just by the trauma of Partition, but also by the need to negotiate and navigate future arrangements with the princely states who comprised nearly 40 per cent of the landmass of India. To offer princely states the freedom to enter into treaty arrangements in order to become part of the new republic required much bargaining. As author Louise Tillin put it, 'While the eventual integration of the princely states did involve the fusing of entities with different prior status, this integration was not a result of equal bargains with the hundreds of individual states.'[8]

By the time the Constitution was being framed, the princely states had already acceded to India, so their integration was no longer a decisive political issue, though it remained legally significant. As soon as they joined the Union, they lost the agency that treaty arrangements brought, accelerating the configuration of the dual polity. This centralising tendency was further reinforced by the perceived need for a stronger unitary structure to facilitate central planning, inter-state transfers as well as major social and economic reforms.

The true preferences of the Congress leadership became evident only after the 1946 Cabinet Mission Plan had been abandoned and Partition accepted. With that settlement, many Congress leaders appeared freed from earlier constraints, most notably Jawaharlal Nehru, who articulated this position when he declared: 'Now that Partition is a settled fact, we are unanimously of the view that it would be injurious to the interests of the country to provide for a weak central authority, which will be incapable of ensuring peace, of coordinating vital matters of common concern and of speaking effectively for the whole country in the international sphere.'[9]

Federalism and Minorities

Legal scholar Bruce Ackerman has written, 'Partition and the creation of Pakistan profoundly shaped India's movement-party constitutionalism. After Partition, India's Muslim population was reduced to about 11 per cent of the total, allowing the Indian National Congress to dominate the Constituent Assembly proceedings. Although the Assembly made a number of significant concessions to Muslims and other minority groups, there was no longer any question that the Indian National Congress was calling the shots. India, in short, serves as a paradigm case involving the constitution of a new regime hegemonic party movement.'[10] What is often overlooked is that this hegemony did not arise solely because the Congress led the struggle for Independence. It was also shaped by the territorial reconfiguration of India after Partition. The new political geography enhanced the prominence of Uttar Pradesh and the wider Hindi heartland—the so-called cow belt—which became central to the Congress's electoral base and political dominance. India had, after the first election, metamorphosed into a one-party state, which, perhaps, was the intent behind the Partition.

This hegemony of the Congress was further entrenched by the process of constitution-making. As it was a nationalist party, it had a compelling interest in forging a strong unitary centre whilst professing pieties about federalism. However, Ambedkar was brutally honest about the basis for the union as distinct from a federation, as that would be the consequence of an agreement, and as such would preclude secession. He said, 'The Federation is a union because it is indestructible. Though the country and the people may be divided into different states for convenience of administration, the country is one integral whole, its people, a single people living under a single imperium derived from a single source.'[11] It is pertinent to know that the term federalism does not even appear in the Constitution. Yet federalism has been traduced, being identified with a weak

State. However, this is emphatically not the case. There are over forty nation-states that are federal in character, including the United States, Canada and Germany, but no one seriously argues that these are weak states prone to secession, quite the contrary.

It is fair to say that post-Partition, the bargaining power of the minorities, particularly the Muslims and Christians, was greatly diminished. It is not as if the Constituent Assembly was not cognizant of these concerns. Indeed, the first draft of the 'Report of the Advisory Committee on the Subject of Certain Political Safeguards for Minorities' placed before the Constituent Assembly in May 1949 was seriously anti-majoritarian. It promised a system of joint electorates with proportional representation for a period of ten years. It suggested that minorities be included in the Cabinet along the lines envisaged by the Government of India Act of 1935, though with the caveat of doing so 'as far as possible'. It even made a declaration that in relation to all-India and provincial services, the claims of minorities ought to be kept in view while making appointments. The report even proposed the appointment of an ombudsman to ensure that these declarations and safeguards were implemented in practice.

From the debates in the Constituent Assembly, we can discern three particular mechanisms for protecting political representation: separate electorates, a variety of proportional representation contrivances, and reserved seats. The Muslim League representatives strongly urged for separate electorates as a means of protecting the interests of a particular minority, as the representative would only be accountable to that minority group which they were supposed to represent. This was rejected by the nationalists who argued in the words of another Constituent Assembly member, Mahavir Tyagi, that 'a state cannot be a confederation of so many religions or sects or groups.'[12] Furthermore, they argued that 'separate electorates' were a relic of colonialism but had no place in a functioning democracy, since the role of representatives in the colonial system was merely advisory and they were not supposed to act as legislators.

The question of a minority quota in the Cabinet or for that matter, any quota or preferment in government service was also rejected. Ultimately, it was Sardar Patel himself who torpedoed the Advisory

Committee's report in May 1949, when he remarked that it was 'no longer appropriate in the context of free India and of present conditions that there should be any reservation of seats for Muslims, Christians, Sikhs or any other religious communities.'[13] And that if such privileges were to be offered, they would be confined to groups such as Scheduled Castes and Scheduled Tribes as far as the reservation of seats was concerned.

In relation to proportional representation, it was forcefully argued by Muslim League leader Z.H. Lari that political minorities are entitled to be represented by representative institutions. 'It is better for us to adopt this principle of proportional representation by means of the single transferable vote or cumulative voting, which is more progressive in instinct and which is really democratic.'[14] The nationalists were uncomfortable with proportional representation for precisely the reason its advocates favoured it: the expectation that it would attenuate 'the tyranny of the majority'. The matter of whether the first-past-the-post system polarised Indian politics is problematical at best. If one looks at countries that have adopted proportional representation, it is not evident that this by itself has precluded polarisation. For example, the 1978 Sri Lankan constitution introduced a system of proportional representation, and that was the prelude to a catastrophic ethnic polarisation that led to a civil war. Indeed, a similar political instability can be seen in Israel, another country which has the proportional representation system in place, that has led to the emergence of numerous small parties which invariably subscribe to extremist positions, causing mainstream political parties to be held to ransom when they form a coalition government. Ambedkar, for one, was obsessed with political stability, as he did not see how a stable government could remain in power if the 'House would be divided into so many small groups that every time anything happened which displeased certain groups in Parliament they could, on that occasion, withdraw their support from the Government, with the result that the Government would fall to pieces.'[15] And yet, India adopted the Westminster system, but with guardrails—a written constitution and judicial review—which became its distinguishing factors.[16]

The move to dismantle all such minority safeguards was sugar-coated and made acceptable by selling the dream of an independent judiciary coupled with the promulgation of a radical constitution. This framework reassured even the most liberal members of the Constituent Assembly that fixed legislative representation for minorities was no longer necessary, as constitutional protections and judicial oversight would suffice. An example of this was the attitude of H.C. Mookerjee, a Christian and the erstwhile chairman of a sub-committee on minorities, who was rather Panglossian in this regard. He said, 'There are certain people who really feel alarmed over the future of their community. Such people want to come to the legislature because they think they can safeguard the interests of the groups to which they belong. But when we have passed the various Fundamental Rights which guarantee religious, cultural and education safeguards—safeguards which are justiciable and can be decided in a court of law—I feel that the presence of people belonging to certain groups is not at all necessary.'[17]

In fact, Mookerjee himself, on behalf of the Christian community, gave up the demand for legislative reservations in exchange for a constitutional right that was central to their identity as Christians: the right to propagate their religion. In that moment of misplaced optimism, Mookerjee conceded the Christian minority's demand for representation in favour of entrenched constitutional rights.

According to Rochana Bajpai, 'The act of abolition of reserved seats for religious minorities was pivotal. Once secured, it had a snowballing effect: the removal of all other political safeguards for religious minorities followed almost as a matter of consequential adjustment. Even the role of the Special Officers was strictly confined to monitoring the "backward classes" and, oddly, the Anglo-Indians—perhaps because they were increasingly irrelevant, as many were migrating in any case.'[18] Patel smugly reflected that the minorities themselves had come to realise 'the evil effects in the past of such reservations.'[19]

Nehru's view on the abolition of reservations for religious minorities was more nuanced; he defended it on the basis that it was a consequence of democracy. What was remarkable post-Independence was the convergence of the Hindu Right, as represented by Patel and secular nationalists like Nehru on the vexed matter of vacating reservations for religious minorities in legislatures. Majoritarianism was integral to this thinking.

Yet, the political leaders of the time showed scant regard to recent history. How one regards difference and pluralism must be viewed through the historical prism of the excesses of the twentieth century. As author Suzanne Schneider puts it,

> It is often assumed that exclusionary political models—you know, the ones that lurk behind the last century's grim history of Partition, ethnic cleansing, and genocide—are remnants of a less civilised past. The reality is that it was modernity and the age of nationalism in particular that rendered the inevitable fact of human difference uniquely threatening. Pre-modern empires regarded heterogeneity as the natural order of the universe. Difference needed accommodation and often careful management, but not eradication.[20]

This is a lesson which was not learnt by the makers of the Indian constitution, despite the appalling genocides committed in the name of nationalism in the last four decades. There was an inevitable prejudice against diversity and the political trajectory was directed at nation-building, showing wilful indifference to the recent history of nationalism in the twentieth century.

Early Federalism and the Original Sin

The early years of the Constitution concealed some of the flaws or, what I consider the original sin in the structure of the Constitution when it comes to federal matters. In the formative years of the republic, there were numerous states with elected leaders who had gained experience of governance when they had been elected in pursuance of the Government of India Act, 1935. These leaders developed their own political followings and gained a deep understanding of their respective states, which is why they did not look to the Union government for support or patronage. This autonomy was reciprocated by the Congress leadership, particularly Nehru, when it came to interactions with state governments. It also helped that there was a Congress hegemony in states which made the issues between the Union and the states merely intra-party differences, which were often resolved amicably.

When Ambedkar called the Constitution flexible, he was referring to a singular kind of flexibility, which could be traced in constitutional developments. For example, it allowed the Parliament to create new states, increase or diminish the area of any state, and alter boundaries or names of states under Article 3. It is remarkable that these powers could be exercised with the approval of a simple majority and, more importantly, without requiring the consent of the state concerned. This article became an important instrument in addressing linguistic issues, with states being largely reorganised on linguistic lines. As per Louise Tillin, 'The creation of linguistic states helped to alleviate potential tensions between an Indian national identity and regional identities shaped profoundly by language.'[21] An instance of this was Parliament enacting the States Reorganisation Act of 1956, which created a composite Bombay state that included the Marathwada region, Vidarbha and the Gujarati-speaking states of Saurashtra and Kutch states. (Later in 1960, the Bombay state was dissolved and the states of Maharashtra and Gujarat were created). This was challenged in the Supreme Court in the case of *Babulal Parate v. State of Bombay.*[22] In its ruling, the court effectively stated that the states had no power to object, as they had no rights under the constitution. It observed that 'none of the constituent units of the Indian Union was sovereign and independent in the sense the American colonies or the Swiss Cantons were before they formed their federal unions. The Constituent Assembly of India, deriving its power from the sovereign people, was unfettered by any previous commitment in evolving a constitutional pattern suitable to the genius and requirements of the Indian people as a whole.'[23]

However, with the drift of Indian public policy towards caste considerations, there emerged a desire to empower Scheduled Castes and Tribes to acquire political salience. This led to the formation of states such as Jharkhand and Chhattisgarh. One of the most recent examples of this happening—also unique in that it was driven by development goals, was the creation of the state of Telangana from the erstwhile state of Andhra Pradesh in 2013. The agitation for this new state was based on unequal economic development, an allegation supported by the findings of the 2010 report of the Committee for Consultations on the situation in Andhra Pradesh, chaired by B.N. Srikrishna, former judge of the Supreme Court. The creation of the new state has been a success story, with Telangana becoming one of the fastest-growing states in India, posting an annual growth rate of nearly 14 per cent per annum over the past five years. As per legal academician P. Ishwara Bhat, 'The formation of Telangana is a strong warning to all the Stares to avoid regional disparity within them.'[24]

The recent Supreme Court judgement on the abrogation of Article 370, insofar as it purports to deal with Article 3, goes further by vesting the Union government with extraordinary powers.[25] The wording of the article makes it clear that it does not permit the Union government to alter the status of the state itself, as the Jammu and Kashmir Reorganisation Act purports to do by reducing it to the status of a Union Territory—a move that the Supreme Court has upheld on the basis of a non-binding assurance given by the Solicitor General that statehood would be restored at some time in the future. As Pratap Bhanu Mehta puts it, 'Performatively, the Court ended up saying, "The whole of the Constitution of India applies to Jammu and Kashmir. But not yet." A curious performance indeed.'[26] In fact, this aspect of the case has created new and horrible vistas for future interference by the Union government interference in states it considers antagonistic to it.

In this case, the court went on to add that it was bound by the judgement in the *Babulal Parate* case and took the view that concurrence of the state legislature was not required for the break-up of the state into two union territories. However, this reasoning is specious when the state is under the president's rule at the time of the break-up; the question being the propriety of the Union effecting such a seismic change to a state without the consent of a democratically elected assembly.

The truth is that the Congress hegemony in politics concealed the true nature of the unitarian nature of the Indian state for at least the first three decades after Independence. Political scientists John McGarry and Brendan O'Leary observe that even when devolution occurs, it still leaves the power with the central authority; it is not a bargain between national or ethnic communities. Power is often in the hands of the dominant nationality or ethnic community and fails to secure what, in their words, amounts to 'a plurinational partnership of equals'.[27] The consequence of this, they conclude, is that India has almost negligible protection for minorities, which would normally align with 'full pluralist federations'.[28]

If we go back to the Government of India Act of 1935, it was responsible for adumbrating the demarcation of powers in three lists: union, state or province, and concurrent. This methodology was adopted in Part XI of the Constitution, with the exception that the Parliament would have the power to legislate on any matter in the state list, if two-third members of Rajya Sabha, present and voting, considered it necessary based on national interest. The Union governments in the past have taken recourse to this provision with great alacrity. This provision undermines Ambedkar's argument of a dual polity. In my view, you either have a strict delineation of powers, or you don't. In the case of the latter, you cannot then say that the nation subscribes to federalism.

Neither Nehru nor Ambedkar had the prescience to see the pervasive centripetal forces that would come to characterise Indian administration and politics—tendencies that have since become deeply embedded in political thinking and that have largely precluded the kind of constitutional architecture built around the American fixation with checks and balances. There was also a marked infatuation with English constitutionalism, reflected in the prominence accorded to constitutional conventions in the tradition of Bagehot and Dicey, particularly in matters such as the role of governors and the vigilance of the judiciary. Legal scholar Gautam Bhatia observes, 'A written Constitution can reduce the extent to which governance relies upon conventions. It cannot, however, eliminate them. The range of human behaviour can never completely be captured in a text.'[29] For that reason, there must be a broad consensus on constitutional principles and morality; given the opportunistic and often criminalised character of the political class, expecting them to voluntarily adhere to constitutional morality remains a dream.

The Misuse of Article 356 and the Judiciary's Abdication of Responsibility

One of the most controversial provisions in the Indian constitution is Article 356, which sought to replicate section 93 of the Government of India Act. Author Arghya Sengupta points out, 'The conceptual foundation for an overwhelmingly strong Union was firmly in place by August 1947. In this light, it should not come as a surprise that despite Sections 93 and 102 of the Government of India Act on the powers of the unelected governor and governor-general being colonial vestiges, they were endorsed by members of the Constituent Assembly with great enthusiasm.'[30] While this provision for president's rule in a state was being contemplated in the Constituent Assembly, there was an attempt to further surcharge it with the power to suspend all fundamental rights, including the right to move the courts for redress. This power would have been draconian in the extreme. Fortunately, the provision that ultimately became a part of the Constitution excluded the power of the president to suspend fundamental rights. And still, Article 356 has been taken recourse to time and again over the years, with uncommon enthusiasm, whenever there has been a perceived 'instability' of state governments. Chief Ministers have been sidelined and democratic institutions suborned. The concept of perceived instability owes its provenance to Germany, where circumstances under which governments may be suspended are carefully and precisely specified, leaving little or no scope for discretion and thereby reducing the risk of misuse. Unfortunately, the vague terminology in the Indian provision accompanied by a marked decline in the character and quality of governors, who are increasingly pliant political hacks rather than persons of integrity, has resulted in the blatant misuse of the provision for president's rule.

In the time of the Indira Gandhi government and now post-2014, Article 356 has been invariably used as a political instrument against opposition or regional parties by the Union government to expand its puissance. During the two tenures of Indira Gandhi, from 1966 to 1977 and from 1980 to 1984, this provision was used around fifty times, and post-2014, around nine times. The most recent instances of such use have been in the case of Jammu and Kashmir, Karnataka and Arunachal Pradesh. It must be stated, as a caveat, that toppling governments by inducing MLAs to defect remains the fastest and most-commonly used tactic.

The president's power under Article 356 was revisited in a nine-judge bench in the Supreme Court case of *S.R. Bommai v. Union of India*[31] decided in 1994. The majority judgement recognised the political realities that had influenced the exercise of such proclamations under Article 356, remarking that state governments had been sacked and legislative assemblies dissolved on 'irrelevant, objectionable and unsound grounds'. Two of the judges (B.P. Jeevan Reddy and S.C. Agrawal) even issued a trenchant warning against the misuse of this power, stating that 'it is not a power conceived to preserve or promote the interests of the political party in power at the Centre for the time being, nor is it supposed to be a weapon with which to strike your political opponent.' The court noted at least ninety instances when this provision was misused against states where the government at the state level was different from the one at the Centre. This was a significant judgement since the Supreme Court, in the words of constitutional law scholar Sudhir Krishnaswamy, 'it identifies the judicial role in the preservation of the federal constitutional arrangement by negating the place of partisan considerations in federal decision-making.'[32]

The *S.R. Bommai* judgement has been consequential in at least reducing the widespread imposition of President's rule, according to author Alok Prasanna Kumar from 100 times between 1950 and 1994 (around 2.5 times annually) to only 29 times between 1995 and 2021 (around once a year).[33] And still, recourse to this provision has not completely stopped. In 2023, NCP MP Supriya Sule reportedly remarked in the Parliament that the NDA government had the 'unenviable record' of toppling nine state governments in nine years.[34] As per Arghya Sengupta, 'For a Constitution that proclaimed itself federal, with a division of sovereignty between the Union and the states, both being supreme in their respective domains, the reversion to a unitary and unaccountable form of government during any disturbance in a state was unexpectedly quick.'[35] It also demonstrates an incorrigible predilection for centralisation of power.

Oddly enough, the *Bommai* case was relied on by the Supreme Court bench hearing cases related to the abrogation of Article 370. An argument was made that the Union could not have made such a seminal change when the state was under president's rule. The chief justice himself recognised that the constitutional arrangement embodied in Article 356 was designed to restore the functioning of the constitutional machinery in the state. And yet, the court failed to see that there has to be a proximate relationship to the object and purpose underlying the suspension of constitutional machinery in the state. President's rule, therefore, ought to extend only to the routine administration of the state. Its use to extinguish statehood would be wholly inconsistent with, and bear no proximate nexus to, the purpose of Article 356. In other words, the Supreme Court ignored the doctrine of implied limitations set out in the *S.R. Bommai* case and opened the prospect of a state under president's rule being converted into a union territory, absent any consultation with the state assembly.

A recent development has been the increasing readiness of state governors to invoke Article 200 of the Constitution, which vests them with the power to grant or withhold assent to bills passed by the state legislature, or to return them for reconsideration. This issue has come to the fore in the context of the strained relationship between the governor of Tamil Nadu, R.N. Ravi, and the state government, particularly following delays in granting assent to several Bills.

In April 2025, the dispute came before the Supreme Court in the matter of *State of Tamil Nadu v. Governor of Tamil Nadu*, where the court held that the governor does not possess unfettered discretion to withhold assent under Article 200, and characterised such delays as erroneous and illegal. It further invoked its powers under Article 142 to grant assent to the pending bills and prescribed specific timelines within which the governor must act.[36]

Subsequently, the Union government sought the opinion of the Supreme Court under Article 143 of the Constitution on the scope of the governor's powers under Article 200, particularly whether the governor enjoyed any discretion in granting or withholding assent to legislative bills. The court felt that there existed such discretion, but it was largely non-justiciable, further observing that no rigid timeline could be prescribed for the exercise of this power. Judicial review, it suggested, would be available only in exceptional cases of prolonged or indefinite delay.[37]

This advisory opinion has significantly diluted the impact of the Governor of Tamil Nadu case, which had been widely regarded as a major boost to federalism for its effect of curbing the Union's ability to obstruct state legislation through a compliant governor. The current legal position thus remains somewhat unsettled. However, a continued and expansive use of Article 200 by compliant governors risks undermining the legislative authority of states and, in effect, sabotaging the federal balance.

The Role of the Rajya Sabha

In a bicameral legislative structure, one would think that the Rajya Sabha (the Council of States or the Upper House) would have a defined role within the constitutional framework. It purportedly represents state interests in that its members are indirectly elected (through a single transferable vote via proportional representation) by the state legislatures. However, the baleful English constitutional influence on its role is apparent as its purpose appears to be confined to reducing the legislative burden—serving as a site for the introduction of bills alongside the Lok Sabha and as a platform for debate, like the House of Lords in Britain. It would have been better had it been modelled more on the US Senate, especially if the federal structure was meant to be taken seriously. The Rajya Sabha does, however, enjoy a veto when a government is seeking to push a constitutional amendment through Parliament. It also has special powers to approve proclamations of emergency (national, state, or financial) if the Lok Sabha is dissolved or cannot approve it within the stipulated time.

It is thus apparent that whilst the Rajya Sabha is meant to ostensibly represent state legislatures, it was never designed to act as a platform for regional demands in any substantive way.[38] Louise Tillin identifies the intrinsic limitations in the form the Rajya Sabha has taken, commenting that 'states are represented in the Rajya Sabha broadly in proportion to their population rather than on an equal basis. As a result, the territorial pattern of representation in the Rajya Sabha largely mirrors that of the Lok Sabha. Members of the Rajya Sabha also tend to vote along party lines.'[39] We thus see the appropriation of the Rajya Sabha by the very same political credo that prevails in the Lok Sabha. The Rajya Sabha's resemblance to the Lok Sabha in its political composition, coupled with its amorphous role as the second legislature, seems like a hugely wasted opportunity. As it happens, the role of the Rajya Sabha is sensationally modest: at the highest, it is an echo chamber of the Lok Sabha; at worst, it is a refuge for placemen and political has-beens.

It would have been entirely possible for the Rajya Sabha to represent the states along the lines of the US senate, where each state, irrespective of its population, is entitled to a fixed number of representatives. The emergence and growth of a multitude of regional parties in India have lent momentum to regional demands and aspirations, creating a political space that the Rajya Sabha could have effectively occupied as a forum for advancing federal principles and reflecting the country's plurality.

The leading Supreme Court judgement on federalism came in the case of *Kuldip Nayar v. Union of India*[40], which questioned the territoriality of representation. The petitioner, a veteran journalist and former Rajya Sabha member, challenged the 2003 amendment to the Representation of the People Act of 1951, which purported to entrench the notion of non-territoriality. He argued that this amendment violated the principle of federalism in that it removed the requirement that a candidate seeking membership to the Rajya Sabha must be an 'elector for a Parliamentary constituency in that State or territory.' The amendment was agnostic as to where the electors came from and imposed no requirement that they should be residents of the state from which they sought to be elected. The amendment was upheld since the Supreme Court took the view that 'the principle of federalism is not territory related.'

The disregard for the Rajya Sabha as a forum for legislative review—arguably the defining function of a second chamber—was starkly illustrated in the passage of the Aadhaar Bill. Notably, an earlier version of the legislation, the National Identification Authority of India Bill of 2010, introduced by the UPA government, had been flagged in December 2011 for substantial revision by the Parliamentary Standing Committee on Finance, chaired by Yashwant Sinha. The NDA government, however, introduced the legislation in a substantially similar form, sidestepping these concerns, and this time as a Money Bill. This classification effectively bypassed the need for meaningful parliamentary scrutiny and debate in the Upper House.

In a challenge before the Supreme Court in the *Puttaswamy* case, the majority judgment adopted a controversial reading of Article 110 of the Constitution, which stipulates that a bill may be certified as a Money Bill only if it contains provisions exclusively relating to specified financial matters. The court, however, appeared to dilute the significance of the word 'only', focusing instead on the 'core' of the legislation—namely, the provision for subsidies, benefits, and services to the public.[41]

Yet, the notion of a 'core' cannot be equated with the constitutional requirement of 'only', which demands strict exclusivity. The idea of a 'core' inevitably admits a broader penumbra of purposes, extending beyond financial matters to include issues such as identity verification for voting or other regulatory uses. On any reasonable interpretation, therefore, the Aadhaar Bill went beyond the narrow confines of Article 110.

It is clear that various reforms have been proposed in relation to the Rajya Sabha, which, as per author Rekha Saxena, were needed for it to shed 'its image of being a parking lot for those who cannot ensure their election from a popular constituency.'[42] This is, unfortunately, Rajya Sabha's current image, and this is not without reason. Saxena also points out that there are over thirty Rajya Sabha MPs whose net worth exceeds INR 10 million, many of whom are non-domiciled candidates and, at least in the last Parliament, fifty-seven of them had criminal cases against them. These facts strengthen the impression of Rajya Sabha essentially being a club where odious plutocrats, such as Vijay Mallya, the now-discredited liquor and airline tycoon, could easily buy their way into the Parliament. A Rajya Sabha seat also expands the scope for political horse-trading, as seen in 2020 when Jyotiraditya Scindia was lured from the Congress to the BJP with the promise of a Rajya Sabha seat and a cabinet position, leading to the collapse of the Congress government in Madhya Pradesh.

The most imaginative of reforms of the federal structure were outlined in the 2010 report of the Commission on Centre-State Relations chaired by retired judge M.M. Punchhi. The report made several path-breaking proposals including the retention of the domiciliary clause for election to the Rajya Sabha and, critically, the idea of granting equal representation to the states, panchayats and municipalities in the Rajya Sabha with the intent of buttressing federalism within the constitutional matrix. This is controversial, as it is difficult to envisage states such as UP, Bihar and Maharashtra divesting their hegemony, and even more difficult to see states concede representation to local bodies such as municipalities. This was a valuable recommendation not only in light of increasing urbanisation but also because it recognised the central role of urban development in driving economic growth. For instance, Mumbai is among the richest cities in Asia and is certainly the wealthiest in India, yet it remains a municipality. Apart from six seats in the Lok Sabha and its indirect representation in the Rajya Sabha through members elected by the Maharashtra Legislative Assembly, it has no independent voice in Parliament.

If wholesale reform of the Rajya Sabha is required, it is pointless to effect such change without extensive devolution of powers not just to the states but, within the states, to municipalities, who should be vested with greater power in relation to raising resources and have autonomy over investment decisions within their jurisdictions. While the Constitution left the structure and scope of administrative decentralisation largely to the states, the process of devolution cannot end at that level. Given India's ballooning urbanisation and the growing centrality of cities, deeper decentralisation is essential. This becomes especially significant since, by 2030, nearly 70 per cent of India's GDP is expected to come from urban areas, which continue to remain inadequately represented.

The prime minister was mindful of the exponential growth taking place in cities and, to address that issue, proposed the development of a hundred smart cities in the 2014 election manifesto. Many found such a vision to be impossibly ambitious, given the sorry state of India's urban infrastructure which called for massive investment to fund solutions with respect to housing, sanitation, water, transportation, education, health and urban pollution. Needless to say, not one smart city that addresses all these issues effectively has emerged, and these projects have become mired in opposition, regulations and apathy. This is the ineluctable consequence of centralised diktats that exclude local participation, where communities are denied a say in their own priorities and are unable to hold their elected representatives accountable for the ownership and execution of these schemes.

The closest example we have of this sort of governance can be seen in the case of Arvind Kejriwal, the former chief minister of Delhi. His government made commendable progress in delivering quality education and health to middle and lower-class Delhi residents, but he was continually undermined by the Centre, who probably felt intimidated by this brand of politics which actually sought to change people's lives rather than deriving momentum from serving a nationalist narrative.

A recent example of disputes which have a North-South dimension relates to the two incipient metro projects the Tamil Nadu government was anxious to promote in Madurai and Coimbatore. The Union government introduced the Metro Rail Policy of 2017 as per which cities with a population of two million and more could plan for mass transit systems including the metro rail. The population was to be computed as per the 2011 census, which created conflict since cities argued that they had grown beyond the 2011 figures but were still being evaluated based on those figures. This requirement was waived in the case of Agra but applied in the case of Madurai and Coimbatore in order to deny these cities the metro rail. This is a clear case of the Union government favouring development in one part of the country over another.

Federalism and the Judicial System

While we have examined how the Indian judiciary has, over time, engaged with the federal question, it is equally important to recognise the central role of a federal judiciary in the functioning of a federal system. India's judicial structure is largely derived from the English model, even though the American system may have been more suitable, given that our courts operate within a written Constitution and are expected to exercise what may be described as a 'constitutional conscience'.

Ambedkar held the view that the 'Indian Federation though a dual polity has no dual judiciary at all. The High Courts and the Supreme Court form one single integrated judiciary having jurisdiction and providing remedies in all cases arising under the constitutional law, the civil law or the criminal law.'[43] This is not entirely accurate as the Supreme Court has special powers under Article 142 to intervene in special cases where it feels the ends of justice need to be served. At the same time, there has been a significant decline in the position of high courts vis-à-vis the Supreme Court. The High Courts of the presidency cities of Calcutta, Bombay and Madras were once institutions of great antiquity and distinction. Their stature is reflected in the example of Justice M.C. Chagla, then chief justice of the Bombay High Court, who in 1949 declined elevation to the Supreme Court, as such an appointment was not then regarded as a promotion. This was before the Constitution came into force in 1950, which significantly enhanced the stature of the Supreme Court relative to the high courts.[44]

Legal scholars Srinath Sridevan and Ananya Pattabhiraman have identified another way in which the executive has diminished the role of the High Courts—through legislation that creates what they describe as 'parallel judicial systems of courts and tribunals, providing for direct appeals to the Supreme Court, bypassing the High Courts'.[45] A particularly relevant example, especially in the context of an emerging kleptocratic tendency, is the Competition Commission of India, established to play a critical role in maintaining competition and preventing monopolies. In an era marked by pervasive crony capitalism, the functioning and structure of such bodies assume particular significance. These commissions are often staffed by former bureaucrats or retired judges perceived to be pliant. Appeals from their orders lie directly to the Supreme Court, bypassing the high courts, over which the executive is able to exercise less influence. A similar concern arises with the National Company Law Tribunal, which now wields significant authority over the corporate sector, including the approval of settlements with banks and third-party creditors—raising concerns in contexts of crony capitalism. NCLT has, at times, functioned as a convenient forum for extending favourable outcomes to those close to the ruling establishment, cloaked in the legitimacy of court-approved settlements. Reliance Communications, led by Anil Ambani, owed INR 47,857 crore to fifty-three banks, yet a settlement was reached under the National Company Law Tribunal for INR 459 crore—less than one per cent of the total debt.[46]

This process of settlement has reached a new apogee in the *Sandesara–Sterling Group loan fraud* case[47] settled in the Supreme Court, where criminal proceedings against the promoters of the Ahmedabad-based company, Sterling Biotech were quashed in lieu of them settling dues worth INR 5,100 crores that they owed to Indian banks from 2017. The order was passed by the Supreme Court as an exercise of its extraordinary power under Article 142 of the Constitution. This sort of settlement raises serious concerns of legal propriety inasmuch as such a settlement decriminalises some very serious criminal activities, allowing the offenders to avoid penalties or imprisonment. Decriminalisation is a worthwhile exercise and should be the norm in many cases, but perhaps not in cases of fraud and money laundering, especially where significant amounts are owed to public banks. The hypocritical stance of Indian courts comes to the fore when you look at sentences given to those accused of cow slaughter or polygamy or even conversions. Needless to say, in cases such as these, it helps to be close to the ruling dispensation. This is deeply worrying and constitutes a major assault on federalism. These are matters to ponder, and it is difficult to disagree with the conclusion Sridevan and Pattabhiraman come to that 'the greater the degree of centralisation of the judiciary, the weaker the federal structure.'[48]

Administrative Federalism and the IAS

Despite pieties about decentralisation in the past, even during the halcyon days of coalitions and strong regional parties, political de-centralisation was never accompanied by any tangible administrative decentralisation, which is critical for the delivery of public goods. (Experience in states such as Andhra Pradesh in the 1980s shows that decentralising sub-districts into mandals significantly improved the distribution of public services at the village level.)

The one substantive impediment to decentralisation which buttresses the unitary character of the Indian state is the Indian Administrative Service (IAS), the successor to the colonial Indian Civil Service (ICS). The IAS is a national bureaucracy, with members who are centrally recruited and then assigned to state cadres. In the Constituent Assembly debates, serious questions were raised about reforming this colonial vestige and determining its future in independent India—issues on which significant disagreements emerged. Nehru wanted to do away with the ICS and replace it with a civil service more attuned to development. It was Sardar Patel who opposed this, arguing that the 'Union will go—you will not have a united India, if you do not have a good All India Service.'[49] Like in most things, he got his way, and India ended up paying the price. This thinking was unfortunately suited to a colonial paradigm, but was not intended for a state active in developing human capital and delivering public goods. As economist Karthik Muralidharan puts it, 'The main goal was not the welfare of the population, but rather to extract surplus from India's land and its people to finance the colonial army and the opulence of its rulers.'[50]

What is often not realised is that the draft constitution vested the right to decide the terms of appointment for civil servants with the appropriate provincial legislatures. This had the merit of making the mandarin class answerable to the state legislatures. If a member of the bureaucracy was found committing a crime or delinquency, they could have been dismissed, provided a written reason had been assigned. Sardar Patel was against this federal model, insisting that there would be constitutional guarantees and safeguards provided to the bureaucracy, mimetic of what the ICS had enjoyed. Though strongly opposed by several chief ministers, including G.B. Pant, Patel got his way and spawned the imperious culture of impunity that continues to plague the bureaucracy to this day, which has cascaded down to middle-ranking officers over the years. The desire for centralisation of bureaucratic services is evident from the enactment of the All-India Services Act of 1951, which empowers the Central government to make rules regarding the recruitment, promotion, and discipline of civil servants. This is possibly why the numbers skew in favour of the cow belt over southern states.[51]

Unfortunately, debates on reforming the IAS have centred around issues such as the generalist qualifications of the recruits, the lack of domain specialists, the need for caste diversity, and the need to insulate the service from political interference. While these are all legitimate concerns, far less attention has been paid to the IAS's role in mediating the relationship between the Union and the states—a dimension that deserves much greater scrutiny.

In 2022, the Union government took the unprecedented step of wresting its share of IAS officers from the states by proposing amendments to cadre rules and increasing direct recruitment. This was seen as an attempt to assert hegemony over the entire administrative service and was termed 'combative federalism'.

In recent times, there has been a noticeable trend of senior state bureaucrats engaging directly with the Union government, effectively bypassing their respective state governments. This tendency is most evident in the practice of the prime minister holding regular meetings with state chief secretaries to review schemes and projects, including those that fall within the state list. This tendency is reinforced by the brute reality that the Union government not only controls recruitment but exercises disciplinary procedures in relation to the highest ranks of the civil service. This fosters a culture of sycophancy where some members of the senior ranks genuflect before the Union government for preferment and even foreign postings.

The importance of certain key and trusted IAS officers is particularly apparent in the Gujarat model of development, which has been imposed throughout India since 2014. The ruling establishment increasingly relies on a select group of trusted bureaucrats to advance policy, often sidestepping political consultation, consensus-building, and even formal cabinet processes. This notion of a trusted bureaucrat and one whose views align with the prime minister may not be new, but it has acquired seminal importance in recent years.

One aspect of bureaucratic reform, as suggested by economist Karthik Muralidharan, is to draw lessons from China, where public officials are evaluated on performance and rewarded accordingly. This approach is coupled with greater autonomy for officials and a more decentralised allocation of budgets.[52] Performance and outcome seem to be at a discount in our bureaucracy where pay grades are risible and the culture is rooted in the colonial paradigm. Even more telling is the size of the bureaucracy. The Indian bureaucracy is grossly understaffed. Muralidharan states that India has only sixteen public employees per thousand people. In comparison, China has over three times as many, Norway has ten times as many, and even the USA has seventy-seven public employees per thousand people.[53] This lack of qualified and incentivised public servants in sufficient numbers derails and undermines governance in India.

However, politicians see things differently. The colonial paradigm suits them as it enables them to get their way and run the government as they wish. The need for compliant bureaucrats acquires heightened political significance in the current Union-state context, where troublesome journalists, opposition politicians seen as potential threats and pesky civil rights activists are sought to be neutralised. The Union government retains control over central agencies such as the Income Tax department, the Enforcement Directorate, the Central Bureau of Investigation and the National Investigation Agency. These agencies afford the Union government the power to raid, investigate and, in some cases, incarcerate potential dissenters or opponents, as was seen in the case of the former chief minister of Delhi, Arvind Kejriwal. As is well-known, the political funding of elections involves access to and retention of large sums of illicit funds. This is the norm for all political parties. However, when the ruling establishment has access to investigative agencies and the full machinery of the state, the temptation to deploy them against political opponents becomes considerable. Reports suggest a stark imbalance in their use, with roughly 95 per cent of such actions directed at opposition figures, compared to about 5 per cent involving members of the ruling party.

The ruling party would aver that there have been no scams or incidents of corruption within its ranks, but given the nature of political funding and many examples of crony capitalism, this is not true. The Union government's response to the occasional media reports suggesting scandal or financial impropriety has often been to brazen it out, whether it be in the context of a defence-related controversy such as the Rafale deal or allegations of privacy intrusions through the use of Israeli spyware, Pegasus. In part, this reflects what political scientist Yascha Mounk describes as the 'moral monopoly of representation', whereby populist leaders sacralise their authority and dismiss criticism from the opposition as anti-national conduct.[54] This aligns also with the position that only opponents of the government are to be investigated and punished. According to senior Supreme Court lawyer Dushyant Dave,

> A pattern emerging over the last seven years shows that only a section of citizens is being acted against by the State. They belong to the Opposition and the minority community, or are activists, dissenters and the like. It is not being suggested that they should be spared if they have violated the laws. But the pattern reveals that the state is merely interested in targeting them without credible evidence and giving wide publicity to its actions, unconcerned with ultimate results.[55]

It is instructive to consider just how pivotal these raids have become. Between 2005 and 2014, during the UPA years, the Enforcement Directorate prosecuted 112 cases. In contrast, from June 2014 to the end of March 2022, it initiated 5,310 cases, conducted around 3,086 searches, and attached assets worth over INR 1,04,700 crore. In most cases, charge sheets were not framed. Writer Prem Shankar Jha remarks, 'How little these arrests have had to do with upholding the law of the land is revealed by the fact that in this entire time the ED was only able to secure 23 convictions—that is less than four to every 1000 indictments!'[56]

Accordingly, a pervasive climate of fear has taken hold in the country, particularly among opposition politicians and regional parties, undermining their ability to function as an effective counterweight to the government.

As is now evident, B.R. Ambedkar's original sin lay in assuming that a federal architecture could remain flexible and self-correcting without sustained investment in federal institutions, capacity-building, and genuine autonomy. Instead, the Constitution permitted a degree of Union encroachment into the state list through various provisions, the use of which has now become routine.

States have been unable to resist this erosion of federalism, constrained by a centralised party system, the absence of inner-party democracy, and the continuing influence of a colonial-style bureaucracy and police apparatus. When states do not conform, the Union can invoke Article 356 to impose president's rule, apply financial pressure, or deploy investigative agencies on tenuous grounds. The result is a pervasive climate of fear, with states disincentivised from acting boldly and taking a cautious role instead, uncertain of when the next lever of control might be applied.

12

RECENT PROBLEMS WITH FEDERALISM, THE FIFTEENTH FINANCE COMMISSION AND THE RISE OF KLEPTOCRATIC FEDERALISM

Retired IAS officer Amitabha Pande has identified three critical trends that have shaped the period from the post-Emergency era to the present, trends that have been markedly intensified since 2014.[1] First, is the spectre of terrorism, closely aligned with the assertive rhetoric of a new nationalism that proclaims zero tolerance. This has, in his view, led to the proliferation of both 'military and paramilitary forces to unprecedented levels.' This subject will be adequately dealt with in the chapter on Asymmetric Federalism. Second, the Union government's control over the design of economic welfare priorities allows it to determine what is necessary and to mobilise resources accordingly. These invariably bear the imprimatur of the Union government, and even the smiling image of a beneficent prime minister. States are reduced to a subaltern status, required to implement centrally determined priorities, significantly diminishing their own agency. This is significant in tracing the progressive 'telos' of the politicisation of economic benefits within the state List and their increasing appropriation by the Union government. Finally, Pande argues that the consequence of this trajectory is the 'emasculation of the capacity of the states to raise their own resources for their own priorities'.[2] Clearly the Centre wants to push its agenda at the cost of the states, and substantively so, which is why the taxing powers of the states have been severely attenuated. This observation is critical as it demonstrates how this creeping centralisation is substantive in character and is designed to further buttress the unitary trajectory that powers this new nationalism. It is for this reason that federalism assumes heightened importance at this juncture in the life of the republic. Indeed, the 2022 World Economic Forum at Davos 2022 identified 'fracture of interstate relations' as a principal risk for India.[3]

It is not just the matter of the Union government encroaching on the domain of the states' autonomy, but since 2014 we have seen a charismatic and powerful leader in place who has aggrandised executive power to a degree that has not been seen since Indira Gandhi was in power. Pande describes him as 'an authoritarian leader who believes he has the people's mandate to impose his will everywhere across the land, and that it is incumbent on all states to follow that without asking questions.'[4] So health and education have suffered, owing in large measure to the lack of funding and the deficiency of administrative expertise in these fields. As historian Romila Thapar remarks, 'The finances are available to the state but have to be deployed on these services rather than on gimmicks like the bullet train, or the tallest statue in the world, or the redesigning of the Central Vista in New Delhi, all of which were and are uncalled for.'[5] These are essentially vanity projects, and showcase where the government's real priority lies, which is invariably in the creation of cynosures of machismo.

We have also witnessed an unprecedented and insidious degree of political intervention in the workings of the Fifteenth Finance Commission and the amendments to the Terms of Reference (ToR). By updating the population figures of states from those in the 1971 census to those in the 2011 census, the Centre has in effect privileged UP and the cow belt at the cost of the southern and eastern states.[6] This change deliberately rewards states which have done the least to control their population growth but which remain politically critical for the BJP.

Whilst this may have been the most egregious alteration in the ToR, there is a pervasive unitary mindset at work which assumes that the Union government knows best. The ToR suggest that the Finance Commission should propose 'measurable performance-based incentives for States' taking into account their 'control or lack of it in incurring expenditure on populist measures'.[7] This is an unfounded assumption based on the glib binary that all central plans are anti-populist and all state plans are populist. Needless to say, there is no proper definition of what 'populism' entails.

This assumption also does a serious disservice to the many states schemes that have proved successful in terms of elevating social development indicators. We only need look at the free meal schemes launched in all panchayat and government-run schools in Tamil Nadu in 1956 by the then chief minister, K. Kamaraj as well as the Employment Guarantee Scheme launched in Maharashtra as early as 1972, to know that these schemes became massively successful and were ultimately approved and encouraged by the Union government. The education system reforms in Delhi and Himachal Pradesh have come into international notice for treating education as a necessity and not a luxury, as evidenced by the unprecedented prominence given to it in the state budgets (25 per cent).[8] When it comes to the Midday Meal schemes that various states run in their government schools, there have been many unintended consequences, such as increased school attendance and improved nutrition levels in children. Better child health metrics and lower infant mortality levels have led to a dramatic decline in the states' birth rates since many parents are choosing to have lesser children. These benefits indubitably outweigh the costs involved.

'Freebies' have also been touted as the most flagrant example of the states' priorities being misplaced. Self-serving examples are given of privileging Punjab farmers with free water and electricity calling this out as blatant policy delinquency. However, this disparagement does not extend to incentives offered by the Union government to industrialists in terms of production linked incentives (PLIs). There is also discrimination in nomenclature, between subsidies that are irredeemably bad and incentives, such as PLIs, which are good.

It is not evident that the PLI schemes, despite the braggadocio which attends the announcements or even the alleged outcomes, are really a prudent use for a government with scarce resources and many competing claims on it. In 2023, the prime minister announced with aplomb that India was a net exporter of mobile phones, when previously, before the PLI Scheme, it had been a net importer. What is omitted, one suspects by design, is that India has actually emerged as a hub for the assembly of such instruments rather than their manufacture, and this entails not only the cost of importing components for assembly but also the burden of government subsidies. Similarly, in relation to a semi-conductor plant in Gujarat which is supposed to generate 5,000 jobs, the government subsidy may amount to INR 3.2 crores per job, an unconscionably expensive way of subsidising jobs.[9] There is major opacity when it comes to data, making it unclear whether the subsidy paid is outweighed by the value added through this exercise, which raises the possibility that all this is done merely for optics.

Apart from paying for these incentives, the public exchequer has to bear the burden of writing off significant loans extended by public sector banks to corporate houses which have turned bad—over a ten-year period ending in 2024, public sector banks and scheduled commercial banks have written off loans worth INR 16.35 lakh crores, according to RBI data.[10] These kinds of write-offs belie the narrative of a government trying to prevent corruption and crony capitalism in the banking system.

This attack on alleged freebies doled out by state governments must be seen as part of a concerted policy by the Centre to cripple state-level attempts at addressing local needs. At the time of writing, Kerala, for example, has been under fiscal strain, reflecting its active commitment to social welfare policies in areas such as health and education. This stands in contrast to states which are ostensibly fiscally prudent but whose social indicators are dire.

This is a likely prelude to a much greater emphasis on centrally sponsored schemes (CSS). The numbers bear this out, as the Union Budget estimate for CSS in the year 2021-2022 was in the region of INR 3.8 lakh crores, in contrast to the Finance Commission transfers—including grants to states—which hardly amount to

INR 2.2 lakh crores. The constitutional stratagem employed by the Union government is to classify these grants under Article 282 of the Constitution, which provides for discretionary grants. This allows the Union government to expand its realm of control through the backdoor into areas it cannot otherwise operate in. The Union government's Swatch Bharat Abhiyan is an example of such a scheme, as the matter of sanitation falls exclusively under the state list. As economist Mihir Sharma states,

> All 'centrally sponsored schemes' were and are an assault on constitutional federal principles. Unsurprisingly, state governments resent the schemes, which are not designed in state capitals with their needs in mind—and, in some cases, are presented as gifts from the political leadership at the Centre, even when the administrative resources used for their implementation belong to the state government.[11]

This centralisation is profoundly unfortunate, as it runs counter to a strong undercurrent in contemporary economic thought that emphasises the efficacy of place-based and context-specific policies, grounded in local identities, loyalties and capabilities.

There are two further examples of this aggrandisement of power which have attracted relatively little attention, even though these have far-reaching ramifications. The first of these is ports, and the second is electricity. The Union government, anxious to burnish its image with international bankers, has been in privatisation mode, and one significant area for this policy is ports. It is not a coincidence that one of the largest private operators of ports in India is the Adani Group, whose meteoric rise is closely associated with the present prime minister's. The Major Ports Authorities Act of 2021 attempts to dramatically change the management model of ports. The oblique agenda is to prepare a blueprint for their privatisation, a concern echoed in the Parliament that such a law would 'provide the backdoor entry to crony capitalists in our ports.'[12]

The other serious transgression of the Union government has been the introduction of the Draft Electricity (Amendment) Bill of 2025, which allows the setting up of private distribution companies that can use the existing infrastructure of public utilities, permitting the consumer to choose their supplier of electricity. This has run afoul of state governments, and rightly so. The chief minister of Tamil Nadu, M.K. Stalin, puts it incisively,

> The state will be giving unbridled access to private place to supply power to select consumers, enabling them to use the already established distribution network of public sector companies, while states PSUs continue to bear the burden of investment in this network. These private companies are being allowed to use it without any investment or any responsibility for its maintenance.[13]

He goes on further to say that this bonanza will allow private players 'to cherry-pick profitable ventures without any social obligation'. Given that electricity is an essential service, this reform cripples the public sector, condemning them to financial distress, while denying them the opportunity to invest in infrastructure and maintenance.

Inter-State Transfers

The priorities of the Union government have an impact on the inequalities between states, which have only increased since the liberalisation of the economy in the early 1990s. Finance Commissions were tasked with the role of resource transfers, with the hope, right from the beginning, that this mechanism would be instrumental in redressing regional imbalances. Even in the 1980s, with the full panoply of the Planning Commission and a semi-command economy in place, this policy of redistributive transfers had signally failed, largely frustrated by resistance from the richer states and the entrenchment of regressive values in the poorer states. According to political scientist Paul Brass, 'the more advanced states have tended to receive higher per capital tax devolution than the less advanced states,'[14] the result being that disparities between states have become accentuated. Journalist Martin Wolf also cautions against the transfer of resources to poorer regions from richer ones, as 'with that is likely to come the dead hand of central control.'[15]

There was always a gap between what we call the cow belt states and the coastal states, but this gap has grown wider over the years. If we take 2014 as the benchmark, an average person in the three richest states—Kerala, Tamil Nadu and Maharashtra—was three times richer than an average person in the poorer states: Bihar, UP and Madhya Pradesh. There is an obvious asymmetry in terms of contribution and disbursal between Tamil Nadu and Bihar, according to economist Mihir Sharma. The differential in a per-head disbursement is INR 3,000, which is modest in absolute terms, but nonetheless significant and growing. Given the deteriorating conditions in the cow belt, what we see is a migration of labour and capital from the northern states to the southern states, even as subsidies flow the other way.

It becomes a source of controversy when the southern states see that the cow belt states show no appetite for adopting sensible policies such as spending more on public goods, improving gender inequalities, women's health, etc., despite being subsidised in the manner that they are. As T.M. Thomas Isaac, the former finance minister of Kerala, has put it, 'We are not against redistribution. All we are asking is: what has been the outcome of decades of redistribution? The Hindi-heartland states continue to remain underdeveloped, both socially and economically.'[16] In fact, in the case of Kerala, the financial crisis in the state was exacerbated, particularly when the Centre reduced Kerala's borrowing limit, forcing it to challenge the Union government's decision in the Supreme Court. The Supreme Court has refused any interim relief, and the case is pending to be heard by a Constitutional bench.

If we look at the growth of the per capita domestic product of states as of 2021, the disparities are only widening. UP, with Yogi Adityanath as the chief minister, clocked an abysmal 0.4 per cent growth in the four-year period of 2017–2021. Admittedly, in the last several years, UP's economic performance has improved, but that cannot be detached from the Union government's largesse to UP, including massive spending on infrastructure growth in the state. It is pertinent that 45 per cent of India's massive highway projects are in UP, which hugely inflates the state's GDP. Despite everything, Adityanath's performance as chief minister has been hailed by the Union government as though he were a messiah of growth and development. In contrast, if one looked at Telangana during the same four-year period, the per capita state domestic product increased by 26.4 per cent. Tamil Nadu jumped by 22.2 per cent, whereas Karnataka and Andhra Pradesh clocked a respectable 15 per cent each. The only bright spot in the cow belt was Bihar, which showed an impressive 21.8 per cent growth rate in the same four years, although on a pathetically low base.

In this context, the greater significance accorded to the state's population, which is apparent in the ToR of the Fifteenth Finance Commission, becomes important. States that have brought their TFR under control to near-European levels feel discriminated against, as states like UP and Bihar, whose TFR rates are substantially higher, are rewarded for their failure to enforce family planning. This lies at the heart of the issue, as a growing population reflects not merely a failure of governance but also reinforces underlying social indicators such as female illiteracy—at 26.8 per cent in Bihar compared to just 7 per cent in Kerala. A demographic divide thus begins to harden into a cultural chasm, further accentuated by linguistic differences, more particularly when Hindi-speaking states seek to assert their hegemony in the name of national integration, including efforts to elevate Hindi as the national language, a spectre likely to snowball in the aftermath of delimitation.

The prospect of imposing Hindi on non-Hindi speaking states, which had remained dormant since the 1960s, has recently resurfaced. At the commencement of the Constitution, English had been allowed to be used as the official language of communication for a period of fifteen years as per Article 343(2). This period would have ended in 1965, but the southern states, particularly Tamil Nadu, were opposed to the imposition of Hindi. This led to the enactment of the Official Languages Act in 1963 and its amendment in 1967, which allowed for the indefinite continuation of English in official communication, with official documentation to be published both in Hindi and English. Recently, another attempt was made to promote Hindi with the draft National Education Policy introduced in 2020, but this was removed after protests.

These fissures were just about tolerable in the national imagination when the Union government was seen as disinterested and fair, but once the venom of politics seeped into the equation, a heady and toxic mixture emerged which was ripe for causing future political turbulence. As economist Mihir Sharma argues, this 'goes to the heart of a central political fault line in India today, one that spans the social and economic spheres.' He argues that:

> New population numbers may mean that these states' share of seats in Parliament will decline, leaving them with little voice in New Delhi's decisions. Inter-regional transfers in India, already high, will increase. One state finance minister has complained that sending local taxes north is 'like throwing money down the well.'[17]

It is thus apparent that the more prosperous and advanced states deeply resent transfers to states that show little or no inclination to undertake any serious social reforms or generate quality public goods. This schism acquires a sharper political edge when it becomes apparent that the present Union government does not need the southern states to continue to remain in power—the support of the cow belt states alone can suffice. The age-old saying that 'the road to Delhi goes through Lucknow' has acquired even greater resonance now. With the spectre of delimitation looming, there is a very real apprehension that the political heft of the cow belt states will be amplified, potentially giving rise to a newly aggrieved minority: the southern states. Delimitation will only serve to exacerbate the growing fissures in a seriously frayed federal compact.

One of the essential features of the federal compact is that there is complete freedom to work in any part of India, a freedom which is enshrined in Article 19(1)(g) of the Constitution. Such freedoms are not readily available in other countries, such as China, where workers cannot go from one state to the other in search of work. Increased migration flow due to the free movement of labour, a non-negotiable principle for the European Union, is considered one of the biggest catalysts for Brexit. With growing economic disparities between the rich and the poor states, there is also increased inter-state migration within India. This has political consequences, prompting certain states to undertake populist measures, such as reserving jobs for locals and making a distinction between local domiciles and persons from other states. This distinction is contrary to the constitutional mandate since it seeks to make a distinction between Indians and restricts the freedoms of movement and work. It also seeks to reserve jobs not on the basis of economic or social needs, but on the basis of domicile. In Haryana, the state government sought to provide 75 per cent reservation for locals in private sector jobs with monthly salaries below INR 30,000. This was challenged in the high court of Punjab and Haryana. The appeal against the high court's order is pending before the Supreme Court.[18] Karnataka has also embarked on this policy. This is emblematic of an all too pervasive parochial mindset which undermines the very idea of India.

These incipient restrictions on internal migration are both unprecedented and extraordinary and have failed to attract the attention they should have. They augur turbulence, as future decades are going to see diminishing water resources in the northern and western parts of India, adversely affecting states like Rajasthan, Gujarat, Punjab, Haryana and UP. This portends to be a future flash point in Indian politics, as diminishing access to water will devastate agriculture and consequently, the employability of residents of these states, and possibly lead to mass migration. This will accentuate the North-South divide.

Encroachment on the Divisible Pool

Even as states are being financially squeezed by the obligation to implement centrally sponsored schemes (CSS) at their own expense, an additional source of resentment has emerged: the Union government's increasingly routine and liberal recourse to cesses and surcharges, which are excluded from the divisible pool of gross tax revenue shared between the Centre and the states. Under Article 270 of the Constitution, the Union government has the power to levy cesses in the event of extraordinary contingencies, such as the occurrence of war or natural calamities, but such cesses have now acquired a permanent basis, reducing the freedom of states to spend from the divisible pool, with the Union government keeping the cess revenues to itself. What is improper is that cesses are mandated to be spent on a specific purpose, but they are not in practice. Since 2014, the Comptroller and Auditor General of India (CAG) has noted that only a percentage of cesses raised have been spent on the purpose for which they were collected; there is complete opaqueness on what has happened to the balance. Economist Karthik Muralidharan argues that to strengthen the fiscal compact, there is traction in linking revenue streams to specific uses, such as petroleum taxes to public transportation.[19] However, given the opacity of government finances, such linkages are often lost in practice.

It is also the case that, up to 2024, the Modi government increased the number of cesses by 153 per cent. The share of cesses and surcharges in gross tax revenue rose from 10.4 per cent in 2011 to an estimated 18.4 per cent over the period 2021–22 to 2025–26. Correspondingly, the states' share in the divisible pool declined from 32 per cent in 2014 to as low as 26 per cent by 2021.

There are also serious issues with the Goods and Services Tax (GST): it was proclaimed as one of the greatest fiscal reforms in independent India, but what it attempts to do is to create a single market through the perverse conceit of shifting taxation from industrialised clusters to consumption areas. This policy only succeeds in reifying the status quo in terms of where industry is based—in states such as Tamil Nadu and Maharashtra, since they are efficient at what they do. This works against states like UP, which have a fledgling industrial base but desperately need to shift their rural workforce into industry and manufacturing. It also has serious ramifications on manufacturing states, which are denied taxing powers and revenue generated from the items they manufacture, as taxation now resides in the place of consumption. GST has further crippled the ability of the states to raise taxes, as their indirect tax rights are emasculated, save for the tax they collect on petroleum products, alcohol and electricity, as now GST serves as a uniform tax system. This particular tax has been lauded as 'One Nation, One Tax', as if it were the normative position worldwide. But as author Nilakantan R.S. observes, the only two other federal structures that are similar to India in terms of their size—the USA and China—do not have a GST or anything similar.[20] This is an important question to ponder.

Thus, through financial legerdemain, the Centre has encroached on the states' capacity to fund their current expenditures. This decline is from the acme of 65 per cent in 1955–56 to less than 38 per cent in 2019–20. Needless to say, the demands made on states have been increasing disproportionately vis-à-vis the growth in revenue, which has been largely static. India has a low direct tax base, forcing it to rely on the most sensationally regressive indirect taxation system in the world: nearly 56 per cent of the total tax revenue comes from indirect taxation. In recent years, there has been a huge windfall in terms of taxation on petroleum products, heavily skewed in favour of the Union government.

It is also relevant that the Union places constraints on the states' capacity to raise monies (INR 5.8 trillion in 2024), imposing a differential interest for market borrowings which is currently 10 per cent for states against the 7 per cent that the Union enjoys. This is wholly discriminatory, as it cripples the states' capacity to raise monies for items on its list. This asymmetry is particularly evident when the states are assigned 60 per cent of the total expenditure, with the Union taking on only 40 per cent.

When certain commentators[21] argue that the CSS trend started much before 2014, and that to blame the present Government for this would be unfair, no mention is made of the role the Planning Commission played as a consultative body for state governments in the formulation of public policy. The Planning Commission was dissolved in 2015, and so far, NITI Aayog has not stepped up sufficiently to perform that role. Also, the Planning Commission used to generate reliable data essential to determining whether policy goals had been met. Now states are dependent on what data the government chooses to disclose.

Instead of developing adequate state capacities to manage critical sectors such as education and health, there has been a greater emphasis on cash transfers to poor beneficiaries in recent years. This was spurred by the momentum created by the digital banking movement, which included the opening of 'Jan Dhan' accounts, which were widely showcased as a flagship initiative of the Modi government. Economist Rathin Roy notes that the Unified Payments Interface (UPI) was projected as a driver of growth, when all it was intended to do was simply to channel welfare benefits to the right recipients, at the same time making it apparent that these benefits were coming directly from the prime minister.

Unfortunately, direct transfers are not a substitute for developing and investing in public services, which only states and municipalities can do efficaciously. In the absence of that, there are serious implications for public policy that are not fully appreciated. As political scientist Niraja Gopal Jayal tellingly puts it, 'In general, the expectation that cash transfers will replace public services by sending people off, coins jingling in their pockets, to shop for food, health, and education on the market is tantamount to shrugging off public responsibility because it is administratively cumbersome.'[22] Politically also, it is not as rewarding since transforming an educational system is not tangible like constructing toilets or roads, and it takes time for the average voter to appreciate the former. So, public goods, such as health and education, get low priority because of intrinsic difficulties in their delivery and the lack of short-term returns which could guarantee success at elections; perhaps, there is also a desire to keep the population at large ignorant.

In India, education was traditionally a state subject, but it was inserted in the concurrent list as part of the Forty-second Constitutional Amendment in 1976. Thereafter, every Union government has been anxious to centralise education, a tendency noted by author Nilakantan R.S., who remarks that 'the three-language formula for schools is an example of India's centralising thrust.'[23] There is, of course, an implicit desire to promote Hindi and Sanskrit at the cost of English. This policy is wholly political in intent and bears no relationship to education. It is prudent to argue that education is best addressed at the state level, given the huge divergence in performance between states. However, the present government, having unveiled the National Education Policy in 2020, is intent on putting in place a single policy for all of India, irrespective of the chasms that exist, in what is termed as GER (Gross Enrolment Ratio), across states, particularly as one progresses from secondary to higher secondary levels. For example, the GER for UP in 2016–2017 was sixty-eight, for Kerala was ninety-nine, for Tamil Nadu was ninety-four and for Maharashtra was ninety-two. The Union government has attempted to coerce certain southern states, such as Tamil Nadu, Kerala, Karnataka to align with the National Education Policy by withholding substantial grants, which are liable to be paid to them under the Samagra Shiksha Abhiyaan, for school education from pre-school to class XII. The reason adduced is these states' refusal to implement the Pradhan Mantri Schools for Rising India (PMSHRI) scheme, which requires the acceptance of the three-language formula, one of which would be Hindi. In the case of Tamil Nadu and Kerala, INR 2,151 crores and INR 1,160 crores respectively were withheld in FY 2024-25, causing a financial crisis in the states' school systems.[24]

It is also relevant to point out that with the 2024 debacle of the 'One Nation One Exam' policy, centralisation of education has become even more controversial and discredited. The NEET exams (medical college entrance exams) conducted in 2024 led to anomalous results, with many students pointing to irregularities in the marking of papers, hinting obliquely at corruption and leading to the possible alienation of more than three million students. This has not helped the cause of centralisation of education.

Not content with the NEET debacle, the Union government has introduced the Draft UGC (Minimum Qualifications for Appointment and Promotion of Teachers and Academic Staff in Universities and Colleges and Measures for the Maintenance of Standards in Higher Education) Regulations of 2025, in terms of which the vice-chancellor for any university would be appointed by the chancellor/visitor of that university from a search-cum-selection committee of three experts also constituted by the chancellor/visitor. Since, in most state universities, the governor serves as chancellor or visitor, this raises concerns about institutional autonomy—given that governors are appointed, and effectively controlled, by the Union government. This sort of step not only devalues the autonomy of universities but also infringes on the principle of federalism. There is clearly an ideological angle at play, and one which only leads to tertiary education being diminished.

No modern society has transitioned into developed country status without substantial spending on human development, which includes education and health, child nutrition and the advancement of women. India spends barely 1.6 per cent on health and 3.9 per cent on education, and these percentages have been decreasing in the last several years but have not created any political furore. Economists Amartya Sen and Jean Drèze have long argued that India's record by all measures of human development has been abysmal, particularly in the post-liberalisation years, causing a great and growing chasm between the rich and the poor. These arguments have been buttressed by the work of economist Thomas Piketty in his magnum opus *Capital in the Twenty-First Century*[25] where he highlights the growing concentration of wealth amongst 0.001 per cent of Indians.

The matter of inequality in India, particularly post-COVID, is one that many economists find difficult to address. According to the World Inequality Lab, the gap between the top 1 per cent of the population and the rest has widened dramatically, with the former category receiving 23 per cent of the annual national income and owning 40 per cent of the national wealth. It points out that India boasts of having 271 dollar billionaires, with a further 94 being added in 2023.[26] This is happening at a time when the latest unemployment report published by the ILO shows a dismal picture of youth unemployment in India, with even the famed IIT graduates not getting jobs.[27] These eye watering disparities in both income and wealth have hugely impacted levels of inequality and opportunity, causing low levels of social mobility across generations. They also adversely affect economic growth, as the immiseration of the middle classes causes a slump in effective demand and a consequent drying up of investment, since there remains no catalyst to propel the virtuous cycle of growth and investment. This leaves India vulnerable to the middle-income trap that other BRICS economies, such as Brazil, seem to be caught in.

The trend towards further emasculation of state finances has been accelerated by the abrupt replacement of the hugely successful Mahatma Gandhi National Rural Employment Guarantee Scheme (MNREGA) with the VB-G-RAM-G Act 2025, an act of economic vandalism rushed through the Parliament in two days without any serious discussion. MNREGA was the flagship programme of the UPA government, the consensus being that it was the most consequential legislation it had passed. According to a study cited by political scientist Pratap Bhanu Mehta, MNREGA's 'general equilibrium effects were substantial: household earnings rose by about 14 per cent, poverty declined by roughly 26 per cent. The programme increased the bargaining power of labour, and led to higher private-sector wages, even for those not directly employed under the scheme.'[28]

MNREGA was genuinely transformative, providing employment to fifty million rural households, and was sought to be emulated by several countries in the global south, including Pakistan. It was particularly helpful during the COVID-19 pandemic, providing a lifeline to millions of people and propping up demand in rural areas. It embedded a rights-based paradigm: anyone who was willing to work could demand employment. Its social impact on women, for example, was singular—MNREGA was availed by women to the extent of 57 per cent, and in Tamil Nadu alone nearly 80 per cent. It also became a spur to decentralisation of power, uniquely empowering gram panchayats in relation to micro projects, such as the building of wells and setting up of plantation orchards.

The main impact of its withdrawal will be felt on the states' finances. The states' contribution to MNREGA was limited to 10 per cent. But the new scheme, as per economist Jean Drèze, requires states to contribute 40 per cent, and if states wanted to spend more on projects than the Centre's state-wise allocation, then would have to fund it entirely on their own.[29]

Even more disturbing is the fact that the new law imposes upon states the legal liability of providing employment or, in the absence of employment, paying unemployment allowance, with no guarantee of requisite funding from the Centre. He concludes by saying that far from revamping India's employment guarantee, the new scheme sinks it 'by demotivating the states and disempowering the workers'.[30]

It is pertinent to note that the Hindu Right gets most intemperate and agitated when it comes to the failure to implement directive principles which relate to UCC and cow slaughter (Articles 44 & 48 respectively) but do not evince the same passion when it comes to Article 39(c), which stipulates that the state shall direct its policy towards ensuring that 'the operation of the economic system does not result in the concentration of wealth and means of production to the common detriment.' Article 38(2) mandates the state 'to eliminate inequalities in status, facilities and opportunities, not only amongst individuals but also amongst groups of people residing in different areas or engaged in different vocations.' These also are directive principles, but manifestly play no role in policymaking and are not often raised in public discourse.

It is not a coincidence that the economies of cow belt states are largely agriculture-based and their populations are mostly engaged in subsistence farming. In fact, what is disturbing is a gradual increase in the number of people working in the agricultural sector—almost 60 per cent, when agriculture only constituted 16 per cent of the GDP in 2024. It has become something of a cliché that the key to spurring economic growth and reducing inequalities lies in the reform of the farming sector, the intent being to move surplus labour from low-income rural occupations into high-paying urban jobs. Making farming efficient is only one part of the problem. The other part, which entails educating the workforce to enable it to become economically productive, is mostly disregarded. Education and skill-development play a central role in enabling people to move up the value chain. We may have missed the boat on that, as many low-skilled jobs are being rendered obsolete by AI and robotics. Unfortunately, other than hosting ubiquitous investment jamborees, there seems to be no real political agenda in the cow belt to break the employment impasse.

If we look at the data, the states that have the least proportion of rural households are the most prosperous, such as Tamil Nadu (35 per cent) compared to UP (75 per cent), one of the poorest states. Kerala has 27 per cent of its households engaged in agriculture compared to Madhya Pradesh, which has 71 per cent. Even more striking is the level of urbanisation in states which are not so dependent on agriculture—in Tamil Nadu it is 48 per cent compared to UP which is 22 per cent.[31]

A state's economic prosperity, development, and urbanisation depend on substantial investments in public goods—quality education and healthcare, clean water and air, a well-functioning judiciary, and most importantly, the greater participation of women in the workforce—all of which require active and effective engagement by state governments. For example, statics released by the Centre for Monitoring Indian Economy (CMIE) show that the female labour participation rate (FLPR) stood at 8.8. per cent in June 2023, whilst in Bangladesh it was 36.668 per cent in 2023 (CEIC Data), a shocking gap between the two countries.[32] Even Afghanistan, prior to the Taliban takeover, had a larger proportion of women in its workforce than India.[33] This discrepancy has great economic resonance, as the empowerment of women is not a mere slogan but has been shown to yield substantial economic gains if implemented. In a 2015 study called 'The Power of Parity: How Advancing Women's Equality Can Add $12 Trillion to Global Growth', the consultancy firm McKinsey captured the huge economic gains countries stand to achieve by extending the involvement of women in the economy, citing a possible surge in the GDP by as much as 5–20 per cent.[34] In this regard, author Swati Narayan has demonstrated that India's poorer neighbours, such as Nepal and Bangladesh, have overtaken India—excluding states like Kerala and Tamil Nadu—in social indicators such as literacy, life expectancy, nutrition and gender equality.[35] Nepal even has a larger GDP than UP and Bihar combined.

In a new and searing indictment of post-Independence economic policies, Princeton economist Ashoka Mody has argued that:

> The bogeyman of the alleged socialist legacy has given India's market-friendly 'liberalisers' license to pursue an economic path that generates ever more inequality while continuing the neglect of public goods necessary for shared progress. Leaders and public intellectuals—irrespective of their rhetoric and professed ideologies—have always paid only lip service to public goods. Particularly worrisome, they have pursued a mythical 'development' that causes possibly irreparable damage to the environment, a public good essential for current and future generations of Indians.[36]

This last part of the observation is directed against the reframing of the term 'development' to refer only to the expansion of physical public infrastructure.

It has been widely suggested that there is an almost umbilical link between the growing inequality in society and the epic surge in corporate profits—rising from around 50 per cent for the top twenty companies in 2011 to 70 per cent in the fiscal year 2020—driven by the centralisation of politics and business. Political scientist Neelanjan Sircar concludes that this political 'consolidation requires the centralisation of political appeal. In order to achieve this outcome, the ruling BJP must mobilise significant political resources, deploying media resources and funding political machinery.'[37] Thus, the growth of an oligarchic kleptocracy poses threats to democracy, market capitalism and society at large, and this is reflected in the growth of dollar billionaires, a phenomenon predicted by Aristotle over two millennia ago.[38]

Journalist Martin Wolf has commented on this development, stating:

> It is a great failing to encourage the emergence of a rigged capitalism, which destroys the legitimacy of the market economy and of the state that protects and promotes it. It is a great failing, above all, to cement power by creating a pluto-populist coalition based on self-seeking at the top and rage at the middle and bottom. It is all too easy to motivate people by hatred and fear, and so by a tribalism that divides the world into the 'good people' like us, and everybody else. But as society becomes more plutocratic, the sinews that bind citizens together snap.[39]

This is an important observation as to the direction in which India is going.

Federalism and a Presidential System

India at present is witnessing the greatest centralisation of government powers than at any other time in the country's history. It is for this reason that talk of having a presidential system has come into vogue.[40] It is proclaimed as the panacea for all our problems, resonating with a latent preference for authoritarianism in much of Indian middle-class thinking and mindset. The Pew Research Center's Spring 2023 Global Attitudes Survey found that even more than the Russians or the Turks, Indians are seduced by the 'strong man' syndrome, that is, rule by a strong leader without interference from parliament or courts, and that as many as 67 per cent of those polled sought this paradigm. Even more remarkable is that 85 per cent of those polled were in favour of military rule.[41]

The BJP has long spoken of ushering in a presidential system, but not in the way it is normally understood. As per political activist Sudheendra Kulkarni, the prime minister 'wants to convert our system into a kind of presidential system where it is him versus all others.'[42] In nations that have a presidential system, such as the United States and Brazil, there is usually a strong upper house, for example, the senate in the US and the federal senate in Brazil. These bodies do not just have a different pattern of representation from their lower houses, but provide space for equal say to all states, a stratagem to maintain the necessary checks and balances. When the matter of having a presidential system is raised in India, it is posited solely as a substitute for the current Westminster-style parliamentary system of representation, in which electorates vote for parties rather than individuals. This vision assumes that such a presidential system would be grafted onto the existing model—retaining a directionless and effete upper house in the form of the Rajya Sabha, which provides little meaningful representation to the states. To compound this, we have the Supreme Court, which, with a few exceptions, operates in the shadow of the executive and tries to avoid conflict, even at the cost of sacrificing constitutional principles. In effect, this sort of presidential system would have no guardrails against a dictatorship.

This model gives rise to great apprehension, as does the preliminary proposal to hold national and state elections simultaneously, which initially appears innocuous and is often justified on the ground of reducing the cost of hosting elections and minimising their disruptive effect on day-to-day governance. This policy has been supported by the 2024 report of a high-level committee headed by former Indian president, Ram Nath Kovind. This argument must be understood as a precursor to a presidential model, with the oblique purpose of denying the Indian electorate an effective choice between voting separately for different parties at the national and the state level. The intent is to belittle state-level issues which would inevitably become subsumed in the national narrative, rendering state-level politics and regional parties which thrive on them irrelevant and marginal to the political discourse. It is true that simultaneous elections were the norm until 1971. However, since then, the momentum of federalism has thrown up a number of regional parties, and as public policy scholar Yamini Aiyar puts it, 'these parties have been far more effective in responding to regional and ethnic identity assertions, and their presence in national politics is linked to their ability to negotiate regional claims on the national stage.'[43]

More practically, there is a concern about the feasibility of such a stratagem, since if the government loses the confidence of the house, the imposition of a straitjacket of fixed terms would invite more horse-trading and corruption. The United Kingdom experimented with this fixed term idea, and after a few years discarded it for being impractical.

The way politics has developed post 2014 is with the centralisation of power in the hands of the current prime minister and Union home minister, who regularly and routinely change chief ministers at the slightest sign of anti-incumbency or at any hint of political assertion. This cavalier approach to Union-state relations, even within the same party, is symptomatic of a broader malaise in which state party units have become subordinate to the national party, stripped of autonomy and subject to the caprice of the central leadership, last seen in the bad old days of the Congress when Congress 'High Command' dominated internal decision-making. In the present case, the BJP government's treatment of state governments led by its own party members is scarcely different.

Federalism and Political Parties

Political parties are seminal to democracy, since they represent communities and ideologies that allow the political process to become a marketplace of ideas, not dissimilar to an economic marketplace. However, despite this perceived centrality, the notion of a 'political party' is itself a surprisingly extra-legal activity. The only statutory recognition of political parties is under section 29A of the Representation of People Act, which includes a stipulation that a political party shall bear true faith and allegiance to the Indian constitution. What is bizarre is that the Indian constitution, despite being one of the most compendious constitutions in the world, which seeks to deal with everything within its purview, including the formation and running of cooperative societies, does not appear to recognise political parties as entities that are required to adhere to any set of rules. There are over 2,500 registered political parties in India, and establishing one is relatively straightforward.

With the increasing feudalisation of political parties without the accompanying civilities and protocols as to succession, a central feature of democracy gets lost. The centrality of inner party democracy at the state level is critical to how the party develops, mobilises support and funding, and formulates the agenda that ultimately shapes its manifesto. In its absence, it is difficult to see how politics can serve any useful purpose in a democracy, beyond becoming a mere validation, a command performance, for an increasingly entrenched personality cult.

One of the advantages of having political parties at the grassroots level was in the area of welfare delivery, where patronage networks facilitated the distribution of benefits, which in turn enhanced the standing of party members and gave them prominence within the community. The shift to direct transfers into bank accounts, enabled by the UPI system and opening of Jan Dhan accounts under schemes exclusively associated with the prime minister, appears designed to burnish his own personality cult. Local party members have been reduced to acting as marketing agents for such schemes without any visible agency within their community. It also has huge ramifications for the federal structure, as it diminishes the role of the local party and grassroots-level politicians in several critical ways which are intertwined. Leakages and corruption in the welfare system may have been attenuated, but it has come at the cost of creating the architecture for a centralised oligarchic kleptocracy which has seized the political and economic narrative.

Even this cynosure policy of the government, Digital India, is now being contested by no less than the Comptroller and Auditor General of India (CAG). In a recent report, it has been pointed out that 'direct benefit transfers' have failed in many critical respects, showing thousands of crores being diverted to ineligible beneficiaries largely due to poor data integration, compounded by defective verification processes. Invariably, these deficiencies affect the poorest of the poor and the voiceless, but the paradigm of a Digital India has transfixed the nation, such that these delinquencies are either neglected or buried on the third or fourth page of newspapers.[44]

These discrepancies likely stem in part from the government's approach to data and statistics, an area where India once stood as a model for the Global South, but whose credibility has in recent years been eroded by attempts to shape statistical outcomes for political ends. These policies have even led the IMF to degrade India's GDP data to C, citing deficiencies in capturing the informal sector and spending patterns in its annual review.[45]

Party Funding and Federal Encroachment

To buttress a powerful regional constituency, local funding to parties is required. Financial restrictions, which otherwise shackle the NGO sector through controls on foreign and corporate funding, do not seem to apply to political parties. It was during Rajiv Gandhi's prime ministership that companies were allowed to fund political parties, which is why raising white monies to spend on elections is much easier. Monies received by political parties is also exempt from income tax. As journalist Devangshu Datta pointedly puts it, 'in India circa 2022, the ease of doing business is moot. The ease of doing charity is non-existent, but the ease of doing politics is as good as it could get, and setting up a party is the smoothest route for money laundering.'[46]

Yet, whilst political parties are critical to the functioning of a democracy, there are no proper regulations on their finances and spending; indeed, no proper stipulations exist as to what they can do or who they can represent. Many openly align with caste or religious formations. Thus, there is a compelling argument to bring political parties within the constitutional framework to ensure they function properly and with propriety.

The importance of raising monies is critical to maintaining local autonomy, and it is the changing nature of electoral funding which is undermining local and regional interests and assisting the centralisers. The costs of elections have been escalating over the last few years, and it was even suggested that in the bitterly contested state elections in West Bengal in 2022, which resulted in a Trinamool Congress victory over the BJP, the budget for each constituency was not less than INR 200 crores per seat. Whether this is true or not is difficult to confirm, but given the scale of constituencies, along with the costs of logistics, publicity, and campaign paraphernalia, electioneering undoubtedly entails enormous expenditure. Accordingly, it is difficult to see how the local BJP cadres could have raised these kinds of monies for elections, and one can assume that funds must have been sent from New Delhi. But it is relevant to note that election expenditure extends beyond campaign costs, to include post-electoral shenanigans such as bribing MLAs to make them defect and horse-trading. This has compounded electoral costs which have spiralled sensationally, partly because of population growth, but also, as author James Crabtree observed, with 'other elements of a modern campaign—pollsters, political consultants, roadside posters, television adverts and Facebook posts—meant that the result fused electoral techniques from the nineteenth and twenty-first centuries, and incurred the expense of both.'[47]

This insidious process of centralisation of big corporate capital and election funding was sought to be turbocharged by a very controversial but wickedly clever device known as the Electoral Bond Scheme introduced in 2017. Electoral bonds secured complete anonymity for the donor, a feature of inestimable value when the reward is access to the control and management of strategic businesses without any accountability. This scheme was controversial on many counts and was successfully challenged in the Supreme Court. The court held that anonymous electoral bonds violated the right to information protected under Article 19 of the Constitution[48] but participants in the scheme faced no adverse consequences.

The need to examine the donors and what a possible quid pro quo would entail was left to *The Hindu* newspaper which showed that forty-one companies, which later came to donate INR 2,592 crores to the BJP, were raided by the Enforcement Directorate and other agencies fifty-six times. Of this amount, INR 1,853 crores were donated through electoral bonds after the raids against them. Even more extraordinary is that some thirty-eight corporate groups received a bounty of government projects worth INR 3.8 lakh crores after donating electoral bonds to the BJP. As our dear Home Minister likes to say, it is important to 'understand the chronology'.[49]

For a Union government obsessed with the aggrandisement of power and a desire for limitless funding for elections the prospect of enabling the encashment of economic rents and the capacity to assist their corporate friends and donors—particularly through the granting of rights that permit the encroachment of promising and lush areas, virgin forests and mineral-bearing regions—can prove to be too tempting to ignore. Centralised funding, channelled through a small group of trusted corporates and enabled by encroachments into the state list, further erodes the autonomy of state governments, leaving them dependent on the party at the Centre for electoral finance. This signals the return of the 'High Command' brand of politics backed and sustained by oligarch kleptocrats, which diminishes the federal impulse.

The standard defence of the Hindu Right is that all this is not new to India. The Congress party, too, fostered powerful relationships with industrial houses such as the Birlas and the Bajajs since the time of the independence struggle. Dhirubhai Ambani, the founder of Reliance, was allegedly close to Indira Gandhi and Pranab Mukherjee, and it is said that much of his stellar rise owes itself to tweaks in policy that favoured his businesses. But the larger issue today is that the private sector is involved in businesses which have strategic importance, such as ports, electricity, oil and gas—all areas which were formerly in the hands of the public sector. Most of the industrial behemoths are family-owned and closely held, which has led to sensational growth in the wealth of certain families.

Given the fact that India's competition and anti-trust laws are at a fledgling stage and are largely considered ineffectual, particularly in the context of domestic companies operating amid stark economic disparities and a contracting middle class, these factors do not bode well for society at large.

The oligarch argument has been surcharged by the observations of the former Reserve Bank deputy governor, Viral Acharya, who has identified the 'Big Five'—Reliance, Tata, Aditya Birla, Adani and Bharti Telecom—companies, he argues, that are growing at the expense of small businesses.[50] He argues that this exponential rise in the industrial concentration of these behemoths has enabled these companies to charge higher product prices than their competitors, entrenching persistent core inflation. According to journalist Rajrishi Singhal, Indian anti-trust laws only find fault with dominance by a single entity and do not consider collective dominance as an economic problem.[51] We return to Adam Smith who, in his book *Wealth of Nations*, wrote that competition favours 'equality, liberty and justice', something sadly absent in our increasingly centralised and mercantilist economy.

Conservatives tend to view the configuration of a renewed federal compact within the revival of the putative Inter-State Council—one of the recommendations of the Sarkaria Commission back in 1983. But this so-called panacea depends heavily on the goodwill of the Union government, a commodity in very short supply these days. It is astonishing that since 1985, the Inter-State Council has met only sixteen times: so much for the consultative paradigm.

It is not as if the government is bereft of the paraphernalia required to widen and enrich the discourse, such as white papers, select committees, parliamentary debates, or structured consultations with the states, supported by relevant data and policy options. Author P. Sainath has alleged that legal teams in the pay of interested corporates such as Adani were involved in the drafting of the controversial farm laws, which were promulgated by ordinance in a manner reminiscent of a medieval fiat.[52] Whether this is true or not we cannot say, but the whole process was undeniably opaque, and as such demonstrates no will or desire on the part of the Union government to engage in discussion. Even after the bloody nose the electorate inflicted upon the BJP in the 2024 elections, partially on account of the displeasure earned by them by the introduction of farm laws, their mindset has not changed. At the time of writing, the Union government is in the process of bringing major amendments to criminal laws and the justice system without any consultation with the states, even though admittedly law and order is a state subject.

What can be done about all this? Perhaps we need to deconstruct our constitutional arrangements to serve the greater cause of federalism, to create new centres of power which would involve much greater devolution. The 'parchment barriers' of the constitution would be respected only when, in the famous words of former US president James Madison, 'ambition is made to counteract ambition.'[53]

A consultative paradigm is at odds with a political trajectory which exercises a gravitational pull to the Centre, and one that is intractably stacked against the states. There was no level playing field to begin with, but the decimation of local politics and state parties, combined with the corporatisation of key sectors such as land, labour and agriculture, has only served to configure a new and ominous compact, one that exists between the Union government and its corporate backers and fundraisers. In this new paradigm, Indian people count for little, except as voting fodder transfixed by the drumbeat of the new nationalism. This is undeniably the nature of this new kleptocratic federalism, one which owes its provenance to the constitutional arrangements arrived at post-Independence.

13

ASYMMETRICAL FEDERALISM

Asymmetrical federalism is generally a type of union in which different constituent sub-states possess different rights; in which one or more of them has more autonomy than the other sub-states although they enjoy the same constitutional status. It is an acknowledgement of diversity and plurality. In this respect, India is not unique in having asymmetrical arrangements in its federal structure. Germany, Belgium, Canada and Spain are all examples of this kind of federalism. However, from the very beginning there has been controversy, as professor of political science Rekha Saxena has stated, 'on the question whether asymmetry in federal structuring is a slippery terrain leading to secession or conducive to national unity.'[1]

In the early years of the Indian republic with the backdrop of a bitter and bloody Partition, there was a pervasive desire for nation-building and the view was that special arrangements for certain states were one-off cases, temporary arrangements to be endured on the way to nationhood. Contemporary thinking is more sympathetic to the asymmetric narrative, seeing it as a means to avoid secession. It is often forgotten that the country that influenced India's federalism the most, the United Kingdom, is itself an example of asymmetric federalism, with separate Scottish and Welsh assemblies Moreover, Scotland has its own distinct legal system, which is rooted in civil law traditions rather than English common law.

The notion of asymmetric federalism is something which, given the nature of the Indian reality, was regrettably discarded in favour of a unitary construct to consolidate and homogenise the country. This shift towards homogenisation becomes even more striking when one considers the inescapable truth that two-fifths of the country, that is the 562 princely states, had never been part of the colonial construct to begin with.

Unlike the relatively fixed borders of many European states, the colonial state had layered and uneven territorial arrangements. There were gradations of sovereignty and control, particularly in regions such as the Northeast. In what later became Pakistan, areas like Baluchistan—formally integrated only in 1955—along with other tribal regions, existed under distinct administrative and legal arrangements that set them apart from the rest of the country. So, then the idiom in the high noon of Nehruvianism was the perceived need for modernity, nation-building and the creation of a socially just and equitable society, a desire that could easily collapse into a more sinister project to impose artificial homogeneity on a culturally and linguistically diverse nation. As philosopher Ernest Gellner has put it, 'Nationalism is the congruence of power and culture.'[2] This raises the issue of whose culture? As culture and power invariably reside together, the prospect of imposition of a uniform culture and language becomes very feasible. To some extent, creating linguistic states in the early part of independent India was an important device to defuse what were seen as fissiparous tendencies, but even this has been overtaken by issues such as tribal needs and economic discrimination.

One of the earliest legal issues arising from asymmetric federalism involved the accession of Sikkim as a state. The accession was done under Article 2 of the Constitution and by way of the Thirty-sixth Amendment Act of 1975, which retained some of the historical features of the princely state. These features included the reservation of seats for ethnic and religious sub-groups through Article 371-F. This legislation was impugned in *R.C. Poudyal v. Union of India*[3] on the grounds that it offended the basic features of the Constitution, which were secularism, democracy and republicanism. The essence of the challenge was that it apparently violated the principle of 'One

Man One Vote', as the degree of reservation was not proportionate to the population of the reserved communities. So, according to legal scholar Sudhir Krishnaswamy, 'the central question in *Poudyal* was the extent to which Parliament's power to admit new States is constrained by the basic principles of Indian constitutionalism and the need to maintain parity between States.'[4] The Supreme Court accepted that whilst Parliament must adhere to the foundational principles of the Constitution, that adherence need not involve complete equality among the states, so the matter of weighted electorates was accepted.

This judgement has raised controversy. One of the leading authorities on Indian federalism, Louis Tillin has characterised Sikkim as an outlier, saying that much like other Northeastern states of India, Sikkim is essentially peripheral to the federal structure. However, as Krishnaswamy rightly observes that by recognising the special status of Sikkim, the court in the *Poudyal* case 'effectively locates a constitutional principle of asymmetric federalism in its interpretation of Article 2.'[5] These are examples of situations where federal laws do not automatically apply. For instance, under Article 371A, central laws have no automatic application to Nagaland unless they are confirmed by the state legislature. In fact, the state enjoys full autonomy in relation to customary practices and laws in relation to land ownership and resources, as does Manipur (Article 371C) and Arunachal Pradesh (Article 371H), the intent being to protect the land and rights of tribals. But examples of states with restrictions on ownership of property are not just confined to the periphery: Uttarakhand, Himachal Pradesh, and parts of Jharkhand and Chhattisgarh all have property ownership restrictions for outsiders trying to buy land in these states.

There has always been a dissonance between areas of post-Partition settlement and areas which were distinctive and inhabited by people who were racially and ethnically different from North Indians. Even during debates of the Constituent Assembly, it was accepted that the people of the Northeast were to be granted autonomous distinct councils.

In India, two areas remained outside of the largely unitary framework: the princely state of Jammu and Kashmir, or the part of it that remained with India and the Northeast. These areas are seen as sources of angst by Delhi, having witnessed violence and separatism; as areas to be subdued and integrated in order to reify the very basis of Indian statehood and nationalism. In the case of Jammu and Kashmir which remains an outlier, being the only Muslim-majority state in India, the abrogation of Article 370—a constitutional provision that had guaranteed a measure of autonomy to the state under the terms of accession—was projected as being a stratagem to include the state within India and forestall any talk of it joining Pakistan. This action taken in August 2019 had long been on the agenda of Hindu nationalists, although in reality much of Article 370 had been hollowed out, with many of the laws applicable in India being automatically replicated in the troubled state. The symbolic importance of this act cannot be understated, as it is a powerful proclamation of the 'puissance' of the unitary state, more so in the way it was done without the pretence of consultation and under a dubious invocation of Article 356.

The legal challenge to the abrogation of Article 370 was dismissed by a 5-judge bench of the Supreme Court.[6] In effect, Article 370 had, over the years, been diluted, but there remained the question whether such abrogation could occur without the consent of the elected assembly. According to the Supreme Court judgement, it could. Pratap Bhanu Mehta says it was done by way of a constitutional legerdemain. He says,

> It was mildly reassuring that the Court held that the modification to Article 367 by Constitutional Order (CO) 272 had the effect of amending Article 370 and was ultra vires [Article 370(1)(d)]. This is an important principle because it prevents the government from introducing a backdoor amendment to an article of the Constitution by amending another article. If an article is to be amended, the amendment has to be specific to it. But given that CO 272 is at the heart of the process, should not the whole exercise be considered to be rendered suspect or malafide?[7]

A very valid question, and one to which there is no plausible answer. Neither is the argument that Article 370 was temporary particularly persuasive when at least nine other states are mentioned in Part XXI of the Constitution, as having 'temporary, transitional and special provisions' applicable to them. There is no explicit expiry date mentioned for all these states, so what happens to all such provisions?

Hamin Ast, a self-proclaimed biography of the controversial Article 370, presents a critical and persuasive review of the legal grounds for abrogation. The main problem it points out with the abrogation is the conflation of the approval given by the governor, a blatantly political appointee, with the concurrence of the people via the means of the Legislative Assembly, a requirement of the provision. At the time when the abrogation took place in August 2019, the J&K state assembly was in suspended animation with the state under President's rule. The representative of the president at the time was the state's governor, Satyapal Malik, a former politician. As the book tersely puts it,

> … when the Governor of Jammu and Kashmir purportedly gave his concurrence on behalf of the Jammu and Kashmir Government, he was not acting in his independent capacity, but rather as a delegate of the President. In practical effect, this amounted to the President seeking his own concurrence before exercising the powers conferred by clause (1) of Article 370. Can such self-concurrence be deemed to satisfy the requirements of law? The short answer is no.[8]

This analysis goes to the root of the matter—the people of the state, represented by their Legislative Assembly, were deliberately bypassed through the use of a compliant governor. In this instance, the governor was effectively acting on behalf of the president, who had initiated the entire process through an ordinance.

In an excellent study of post-abrogation Kashmir by the journalist Anuradha Bhasin, she dismissed the hoopla attending the abrogation, concentrating instead on the shocking policy of shutting down local protests and media. She says that 'the world's largest democracy has fully integrated an entire region by turning it into a vast prison to ensure compliance to the new mantra of absolute silence and supreme subjugation.'[9]

The state of Jammu and Kashmir has been reduced to a union territory, albeit one with a legislative assembly, whilst Ladakh is a union territory without a legislative assembly. Delhi is another union territory, and a controversial one at that. I say controversial because in 2021, the Union government enacted the Government of National Capital Territory of Delhi (Amendment) Act which clarified that the expression 'Government' referred to in any law to be made by the Legislative Assembly shall mean the 'lieutenant governor'. The new law vests the lieutenant governor with the power to override laws passed in the Legislative Assembly, thereby disempowering elected MLAs. The original argument for the creation of union territories was that they were either too small for full statehood or, for reasons of cultural autonomy, could not be merged with an adjoining state. However, it has now metamorphosed into a device for imposing centralised rule on certain areas and to undermine the federal paradigm.

The perplexing part of the narrative against asymmetric federalism is that it is not founded on any principle. Even at the time of writing, when the country is in the feverish grip of the most virulent nationalist sentiments and people who speak of greater autonomy of states are branded as anti-national, there is little constitutional basis for the claim that only a single unitary structure with a homogeneous cultural narrative is legitimate. This ignores the State's discussions with persons representing the Nagas, for example, making allowances for Nagas to have a separate flag, coinage, currency, and substantive state autonomy. Ironically, the very same thing would be considered treasonous if discussed in relation to Kashmir.

There is a strong and compelling argument in favour of asymmetric federalism which is independent of any security or religious considerations: that people who share a common linguistic and cultural identity may want to preserve it and not want to be swamped by the rest of India. If we look at citizenship laws, a new category of citizenship was introduced vide section 6A of the Citizenship (Amendment) Act of 1985 at the instance of the state of Assam, to address the influx of Bangladeshi refugees post the 1971 war, the logic being that Assamese culture should be protected from being undermined by Bengali migration.

Similarly, whilst the Constitution made extensive provisions for affirmative action in favour of scheduled tribes throughout India, provisions made for scheduled tribes in the Northeast were very different from those for the rest of India. According to political science professor Sanjib Baruah, in this way 'the indirect rule regime of the colonial era was given a new lease of life.'[10] The Sixth Schedule of the Constitution provides for autonomous districts and autonomous regions, to be governed by elected councils with the authority to levy taxes and to establish courts for the dispensation of justice according to customary law. However, because of the Naga insurgency, elections to the hill district councils were never held. When the state of Nagaland was created in 1963, Article 371A was inserted into the Constitution, which broadly provided the same protections as the Sixth Schedule. In reality, of course, there was a paucity of state institutions to exercise and legitimise this autonomy, which meant that the governor of the state, appointed by the Union government, would effectively exercise power. This pattern has recurred intermittently in Kashmir since Independence, with the Union government in Delhi periodically undermining the democratic process. In fact, the liberal recourse to the appointment of such governors is mimetic of colonial rule.

Whatever paper concessions were offered to communities in the Northeast and in the state of Jammu and Kashmir, in an attempt at asymmetrical federalism, are greatly outweighed by the denials of basic human rights which most Indians, until recently, would regard as part of the State's patrimony. So, AFSPA, an acronym for the Armed Forces Special Powers Act, has been liberally enforced in these states. This colonial legislation (revived by Nehru in 1958) is highly controversial in that it vested the most sweeping powers on government security forces, including the police and military, giving them 'carte blanche' to open fire on civilians on subjective grounds such as the need to maintain public order. These powers further extended to destroying any property, including a house or a dwelling area, which, in the security forces' view, may be a place where an attack may be launched, as well as to arresting persons without warrant on mere suspicion. Recourse against the misuse of AFSPA is negligible, and there are no reported cases of any substantive redress.

The conclusion one can draw as to asymmetrical federalism is that it is used invariably as a cynical political stratagem by politicians for purely opportunistic reasons. In states where minorities (with respect to the general populace) are either a majority or have a large presence, such as in Kashmir, Assam or Manipur, nationalist rhetoric, alleged security concerns and jingoism are often amplified. In this process, the concerns and interests of local inhabitants are pointedly ignored, and they are not treated as citizens. The Manipur crisis illustrates the danger of Hindutva partisanship in penalising a Christian minority, the Kukus.

Colonial laws in relation to security are imposed almost on a permanent basis as if constitutional rights can be suspended at will. It is in these peripheral areas such as Kashmir, Assam and the states in the Northeast that the matter of citizenship is the most fraught with controversy arising from their histories. But these tensions have deepened by virtue of government policy, aided by the Supreme Court's judgement as regards the abrogation of Article 370. As Pratap Bhanu Mehta pointed out, the abrogation by stealth is a new form of repression 'reminiscent of the Reichstag or Chinese constitutional ideology that sees federalism as an obstacle to a strong state and homogenous culture.'[11] If unchecked, he foresees India becoming a union of union territories, reshaped at the whim of the Centre, driven by a deep anxiety about division and secession.

To put matters in perspective, it is a vainglorious conceit that India has endured as a single political entity from 1947, something which our political class exults in, unlike Pakistan which has gone through a division. But historian Perry Anderson[12] points out that many post-colonial states persist, notwithstanding how heterogenous they are or how artificially their borders were defined. He gives the example of Africa where, other than Sudan and now possibly Libya (likely because of Western intervention), all the other fifty-one countries continue in the same form as they were when colonial powers departed from the continent. Similarly, in Asia, other than the division between Malaysia and Singapore, the same countries persist. So it would be safe to say that the unchanged status of India is the norm and not the exception.

14

CITIZENSHIP AND THE CITIZENSHIP AMENDMENT ACT

In colonial times, the question of citizenship was inextricably linked to the idea of a nation, and as the colonial masters repudiated the idea that India was a nation, Indian citizenship was a chimera. The idea of citizenship in India, then, is a post-colonial concept where the founding principle is 'jus soli'—citizenship by birth—in contradistinction to what is known as 'jus sanguinis', that is, citizenship through ancestry. These two legal concepts have different origins. 'Jus soli' is a common law principle which prevailed in the Anglo-Saxon world. 'Jus sanguinis' is based on civil law principles. In view of the fact that India was a multi-ethnic society, 'jus soli' made admirable sense. As political scientist Niraja Gopal Jayal put it, 'India affirmed the possibility of citizenship as a political identity without an anchorage in culture.'[1]

Citizenship as a concept is controversial and much contested in academic circles. In established nation-states, the notion of citizenship, according to sociologist T.H. Marshall, is a constant striving for 'status bestowed on those who are full members of a community. All who possess the status are equal with respect to the rights and duties with which status is endowed. There is no universal principle that determines what those rights and duties shall be ...'[2] This is a citizenship which is singularly aspirational and contingent on belonging to a particular community in order to claim its rights. But in the modern era, the acquisition of citizenship has become increasingly invaluable, turning into a powerful instrument of exclusion. The controversial amendments introduced in 2019 to the Citizenship Act of 1955 have incited much disquiet, as they have sought to introduce religion as a factor in granting citizenship in certain circumstances.

Given the colonial baggage, the clear principle of jus soli had to be compromised, compelling the new republic to accommodate the interests of around four million Indians who had settled in what became the British Commonwealth. After all, the British 'imperium' allowed migration for work and residence throughout the colonies, and many Indian subjects took advantage of these opportunities. So, there were large settlements of Indians in Ceylon (mainly Tamil plantation workers), Malaya and, of course, Burma, which was part of British India until 1935. These countries subscribed to different principles while granting citizenship, which invariably resulted in Indians being offered inferior or second-class citizenship. This created a dilemma for Nehru who was cognizant of the problem but took the orthodox view that people who have settled in a different country should owe allegiance to that country and there should not, as a matter of principle, be a case of divided loyalties. In this respect, Nehru's views were not very different from British politician Norman Tebbit's famous 'cricket test', as per which if you insisted on supporting the test cricket team of your country of origin while living in England, you were being disloyal and unpatriotic to England.

In view of the demands of Indians living overseas, the jus soli principle came to be enshrined in Article 5 of the Constitution, supplemented by domicile and descent-based qualification—not unlike English law. This was developed to accommodate the needs of the Indian diaspora who needed the guarantee that they would be able to take Indian citizenship in the event of a possible abrogation of their rights in the country of their domicile. This was not fanciful, as can be seen from what happened in Uganda in 1974 when the Asian community—primarily of Indian descent—was displaced and expelled from the country under the orders of the brutal dictator

General Idi Amin. The complication has always remained with the status of Pakistanis, most of whom would qualify for citizenship under the principle of jus soli, but are excluded because of the creation of Pakistan. The controversies which led to the formulation of Articles 6 and 7 of the Constitution were based on the great migrations from Pakistan to India, both pre- and post-Partition. By setting out the matrix of citizenship, the Indian state was affirming its sovereign powers.

These migrations gave rise to numerous challenges, including the rehabilitation of refugees and the recovery of women who had been abducted on a massive scale in Punjab during the Partition. The gravity of these concerns ultimately led to the Nehru–Liaquat Pact of 1950. This bilateral treaty between India and Pakistan permitted refugees to return to dispose of their property, provided for the recovery of abducted women and looted assets, derecognised forced conversions, and affirmed the rights of minorities in both countries. It attempted to set a time limit that would enable both countries to maintain the religious demographic status quo. In effect, it attempted to repudiate Patel's mischievous policy of encouraging minority migration to create some form of majoritarian spatial regrouping along the lines of the two-nation theory.

There is an inherent complexity in the nature of colonial borders and the grant of citizenship, particularly if territoriality is the basis of citizenship. So, if you were crossing the border or migrating administratively, there had to be a category for it. This was particularly evident in the East where many Hindu Bengalis saw the partition of India in 1947 as a temporary phase rather like the partition of Bengal in 1905, post which they had continued to live in East Bengal. Once East Bengal became a part of Pakistan, they could not legitimately cross the border, so a special administrative category was created for them called termed 'displaced persons'. Anupama Roy, professor of political science, states, 'The Ministries of Home, External Affairs, Rehabilitation, Law, and the Election Commission of India acted in concert to complete the registration of displaced persons as Indian citizens expeditiously.'[3]

The Indian government passed the Administration of Evacuee Property Act of 1950, the intent of which was to provide rehabilitation to the Hindu and Sikh refugees who had migrated from West Pakistan to India and the Bengali refugees who had come from East Bengal. The matter of citizenship was influenced by this factor, as Muslims who had migrated to Pakistan but had come to India in order to dispose of their properties were interrogated to find out whether they had been allotted property in Pakistan. If that were the case, they were classified as 'evacuees'. But the bureaucracy went one step further and devised an ingenious category known as the 'intending evacuee' which included persons who had not yet migrated to Pakistan but had taken actions indicating an intent to do so. Their property automatically fell under the custodian's authority. Salman Khurshid has spoken of how this draconian legislation affected joint family properties.[4] Several Muslim families owned properties as co-parceners by reason of Sharia laws of inheritance, making this kind of provision particularly prejudicial to them. It placed the burden of proof on them to prove that they were not evacuees, nor did they harbour any future intention to migrate to Pakistan. Records from that time disclose many cases where bureaucrats with political patronage acted in an arbitrary or capricious manner in the appropriation of such property.

These laws had a profound impact on the psyche of Indian Muslims living in northern India. Mushirul Hasan has called these laws most inequitable, stating:

> Muslims could not easily dispose of their property or carry on trade for fear that the long arm of the property law might hold them in its grip. The laws restricted business opportunities and crippled large numbers of Muslims especially in the north and west of India.[5]

In fact, under the creative rubric of the 'intending evacuee' category, a number of Congressmen who had sent small amounts of money to relations in Pakistan were also included in this category, despite having no explicit intent to migrate. This made even their property liable to fall under the custodian's aegis.

Assam, Citizenship and Statelessness

If the difficulties faced by Muslims living in UP and their stigmatised and fragile citizenship were a source of fear, this was negligible in comparison to the plight of Assamese Muslims. These concerns predate Independence. Assam was famed for its tea plantations, and for that reason, colonial tea planters had brought in low-cost labour from all over India, a parallel to the Tamil labourer influx into Ceylon in the nineteenth century. Further, land reclamation attempted by the colonial administrators required plentiful labour, which was drawn principally from East Bengal. Even in colonial times, there was a large population of non-ethnic Assamese people who had been settled in Assam for several generations. Many of these non-ethnic Assamese, a majority of whom were Muslims, had adopted the Assamese language and assimilated, as far as possible, into the region's cultural practices. Over time, they came to be referred to as 'Miya Muslims'.

It is apparent that the recent targeting of Miya Muslims who had consciously adopted Assamese as their first language was meant to serve a larger political agenda. It sought to galvanise tribes such as the Bodos to agitate against Miya Muslims on the ground that they were not ethnic Assamese. The premeditated expulsion of Muslims from Assam predates the growth of the United Liberation Front of Asom (ULFA); it can be traced to the Nehruvian era. In a new study, author Pratinav Anil has shown from official figures that in Nehru's second and third terms, around 35,000 Assamese Muslims were deported or given notice to leave the country. The 'modus operandi' for these expulsions involved, according to him, Muslims being driven out of their homes to makeshift camps set up at the border, where they were forced 'to sign papers declaring falsely that they were Pakistanis.'[6]

This impetus towards communalisation of Assam is now at its apogee with BJP in power in the state, following a policy which seeks to stigmatise Assamese Muslims on the allegation of being Bangladeshi infiltrators, in many cases without any regard to the facts. It is not a coincidence that the size of the Muslim population in Assam, being about 34 per cent at the time of writing, magnifies this issue. The state has the second largest Muslim population after Jammu and Kashmir. Labelling Muslims of Assam as 'Bangladeshis' creates a basis for questioning or denying them citizenship.

However, as Sanjib Baruah says, amidst much of this cacophony of allegations of illegal migration and the perceived perfidy of politicians seeking to enrol illegal migrants on the electoral list, the fact that 'Assam's contemporary religious demography is the result of a migration flow that began more than a century ago'[7] is pointedly ignored. The present political class has a vested interest in creating as much confusion as possible over the identity and provenance of these inhabitants, in order to avoid facing the incontestable fact that many of these persons have been residents in Assam from colonial times, and that many of the migrants who have crossed over in recent times from Bangladesh, particularly from Sylhet, are actually Hindu Bangladeshis. It is this paradox in the narrative that the BJP-led government at the centre has sought to address through the Citizenship Amendment Act (CAA). The desire is to regularise what has been a policy followed by the Assamese Government for many years: to class Hindu migrants as 'refugees' and Muslim migrants as 'infiltrators', which according to a recent study would apply to all resident Muslims living in Assam post-Independence.[8]

The Assamese agitation from the late 1970s to the mid-1980s set off a succession of other agitations in other Northeastern states with demands being made that migrants be dealt in a similar manner, even though migrations in these states were negligible and there was minimal demographic impact. In Arunachal Pradesh, communities such as the Chakmas and Hajongs, who had migrated from what was then East Pakistan in the 1960s, along with Tibetans who had fled with the Dalai Lama in 1959 have been targeted as illegal migrants.[9]

Even more bizarre are entities called 'chitmahals', which are enclaves of Bangladesh within the territorial borders of India and vice versa. At present, there are some 130 Indian chitmahals within Bangladesh covering around 21,000 acres and around 95 Bangladeshi chitmahals within Indian territory. The people living there are practically stateless and have no access to any security.[10]

All this is to say that the complex histories of partitions and migrations in the border states of India have muddied the waters of citizenship of people living in these states.

The Citizenship Amendment Act, 2019

The matter of citizenship came into public prominence with the passing of the Citizenship Amendment Act in 2019—an invidious statute that made it clear to those who continue to believe that India is a secular republic that this is palpably not the case. The act openly discriminates in the grant of citizenship to those who seek it, refugees and migrants, on the grounds of religion. This is manifest from a plain reading of the amendments introduced which exempt any Hindus, Sikhs, Buddhists, Jains, Parsis, or Christians, who have entered India prior to 31 December 2014 from Afghanistan, Bangladesh or Pakistan, from being treated as illegal migrants.[11]

It is noteworthy that this exemption has not been extended to persons belonging to the Muslim community. The Union government argued that this amendment gave a one-time amnesty to those who had faced religious persecution in these three countries and sought refuge in India prior to 31 December 2014, but did not have the necessary documents. It is further relevant to note that the amendment pointedly excluded migration from the tribal areas of Assam, Meghalaya, Mizoram or Tripura as included in the Sixth Schedule to the Constitution.

The enactment of the CAA provoked massive controversy, leading to major demonstrations in Delhi largely led by Muslim women. At that time, the fear had been that this law would be used for the purposes of creating the National Register of Citizens (NRC) through which the government would seek to determine who qualifies as a citizen and who does not, adversely affecting the poor, the powerless and those without papers could be disenfranchised. The NRC had been made part of the Citizenship Act through an amendment introduced in 2003. The intent was to identify the citizens, issue them identity cards, thus creating a comprehensive register of all citizens of India. Assam, a state where illegal migration was an incendiary topic, became the laboratory for this potentially gargantuan exercise. Although not expressly stated, the oblique purpose seemed to identify illegal migrants, particularly those from Bangladesh. Writ petitions had been filed seeking directions to the Assam government to implement the NRC, causing the Supreme Court to give a deadline of 2016 for identification of citizens and deportation of those found without documents, in consultation with the Bangladesh government. Eventually, when the list was published in 2019, the process excluded over 1.9 million people who were constrained to appeal to the Foreigner Tribunals set up in Assam. To the embarrassment of the then BJP-led government in Assam, the list of persons unable to prove their citizenship included far more Bengali Hindus than Muslims. Later, the chief minister of Assam, Himanta Biswa Sarma, declared the list to be illegitimate, probably because the outcome did not align with their agenda.

Many people were excluded from the list for not being able to provide the requisite documents. Sanjib Baruah points out that the exercise was not entirely dependent on documentation, but there was further discretion vested in local administrators to deem entire settlements and communities as 'original inhabitants'. It is not clear on what basis this discretion was to be exercised, but given the political agenda of the then Assam government, one can reliably guess what it would be.

The head of BJP's IT cell and the party's spin doctor at large, Amit Malviya, seeks to create a revisionist narrative in order to give some intellectual credence to the CAA. He liberally cites instances of Congress politicians lamenting the plight of Hindu refugees from Bangladesh or Pakistan. Indubitably, there has been a steady migration of Hindus from these countries, but that does not mean that such migrations were necessarily prompted by religious persecution. For many persons who can prove religious persecution, it would be more sensible to migrate to countries that have refugee laws and asylum procedures in place than to come to India which offers no such safeguards (India is not a signatory to the UN Refugee Convention). Malviya seems to be confused between migration arising out of religious persecution and migration for economic reasons, in search of better opportunities.

The purpose behind Malviya's revisionism is clearly to burnish the two-nation narrative, a narrative which was firmly and indubitably rejected by the Constituent Assembly. As constitutional law scholar Gautam Bhatia so trenchantly puts it, the CAA discriminates 'between people on the basis of the characteristics that they cannot control.'[12]

Even if one disregards Malviya's revisionism, the other apologist for this legislation falls into a more exalted category. Harish Salve is one of India's most highly paid and sought-after lawyers and now serves as a King's Counsel in England, the ultimate accolade. The argument made was that any criticism of the CAA is an oblique attack on the capacity of the State to make classifications. He argued, 'If a law deals equally with members of a defined class, it is not open to the charge of denial of equal protection [of the law] on the ground that it has no application to other persons.'[13] It is, according to him, a law based on a rational criterion. That criterion is confined to religious persecution.

But as senior Supreme Court lawyer and politician, Salman Khurshid, points out, 'we will still need to know why religious persecution meets the test and not persecution per se.'[14] Even Salve would agree that persecution as such was not a good thing, but on what basis could the protections be narrowed down to the ground of religious persecution? This is not fanciful, as the treatment of Tamilians in Sri Lanka is a pertinent example. There is no doubt that the Tamil community was and is discriminated against by the majority Sinhalese community in Sri Lanka, not on religious grounds, but ethnic ones. If so, why should Tamilians, who indubitably originally hail from India, irrespective of whether they are Hindu and Muslim, not enjoy the same rights as a Hindu in Pakistan who faces persecution? Why is Sri Lanka excluded from the list of neighbouring countries? It cannot be because it was not part of British India, as neither was Afghanistan, which is one of the three countries identified under the CAA. On the other hand, Myanmar, which has seen large-scale persecution of Rohingyas on religious grounds, was part of British India until 1935. The distinction which, according to Salve, is based on a rational criterion, does not seem to take into account that a different kind of persecution of persons of Indian ethnicity might also require the intervention of the Indian state. For instance, Rohingya Muslims in Myanmar, who are being persecuted by the Buddhist majority, clearly fall in the same category as Hindus being persecuted in Afghanistan, Pakistan and Bangladesh, and hence should also be protected. The fact that one category is welcome within India and the other is not is frankly perverse and restrictive.

If his argument is that religious persecution or discrimination cannot take place within a religion, then on what basis have reservations been provided for Dalits and Scheduled Castes who fall under the Hindu religion? What about atheists and apostates? What protection do they have, as they are also subject to religious persecution? The very notion of religious persecution adopted in this law is, in my view, selective and perverse.

One detects an Islamophobic strain in the rhetorical question put by His Majesty's Counsel, 'Do we really need proof that minorities are persecuted in these Islamic Republics?'[15] This seems to imply that, because these are Islamic countries, religious persecution of minorities is a prerequisite of their existence. He then proceeds with seamless logic to inquire, 'How can Parliament be faulted for coming to a conclusion that such minorities in the three named neighbours need to be protected?'[16] So, he made two faulty assumptions. First, because these countries are styled as Islamic states that make religion the basis for their laws, persecution of minorities in these states would necessarily be involved. If such were the case, then relying on a similar hypothesis, protections should also be extended to Hindus or Christians living and working in numerous Islamic states like the United Arab Emirates, which too has made Sharia the basis of its constitution. The fear of persecution from an Islamic state has not prevented several Hindus and Christians from India, who are living in Dubai, from applying for the 'Golden Visa' programme, which grants them the right of residence. Secondly, as discussed earlier, if the concern is to prevent religious persecution in the neighbourhood, why does the law exclude Sri Lanka and Myanmar? Is it perhaps because these are Buddhist countries and the belief is that Buddhism is a religion of peace while Islam is a religion of war?

What the proponents of CAA ignored was the fact that whilst over decades, India has seen a net migration of people from its shores, who wish to improve their prospects in foreign countries, the migration numbers have seen a significant increase in recent years. In 2022, a total number of 225,620 Indians reportedly gave up their citizenship, the highest in the last twelve years. More than 1.66 million Indians have given up their nationality since 2011.[17] This hardly makes the case for the narrative that Indians are being persecuted in other countries, most of which are nations where Hinduism is not the prominent religion.

Is it possible to decontextualise these laws from political debates, promises in manifestos and speeches that surround and shape them? To attempt to detach these laws from the political background is an erroneous conceit, one favoured by the Hindu Right to camouflage the real purpose of this amendment, which is to embed issues such as migration and asylum in a religious matrix. It is perhaps a precursor to replicating the Israeli law of return, which would extend citizenship to any Hindu living anywhere in the world, irrespective of how tenuous their connection with India is.

When Donald Trump became the US president in 2017, one of his first acts was to issue a proclamation imposing a travel ban, restricting migration from Muslim countries. In the course of arguments in the US Supreme Court in a challenge to the travel ban, there was much reference to President Trump's overt animus towards Muslims and to the fact that his main intent was to make the entry of Muslims into America almost impossible. While the US Supreme Court upheld the travel ban, one of the judges, Justice Sonia Sotomayor, gave a powerful dissenting opinion in which she concluded that none of the features of the proclamation highlighted by the majority supported the government's claim that it was rooted in genuine security interest. What the evidence actually showed to the reasonable observer was that its primary purpose was to ban all Muslims from entering the US. In fact, she roundly stated that 'no matter how many officials affix their names to it, the Proclamation rests on a rotten foundation.'[18]

This kind of courage and outspokenness seems to be lacking in the citizenship-related judgments given by the Indian judiciary. This is evident not only from the lack of urgency shown in matters of such high constitutional importance, but also in the judiciary's hesitation in describing such perversions of law in a blunt and straightforward manner, especially when the arguments of the government are demonstrably dishonest and unconstitutional. For example, in the infamous *Sonowal* case[19], the Indian Supreme Court, while striking down the Illegal Migrants (Determination by Tribunals) Act of 1983, chose to describe migration as not merely an illegal entry into a foreign territory, but also as 'an act of aggression'. This remarkable non sequitur relied on the prejudicial belief that illegal Muslim migration led to religious fundamentalism and posed a threat to national security, similar to President Trump's characterisation of illegal migrants as criminals, rapists and drug dealers. According to academic Anupama Roy, the court discussed the influx of migrants 'not in terms of changes in the linguistic profile of the State but in terms of its religious profile, emphasising the increase in the Muslim population, and the threat it posed not just to Assam but to all of India.'[20] It is hypocritical that the Indian government, which condemns the practice of illegal migration, does not show the same indignation when thousands of Indians illegally enter other friendly countries. In fact, the refusal to take back what are clearly unlawful immigrants is a matter which ended up derailing the Indo-British trade deal for many years.

At any rate, the CAA has been seriously defanged, and the prime minister has unceremoniously dumped the controversial NRC.

Ironically, a similar tactic has ominously resurfaced with the special intensive revision (SIR) exercise, a process under which the Election Commission (EC) scrutinises existing electoral rolls. This has justifiably attracted controversy, as it purports to reverse the burden of proof in terms of voter qualification whereby all existing voters are compelled to adduce evidence proving their entitlement against old records or based on arbitrary criteria imposed by the EC (such as your grandfather's birth certificate). This is clearly a case of overreach since the EC is not vested with the powers to determine citizenship—that falls under separate statutes, the Citizenship Act and the Foreigners Act. This shift in the burden of proof in the SIR exercise, which was carried out first in the state of Bihar, greatly imperilled the enfranchisement of married women, migrants and the poor in general. So, citizenship is compromised through the backdoor, since you may reside in a place where you don't have the right to vote, making this exercise a harbinger of being identified as an illegal migrant.

The need of the hour is for a proper legislation on refugees and asylum seekers that distinguished between migrants who are victims of persecution, whether it be religious, ethnic or linguistic, and economic migrants who come to India for better work opportunities and end up working in the unorganised sector. India has been remiss in being one of the few 'soi-disant' liberal democracies that have not signed the UN Refugee Convention of 1951, and, whilst several model laws have been drafted by the National Human Rights Commission of India, they remain on the shelves gathering dust.

Author and politician, Shashi Tharoor, who has been trying to pilot one such legislation through the Lok Sabha, points out how there is complete confusion over laws relating to refugees in India. As he puts it, 'We have a cocktail of laws such as the Foreigners Act, 1946, the Registration of Foreigners Act, 1939, the Passports Act (1967), the Extradition Act, 1962, the Citizenship Act, 1955 (including its controversial 2019 amendment) and the Foreigners Order, 1948—all of which club all foreign individuals together as "aliens". Because India has neither subscribed to international conventions on the topic nor set up a domestic legislative framework to deal with refugees, their problems are dealt with in an ad hoc manner, and like other foreigners, they always face the possibility of being deported.'[21] This gives rise to arbitrariness and capriciousness, which seems to suit this government's mindset of minimum governance, maximum harassment.

15

THE INDIAN DIASPORA

An important factor propelling this virulent nationalism is the role played by the Indian diaspora, that is, people of Indian origin living outside India, encompassing both citizens residing abroad (NRIs) and foreign citizens with Indian ancestry (PIOs/OCIs). One would assume that people who, whether personally or through their ancestors, chose to leave a country might no longer feel a strong attachment to it. Instead, they would likely be more focused on building a new life and integrating into their new home. Oddly though, the Indian diaspora continues to have powerful linkages with India in ways which are not particularly helpful or benign.

It is important to understand the size of this diaspora. According to one figure, the number of migrant workers totals more than 281 million internationally, of which 18 million are of Indian origin.[1] This is a substantial figure by any standards; in fact, it approximates the population of a small European country such as Netherlands. They remit substantial funds to India—in 2022, this exceeded USD 108 billion, around 3 per cent of India's GDP, which is more than the remittances made to any other country. The Indian diaspora is a serious contender for attention from the Indian government, a fact that is demonstrated by the concessions offered in the form of the

OCI (Overseas Citizen of India) status, allowing foreign citizens of Indian origin to live, work and travel to India indefinitely without needing a visa or local police registration. The only right they cannot exercise is the right to vote.

The introduction of the OCI card recognises putative citizenship anchored in culture and ethnicity, which aligns with much of the modern trajectory of globalisation, migration and technology, where the role of the nation-state is demonstrably diminished and recognition is given to de-territorialised citizenship. India, much entranced by the role the Chinese diaspora had played in the growth of the Chinese economy, wanted to emulate this model and thus sought to introduce the OCI card.

It is, in turn, a nod to the indispensability of Indian migrants and their indubitable success, particularly in the US, where they are the highest-earning migrant group with a median household income of USD 150,000, double the national average. Among their numbers, they include the heads of twenty-five S&P 500 companies. With such economic success comes political leverage. As *The Economist* put it, 'A stunning example of this came in 2005, when America struck an agreement that, in effect, recognised India as a nuclear power, despite its refusal to sign the Nuclear Non-Proliferation Treaty (along with Pakistan and Israel). Lobbying and fundraising by Indian-Americans helped push the deal through Congress'.[2]

It is common knowledge that the diaspora plays a seminal role in the emergence of the new nationalism in India and, paradoxical as it may sound for a people who have left India, they are the most ardent supporters of the Modi government and its nationalist narrative. In a post-colonial world, where many host countries remain reluctant to revise their national or colonial narratives, there is an inherent tension between the pride these countries take in their past and the impulse among migrants to reconstruct or revive pride in their own countries of origin. It can, of course, go either way; many successful migrant families want nothing to do with the country they came from, but many do. To some extent, this process has been hastened by the spread of modern technology and the growth of social media.

Support for Hindutva from the NRI population has been both vociferous and pervasive, even extending to local political choices which NRIs have to make in the countries where they live. Many NRIs in the US work in the tech industry with little background in liberal arts and invariably import their entrenched high-caste prejudices, which can align uncomfortably with the Islamophobic currents already present in American society.

What is surprising, though, is that Islamophobia extends even to Islamic countries such as the UAE and Oman, which have traditionally had good relations with India and have had no difficulty in allowing the Hindu diaspora in their country to practice their religion freely and prosper. Many Hindu businessmen who have thrived in these countries express the most virulent Islamophobic views. This is perplexing as there is no ostensible provocation for this mindset. It is not as if these highly privileged people are confined to ghettos or persecuted in any manner.

These attitudes contrast with the perception in the Global South about Nehruvian India, which was regarded as an exemplar, a paragon and a benchmark that other post-colonial societies could aspire to.

I say this by way of background, as there was undoubtedly a degree of empathy between the Indian middle-class and the larger post-colonial third world, which has now diminished. The Indian middle class now consciously identifies with the interests of the US, Europe, Israel and the global right. This is not just because of economic liberalisation and foreign direct investment pouring into India, but also on account of the hypnotic allurement of American soft culture. I believe that this identification is also, regrettably, based around a subconscious Islamophobia fuelled by the 'clash of civilizations' thesis of political scientist Samuel P. Huntington, which predicted that people's cultural and religious identities would become the primary source of conflict in the post–Cold War world, thus placing the West and Islam as irreconcilably opposed to each other. The Indian middle classes' identification with the Western world is also influenced by a vainglorious perception that India is not really a third-world country, since it has a vibrant IT sector, a space programme, nuclear arsenal, however these things are merely proof of its exceptionalism, but overlook the everyday realities faced by the majority of Indian population.

Author Nitin Pai makes a very valid point that this desire of the diaspora to identify with the country of origin can pose risks, and that 'Indian leaders should take extra care not to conflate Indian origin with loyalty to India, or to religious or ethnic sectarianism. An important reason Indian immigrants have done well in politics, culture and business overseas is that they have always been—and been seen—as bona fide members of the local political community, with no divided or extra-territorial loyalties.'[3] Unfortunately, Indian politicians at the time of writing, including the prime minister, revel in NRI diaspora gatherings and harvest the popularity demonstrated for their political needs at home.

It is an extraordinary paradox and irony that the ideology of Hindutva derives its mojo from its categorisation of Indian minorities on the basis of where their most sacred places of worship are and uses, this to stigmatise the citizenship of minorities. Yet, it does not seem to occur to many of these NRIs and Hindutva ideologues that encouraging or fostering political loyalty to India for being their home country might create complications in the countries where they live and often hold citizenship.

NRIs also seem to ignore the fact that they cannot escape racism and the toxic ideology of white supremacy that is all too pervasive in various Western countries where they have settled. The infamous examples of Sikhs being attacked in America and some being killed post-9/11 after being wrongly identified as Muslims illustrate not just the ignorance of white supremacists, but also their fetish with race. The Russian invasion of Ukraine prompted a huge outpouring of sympathy for Ukrainians to the point that several Western countries relaxed all immigration restrictions for Ukranian refugees. This stands in stark contrast with their attitudes towards Syrian and Afghan refugees, persons who, ironically, have had to flee their country because of botched Western interventions.

It is thus convenient for many NRIs to hold Islamophobic views and, as a consequence, support a virulent nationalism which seeks to portray India as a potential superpower, radically different from the image the West holds of India of being poor, corrupt and weak, particularly in relation to its immediate neighbour, China.

As Nivedita Menon points out, 'Hindutva is now a global phenomenon, and one of the key projects of Hindutva in the global North is to present Hindutva as coterminous with Hinduism—as a belief protected by the multicultural norms of these countries.'

As such, it enables Hindutva organisations to claim that any critique of Brahminism, caste discrimination, or patriarchy amounts to Hinduphobia. In this, she observes there is a co-victimhood with antisemitism.[4] For the Hindu Right, criticism of the religion and the State overlap seamlessly.

PART V

THE ROLE OF THE JUDICIARY AND MAJORITARIANISM

16

THE HISTORIC ROLE OF THE JUDICIARY POST-INDEPENDENCE

Minorities reposed their faith in the guarantee of fundamental rights, trusting that these rights would remain beyond the reach of legislative encroachment and be safeguarded by an independent judiciary. The whole concept of fundamental rights and judicial review of legislation by a constitutional court had been largely imported from America, following the landmark US supreme court judgement of *Marbury v. Madison* passed in 1803. In the US, the supreme court assumed extensive powers of reviewing legislative acts under the cover of a liberally interpreted 'due process' protected by the Fifth and Fourteenth Amendments to the US constitution.

A striking and illuminating example of such a dialogue on fundamental rights comes from the period prior to the American Civil War when the Confederate states sought to make citizenship contingent on race, thereby excluding African Americans. This dialogue ultimately affirmed a foundational principle: that legislatures, even when backed by numerical majorities, cannot curtail constitutional rights of a fundamental character. Thus, the US Constitution enshrined the principles of entrenched rights and repudiated what Ronald Dworkin has termed the 'majoritarian premise'.[1]

Since the 1950s, the US Supreme Court has played a stellar role in expanding rights and entitlements of the citizens—bringing an end to racial segregation in public schools, decriminalising same-sex relationships, recognising same-sex marriage, and affirming abortion rights, among other landmark interventions. The importance of the US supreme court can be gauged from the seriousness American politicians afford their power to nominate judges to the court whose politics align with their agenda, and to the promises they make to their electoral base that they will do precisely that.

The concept of judicial review of legislation by constitutional courts was adopted in India, but with one important difference. In India, much of the bite of fundamental rights was diluted by the dichotomy created between fundamental rights and directive principles, the former being enforceable in court and the latter being principles which are idealistic but legally non-binding. As constitutional law scholar Arghya Sengupta has pointed out, many of the radical socialistic ideas were dumped in the category of directive principles. In his words, directive principles provided 'a convenient receptacle of accommodation' to enable fundamental compromises on ideology.[2] For instance, in spite of Congress party's desire for economic redistribution, all such ideals were dumped in the directive principles category, partly owing to the fact that Sardar Patel had already as Chairman of the Advisory Committee on fundamental rights recommended that the right to property be made a fundamental right.

What we have in the Indian supreme court, is a glorified appellate body which, rather unsatisfactorily, doubles up as a constitutional court as and when a larger bench is formed to hear matters of constitutional importance. However, many judges, having largely dealt with civil or criminal litigation before their elevation to the Supreme Court, do not possess adequate experience in constitutional adjudication. In an interesting new study, it was established that special leave petitions (petitions through which cases are brought before the Supreme Court) constitute 92.4 per cent of all cases pending in the Supreme Court, whereas constitutional cases comprise less than 4 per cent of the total cases. It is noteworthy that while a few special leave petitions can involve minor constitutional issues, the majority of them serve as appeals from judgements of high courts on criminal and civil issues.[3] In addition, there is a requirement of 'acceptability' of court judgements. As Pratap Bhanu Mehta puts it, 'The Supreme Court of India now occupies a position of extraordinary authority in the Indian polity. It often seems that nothing is beyond the scope of the Court's power and jurisdiction. "Promiscuous" is perhaps the right description of its role, suggesting that its reach is both wide-ranging and largely dependent on the Court's own whims and pleasures.'[4] The ideological fixation with suitability of judges has exacted a huge price on Indian society augmenting the backlog, which now stands at 52 million cases until mid-2025.

The Supreme Court sits at the apex of the judicial system and is valorised as one of the three constitutional pillars which guarantee the separation of powers. In such capacity, it sits over the high courts, some of which were set up under a royal charter, much before the setting up of the Supreme Court. The high courts of Calcutta, Bombay and Madras have a history and pedigree that goes back to the eighteenth century. This is often forgotten in the face of the vice-like control the Supreme Court exercises over high courts which has had a detrimental impact on their functioning and, in consequence, their standing.

At the time of constitution-making, there was inevitably an existential dilemma: how to reconcile the process of appointment of judges to courts with the imperative to maintain the independence of the judiciary. This was even more important when the judiciary had been vested with pivotal constitutional powers of judicial review of executive actions. The critical aspect of this debate is fundamentally the scope of judicial review of government legislation. Constitutional bodies are not absolute—they owe their existence and legitimacy to the Constitution. This is expressly provided in Article 13, which pointedly limits legislative power, making it subject to fundamental rights. In the words of Gautam Bhatia,

> 'The primary role of the Court was that of a counter-majoritarian institution. It existed to check the excesses of majoritarianism, on the understanding that true democracy meant something more

> than brute majority rule ... it were these minorities that faced the greatest difficulties in articulating their interests through the normal channels of (majoritarian) democratic governance. The task of the Court, essentially, was to come to the rescue of those whom the political process – formally or effectively – excluded from equal participation.'[5]

He gives the example of same-sex relations, that where such relations are viewed with great disfavour by many, the court would be justified in examining such laws which target this community with stringent scrutiny.

Thus, the matter of the composition of the Supreme Court is pivotal, as many judges are not necessarily interested in promoting constitutional morality and rather prefer to avoid confrontation with the government. Shashi Tharoor, in his biography of Ambedkar, says that the Constitution predicated the shift from an administration of law and order centred on imperial despotism to one centred on constitutional morality.[6] What concerned Ambedkar was that constitutional morality should be privileged and legalised over the traditional religiously derived morality of Indian society, which embraced the caste system. He saw constitutional morality to be a 'commitment to constitutional means, to its processes and structures, alongside a commitment to free speech, scrutiny of public action and legal limitations on the exercise of power.' Unfortunately, this paradigm is under threat—not only by an assertive executive intent on shaping the judiciary through the appointments process, but also by a deeper structural failing: the persistent neglect of diversity in judicial appointments, a concern that has never commanded the same seriousness accorded to it in other domains of public life. Judges at the highest levels continue to be drawn from a pool of largely upper middle class, high caste male, which shows that it was shortsighted of Ambedkar to even imagine that an upper-caste judiciary would promote constitutional morality if it conflicted with their entrenched beliefs. It is relevant that out of the forty-seven chief justices that the Indian supreme court has had, at least fourteen have been Brahmins. It is further relevant that it was not until 1980 that a judge from OBC or SC/ST communities became the chief justice.[7]

Legal scholar and academic Mohan Gopal presents a dire and disturbing presentiment of the future of the Indian constitution, the crux of his argument being that the struggle between the executive and the judiciary in relation to the choice of judges—which we are increasingly seeing—is an existential one, as the government appears intent on hollowing out the secular foundations of the Constitution and supplanting them with a vision more congenial to the idea of a Hindu Rashtra.[8] It seems that the best way to do that is to pack the courts with judges of a theocratic disposition, judges who look to ancient Hindu scriptures, to the 'Sanatana Dharma' (eternal law) or to the Vedas as the source of law, the 'grundnorm' as it were, rather than to the Constitution. This is already apparent in the composition of the Supreme Court, where there are at least five such judges who are so inclined at the time of writing. Mohan Gopal identifies this tendency by quoting from the recent *Hijab* judgement where one of the judges opined,

> The use of word "panthnirpeksh" in the Constitution brings out the difference in the terms "Dharmanirpeksh" and "Panthnirpeksh". "Panth", or sect, symbolizes devotion towards any specific belief, way of worship or form of God, but Dharma symbolizes absolute and eternal values which can never change, like the laws of nature. Dharma is what upholds, sustains and results in the well-being and upliftment of the Praja (citizens) and the society as a whole.

Mohan Gopal suggests that what the judge was actually saying was that dharma means 'Sanatana dharma' and that in applying our constitutional law, 'Sanatana dharma' ought to be taken into account. He speculates on the 'telos' of this conceit, suggesting that by this clever manipulation of language, a 'homa' (ritual prayer) may be permitted in a government school as that is part of 'dharma', but the wearing of hijab is not, since that is a part of religion.[9] To many, this would be a meaningless distinction. This is an interesting and disquieting take on secularism as it introduces 'Sanatana dharma' as a source of law through the back door. So, there may not be a need to amend the Constitution, as, in effect, that can be done through the appointment of such theocratic judges. This understanding is buttressed by the fact that in Article 13 of the Constitution, the definition of laws includes 'custom or usages' and as such, 'dharma' may well be construed as 'custom' and not religion.

These examples show, and demonstrably so, the diffidence in the judiciary when it comes to addressing serious constitutional issues. Much of this reluctance to confront the executive stems from an overinvestment in the idea of elections and majority rule. Under this view, the executive derives its authority directly from the will of the people who elect it, whereas the judiciary does not. Because judges are appointed rather than elected, it is argued that they lack the same democratic mandate. The late BJP politician, Arun Jaitley, who himself never got elected to the Lok Sabha, often spoke of the 'tyranny of the unelected' whenever court judgments did not meet his approval, as if merely being elected could negate an evil.

It must be recalled that in the seminal constitutional judgements on fundamental rights, such as the *Golaknath* case in 1967[10] and the *Kesavananda Bharati* case in 1973,[11] the Supreme Court had observed that even a new constituent assembly could not change the basic structure of the Constitution, in which the court included secular and democratic values and fundamental rights. In this context, to view the Supreme Court as a bastion for the protection of democracy and democratic values, including secularism, is not fanciful. However, the manner in which the government has managed to influence the Supreme Court creates the impression that no formal rewriting of the Constitution is necessary. By elevating opportunistic judges—often rewarded with post-retirement sinecures—or, more troublingly, appointing those with an overtly theocratic disposition, the constitutional order can be subtly recast from within, without a single amendment being passed.

The conflict, therefore, is not merely about whether any residual constitutional conscience still holds sway. It is also about the Supreme Court's record: in matters concerning minority communities, its judgments have often reflected a distinctly majoritarian impulse. Yet even these decisions may fall short of what a court determined to enforce the full doctrinal framework of 'Sanatana Dharma' and Vedic texts, aligned with the vision of a Hindu Rashtra, might seek to accomplish.

It was these concerns about majoritarianism and the suffocation of homogenising values that Ambedkar had warned, when he had said,

> In politics we will be recognising the principle of one man one vote and one vote one value. In our social and economic life, we shall, by reason of our social and economic structure, continue to deny the principle of one man one value. How long shall we continue to live this life of contradictions? How long shall we continue to deny equality in our social and economic life?[12]

I will now examine four areas where, as per me, the Supreme Court has acted with the greatest promiscuity in applying constitutional principles to the matter of minority rights.

17

THE ELEVATION OF THE COW

If we look at the manner in which cow slaughter has been stigmatised post-Independence, we are confronted by an issue which holds more ramifications than just to assuage hurt religious sentiments, which, in my view, have been egregiously privileged. It relates to choices of diet and nutrition, an important factor in a country where a shocking proportion of the population suffers from poor nutrition. It relates to jobs and economic welfare, for minorities as well as for the majority community, in a society where unemployment has reached epic proportions. It relates to financial priorities, as providing for cows post their milk-producing age becomes hugely expensive for both the farmer and the government. It relates to the rule of law, as legislations have been passed that attempt to make a mockery of due procedure and rules of natural justice, reversing the burden of proof and treating something which is intrinsically innocuous, at par with dangerous narcotics as an excuse to incarcerate or kill people.

I will seek to demonstrate that irrespective of its huge economic and political ramifications, the sentiment of a minority has been greatly privileged over the rights of the many. It is worth mentioning that most Indians—as much as 75 per cent of the population—are non-vegetarians in their dietary habits.[1] Admittedly, there may be many non-vegetarians who do not eat beef, but this curated image of Indians being largely vegetarian is a myth.

Historically, the British allowed Muslims to slaughter cows, particularly at the time of Eid al-Adha (the Eid of the sacrifice). Many Hindus opposed this policy, and in 1928, the Allahabad High Court ruled that cow slaughter by Muslims was not illegal.[2] The British, of course, were not entirely neutral in this matter. They wisely sought to distance themselves from the controversy, distracting attention from those who consumed beef to those who slaughtered the cow (invariably Muslim butchers). The plain fact was that the largest consumer of beef was the British Army. Queen Victoria admitted as much in a note to Viceroy Lord Lansdowne on 8 December 1893, 'Through the Mohammedans cow killing is made the pretext of the agitation, it is in fact directed against us, who have killed far more cows for our army than the Mohammedans.'[3]

During the Independence movement, Gandhi strongly advocated the prohibition of cow slaughter. Yet, he was clear-eyed enough to recognise that the issue was not inherently communal in the way the Hindu Right sought to frame it, and he resisted reducing it to a matter of religious antagonism. He pointed to the very lucrative trade of cattle export from Gujarat to Australia, undertaken by the Hindu merchants of Kathiawad. He remarked, 'The cows find their neck under the butcher's knife because Hindus sell them. If they did not do so, there would be no slaughter.'[4] Post-Independence, cow slaughter was banned in three Congress-ruled states: UP, Bihar and Madhya Pradesh. The cow protectionist lobby, under the tutelage of Rajendra Prasad, sought to enshrine the banning of cow slaughter in the Constitution. Well before contemporary debates on animal rights—such as those later advanced by Peter Singer[5]—Ambedkar remained unpersuaded that cows could be bearers of rights. In his view, rights inhered in citizens, and since animals were not citizens, they could not be vested with rights in the constitutional sense.

Despite Ambedkar's position, he sought to accommodate the cow protectionist lobby which spoke the language of emotion—one member of the Constituent Assembly, Raghu Vira, went as far as privileging the cow over the children of the family, as the cow was the mother of the nation.[6] With such emotional froth, a compromise had to be reached. That compromise was embodied in Article 48 of the Constitution which read, 'the state shall endeavour to organise agriculture and animal husbandry on modern scientific lines and shall, in particular, take steps for preserving and improving the breeds, and prohibiting the slaughter of cows and calves and their milch and draught cattle.' It is relevant to note that the language used in this provision has no religious character but took refuge in the idiom of agricultural economics. This is peculiar, as the protection afforded to the cow in India is perhaps unique and finds no parallel in any legislation internationally.

The fact that not even Gandhi took this pseudo-scientific verbiage seriously is evidenced by the fact that his insistence for cow protection extended only to the provinces of Gujarat, Marwar, UP and Bihar, as these were the provinces where the cow was worshipped. Clearly, if one were looking to uphold a religious principle, then cow protection would have had universal application.

Litigation ensued upon the state governments of Bihar, UP and Madhya Pradesh enacting legislation banning cow slaughter in the 1950s. The Supreme Court heard the challenge in the landmark case of *Mohammed Hanif Qureshi v. State of Bihar.*[7] The legislation enacted by Bihar even banned the slaughter of buffalos. The argument raised by the petitioners (mostly Muslim butchers) was that this law violated not only their right to the free exercise of their religion but also to pursue an occupation and livelihood of their choice. In relation to the first part of the challenge, without seeking any expert evidence and relying on the work of an English orientalist, the Supreme Court came to the conclusion that it was not essential for Muslims to slaughter cows on Eid and that the slaughter of a goat could suffice. In relation to the second part of the challenge, the Supreme Court held that laws admittedly did regulate and restrict these occupations however, that in itself did not deprive butchers from practicing the profession of butchery. The slaughter ban was not an absolute restriction, and butchers could continue to slaughter bullocks, goats and sheep.

What is remarkable about this judgement is that it never sought testimony from any expert on Islamic law. Instead, much like the English judges of the Privy Council in pre-Independence times, it relied largely on secondary sources and commentaries rather than authoritative scholarly testimony. The court also ignored history, since as author Abhinav Chandrachud points out, 'In British India, Muslims were allowed to sacrifice cows during the festival of Bakr Id (the word bakr is Arabic for cow), though Hindus worshipped cows.' The court also failed to consider the broader societal impact, overlooking what the noted American scholar Donald Eugene Smith observed that 'the cow issue is not a simple matter of religious belief but a means of asserting Hindu dominance.'[8]

In fact, the Supreme Court takes it as axiomatic that in Hinduism, beef eating and the slaughter of cows is forbidden, without undertaking any substantive examination of the theological or historical basis for such a claim. In the judgement, it states, 'There can be no gainsaying the fact that the Hindus in general hold the cow in great reverence and the idea of the slaughter of cows for food is repugnant to their notions and this sentiment has in the past even led to communal riots.' The court could also not detach the potential for public disturbance from the judicial pronouncement and said, 'While we agree that the constitutional question before us cannot be decided on grounds of mere sentiment, however passionate it may be, we, nevertheless, think that it has to be taken into consideration …' Once again, this matter of hurting religious sentiments comes into the picture, irrespective of any interrogation of such sentiments, a point remarked upon by legal scholar and professor, Upendra Baxi,[9] who was constrained to comment on the fact that the court did not apply the same onerous standards to determine whether cow slaughter was contrary to Hinduism as it did to determine whether cow sacrifice was optional in Islam.

So let us examine whether there is any religious sanction to this practice. The consumption of beef in Vedic times is well documented. The late historian D.N. Jha has not only cited the Vedas, Upanishads and sutras to substantiate his argument that beef eating was pervasive in ancient Hindu culture amongst Brahmins, but has also said that this dietary habit extended even to the Jains and Buddhists.[10] His research shows that this practice continued until the nineteenth century and even afterwards. He maintained that even such historians that the Hindu Right claims as its own, such as R.C.

Majumdar and K.M. Munshi, have 'never disputed that ancient Hindus ate beef.' These findings have been further fortified by a recent study[11] that found the presence of animal products, including cattle and buffalo meat, in ceramic vessels dating back approximately 4,600 years. The findings come from seven Indus Valley civilisation sites located in present-day Haryana and Uttar Pradesh, lending archaeological weight to the historical evidence.

Indologist Wendy Doniger, in her book on the Hindus,[12] questions whether cows were sacred in Hinduism. She concedes that they were special animals and were not publicly killed in certain regions. But she questions the term 'sacred cow' and argues that 'few of us kill or eat our children, but no one would argue that they are sacred. There are few, if any, Hindu cow goddesses or temples to cows. Hindus do not always treat cows with respect or kindness; cows are sometimes beaten and frequently half starved; Hindus will often treat cows in ways that sheltered Americans, who eat beef that comes neatly wrapped in plastic, regard as cruel.'[13]

An important aspect of the cow slaughter ban case was that there was no reference to the impact the ban would have on the livelihoods of members of the Qureshi community of North India, a community that traditionally did not slaughter any other animals than cows and bullocks. Legal scholar Rohit De has pointed out that this judgement adversely affected the two million-strong Qureshi community.[14] All these nuances, practical concerns and cultural taboos were pointedly ignored by the court who, in the words of Rohit De 'chose to treat the category of butcher as an economic agent who was free to adapt his methods according to the shifting contours of regulation. The Court was caste-blind and in doing so ignored the limits that the economy and community placed on the Qureshis' ability to branch out into slaughter of other animals.'[15] This is a very serious example of judicial myopia, given the size of the community affected and the pivotal role they played in the supply of food as well as in the production of ancillary goods such as leather items and hides. Their fundamental right to pursue their livelihood was abrogated on the inchoate notion of 'sentiments being hurt'. It is not a coincidence that this judgement relates to UP, which has had the largest cattle population over the years and where the cow protection movement had been active for more than a century.

Regrettably, this judgement has largely influenced later judgements on this issue and a 2005 Supreme Court judgement entitled *State of Gujarat v. Mirzapur Moti Kureshi Kassab Jamat*[16] went even further. The Gujarat government had enacted a law which placed a total prohibition on the slaughter of bulls and bullocks irrespective of whether these animals were useful or not. This legislation was challenged on constitutionality before the Supreme Court. In a disappointing judgement, the court held that even cattle which were no longer useful had served human beings hence, they were entitled to compassion in their old age. Unfortunately, the treatment of old cattle shows that compassion is sorely lacking. The court failed to consider who would fund the upkeep of the old cattle, which could no longer be put to use, a matter which has assumed great contemporary importance.

While giving these judgments, the Supreme Court has disregarded the many political debates which had attended the controversial matter of cow slaughter, including the remarks of Gandhi, who had said, whilst cow protection was a laudable sentiment, it 'must come through self-suffering, through tapasya, not through the imposition of law on those who do not accept it.'[17] He even drew a parallel with Pakistan, saying that if India bans cow slaughter, 'what prevents Pakistan from prohibiting idol worship on similar grounds'.[18] The many cow slaughter legislations mark the beginning of universalism turning intolerant on the absurdly specious argument that such activities would 'hurt religious sentiments'.

What we are seeing is an attempt to impose, what is best described as a taboo, on persons who do not subscribe to that taboo. It is not as if any moral argument is being presented, since the prohibition of the slaughter of living creatures is not being sought; it is only the slaughter of cow/buffalo that is being prohibited. In traditional societies, the breaking of a taboo involves self-pollution, which needs the purification of the self. That is what distinguishes a taboo from a moral demand. As philosopher Kwame Anthony Appiah states, 'A final difference between taboos and moral demands is that breaches of them pollute mostly you: they aren't fundamentally about how you should treat other people; they're about how you should keep yourself (ritually) clean.'[19] There are a few other countries that seek to impose their taboos on people who do not necessarily subscribe to them. The Kingdom of Saudi Arabia is one such country, as are Afghanistan and Iran. India now falls into this unsavoury club of theocratic intolerance by seeking to extend personal religious sentiments as dietary taboos on people who do not subscribe to them.

Ramifications on the Economy

Apart from the specific impact on the Qureshi community, these judgements have had huge ramifications on the agricultural economy, the leather industry, and the livelihoods of many millions of Muslims and Dalits. As of 2023, India was the second largest exporter of beef in the world, whereas the leather industry was one of the largest exporting industries and a huge employer of labour in the informal sector. As of 2025, the leather industry, which is around USD 16 billion, has been threatened by the ban on slaughter. According to some reports, 3.5 million job losses had occurred by 2017 in UP alone due to the draconian anti-slaughter laws. This number would have substantially increased almost nine years later.[20]

The fact that many on the Hindu Right have been conscious of the huge economic cost involved in this project is evident. As far back as 1955, the Gosamvardhan Inquiry Committee appointed by the UP Government to examine the issue of cow protection concluded, 'The problem of the cow demands as high a priority as national defence. It is the biggest problem that confronts the nation and must be tackled irrespective of the heavy expenditure involved in this undertaking, totally unproductive though it might appear for years to come.'[21] In fact, JNU professor and author Vikas Rawal has cautioned that the cost of looking after 27 crore unproductive cattle in India would cost the nation INR 5.40 lakh crores per annum, which is five times higher than the current defence budget.[22] As it happens, there is little in the way of 'gaushalas', which has meant that the excessive cattle population has become a source of nuisance. Former IAS officer and environmentalist Avay Shukla says that those calculating the costs to farmers of maintaining unproductive cattle warn that on the other hand '[i]f allowed to roam free, these cattle would devastate farmers' crops and create an agrarian crisis.'[23]

Quite apart from these economic costs, the ban also disrupts the renewal cycle under which farmers would sell cows and buffaloes which had outlived their use for cash to buy new livestock. Environmentalist Sunita Narain observes, 'Livestock is the most important security of farmers in our world. Indian farmers practice agro-silvo-pastoralism, that is, they use the land for crops and trees, as well as for livestock. This is their real insurance system, not banks. Livestock is also not kept by large meat businesses but by big, small, marginal and landless farmers. It works because the animals have a productive purpose: first, they give milk and manure and then, meat and leather. Take that away and you will take away the base of economic securities of millions in the country, greatly impoverishing them.'[24]

Communal Violence and Persecution of Minorities by these Laws

In UP, the Prevention of Cow Slaughter Act of 1955 and its apparent misuse by the state government provoked the Allahabad High Court to observe that 'the Act is being misused against innocent persons.' It went on to state that in these cases, 'whenever any meat is recovered, it is normally shown as cow meat (beef) without getting it examined or analysed by the Forensic Laboratory.'[25] UP government's data for the years 2018 to 2020[26] shows that nearly one-third of the arrests recorded under the draconian National Security Act (NSA) were under the rubric of cow slaughter independent of the NSA and that 1,706 cases were registered and over 4,000 people arrested and incarcerated in relation to cow slaughter. It is pertinent that out of the 120 cases brought under the NSA, 94 were quashed. Unfortunately, there is no breakdown as to how many of these cases are against Muslims or Dalits. However, since action is directed at those involved in the trade, it is reasonable to assume that a large proportion belong to these two communities.

The matter of cow slaughter has generated a phenomenon known as cow vigilantism, where persons who style themselves 'gau rakshaks'. They are often patronised by political actors and take it upon themselves to enforce the law by raiding houses, disrupting the transport of livestock and physically attacking, and, in some cases, killing persons who are engaged in this business. These people have almost carte blanche, as no one really seems to know the law, particularly when cattle are transported through different jurisdictions. As activist Aakar Patel observes, 'There is confusion arising from a full ban in some states to no ban in some and partial bans in others. There are bans on beef eating in some states, but not in other states. There are bans on the slaughter of some species of bovine but not others, on some cattle of a particular gender but not the rest. There are bans on beef possession in some states and no clarity on this in other states, and bans on transport in some places, regulations on time and temperature and carrying conditions elsewhere. There is little logic or coherence to any of it.'[27] Amidst this welter of confusion, there are individual operators who, with tacit political support, become vigilantes and act against mostly Muslims engaged in the trade as a means of spreading terror and fear.

I have dwelt on this topic, not just because of the manifest malign intent of these laws to actively persecute Muslims and Dalits, but also due to the huge economic ramifications which gain importance, given the fact that 60 per cent of our workforce is engaged in agriculture. It involves coercion and violence on the poorest of our population, and this does not seem to have attracted any serious attention in the public space. In fact, to discuss this subject, as Professor Jha discovered, 'is an area where angels fear to tread, and is emblematic of how "culture" has displaced religious scripture in constituting "the people's sentiment" as the law. It has also highlighted the craven pusillanimity of judges when it comes to applying constitutional principles, vacating this mandate in favour of avoiding hurting sentiments.'

18

THE ESSENTIAL RELIGIOUS PRACTICES TEST

This has been an issue in India with both the principal religions, Hinduism and Islam. The freedom to practice one's religion being a fundamental right means that if the customs of society regulate matters such as marriage, diet, and the right to adopt another religion, then all these matters become subservient to religious beliefs. So, in the event that such custom or practice becomes controversial and is subject to a legal challenge, the court has assumed the role of determining the important question of what constitutes the core of the religious belief and custom.

The critical issue is what exactly comprises the essence of religion and what may be a custom. Indian courts have, in such matters, taken recourse to the 'essential religious practices' test (ERP) as the operating factor for seeking the protection of Article 25 and 26 of the Constitution. A plain reading of Article 25 shows that it demarcates activities that are religious and those that are secular but may be associated with religious practices. As such, it vests courts with the power to distinguish between the religious and the secular. This extraordinary power is replicated in Article 26(b) which permits 'a religious domination' to manage its own affairs and the properties which it owns in accordance with law. Time and again, courts have attempted to distinguish between the religious and the secular.

The ERP test was first defined by the Supreme Court judgment in 1954 in the case of *The Commissioner, Hindu Religious Endowments, Madras v. Sri Lakshmindra Thirtha Swamiar of Sri Shirur Mutt*.[1] The commissioner had taken action against the Shirur mutt over financial irregularities. The mutt had invoked Article 26 insofar as it allows religious denominations to manage their own affairs. To an argument by the State that all secular activities, associated with religion but not really an essential part of it, would be amenable to State regulation, the Supreme Court observed, 'In the first place, what constitutes the essential part of a religion is primarily to be ascertained with reference to the doctrines of that religion itself.'[2] This became the 'essential religious practice' test.

The landmark case on this issue is the 1962 case of *Sardar Syedna Saifuddin Saheb v. State of Bombay*.[3] The head of the Dawoodi Bohri community had challenged the Bombay Prevention of Excommunication Act of 1949, which was enacted to negate the effect of an earlier Privy Council judgment [*Hasanali v. Mansoorali*] which had upheld the right of the Dai-ul-Mutlaq (the supreme spiritual and administrative leader of the Dawoodi Bohra community) to excommunicate any member of the community after following a procedure laid down by the Privy Council. The act sought to disable the Dai-ul-Mutlaq from exercising such a power and hence, was challenged for being in violation of Article 25 and 26. The Supreme Court found in favour of the challenging party and ruled that the power of excommunication was a necessary attribute if the community is to be kept together as a cohesive body. Reliance was placed on two observations of the Privy Council: The first that the protection of Article 25 and 26 was not limited to matters of doctrine or belief but also extended to acts done in pursuance of religion, thereby guaranteeing the protection of rituals, observances, ceremonies and modes of worship that constitute integral parts of a religion. The second was that when the court considers what constitutes an essential part of a religious or religious practice and what does not, it can do so with reference to the doctrine of a particular religion and also include practices which are regarded by the community as a part of its religion.

There was one dissenting voice in the *Sardar Syedna Saifuddin Saheb* judgment, that is the then chief justice of the Supreme Court, Bhuvneshwar P. Sinha. He pointed out, quite correctly, that excommunication would have far-reaching secular consequences for the concerned individual, affecting rights such as burial in the community burial ground, marriage within the faith, and acceptance within the community. The majority judgment deserves reconsideration, as it does not clearly demarcate the religious from the secular and may end up legitimising practices that are inhumane. For example, the customary practice of female genital mutilation (FGM) associated with Bohri women. Purely relying on the court's interpretation that Articles 25 and 26 include all customs, rituals and ceremonies, modes of worship of a religious community as integral parts of the religion, even the heinous practice of FGM could be considered acceptable.

A recent Bombay High Court judgment on the entry of women into the sanctorum of the Haji Ali Dargah in Mumbai,[4] illustrates that Muslim women are no longer afraid to exercise their constitutional rights irrespective of religious doctrine and customary practices. The trust in charge of the Haji Ali Dargah contended that the Quran and the 'Hadith' (the sayings of the Prophet) prohibited women from coming close to a tomb of a male saint, regarded women who were menstruating as unclean and required the segregation of men and women at holy sites. Various verses from the Quran and Hadith were enlisted and placed before the court to substantiate these arguments, to no avail. The court was of the opinion that these texts did not prohibit proximity of women with the tomb of a male saint or render it sinful. The question whether the exclusion of women from the sanctum sanctorum constituted an essential or integral part of the religion of Islam or not was also considered, and it was found that it was not an integral part. After all, one of the several equalities that humans are entitled to is equality before God and, as such, the right to perform prayers and rituals constitutes an important fundamental right.

The most recent example of the Supreme Court putting the ERP test to use is the hijab case, arising from a ban in Karnataka on female students from wearing the hijab whilst attending class. The high court in *Resham v. State of Karnataka*[5] upheld the ban on the ground that the practice of wearing the hijab did not constitute an essential practice of Islam and hence, a ban would not be a transgression of the right to freedom of religion. The court also took the view that there was no substantive right to freedom of expression and privacy and, finally, that such a ban was not inherently discriminatory. Subsequently, when the case reached the Supreme Court, there was a split judgment, with one judge supporting the school's right to impose a uniform, and the other allowing the wearing of hijab, emphasising that it was a matter of choice.[6]

In my view, the finding that the practice of wearing a hijab was not 'essential' to Islam was ill-advised. The court undertook a theological study without the benefit of testimony from expert witnesses. Academic Faizan Mustafa has pointed out that even this reading may be flawed, as there is nothing to say that religions cannot change their practices.[7] It also ignores the manner in which religions become localised and adopt local practices such as celebrations at Sufi shrines of Hindu festivals such as Diwali and Holi. Contrary to the Hijab case, when dealing with cases of cow slaughter, the Supreme Court has been content to merely observe that the consumption of beef hurts the sentiments of Hindus. The court failed to consider any ancient texts, even though Shastric texts speak of early Hindus consuming beef, which is very much at odds with what modern Hindus seem to consider the basis of their religious beliefs. If at all the Supreme Court seeks to use the ERP test in cases of this nature, it must follow one common rule, instead of cherry-picking cases where it will look at ancient texts and where it will not.

When the ERP test was invoked in the hijab case, it was not a case that there was a clash between individual and group rights. Those in favour of wearing the hijab argued that it was a matter of freedom of conscience, a freedom enshrined in Article 25. The court rejected the claim on the specious ground that the petitioners had not furnished material particulars to show how wearing the hijab was an overt act of conscience for them or how being asked to remove it violated their conscience, holding that a mere assertion to this effect was insufficient. The judgment goes much further and makes an extraordinary assertion that freedom of conscience concerns the inner realm of belief, while profession, practice and propagation are its external manifestations, therefore any claim of freedom of conscience under Article 25 would also have to be tested on the altar of essentiality. This is a problematic position since, as lawyer and author Suhrith Parthasarathy notes, 'it is possible, for example, that the hijab may not be essential to Islam, and yet that Muslim women wear it as an exercise of their own individual beliefs,' in which case their freedom to wear the hijab would still merit protection.

Personally, one may find the wearing of the hijab regressive and contrary to the texts of Islam, but must also be alive to the fact that the wearing of hijab empowers many young women who, otherwise, might not be allowed to attend college. In a few cases, such as *Jeeja Ghosh v. Union of India*[8], the Supreme Court has adopted the 'reasonable accommodation test'. The same approach should have been adopted in the hijab case, as the ban risks jeopardising women's access to education, a far more significant concern than tolerating a supposedly regressive dress code.

In a recent controversy, a Christian army officer was dismissed for refusing to enter the sanctorum of the regiment temple. Even when he challenged his dismissal in the Delhi high court and the Supreme Court, his plea was rejected. The matter did not relate so much to the question of his religious belief, but to the matter of military necessity and the powers granted under Article 33 of the Constitution, which allows for the abrogation of fundamental rights of members of the Armed Forces, police, intelligence agencies, and similar forces. The fact remains that the officer had neither been disrespectful to the regiment's tradition, nor had he shirked his duties or left his post. His objection had been that as a Protestant Christian who was committed to monotheism, he could not enter the inner sanctum and perform puja, havan or aarti without violating his conscience. Senior advocate Sanjay Hegde has said that this matter should not have come to court at all, instead the senior leadership in the army could have solved the issue with 'one conversation, one directive, or one thoughtful accommodation'. He correctly, in my view, drew a parallel with the case in *Bijoe Emmanuel v. State of Kerala*[9] concerning children, who being Jehovah's witnesses had refused to sing the national anthem but had been protected because they had stood by respectfully.[10] Justice Chinnappa Reddy singled out tolerance as being the lodestar in such cases. Hegde concludes by quoting Justice Reddy that our Constitution practices tolerance, and adds, 'We honour that practice not by enforcing uniformity, but by understanding when uniformity need not be enforced.' Sadly, an officer was dismissed from the army without pension or gratuity, in spite of any manifestation of disrespect.

Gautam Bhatia[11] argues that the ERP test has overreached itself by transforming from merely being a test that qualified whether a particular practice was religious or secular to one that qualifies its significance within the religious matrix. This vests Indian courts with the power to determine theological matters, just the way the Vatican papacy does. More than this, in the split judgment of the Supreme Court, the one judge who set aside the Karnataka high court judgment, discarded ERP on the basis that there will always be more than one viewpoint on a particular religious matter, and nothing gives authority to the court to pick one over the other. This is legitimate and Bhatia concludes that the ERP doctrine, as such, extirpates religious dissent and pluralism within a religion, as it assumes one truth.

19

CONVERSIONS BECOME CRIMINAL

The matter of conversions is intimately connected with majoritarianism, as there is an enduring belief amongst many Hindus that if conversion is allowed freely, it would result in the loss of the Hindu majority in India. An eerie parallel can be drawn with the 'Great Replacement Theory' touted by the European far right, as per which the white race is slowly being replaced by coloured migrants in Europe and the US. Thus, the issue has acquired a political character, with anti-conversion laws being passed in many state legislatures, which impose criminal penalties on persons who seek to convert. At the time of Independence and until 2014, the prime target of such laws were the Christian missionaries, but now the scope of anti-conversion laws extends to Muslims who are accused of being complicit in a 'love jihad'. What is interesting is that as a matter of practice, any conversion from Islam or Christianity to Hinduism is not a considered a conversion, but is rather termed as 'ghar wapsi'.

Initially, owing much to the efforts of the Christian Congress party member, H.C. Mookerjee, the right of a person to propagate their own religion was inserted in the Constitution itself. During the time of Partition, there was sympathy for the Christian point of view, as Christians had opposed the Muslim League's demand for Pakistan.[1] Oddly, even Sardar Patel emerged as an unlikely champion of conversion in his capacity as the chairman of the Advisory Committee on Fundamental Rights, Minorities, and Tribal and Excluded Areas. In the draft article on freedom of religion, the key word 'propagate' was included.

The disagreements in the Constituent Assembly centred around introducing caveats seeking to reduce the scope of such propagation by annulling conversions if they were induced by fraud, coercion or undue influence. This was not considered unreasonable as this would apply to any contractual relationship as such, which gets vitiated in case any of these factors came into play. The Hindu Right lobby in the Constituent Assembly, led by Congress party member P.D. Tandon, stated unequivocally that they 'deemed it very improper to convert from one to another religion or to take part in such activity.'[2] They also questioned the conversion of children under 18. The objection caused a furore amongst Christians who saw the intent to delete the word 'propagate' as 'cutting at the root of family life'.[3]

As a compromise, finally Article 25 was adopted which read as follows, 'Subject to public order, morality and health and to the other provisions of this Part, all persons are equally entitled to freedom of conscience and the right freely to profess, practise and propagate religion.'

However, this right to propagate religion has been steadily whittled down, and important laws have been passed over the years that discourage conversions. For example, a Hindu woman who had converted was not entitled to maintenance. Conversion could also have adverse implications for the person converting if they happened to belong to a Scheduled Caste community which was entitled to affirmative action. The Constitution (Scheduled Castes) Order of 1950 issued by the president contained a rider that 'no person who professes a religion different from the Hindu or the Sikh religion shall be deemed to be a member of a Scheduled Caste.' (Buddhist was added in this category by an amendment in 1990.'[4]

It is also relevant that in passing the Hindu Marriage Act in 1955, one of the nine grounds on which divorce could be sought was if the other party ceased to be a Hindu by conversion to another religion. This was a matter dear to the heart of the Hindu Right.

Author Swaminath Natarajan remarked that while the provision was understandable from the viewpoint of Hindu marriage being a religious sacrament, he found it odd that 'a secular state should not insist on further proof to establish that the conversion interferes with the religious life and practices of the other party'.[5]

Professor of law Marc Galanter found this to be a discriminatory anomaly, given the factual matrix of Hinduism and observed, 'Heterodox practice, lack of belief, active support of non-Hindu religious groups, expulsion by a group within Hinduism—none of these removed one from the Hindu category, which included all those who did not openly renounce it or explicitly accept a hostile religion.'[6]

State Legislation Reducing the Scope for Conversion

One important factor which continues to cast its malevolent influence was the report of the Niyogi Committee (Christian Missionary Activities Enquiry Committee) issued in 1956 that concluded that Christian evangelism had the agenda of taking advantage of the constitutional freedoms to propagate religion with the aim of creating 'a Christian party in the Indian democracy on the lines of the Muslim League, ultimately to make out a claim for a separate State, or at least to create militant minority.'[7]

This report had its repercussions as from the 1960s onwards, it propelled efforts to introduce legislation to attenuate the scope for conversion and abridge Article 25. This was certainly the case in Madhya Pradesh and Orissa—both states had a significant presence of Christian missionaries and a large number of tribals—where upper-caste Hindus were concerned at the increasing number of conversions and attempted to make them difficult by placing caveats around them, such as that conversions could not be procured by force, allurement or fraud. Legislation was passed in both states to regulate such conversions under the misleading title: Freedom of Religion Act. This stipulated a requirement that the concerned priest, or whoever converts any person from one religious faith to another, inform the District Magistrate that such a conversion had taken place, so that, presumably, the converted person could be questioned as to why they had chosen to leave their religion and whether there was any kind of inducement/allurement offered to effect such a conversion. The term inducement/allurement is one rich in ambiguity, as it is not confined only to a material inducement; it could be a religious one, for example, an assurance of a passport into the 'Kingdom of Heaven' would suffice as an allurement. If anyone ran afoul of these laws, they could face imprisonment of up to one year, rising to two years in cases involving the conversion of a minor, a member of a Scheduled Caste or Scheduled Tribe, or—rather oddly—a woman. Apart from the egregious criminalisation, the underlying assumption that women and people from lower castes have no agency or capability to make rational choices in matters of religion is gravely problematic.

When challenges to these legislations reached the Supreme Court, they were heard in the case of *Rev. Stanislaus v. State of MP*.[8] The court was asked to consider the constitutionality of the impugned anti-conversion statutes for being contrary to Article 25 of the Constitution. It was further argued that the right to propagate would include the right to convert. In what can only be called an anomalous judgement, the Supreme Court decided that the right to propagate was not coterminous with the right to convert, restricting the term 'propagate' to mean merely the transmission or spread of one's own religion by the exposition of its tenets. The judgement denied a right to convert on the specious ground that allowing the same would vitiate 'the freedom of conscience' also guaranteed by Article 25. As regards this judgment, constitution law scholar Abhinav Chandrachud has remarked that the Supreme Court forgot that 'there are two people involved—the preacher and the listener. While the preacher's right to propagate religion may not include the right to convert the listener, the listener's right to conscience under Article 25 includes the right to convert to another religion after listening to the preacher.'[9] This is a valid observation and once again shows the Supreme Court's bias in favour of majoritarianism while upholding laws which clearly abridge important constitutional rights.

It is pertinent to note that this judgement given in 1977 became the catalyst in emboldening other state legislatures such as Tamil

Nadu, Andhra Pradesh, Arunachal Pradesh, seeking to restrict conversions along the lines set out in the Orissa and Madhya Pradesh legislation in a spate of competitive regressiveness. The most draconian law against conversions which in effect completely abrogates the right to conversion, unsurprisingly emanated from Gujarat in 2023. It effectively vested the bureaucracy with the power to determine whether a person can or cannot convert based on undisclosed criteria.[10] It is an extraordinary piece of legislation that required individuals intending to convert to submit a form to the District Magistrate detailing their reasons for conversion, occupation, monthly income, caste status—whether they are Dalits or Adivasis—the date and time of the conversion, and other particulars. If they failed to do so within ten days of conversion, they faced one-year imprisonment. The law further enhanced the punishment for propagation to three years (with an additional year if they converted a woman, Dalit or Adivasi). The law is so draconian that, according to journalist Aakar Patel, 'the Catholic Church in Gujarat has stopped offering the baptism ceremony to individuals wishing to take it. The Church only baptises the children of Christians.'[11] It is evident that the constitutional right to privacy clearly does not apply to the much-vaunted 'Gujarat model'.

It must be noted that these anti-conversion laws have been attracting international opprobrium. The annual report of the United States Commission on International Religious Freedom, issued in 2021, singled out these laws that criminalised conversion as instances of of denial of religious freedom. The authors had the controversial matter of 'love jihad' in mind, looking at the spate of such laws passed in BJP-led states such as Gujarat, Himachal Pradesh, Uttarakhand and Madhya Pradesh.

However, 'ghar wapsi' or conversion to Hinduism does not seem to earn similar opprobrium. The anti-conversion law in Chhattisgarh specifically excludes conversion to Hinduism, and so does a law recently enacted in UP. In fact, the so-called 'ghar wapsi' movement is gaining momentum with the VHP leader Pravin Togadia alleging that his organisation has converted more than 500,000 Christians and 250,000 Muslims to Hinduism during the last ten years.[12] This does not take into account the substantial number of Dalit and Adivasi conversions and is therefore likely to be a significant underestimate, assuming that what Togadia states is correct.

The British were undoubtedly interested in religious conversions, but after Queen Victoria's proclamation of 1858, which ended reprisals against the rebels of the 1857 violence and announced a policy of tolerance and non-interference in India's religions, they tempered this impulse. Thereafter, the evangelical dimension of British rule was deliberately downplayed, except in certain tribal regions. The tribal hinterlands are where the missionaries remained active, particularly in the Northeast, Madhya Pradesh, Chhattisgarh, and parts of the Dang region of Gujarat. In all fairness, many of the people in these areas who converted to Christianity had led impoverished and squalid lives. Christian missionaries provided education and an opportunity to better their lives. Several of the tribes mentioned above practice animism, that is, they do not worship any of the gods from the Hindu pantheon. They do not pray in temples but in sacred groves which are called the 'Jaherthans'.[13] Many Adivasis have even named their religion, calling it 'Sarna' or Sarnaism, in an attempt to obviate their identity from being subsumed into Hinduism. In colonial times, there was a provision for tribals to choose 'Aboriginal' as an option for their identity, which post-Independence was denied to them. It must be noted that in the context of the Hindutva fetish of claiming that Aryans were the original inhabitants of India, it is Adivasis who, according to author Tony Joseph, 'share as much of the population genetically since they carry the ancestry of the First Indians, and they ought to be seen as the foundational population for India as it is today.'[14]

As a consequence of the government's policy on conversions, there has been a concomitant restriction on the role of NGOs, some of which have traditionally been associated with the Christian church and accused of promoting conversions.[15] Post 1961, Christian organisations in Goa were targeted as they were seen to be identified with the Portuguese and were alleged to be causing instability. Even Nehru was impressed by this argument. This is not the first example of such a right being abrogated at the altar of national security. It must be recalled that in the 1950s and 1960s, when the age of the well-funded corporate NGO had not yet started, the main non-governmental entities were religious organisations. The Foreign Contribution (Regulation) Act of 2010, which regulates and oversees funds raised by NGOs from sources outside of India, was further amended in 2020 during the peak of the first wave of COVID-19, putting in place restrictions that allowed for payments to be made through only one bank in New Delhi. This came after a sweeping cull of NGOs and the introduction of additional requirements that rendered FCRA registration increasingly difficult.

The argument of the government was that this amendment would enhance 'transparency' and 'stop the misuse of foreign funds by some people'.[16] This amendment was challenged in the Supreme Court, which upheld the law, largely on the bogey of misuse of funds to threaten national security.[17] It is relevant that the Supreme Court restated the government's arguments without citing any evidence in support of this alleged threat to national security. This judgment further undermined the notion of freedom of association, a principle enshrined in Article 19(4) of the Constitution.

These amendments were ill-timed, since at a time of great suffering they precluded NGOs operating in India from passing on foreign contributions to other organisations or unregistered NGOs, a common mechanism used to circumvent the stringent requirements for registration under the FCRA. In a BBC report, Jennifer Liang, co-founder of the NGO 'The Ant', said that the legislation had cost lives during the deadly second wave of the pandemic in April–May 2021, when thousands were dying for want of oxygen. Because her organisation was unable to open a new bank account in Delhi, it could not distribute oxygen concentrators received from foreign donors to the government.[18]

It is profoundly unfortunate that the matter of conversions has become so controversial that it attracts criminalisation and fundamentally repudiates the idea of freedom of religion, freedom of association and freedom of those choices that were once considered the bedrock of the Constitution. The stigmatisation of conversion has expanded to encompass social relationships between young people of different religions, which are sometimes brought under the charge of 'love jihad'. Not only has the attitude of the majority community denied people legitimate choices on how they want to live their lives, it has also cast suspicion on the NGO sector, which is being closely monitored amid allegations that it is involved in clandestine conversions.

According to author Aparna Pande, NGOs are denounced because of the belief 'that foreign non-governmental organisations (NGOs) and churches convert these individuals by offering money, jobs and opportunities to study abroad.'[19] In other words, NGOs are blamed for encouraging social mobility—an anathema to the Hindu Right—assuming that this is even true. The real target of this NGO crackdown seems to be environmental activists who pose a threat to the resource kleptocracy that India is fast becoming.

20

RELIGION, ELECTORAL POLITICS AND THE DISAPPEARANCE OF MINORITIES FROM THE PUBLIC SPACE

A question critical to the functioning of democracy is whether appeals for votes should be allowed to be made in the name of religion. This is a crucial element of the majoritarian agenda, as it seeks to normalise the use of religious tropes and symbolism in electioneering, with the intention of consolidating a vote bank based on religion, essentially a vote bank on stilts.

The conundrum of religion in politics is one that is not unknown to the West, as there has been a lively debate on the use of religious sentiments and tropes to attract votes in the name of religion. On the face of it, such appeals in a society which is multi-religious have the indubitable effect of shutting out people who either belong to a different faith or are non-believers, atheists, etc. The philosopher, John Rawls, equated electoral battles to appeals to 'public reason',[1] arguing that appeals to religious identity should be excluded. Legal scholar Michael J. Perry has argued, 'A proper pluralistic conception of politics should include space for religious-moral discourse; citizens should not be required to translate their deepest moral convictions into a purely secular vocabulary before they may participate in political debate.'[2]

In this regard, given the violent history of Partition, which as historian Shruti Kapila argues, represented an expression of the general will of the Indian nation, there remains the unsettling possibility that the people, that is the 'sleeping sovereign', retain the capacity to rise once again in anger and violence. It was therefore necessary to create institutional safeguards to forestall such outcomes, including the establishment of the Election Commission of India and the development of a Model Code of Conduct, institutions that have only recently been significantly weakened.[3]

India's election law does not permit appeals to be made in the name of religion since the founding fathers were fully aware of the incipient dangers this brand of politics posed to the future of democracy. The authoritative text on this issue is the opinion given by the late Justice P.B. Sawant as a member of the seven-judge bench hearing the case *S.R. Bommai v. Union of India*.[4] In connection with the Representation of the People Act of 1951, Sawant pointed out, 'When the State allows citizens to practise and profess their religions, it does not either explicitly or implicitly allow them to introduce religion into non-religious and secular activities of the State. The freedom and tolerance of religion is only to the extent of permitting the pursuit of spiritual life which is different from the secular life. The latter falls in the exclusive domain of the affairs of the State.' The court relied on sections 123(3) and 123(3A) of the act which broadly prohibit the appeal by a candidate, their agent, or any other person with their consent, to vote or refrain from voting on the ground of religion, race, caste, community or language, or the use of religious or national symbols—such as the national flag or emblem—to promote the election prospects of a candidate or prejudice another candidate. During the hearing, senior advocate Ram Jethmalani had argued that what was prohibited was not an appeal to religion as such but an appeal to the religion of the candidate and soliciting votes in the name of said religion. According to him, candidates were not prohibited from soliciting votes in the name of a religion to which they did not belong. However, Supreme Court did not accept this contention and held that seeking of votes in the name of any religion was expressly prohibited.

However, in a series of later judgements of the Supreme Court, the majoritarian agenda of bringing religion into politics has managed to sneak in through the back entrance. The landmark judgement on this is the one in *Dr. Ramesh Yeshwant Prabhoo v. Shri Prabhakar Kashinath Kunte*,[5] which marked the beginning of the rot. The charge was the violation of the Representation of the People Act based on several incendiary speeches made by Shiv Sena leader Bal Thackeray in November and December 1987. The speeches repeatedly invoked the protection of Hinduism, dismissed the need for Muslim votes, and proclaimed that the Shiv Sena would implement a Hindu ideological agenda. In court, Thackeray was defended by Ram Jethmalani who argued that the act would stand infringed only if a direct appeal for votes was made on the ground of religion and that, too, would be subject to the appeal's propensity to disturb public order—a point he had also argued in *S.R. Bommai*. He had further argued that Thackeray had sought to secure votes not by invoking Hinduism, but rather Hindutva, which, according to him, was not a religion but Indian culture itself. The first argument had been expressly rejected in *S.R. Bommai*, yet Justice J.S. Verma, who pronounced the judgement in the *Ramesh Yeshwant Prabhoo* case, distinguished that ruling without offering any coherent justification.

The lawyer for the respondent had correctly emphasised on the understanding of Hindutva as elaborated in Savarkar's writing. To examine Hindutva without reference to Savarkar's views, which is what the Supreme Court did, is a rather curious conceit. It was like discussing the Shakespearean play *Hamlet* without talking about the prince in Denmark.

It conflates the idea of Hinduism as a 'way of life'—drawn from an earlier Supreme Court judgment[6] dealing with Dr Radhakrishnan's capacious definition of Hinduism—with Hindutva, a far more exclusionary ideology. The court stated that it was 'difficult to appreciate how in the face of these decisions the term "Hindutva" or "Hinduism" per se, in the abstract, can be assumed to mean and be equated with narrow fundamentalist Hindu religious bigotry, or be construed to fall within the prohibition in sub-sections (3) and/or

(3A) of Section 123 of the R.P. Act.'[7] The Supreme Court went even further in the *Manohar Joshi*[8] case, where it remarked that it would be wrong to assume that references to Hindutva were axiomatically repugnant to non-Hindu faiths. This observation overlooked the central premise of Hindutva—that it accords primacy to Hindus over adherents of other religions in India. In fact, the magazine *Organiser* (the mouthpiece of the RSS), while speaking of about the *Ramesh Yeshwant Prabhoo* case, had no hesitation in saying, 'The Supreme Court has put its seal of judicial imprimatur on the Sangh ideology of Hindutva by stating that it is a way of life or state of mind and that it is not to be equated with religious fundamentalism.'[9]

The Supreme Court in the *Abhiram Singh v C.D. Commachen* case[10] gave a split verdict, with four judges favouring the approach adopted in the *S.R. Bommai* case. The majority judgement (through Justice Madan Mohan Lokur) stated that 'sub-section (3) of Section 123 of the Representation of the People Act, 1951 must be given a broad and purposive interpretation thereby bringing within the sweep of a corrupt practice any appeal made to an elector by a candidate or his agent or by any other person with the consent of a candidate or his election agent to vote or refrain from voting for the furtherance of the prospects of the election of that candidate or for prejudicially affecting the election of any candidate on the ground of the religion, race, caste, community or language of (i) any candidate or (ii) his agent or (iii) any other person making the appeal with the consent of the candidate or (iv) the elector.' The then chief justice, T.S. Thakur, also clarified that 'India is a secular state is no longer res integra. Secularism has been declared by this Court to be one of the basic features of the Constitution ... An interpretation which has the effect of eroding or diluting the constitutional objective of keeping the State and its activities free from religious considerations, therefore, must be avoided.' But by then the genie was out of the bottle.

The practice of using religious symbolism in electoral politics to garner votes is connected with representation at the level of both the Parliament and state legislatures. Representation has a crucial influence on power and decision-making, as, naturally, politicians tend to favour people who vote for them in the not unreasonable expectation that these voters will continue to support them in future elections. Judicial rulings that allow recourse to religious symbolism in election campaigns consequently amplify, and even weaponise, the mobilisation of people's insecurities, fears and prejudices. It is not an accident that BJP at the time of writing, has not a single elected Muslim MP and very few Muslim representatives at the state level.

The consequences of privileging this kind of religion-centric politics in which unalloyed appeals are made in the name of religion and minorities are demonised, that spawned after the *Ramesh Yeshwant Prabhoo* judgement, has been consequential; it has opened the floodgates for the abuse of minorities, normalising it to a great extent. Emblematic of this attitude is a reference made by the successful chief ministerial candidate in the 2022 Uttar Pradesh state elections, who had invoked the slogan '80 versus 20', a shorthand widely understood to refer to Hindus versus the minorities.

The strategy of showcasing the principal opposition party, that is the Congress, as a Muslim party by BJP, has been highly successful in not just winning over Hindu voters to the BJP's side, but has also inflicted collateral damage on the Muslims. They have been rendered even more isolated and besieged, as the Congress and other secular parties, anxious to avoid this charge, engage in competitive Hindu majoritarianism and consciously refrain from choosing Muslim candidates and raising issues affecting Muslims.

This has created a situation in which Muslims, whose presence in Parliament and state assemblies was already minor or token for decades after Independence, are now being increasingly excluded from the public sphere. In 1952, in the Lok Sabha, their representation was 8 per cent when their population share was 11 per cent. In 2014, Muslim representation in Parliament declined to 4 per cent, despite Muslims constituting roughly 14 per cent of the population, and there was not a single Muslim MP from the ruling party in Uttar Pradesh, where Muslims make up about 19.26 per cent of the population.[11] The absence of proper representation proportionate to their population has greatly prejudiced Muslims on matters that affect them in a singular way, including security and communal conflagrations, reservations and personal law.

These examples demonstrate how religion, often disguised as custom and practice, has expanded since the Constitution's founding, with the Supreme Court repeatedly playing a complicit role in building the legal infrastructure of majoritarianism that has prepared the ground for the present dispensation. The term 'secularism' has been corrupted, but not in the way the Sangh Parivar argues that minorities are being privileged and pampered. As journalist Aakar Patel puts it, 'India's secularism is used as a carapace under which Hindutva abuses India's minorities. This contradiction is Hindutva's weakness. It is dishonest about its bigotry.'[12]

PART VI

THE AFTERMATH OF PARTITION, KASHMIR, PAKISTAN AND THE PLIGHT OF INDIAN MUSLIMS

21

THE AFTERMATH OF PARTITION

The Partition witnessed the migration of around 7,249,000 Hindus and Sikhs from Pakistan to India and a migration of 7,226,000 Muslims from India to Pakistan.[1] In Bengal, as per the 1951 census, 700,000 Muslims migrated from India and 1.5 million Hindus migrated to India from East Pakistan.[2] It is important to realise that to focus solely on Partition riots, as many commentators do, is to miss the full enormity of the tragedy, as it pointedly excludes the terrible massacres that occurred in the princely states, such as Jammu and Alwar, as well as the pogrom unleashed by Sardar Patel in the Nizam of Hyderabad's territories, which was euphemistically called 'police action'. This wider conspectus gravely undermines the curated mythology of a seamless and peaceful transition of power from 1947 to 1950—it demonstrates how violent this period was and that, in some ways, what happened was tantamount to a civil war. But was this violence a harbinger of the future of Partition?

Political scientist Pratap Bhanu Mehta makes the point that the Partition of India could only work if three conditions were met.[3] The first being that 'internal conflicts in each of the states would not radically spill over into the other states.' The fragile configuration of Pakistan post-Partition was always likely to create issues going to the very tenability of the state. This surfaced with a vengeance in 1971 with the bloody creation of Bangladesh, with assistance provided by India. There is also the matter of Jammu and Kashmir and the border issues with Pakistan which remain unresolved. Secondly, that successor states would attempt to behave in as normal and conventional a way as possible, encouraging trade and commerce. It is entirely possible that the two separated Punjabs could have made some kind of peace despite the carnage. There were ineffable cultural and economic ties that would have compelled the Punjabs to cooperate, but, unfortunately, owing to the Kashmir dispute, normal relations have not been possible. The third condition that Mehta points out is the seminal role India ought to have played in the subcontinent. Because of India's size and population, it was always going to be the big brother in the equation, and in reaction to communalism in its neighbourhood elsewhere it ought to have reaffirmed its own secularism more deeply. But that has been wrecked by the 'ascendency of Hindu nationalism ... [which] looks for pretexts to target Muslims, deepen internal divisions, and construct a seamless spectre of Muslim threat.'[4]

This has only led to further aggravation of already troubled relations between neighbours; even a state like Bangladesh, which sought to maintain normal relations with India, is deeply aggrieved at the anti-Muslim rhetoric of Indian politicians. This has been compounded by the toppling of the authoritarian Sheikh Hasina government in Bangladesh, a regime with close ties to the government in power in Delhi. This has not only had the consequence of compromising Bangladesh's already stigmatised secularism but has also had a malign domino effect throughout the subcontinent, encouraging fundamentalists of all hues to compete in expressing intolerant sentiments and making inflammatory speeches.

The Indian state, which has been plagued with border troubles since Independence now faces hostile forces on both its western and eastern borders. It also has a major military commitment in Kashmir to sustain, and by adopting a policy that alienates its largest minority, it has stoked up problems for the future. Partition also imposed a unitarian configuration on the Indian state, giving supremacy to cow belt states, particularly UP and Bihar, which has helped propel reactionary conservatism and the vivification of religion, bringing with it, the attendant social impoverishment. And now, with the prospect of delimitation, even greater political heft is likely to be given to northern states, which in all likelihood will foment serious issues with states in the south. All in all, the virulent nationalism that has taken hold is consuming Indian institutions and democracy.

For Pakistan, the outcome has been an unmitigated disaster, effectively reducing it to a garrison state because of its own paranoia, increasingly functioning as a device to enrich the military. Bangladesh and its stellar economic development in the last few years have been a surprise, but its performance is only remarkable in the context of a subcontinent growing at sub-optimal levels and, despite 1971, there still lurk the malign forces of religious reaction. Some of this concern has come to pass in Bangladesh, with the growing alignment between religious fundamentalism and democratic politics, which appears to be a direct reaction to the secular but corrupt and authoritarian leadership of Sheikh Hasina.

A key omission in discussions about the consequences of Partition is the fact of the dismantling of what was the British Indian army and its wider geopolitical ramifications. This was the largest volunteer army in the world, numbering over 2.5 million men in August 1947. Whilst the sycophants of Hindutva wax eloquent on Nehru's alleged blunders on Kashmir, the reality is that it is unlikely it would even have been a part of India but for Nehru. Also, what they do not speak of is Tibet, which was annexed by China in 1950. In my view, the Chinese would have been reluctant to disturb local equations and invade Tibet in 1950 if there had been a serious deterrent in the form of a united Indian Army.[5] The present-day ramifications of that are that India would never have had to share a border with China, if Tibet had not been overrun and annexed. This is not to exculpate Nehru but to point out that the Hindu Right are far from blameless in maintaining an adamantine stand on majoritarianism, thus hastening Partition, and should have to bear blame for some of the consequences that haunt us to this day.

Pakistan

The Partition led to the creation of Pakistan as a sovereign State with two wings: West Pakistan and East Pakistan. At that time, there were serious doubts if it would even be able to survive as a country. It had 27 per cent of the land space of undivided India, with 17.5 per cent of its resources. More than a thousand miles of Indian land lay between its two wings, which had both been entry points for foreign invasions in the past: from Afghanistan and Central Asia in the West and Japan in the East. For Pakistan, this denouement made no sense at all, and as British policy analyst Anatol Lieven points out, the demand for an East and West Pakistan was 'dictated at first instance by the need to keep all Muslims together so as to form the largest possible block against the Hindus within an Indian Confederation.'[6] He goes on to observe that 'as a homeland to all Muslims of South Asia, that meant that enormous political and emotional capital was invested in trying to maintain Pakistan as one State—when two friendly allied states would have made more sense.'[7] This epitomised Jinnah's failure to fully grapple with the practical realities of Pakistan as a nation-state and his obtuse insistence on treating Bengalis as inferiors without any agency. The latter is evidenced from the diktat that Urdu be the language of the entire state despite there being a significant number of Bengali-speakers in Pakistan. It also exposed the contradiction between his argument in favour of cultural pluralism in India and his insistence on linguistic and cultural homogeneity in Pakistan.

The need, in the words of Anatol Levien, to 'balance, conciliate or suppress'[8] East Bengalis has had a hugely detrimental influence on Pakistan's trajectory as a nation and has contributed to its stunting as a democracy. East Pakistan's small majority of Bengali Muslims would have meant that in fair and free elections, power would have shifted to a Bengali party, a prospect which the West Pakistanis would never have countenanced. East Pakistan became restive, particularly after the 1965 presidential election, where Fatima Jinnah was defeated by Ayub Khan in a rigged election which was sought to be legitimised by a disastrous and unnecessary conflict with India. Five years later, once again the popular mandate threw up a Bengali-speaking candidate, Mujibur Rahman of the Awami League, as the victor of the 1971 prime ministerial election. Yet again, the popular mandate was ignored, and that became the genesis of the Bangladesh Liberation War. Over the years, the Pakistani military has managed to establish successive dictatorships, entrenching itself in power as well as becoming addicted to it. Author Salman Rushdie has put it pithily: 'The idea of Pakistan suffered from insufficient imagination.'[9]

This baleful influence of the military in Pakistan has also had the unsettling effect of ratcheting up episodic tensions in Kashmir. The onset of conflicts started at the very birth of the two nations, with the Jammu genocide and the entry of tribal irregulars into Kashmir in 1948, instigating Indian reaction in order to protect the Valley, Jammu and Ladakh. Pakistan also had to deal with a disputed border with Afghanistan and the challenges of Pakhtun nationalism. The need to avoid a two-front war shaped strategic thinking within the Pakistani elite, with long-term consequences for regional stability, including conditions that later facilitated instability in Afghanistan and the rise of the Taliban. The Pakistani elite, from the very beginning, feared that India would seek to enforce what the RSS termed as 'Akhand Bharat' (greater India), since there existed a strong constituency in India that was unwilling to accept the creation of Pakistan.

Author Sudipta Kaviraj, writing on the Partition as a territorial phenomenon, points out that 'the most fundamental damage to political imagination was done perhaps by the idea underlying Partition that minorities can only secure themselves only in a state of their own, that is only if they turn themselves into a majority.'[10] That is unfortunately the great takeaway of Partition, that people of different religions cannot live together and that the only way societies can be formed and nations consolidated is by reference to an avowedly religious praxis.

22

KASHMIR

The main issue which seems to have galvanised both countries and vitiated the possibility of any civil relationship between India and Pakistan, as envisaged by both Gandhi and Jinnah, has been the Kashmir dispute. The Kashmir Valley is 97 per cent Muslim, whereas Muslims constitute 64 per cent of the population of the entire state of Jammu and Kashmir. It was the last of the princely states to accede to India, although Pakistan disputes the validity of the accession. For purely demographic reasons, it should have gone to Pakistan on the basis of it being a Muslim-majority province, a view held by Sardar Patel. The complication lay in the fact that the ruler of Kashmir, Maharaja Hari Singh, was a Dogra Hindu who wished for Kashmiri independence to retain his sovereignty, and to this end, he kept playing off the Congress against the Muslim League, refusing to go with either. Unfortunately for him, he left matters unresolved until the Poonch uprising, which started in August 1947 and by September had become a full-blown revolt, resulting in widespread communal violence. The Dogra army took the lead in committing atrocities and violence against Poonch Muslims. They were opposed by the self-proclaimed Azad army, who sponsored tribal forces which had, in their own words, already 'liberated' a substantial part of Mirpur and Poonch from Dogra rule by that time. As historian

Chitralekha Zutshi puts it, 'it was this insurrection against Dogra rule rather than the incursion of the Pukhtoon tribesmen that set the stage for the division of the state.'[1] This revisionism, associated with political scientist Christopher Snedden, which traces the tribal rising as a reaction to the pogrom in Jammu, greatly changes the narrative through which we see the genesis of the Kashmir dispute.[2]

Maharaja Hari Singh was constrained to seek Nehru's help, who took the decision to intervene militarily and force the invading tribesmen back. A massive airlift of soldiers and equipment took place from Delhi in October 1947 in exchange for Hari Singh agreeing to sign an Instrument of Accession to become a part of India. There are all manner of academic debates over the validity of this instrument, which I do not wish to go into, save to say it was not uncontroversial.

Mountbatten had to validate the accession treaty in his capacity as governor-general, and he did so with the qualification that such the accession should be ratified in accordance 'with the wishes of the people of the State.'[3] This became the genesis for the demand of a plebiscite in Kashmir. Nehru accepted this condition, as this was the protocol adopted in the case of Junagadh and the Northwest Frontier province as well. In Junagadh, there was a Muslim ruler who ruled over a largely Hindu population and decided to accede to Pakistan. In that case, the instrument of accession was rescinded, and a plebiscite was agreed to by Pakistan. In fact, at the time Sardar Patel in Junagadh made a speech that 'The State is no property of any individual. Paramountcy has lapsed not by the efforts of the Princes, but by those of the people.'[4] These words would have equal resonance in relation to Kashmir. In any case, Nehru was close to the pre-eminent political leader of Kashmir, Sheikh Abdullah, who was confident of getting support from the Kashmiris. A charismatic leader and the son of a shawl trader, Abdullah was imprisoned in 1946 for leading a popular movement against Maharaja Hari Singh. In any case, Nehru's room to manoeuvre on this issue was limited, given that Mountbatten's approval of the ascension was conditional.

Logically, Kashmir should have become a part of Pakistan given its largely Muslim population, however, being a princely state, different rules applied to it. Journalist Kuldip Nayar wrote,

> While it is true that Nehru was keen on Kashmir's accession to India, Patel opposed it. Sheikh Abdullah told me in an interview later (21 February 1971) that Patel argued with him that Kashmir was a Muslim-majority area and should go to Pakistan. Even when New Delhi received the Maharaja's request to accede to India, Patel said, 'We should not get mixed up with Kashmir. We already have too much on our plate'.[5]

Whilst Patel remained consistent and the Congress position was clear in relation to princely states with Muslim rulers and Hindu majority populations, such as Junagadh and Hyderabad, Nehru's emotional bonds with Kashmir had to be contended with too. As per Patel's records, even as he had tried his best to dissuade Nehru, the latter 'had broken down and wept, saying that Kashmir meant more to him at that moment than anything else.'[6] This concern was further recorded in a letter Nehru sent to the prime minister of the princely state of Jammu and Kashmir, M.C. Mahajan, in which he expressed his view on the future accession of the state, lamenting 'for me it is both a personal and a public matter. It would be a tragedy for me if Kashmir went to Pakistan.'[7]

Post the hostilities that started in 1948, a ceasefire was declared on 1 January 1949. At the time, Pakistan held Gilgit, Baltistan, and a sliver of Kashmir including Poonch and Mirpur, whereas India held Jammu, Ladakh, a part of Poonch and the lion's share of the Valley, including Srinagar, which was the capital. There was no serious equivalence between the territories each held: India had got the glittering prize of the Valley, while Pakistan was left with largely uninhabitable mountainous regions, which later came to be called Pakistan-occupied Kashmir or PoK.

The Hindu Right has always excoriated Nehru for what they call his weakness in agreeing to a ceasefire and not proceeding to annex PoK too. This accusation has acquired new resonance with the Modi government abrogating Article 370 of the Constitution. An argument is made that this compromise amounted to what current home minister, Amit Shah, calls 'a Himalayan blunder', referring specifically to the decision to take the Kashmir issue to the United Nations and agreeing to a plebiscite. In relation to the first accusation, contemporaneous correspondence with the then commander-in-chief of the Indian Army, Sir Francis Robert Roy Bucher, largely absolves Nehru, since he agreed to the ceasefire on the advice of his army chief. Bucher wrote on 28 November 1948 that there was fatigue on the part of the Indian troops in Kashmir and that 'an overall military decision is no longer possible ... Army personnel evince two weaknesses: lack of training in the junior leaders and tiredness and ennui in the other ranks ... In brief, the Army needs respite for leave, training and revitalising.'[8] Bucher himself suggested that a political approach to the problem was best. Even though, very conveniently, the Bucher papers have been embargoed by the NDA government, the *Guardian* newspaper was still able to access some critical letters.[9]

As referred to earlier, Mountbatten had placed an important caveat while approving the instrument of accession, that it should be settled by reference to the people. According to journalist Anuradha Bhasin, this meant the accession was not 'permanent and irrevocable.' It had to be settled by a referendum which was principally agreed to by the Indian government before and even after the dispute went to the United Nations.[10] Referendum as an instrument had been earlier employed, in the case of Sylhet, part of Assam in British India—the question there was whether this predominantly Bengali-speaking enclave should be part of India or Pakistan, and it agreed to go to Pakistan.[11] So, this idea of having a referendum of the people was clearly not conjured up as a means of Muslim appeasement. It had started with Junagadh and was used on a few other occasions.

If there was any doubt about the likely outcome of the plebiscite in 1948, the fact that Pakistan refused to unconditionally withdraw its troops from the areas it occupied, in accordance with the UN Council resolution 47, is the best evidence that Pakistan itself never wanted a plebiscite at that time. In respect to taking the Kashmir issue to the UN, this was explicitly supported by Sardar Patel.[12]

Pending the outcome of a plebiscite, the (in)famous Article 370 was added to the Constitution in 1949 as a stop-gap measure. It is relevant that Article 370 was passed almost unanimously in the Constituent Assembly, save for one dissenter, Maulana Hasrat Mohani, a communist, who objected to the grant of special status to

Kashmir on the grounds that it discriminated against the other states of the Indian union, which also deserved greater autonomy to realise the objective of federalism. Thus, contrary to popular mythology, there was no other dissent to Article 370; in fact, it was presented in the Constituent Assembly by Sardar Patel and seconded by Syama Prasad Mookerjee.

Furthermore, as legal scholar Faizan Mustafa points out, 'Some critics of Article 370 have argued that Kashmir joined India in 1947 without any conditions and, that Article 370 unnecessarily gave it special status. However, the Constitution was adopted on November 26 1949, and Article 370 had already been included before that.'[13] The fact is that Article 370 was negotiated by Sardar Patel while Nehru was away to the US. It was Patel who proposed it in the Lok Sabha, and any statements to the contrary are only designed to create a false binary between Patel and Nehru on this issue.[14]

Whilst Pakistanis have a different view of why the plebiscite did not take place and blame Indian intransigence, the point which is missed is that the Kashmir Valley itself was changing at this time, because of the introduction of radical land reforms by Sheikh Abdullah in 1950, which were well received and widely popular. There is nothing to suggest that Kashmir would not have voted to stay with India in that period.

With the assassination of the then prime minister of Pakistan, Liaquat Ali Khan, in 1951, all gentlemanly protocols and civilities that marked inter-State relations between India and Pakistan came to an end. In any event, the Pakistani elite went through a transformation. The Muslim League had never had strong roots in the provinces which were to become Pakistan, and in the absence of a robust political class, and indeed a vibrant civil society, power gravitated towards bureaucrats, the military and career politicians from elite backgrounds, whose survival was contingent on army support. Zulfiqar Ali Bhutto was the prime example of such a politician, and he was the instigator of much that has gone wrong with Indo-Pak relations. One of his most dramatic gestures was signing a border agreement with China in which he ceded over 2,000 square miles of the former state of Jammu and Kashmir to China, the area known as Aksai Chin, making the Kashmir dispute tripartite—something that

India has belatedly realised after the abrogation of Article 370. The unwisdom of this abrogation surfaced in the Galwan Valley barely ten months afterwards with the brutal strike on twenty Indian soldiers by the People's Liberation Army (PLA) and an intrusion into what India considers its territory in Ladakh. As journalist Manoj Joshi explains, the creation of the union territory of Ladakh so antagonised China that it attempted to raise the issue of Jammu and Kashmir as an India-Pakistan dispute in the UN Security Council for the first time since 1971.[15] In fact, the Chinese UN spokesperson Wang Wenbin stated clearly that 'China does not recognise the so-called Union Territory of Ladakh illegally established by India and opposes infrastructure construction in disputed border areas for military control purposes.'[16]

There were talks in the 1950s between Nehru and the new Pakistan prime minister, Mohammad Ali Bogra, which yielded nothing. What also became irksome for Nehru was the attitude of his erstwhile ally, Sheikh Abdullah, whose support had been crucial in securing the larger part of Jammu and Kashmir to India and in lending legitimacy to this exercise. Sheikh Abdullah was very much his own man and was confident enough to even suggest that independence was a feasible option for Kashmir. This suggestion provoked the displeasure of Nehru's cabinet and persuaded the government to keep him under arrest for nearly two decades. Chitralekha Zutshi ascribes this conduct to India's growing reluctance to hold a plebiscite, particularly in light of the pro-Pakistani position the US had adopted. This made even a popular chief minister like Sheikh Abdullah supremely dispensable. She argues that between 1953 and 1989, 'a succession of quisling governments sustained themselves through corruption, nepotism, and the suppression of dissent and opposition.'[17] This brute authoritarianism was epitomised by the introduction of the death penalty 'for those suspected of pro-Pakistan leanings' during the prime ministership of Bakshi Ghulam Mohammad in Kashmir.[18]

Belatedly, Nehru woke up to the fact that alienating Pakistan made no sense, as it was driving the country into the arms of a resurgent and triumphalist China which had tasted military success in 1962 and, after the annexation of Tibet, boasted of having the longest international border with India. The countries were sharing a border for the first time, and China posed a very tangible military threat to India, particularly as other border issues were also not resolved. Nehru wanted to avoid a two-front war with Pakistan and China at all costs and accordingly held negotiations with Pakistan in 1963, sending his cabinet minister Swaran Singh to negotiate with Zulfiqar Ali Bhutto on a resolution for Kashmir. Bhutto, as was his wont, scuttled the possibility of a settlement, although Ayub Khan, in principle, had been in favour of it.

Nehru was at his wit's end, but eventually came up with an innovative solution. He played the Sheikh Abdullah card and released his old friend from jail in order to send him to Pakistan to negotiate with Ayub Khan and finalise a tentative agreement. But the Sheikh was what one could politely describe as a bit of a loose cannon and made the extraordinary suggestion of a confederation of the three entities: India, Pakistan and Kashmir. This solution was entirely self-serving but provoked the suspicions of the Pakistanis, who were forever paranoid about India's intentions. In any case, Nehru passed away in 1964 whilst Sheikh Abdullah was in Pakistan, and on his return he was again arrested and imprisoned.

Ayub Khan attributed the 1965 war to India's intransigence over Kashmir, which led to the catastrophic attempt by Pakistan to wrest Kashmir from India by force through a military operation called 'Operation Gibraltar'. However, this war was actually triggered by domestic compulsions in Pakistani politics. Bhutto had successfully rigged the presidential election between Ayub Khan and Fatima Jinnah. He then persuaded Khan that a decisive military victory over India, one which involved the taking of Kashmir, would be needed to legitimise this constitutional perfidy. Ayub Khan had the support of China and was also conscious of the Indian Army's rearmament efforts post the Chinese war debacle. He saw this as the last window of opportunity to take on India before it regained its military strength. The war ended in a disaster, with the Pakistanis narrowly escaping complete defeat as Indian tanks approached Lahore and supply lines started becoming non-existent. Ayub Khan had wrongly assumed that the initial attack would not lead to an all-out war, relying also on Bhutto's assurance that Indian troops would not cross the international border. Pakistan had also gambled on an all-out revolt by the Kashmiris against India, which never happened. Despite the imprisonment of their most popular leader by the Indian state, in the words of academic Radha Kumar, 'Kashmiris surprised both India and Pakistan by cooperating with Indian troops to repel the guerrillas.'[19] Similar to 1948, it was the active support of the Kashmiri people that forestalled Pakistan from acquiring Kashmir, a fact that the Hindu Right contumaciously ignores.

As this is not a book on the rights and wrongs of what happened vis-à-vis Kashmir, I do not propose to deal with the events post the Soviet withdrawal from Afghanistan and the cynical use by the Pakistani establishment of the many spare foreign fighters and 'jihadis' who had remained behind, to infiltrate the Valley and foment violent instability which, even after thirty years, Kashmir is still recovering from. Instead, I will deal with a pet bugbear of the Hindu Right, which is the treatment of Kashmiri Pandits. This is an issue which the Hindu Right constantly raises, ascribing the killings and ethnic cleansing of Kashmiri Pandits by Kashmiri Muslims. I, for one, am not persuaded that this claim is justified. Recently, an extraordinarily incendiary piece of propaganda, masquerading as a film called *Kashmir Files*, was released, which depicts, in the most luridly grotesque manner, Kashmiri Pandits fleeing from the Valley because of genocidal violence unleashed on them in the early 1990s. This alleged genocide does not square with the data released by the Srinagar District Police Headquarters in response to an RTI filed in 2022. The figures clearly indicated that since the inception of militancy in 1990, Kashmiri militants had killed around 1,724 people in Jammu and Kashmir of which 89 were Kashmiri Pandits, while the remaining belonged to other faiths. There were admittedly four prominent Kashmiri Pandits who were killed—Tika Lal Taploo, a BJP and RSS leader; Lassa Kaul, Director of Srinagar Doordarshan; Sheela Tikoo and Justice Ganjoo (who had pronounced the death sentence on Kashmiri separatist, Maqbool Butt). Three of these killings were politically motivated rather than about the fact that they were Kashmiri Pandits.

The issue of why so many Pandits migrated out of Kashmir is a complex one, but the malevolent role of Jagmohan, the then governor of J&K, has often been cited as having encouraged the migration. It is undoubtedly true that over 300,000 Pandits left the Valley in 1990, but to ascribe this to imaginary mass killings and genocide is unfounded. It is equally true that successive governments over the years have not seriously attempted to rehabilitate the Pandits back in the Valley, something perplexing given the size of India's military commitment to the state. This becomes even more striking in light of the presence of a substantial Sikh population, estimated at around 70,000 to 80,000 in the Valley, which sits uneasily with any simplistic jihadist framing of the situation.

23

PAKISTAN

The 1965 war had serious implications on Indo-Pak relations, causing the Indian government to view Pakistan as a hostile state. This, unfortunately, also had huge ramifications on India's large Muslim population. With Nehru's demise in 1964, India's Muslims had lost someone they saw as a genuine friend and protector. The hostility consequent on this unnecessary war collapsed into distrust for Indian Muslims. A result of this was the enactment of the Enemy Property Act, 1968, as per which properties identified as having any Pakistani interest were attached and vested in the custody of the Custodian of Enemy Property for India. As of 2018, the status of these properties appears to be legal appropriation by the state. Attaching enemy property in times of war is not unusual; what is exceptional is that this law has persisted indefinitely, even after the end of hostilities, and has now metamorphosed into an instrument of acquisition. It is an act of collective punishment, in most cases affecting Indian Muslims who chose to stay back post-Partition. Given the nature of heirship under Sharia law, it was inevitable that some properties would include shares belonging to family members who had migrated to Pakistan, thereby rendering such assets liable to attachment as 'enemy property'.

The Enemy Property Act of 1968 followed in the wake of the abolition of zamindari in 1951, a reform that disproportionately affected the Muslims of UP. This was despite assurances made by Nehru to Muslim rajas and taluqdars; as journalist Saeed Naqvi notes, Nehru promised 'that zamindari abolition would not follow so soon after the trauma of Partition. Even the smaller landlords felt reassured by this promise, only it turned out to be false.'[1] This is not to say that land reform was not a laudable step, but in the context of Partition and with a threat posed to their properties and businesses, Indian Muslims were left feeling besieged. If the abolition of the Zamindari disproportionately hit the Muslims of UP, the arbitrary and, in some cases, corrupt conduct of the Custodian of Enemy Property towards them deepened their distress. This greatly disturbed Nehru, causing him to remark in 1949—'I have been upset about many things, but these recent developments in regard to Muslims, evacuees or others, have come as a great shock to me.'[2]

It is extraordinary that members of the Pakistani establishment, while formulating their national policy, failed to consider its adverse impact on their co-religionists in India, even adopting an unremittingly hostile attitude towards them. There was never any realistic prospect of physically accommodating pre-Independence India's vast Muslim population in Pakistan but, at least, if the countries had good relations, the Hindu Right's ability to mistreat India's Muslims, on the pretext of Pakistan's delinquencies and excesses, would have been considerably reduced.

The sense of exceptionalism felt by West Pakistanis, particularly in the Punjabi-dominated military, is evident in their attitude towards Bengalis living in East Pakistan and, by extension, towards Indian Muslims. This mindset arose from an ethnic sense of exceptionalism and a deeply militaristic attitude, which had violent consequences in 1971. Many of the Punjabi Muslims, who had bought into the notion of belonging to a martial race, considered Muslims from East Pakistan and UP as weak and inconsequential.

There was within Pakistan's elite an underlying unease towards India, reinforced by the events of 1971 and India's role in the secession of East Pakistan to form Bangladesh. It was unfortunate that India became mired in this episode, giving ample ammunition to Pakistani military hawks and credence to the narrative of India's perfidious intentions. The fact, though, was that the genocidal conduct of the Pakistani Army towards the local population of East Pakistan, many of whom were Hindus, caused an exodus of refugees to India, leaving the Indian government with no alternative but to step in. In fact, prior to 1971, it suited India's interests to maintain the status quo, as Pakistan was dependent on the Indian landmass for transportation and logistics links between its two wings. Moreover, Bengali political influence acted as a corrective to the palpably anti-Indian mindset of the predominantly Punjabi army. In retrospect, this third partition was destined to happen, given the condescension with which West Pakistanis looked on their Bengali brethren, treating them as culturally inferior and as less authentic Muslims.

In any event, what became evident in Pakistan was an organic collaboration between a Punjabi-dominated bureaucracy and army on the one hand, and the landed families from the Punjabi province on the other. As per historians Tai Yong Tan and Gyanesh Kudaisya, 'One of the outcomes of this association was the militarisation of the administration of the Punjab, characterised by the conjunction of the military, civil and political authorities into a unique civil-military regime.'[3] This was a precursor to the embedded role of the army in civilian administration in Pakistan, which sadly continues to this day.

After the 1971 war and the creation of Bangladesh, the two-nation theory was discredited beyond repair. If there was any doubt about the Pakistani establishment's insouciance towards the suffering and displacement of fellow Muslims, it was dispelled by the appalling treatment meted out to Urdu-speaking Biharis stranded in Bangladesh after the 1971 war, who were denied accommodation by Pakistan in the self-proclaimed Muslim homeland. No such hesitation was shown to the Afghan refugees streaming across the border into refugee camps as a consequence of the Soviet invasion, as that aligned with the army's strategic interests. Such brutal inhumanity was recently again on display in 2023, with the dramatic overnight expulsion of Afghan refugees by the Pakistan Government, many of whom had been born in Pakistan and had no tangible connections with Afghanistan.

These issues are particularly pertinent to India in light of the question of Kashmiri Muslims. Several Indian citizens fled from Kashmir in the 1990s amid the army's crackdown on militants, during which many civilians were also suspected of aiding insurgents. Around 35,000 Kashmiri Muslims fled to Pakistan Occupied Kashmir (PoK) in that period. Pakistan has not given them citizenship, and they are essentially treated as stateless refugees. This migration has to be looked at in the context of civil strife that took place during that period, and the imposition of AFSPA which denies them due process. Yet the persons who have fled, for whatever reason, continue to be Indian citizens languishing bereft of any rights in PoK. They deserve, at least, a right to be heard.

The 1971 catastrophe caused the Pakistanis to rethink the nature of their Islamic identity, and to this extent, a new fetish surfaced with a faux sacrality afforded to Kashmir. As author Farzana Shaikh puts it, 'Kashmir was recast as sacred territory awaiting liberation through jihad—thus authenticating Pakistan's identity as the protector of Islam.'[4] It is for this reason that the Pakistani establishment is so fixated with Kashmir, as it reaffirms its own Islamic identity. For more mundane reasons, it also gives the army license to interfere in and take control of the Indo-Pakistani discourse, effectively setting the ground rules that there can be no peace with India without a resolution of Kashmir. This in turn means that the army has secured for itself a disproportionate share of the resources of the State, sustained by the beguiling fiction that Kashmir is the battleground and that the army has to be in a state of constant military preparedness.

If Zulfiqar Ali Bhutto was the wily and opportunistic operator responsible for hitching Pakistan's star to China as well as for creating conditions that entrenched the poison and toxicity of Partition, his assassin and successor General Zia-ul-Haq was even worse. He sought to reshape a largely feudal and Sufi society in the image of a South Asian Saudi Arabia, albeit without the oil wealth that Saudi Arabia enjoys. He belonged to the 'Jamaat-e-Islami' persuasion and had the overweening desire to impose Sharia law on Pakistan, most notably through the 'Hudood' ordinances that imposed particularly barbaric punishments. These laws were of symbolic effect as they were rarely used in practice, their ostensible purpose being to banish and efface all vestiges of modernity, secularism and democracy. General Zia, behind a jovial Terry Thomas visage, harboured a most regressive mindset, allegedly proclaiming that had Islam not been central to the idea of Pakistan, all those who migrated might have continued to remain in India.[5] For the first time in Pakistan's brief history, an Islamic ideologue had come to power, who had untrammelled authority to impose his will and to mould the bureaucracy and judiciary under the rubric of Islamicisation. He got only eleven years to carry out his mission until he died in a mysterious air crash in 1988 caused most likely by a bomb hidden in a crate of mangoes.

General Zia's legacy lies not only in the injection of a particularly virulent strain of Islamicist thinking into the body politic, but also in transforming Pakistan's strategic geographic location into a source of revenue, effectively renting it out to global actors, from the Americans in the 1980s to the Chinese most recently, particularly in relation to China's Belt and Road initiative.

However, the damage has been done. Pakistan has been in gradual decline, demonstrated by its abysmal investment in developing manpower skills, and science and technology, with the hegemony of religion having extirpated all rationality. Military expenditure exceeds 26 per cent of the GDP—this is probably a gross underestimate, given the disguised outlays on things such as pensions. What is extraordinary is the extent to which Pakistan's military assets have grown—by 115 per cent between 2011 and 2022, yielding an annual income of over USD 2.7 billion. The Pakistani army has huge investments in real estate, food processing businesses, clubs, transportation and logistics companies, etc., and all these are given preferential tax treatment. This even though the country's finances are in a dire condition, reducing it to the status of a mendicant, having to borrow from the Saudis, the World Bank, China and other lenders.

24

THE PLIGHT OF INDIAN MUSLIMS

In the real sense, Indian Muslims were the orphans of Partition. Their political leverage ceased to have any traction; they were stripped of separate electorates and reserved positions post-Independence, and Pakistan was cynically presented as a gift to the Muslims of India, and having 'given' them that, it was argued that there were no further reasons to accommodate them. The left-leaning members of the Congress party busied themselves with what they saw as reform of Hindu society, whereas the right-leaning members of the Congress party sought to obstruct or undermine such reforms. Muslims in India were largely left to fend for themselves.

One of the many intractable problems faced by Muslims is that they are viewed by the majority community, particularly in the North, solely through the prism of religion, and this, in my view, is the origin of their stigmatised citizenship. Where does this perception come from? In North India, we would have to go back to the Khilafat Movement as the turning point in Hindu–Muslim relations in the period preceding Partition; strangely, this movement became integral to the nationalist struggle.

In pre-Independence India, the Khilafat Movement proved to be one of the most fraught events for the Muslim community of India, as it brought into sharp focus the divide between, on the one hand,

Muslim thinkers such as Sir Sayyid Ahmed, who believed that the future of Muslims in India would be best secured under continuing British rule, and, on the other hand, those Muslims who were of an incorrigibly anti-Western mindset and religious disposition, and regarded colonial rule as an affront to them. This was the obvious demarcation. But within the community there was also an emerging Western-oriented middle class, which may have been politically and numerically inconsequential, but found in a leader such as Jinnah a spokesman who was a nationalist but was also chary of intertwining politics with religion and global Islam, as he saw this as intrinsically fraught with danger. There is a larger controversy which this issue opens up: what exactly was the relationship between Indian Muslims and global Islam? This is an issue which has not quite been resolved even now.

I say this because much of the intellectual framing for the insidious Islamophobia, which regrettably frames the narrative in India today, owes its origins to the West. It is fair to say that other than the Kashmir dispute and Pakistan's involvement there through surrogates, this Islamophobia is a consequence of a peculiarly Western viewpoint which is manifest in media coverage and in the narrative of the new right. The ideas of historians such as Samuel Huntington gained traction in the aftermath of various random acts of violence and terrorism committed by discontented Muslim groups in the West and the Middle East, contributing to the configuration of a new enemy in the post-Cold War world. But many consider the Khilafat Movement as the root of the Partition, for having surcharged political Islam and ultimately resulting in the passing of the Lahore Resolution. An argument is often made, controversially, that the present state of radicalisation in India could be traced back to these events; this is a very serious charge and one which has to be addressed.

At one level, it was opportune for the Congress leadership under the Gandhi to raise the issue of support to the beleaguered Ottomans as they were at war with the British empire. The fact that they were guardians of the holy places, Mecca, Medina and Jerusalem, gave a legitimacy to the Caliphate which transcended everything else. It was an easy and obvious way to garner support amongst the religious Muslims of the subcontinent and to win them over to the nationalist movement without conceding much in practical terms. It was also significant in that it brought communities together, both Hindus and Muslims, on one nationalistic platform. As philosopher Akeel Bilgrami puts it, this movement was 'a genuinely pluralistic and inclusive movement against imperial force,'[1] and the Khilafat Movement allowed for mass engagement with Muslims to garner their support for the nationalist movement in an idiom they could understand. The immediate consequence of the Khilafat Movement was to alienate Jinnah from the Congress, however would be some years before the formal separation occurred. Ironically, in light of Jinnah's future political trajectory, he was genuinely disturbed by the unwelcome intrusion of religious tropes and slogans such as 'Islam in danger' in the then civilised political discourse which had till then been monopolised by the upper echelons of Muslim society. Bilgrami argues that there was, in any case, no authentically Indian secularism at the time, at least as understood in the West, and to blame the Khilafat Movement for introducing the controversial element of religion into politics would be fanciful and historically incorrect. In arguing this, Bilgrami is broadly accurate. In support of this argument, one can allude to Tilak's promotion of the Ganesh festival, along the lines of the Muharram Taziya processions in Maharashtra, as a catalyst for energising the masses.

A counter to this argument is that the Khilafat Movement was something of an egregious distraction. It distracted the UP Muslims, for example, from defending the existing pluralistic culture, which was the only way the communities could have truly coexisted. Instead, their energies were channelled into a cause which, by 1918, was already lost and mostly irrelevant to their lives. It also caricatured the community as one owing fealty to a foreign sovereign, the Ottoman Caliph, and thus being potentially disloyal to India. It was this aspect that perhaps prompted Savarkar to distinguish Indian Muslims and Christians from Hindus on the basis of where they owed their religious allegiance.

The Demise of the Cultural Muslim

My own take on this is that the Khilafat Movement may well have been inclusive and pluralistic at the time, but it had resonance only because of the spectre of colonial oppression—it was aimed against a common enemy. But it did not bode well for the future of Muslims, as it reduced them to a community for which only religious demands were paramount. This appealed to Hindus politicians: it ghettoised Muslims, confining their demands to the religious sphere, most of which did not gravely prejudice Hindus, other than their demand to retain their personal laws which purportedly posed an obstacle to the chimera of a uniform civil code. Thus, the cultural and economic rights of Muslims were not taken seriously: for example, the demand to have Urdu as an official second language in UP was disregarded, and it was marginalised to the status of a third language after Hindi and Sanskrit.

The fact that Muslim demands were considered to be confined to religion had itself important implications for the leadership of the community. In general, the spread of Westernisation and English education in India had the effect of distancing elites from the masses in all communities. In most cases, it fostered a process that secularised the elites, in that religion became a personal matter for them, if it mattered at all. That led to the emergence of a new group of Muslims that could be called 'cultural Muslims'—they were not very different from Hindus, Christians and Sikhs of the same class and education level, who believed in rationalism, progress and equality. In this way, they sharply differed from many of their poorer and less cosmopolitan brethren who took pride in their identity and religion, almost wearing it on their sleeve. The difficulty these cultural Muslims encountered was that the political agenda for secularism had hardened into the straitjacket of cultural uniformity in the name of 'nation building.' At the same time, religious demands—those that did not affect the majority community—were acceded to, allowing politicians to buy votes relatively cheaply and keep the mullahs happy. In such a political milieu, the cultural Muslim was seen as elitist and increasingly irrelevant, whereas the fundamentalist was given prominence.

In fact, this caricature of the community became even more pronounced with the expansion of employment opportunities in the Gulf in the 1970s and the growing influence of the Wahhabi strain of Islam on many poor Muslims. Imported from Saudi Arabia, Wahhabism is an aridly puritanical version of Islam, which pointedly looked down on what they categorised as un-Islamic behaviour, such as drinking alcohol, listening to music, or engaging in any form of saint worship. In many ways, this dramatised what had been an existential and historical struggle for the soul of Indian Islam, particularly between the Deobandis and the Barelvis, the former seeking to Arabise the religion, and the latter, who believe in veneration of the Prophet, Sufism and saint worship. It can also be seen as a broader agenda to detach Indian Muslims from their roots in what was a syncretic culture. The consequence of this Arabisation of Indian Islam was that it profoundly contracted and reduced the cultural footprint of Muslims, since being a Muslim was increasingly being seen through a religious prism, one that was greatly influenced by Wahhabi thinking.

If I have raised the issue of lack of agency of Indian Muslims, one cannot ignore the blight of the new fundamentalist ideologies which have been imported from the Middle East in which religion is not only ritualised, it is reduced to what has been described as the 'objectification of Muslim consciousness'.[2] It purports to provide 'a self-contained system that its believers can describe, characterise and distinguish from other belief systems.' Much of these writings refers to anecdotes from the life of the Prophet and his companions which believers are called upon to emulate. The purpose of this is to identify with the imagined persona of the Prophet and of his era; it is irredeemably revanchist in character. This atavistic thinking infects the community in terms of their attitudes and priorities as well as creates a chasm with the majority community.

The danger is that believers are drilled into thinking that the temporal world is a mere illusion which distracts from the practice of true religion. Such an attitude influences perceptions of the future. For a society and its people to attain success, not only is the acquisition of education and practical skills essential, but a belief in a future which will involve planning and a sense of the long term is also needed. Admittedly, there are societies such as Israel and Saudi Arabia that are rich enough to fund large numbers of people who wholly devote themselves to religious practice at the cost of their livelihoods. This is not an option for many Indian Muslims, but unfortunately this anti-materialist sentiment combined with a disdain for Western education conspires to keep the community backward.

One of the effects of this typecasting of Muslims—as essentially religious beings, who have no claims on modern society other than asking to be left alone to practise their religious beliefs—was the diminishing of the role and influence of cultural Muslims, who came to be regarded, not just by the Mullahs but even by the majority community, as not really authentic Muslims. This leads to the unspoken assumption that there are real Muslims and fake ones, and that the latter should have no real say in the future of the community. This fate is not uncommon, as other religious communities have also suffered from this suffocating attitude—the Jews spring to mind. In a biography of Sir Isaiah Berlin, there is a passage that is worth repeating.

> One Jew may find his identity in Israel, another in Britain; one may find it in religious faith, another in the observance of Jewish customs, and yet another in abandoning Judaism altogether. It is a form of intellectual tyranny to suppose that one of these choices must be right for everyone. If the claims of religion and tradition were to prevail over an individual's right to shape his own life, Jews would merely exchange the externally imposed servitude they had long endured for a self-imposed one within their own community.[3]

I think this quotation is poignant and hugely relevant as it acknowledges the autonomy of individuals to practice their faith in the manner they want, and though this autonomy is granted to persons who belong to other religions, it is worth asking why it is denied to Muslims?

The idea of the 'elite' Muslim sits uneasily with historical reality. If one examines North Indian culture, one sees the extraordinary contribution the Muslims have made, whether it be to handicrafts, textiles, art, literature, drama, poetry, classical and folk music, culinary arts, or cinema. With the Partition, there was a rise in fundamentalism and a decline in this sort of contribution. It is as if the narrative that Muslims are labelled with, of religious beings who are forbidden from participation in the arts, is being taken seriously. And that is not just a loss for Muslims; it is a diminishment of Indian culture.

The Rise of the Religious Right

The rise to prominence of the All India Muslim Personal Law Board (AIMPLB) as a leader of the Muslim community in the North is a consequence of the *Shah Bano* case and the Ayodhya dispute. This self-appointed body purports to represent the interests of the North Indian 'Ashrafs', the traditional upper-class Muslim North Indian elite. To a large extent, the *Shah Bano* judgement gave legitimacy to this body as interlocutors who were able to protect Sharia law from any reform or interference from a secular government. It also buttressed the narrative that all that Muslims were interested in were religious matters, such as preserving Sharia law and safeguarding mosques. This narrative was hugely damaging to all Muslims in the long run, as Professor Devji observed, 'they generally ended up holding Muslims in different parts of the country hostage to North Indian concerns, and thus shut down political diversity within the community.'[4] The AIMPLB, in its attempts to defend the Sharia and the Babri Masjid, played into the hands of the Hindu Right, as it projected a united Muslim coalition of interest at an all-India level which only instigated the consolidation of a much larger Hindu coalition. This transformed the political discourse in the country, bringing Hindu nationalism to the forefront.

The treatment of Indian Muslims by the majority community is often viewed through the prism of an indulgent majority having to deal with a recalcitrant minority who stubbornly do not wish to 'integrate,' who stand out because of their dress, their excessive religiosity and their desire to cling to their personal law. The Sachar Committee Report on the state of the Indian Muslims has been an eye opener as to the extent of the backwardness and poverty of the community. Perversely, this view has been used by the Hindu Right to blame the secular Congress for the state of affairs without offering an alternative vision.

I have placed the plight of Indian Muslims in the context of the subcontinent, as I think that is the only sensible way of understanding their problems. In this regard, the focus is unapologetically on North India and the Deccan, as there is a historic continuum. It is not possible to detach Partition and its aftermath from their present fate, whether it be the separation of families, the migration of the best and brightest, the stigmatised citizenship or a besieged culture. These factors cannot be disregarded, particularly when seen alongside burgeoning Hindu triumphalism and attacks on peculiarly Muslim businesses, such as butchery and the leather trade, through draconian cow slaughter laws. The tentacles of the Enemy Property Act extend to landed Muslims, and the stubborn refusal to give reservations to Muslim Dalits and other Muslim Scheduled Castes exhibits a desire to discriminate against Muslims of all classes. These concerns are only exacerbated by the slow but inexorable disappearance of the Muslim voice in the political space and its absence in the media, save for the dwindling Urdu press.

In fact, the Hindu Right's narrative has gained considerable traction, casting India's Muslims as disloyal to India, pro-Kashmiri, insistent on special minority protections, resistant to a Uniform Civil Code, thus undermining national unity. So much so that the image conjured up typically portrays Hindus as besieged in their own country by a demanding, disloyal and ungrateful minority who, according to many, should not be here in the first place; instead, they should all be in Pakistan.

Author Nirad Chaudhari has said that he always thought of the Poles as an unhappy people but 'I do not consider that even their fate has been tragic as that of the Muslims of India.'[5] Today most people look at their economic and social conditions and feel a sense of despair. But for Indians of an earlier generation, it only reflects part of their contemporary destitution. Author Sudipta Kaviraj puts it well when he says,

> As a community, the Muslims suddenly lost their status as a culturally and socially leading group, forced unjustly to be on the defensive, despite Nehru's attempt to celebrate their decision to stay as a triumph of secularism. Once they had been among the groups which used to dominate society; now they had to be protected by the state.[6]

This is a very insightful observation, but does not quite capture the true extent of their denigration and decline, as, along with their community, their culture is also sought to be banished and their history effaced from school textbooks.

It is often forgotten that Muslims, particularly those from Bombay, played a significant role in Indian nationalism. Figures such as Badruddin Tyabji, the first Muslim president of the Congress, along with the Ali brothers and Abdul Ghaffar Khan, popularly known as the 'Frontier Gandhi,' exemplify the many who sacrificed themselves for the cause of India's freedom. Muslims from India have also distinguished themselves in commerce—the 'Khoja, Memon and Bohri' communities from Gujarat have not only established thriving businesses in India, but in Africa and in the Far East.

The cultural contributions of Muslims have been immense in music, art, theatre, cinema, education and handicrafts, including textiles. This cultural contribution has had a major knock-on effect on popular culture, especially in Indian cinema, shaping film production, scriptwriting and music, particularly during cinema's 'Golden Age'. I state this only to underscore the extent of the community's subsequent decline, a trajectory that, rather than being reversed, appears to be further exacerbated by the current government's approach.

For a population of over 200 million, the fact that the number of Indian Muslims who have joined extremist organisations is minuscule is one in which the Indian establishment should take great comfort. Instead, it pointedly chooses to ignore this as it does not align with its narrative. India is probably the only country in the world which, despite having a largely docile Muslim minority population, is transfixed by an imaginary existential threat of Muslim fundamentalism. So much so that it acts as the lightning rod of its foreign policy almost to the point of collective paranoia. This fear and trepidation are apparent on the news and television coverage, where nary a day passes without the dredging up of some Islamophobic reference or the highlighting of some stray incident in Kashmir to show Pakistan's perfidy. One would imagine that there were no other problems in India save for being the target of international Islamic terrorism, the only spoiler in an otherwise trouble-free existence.

The Alienation of Indian Muslims

Whilst it is true that from the time of Independence to around 2001, there have been instances of episodic violence between Hindus and Muslims, with riots and massacres taking place in Hashimpura in UP, Nelli in Assam, Bhagalpur in Bihar in 1989, Bombay in 1992, Gujarat in 2002—all of which represent an unsettling new and sinister twist in the 'confrontations.' In the past, episodes of communal violence and massacres involving minority communities, whether they be Muslims or Sikhs, were accompanied by cover-ups, with some degree of political choreography and police complicity. But the Gujarat conflagration brought in a new dimension when allegations were made that there was Pakistani involvement in the death of the pilgrims who were returning from Ayodhya. The allegation that the terrorist organisation Lashkar-e-Taiba was involved in the attacks is bereft of any tangible evidence, but it ended up transforming a quotidian Hindu–Muslim clash into one in which the Indian state was pitted against a global evil jihadi conspiracy, warranting violent retribution on local Indian Muslims by way of collective punishment handed out by vigilantes and non-state actors. This is the Kashmir playbook, the Putin playbook in Chechnya, as well as the Israeli playbook in Gaza and West Bank.

The alienation of Muslims, particularly in the heartland, is growing apace, particularly with the police being emboldened by Hindutva policies. We saw the recent example of Muslim boys who were breaking their fast during Ramazan being arrested because they were accused of throwing the remains of allegedly chicken biryani into the Ganga. The fact that the river is the recipient of huge quantities of sewage and industrial waste, for which no one gets pulled up is jarring. It is also material that Muslims number disproportionately amongst imprisoned undertrials: in UP, for instance, Muslims constitute about 19 per cent of the population, yet they accounted for roughly 28.3 per cent of those languishing in prison in 2020—a disparity that appears anomalous.[7]

The plight of young Muslims has been brought into sharp relief by the recent findings of the All India Survey of Higher Education. In comparison to Dalits, Adivasis and OBCs, the enrolment of Muslim students has dropped by 8 per cent since 2019–2020. Interestingly, the decline is most pronounced in UP (around 36 per cent), Jammu and Kashmir (26 per cent), and Delhi (20 per cent). This can be contrasted with traditionally backward communities, like the Dalits, whose enrolment has increased by 4.2 per cent, the Adivasis by 11.9 per cent, and the OBCs by 4 per cent. Interestingly, states in which Muslims are given reservations both in jobs and higher educational institutions, such as Kerala, which affords 10 per cent reservations in government jobs and 12 per cent in educational institutions, show a more positive trend.[8] Political scientist Christophe Jaffrelot ascribes this disturbing trajectory to the rise of Hindu majoritarianism in terms of discrimination in jobs, as it is almost worthless to acquire an education without the prospect of gainful employment. He also attributes this situation to the increase in day-to-day violence towards Muslims, which has forced them into ghettos in most Indian cities. He bases this view on research conducted that showed that CVs with Muslim names attracted the least interest.[9] His conclusion is that we are witnessing the manufacturing of second-class citizens, which does not bode well for social harmony.

Historian Ali Khan Mahmudabad observes that the 'lethal combination of political, institutional, legal, economic and social exclusion promises to sow the seeds for a conflict that will destabilise India for the years to come.'[10] He also points out that nearly 50 per cent of the Muslim population is below nineteen years of age, underscoring the potential long-term consequences for this young community, that is growing up in an atmosphere of 'hate and intolerance,' and as a generation will have known nothing but exclusion and alienation. With the BJP making Indian politics increasingly more right-wing, it is more than likely that young, alienated Muslims will not look to the secular opposition as their role model; they may very well look to Muslim extremism for succour. Yet the majority community remains insulated from any blame; in fact, the argument is that the real problem has been the excessive indulgence shown by the majority to the minority. This is one of the reasons that post 2014, India has elected a government and a party which cannot be accused of such misguided policies. The Muslims have been shown their place.

The problem with this fetish with Islamic fundamentalism is that it borrows much from the Western narrative, seeing the problem as being integral to Islamic thought which promotes jihad and justifies terrorism and violence, rather than seeing it in the context of the twenty-first century. It is important to note that the concept of 'jihad' received prominence only in the twenty-first century. Faisal Devji, in his incisive study on militant Islam, makes the point that 'local forms of Islamic militancy are... increasingly mediated by global conditions rather than the other way round.'[11] This argument is further reinforced by the brilliant work of author Suzanne Schneider where she examines jihad not in the context of some historical continuum from the seventh century, but rather argues that to truly understand it one has to look 'sideways at the contemporary world.'[12] This is necessary as it upends the narrative which views Western violence, as witnessed in Afghanistan, Iraq and Gaza, as being rational and proportionate, as distinct from jihadi violence, which can only be terrorism.

The only way forward is for the Muslims of North India to discard their fetish with outdated interpretations of the Sharia and to recover their agency through more calculating and self-centred political alignments, as we have seen in the South. The BJP has been promising assistance to those referred to as Pasmanda Muslims, that is, those Muslims that have been socially and economically left behind, but there has been little follow through. At the same time, this may be a political dead end as it probably involves nominal caste-based reservations, and yet, as experience with OBCs has shown, it is not as if these reservations guarantee outcomes.

A more promising avenue may lie in the reform of Waqf laws. As Faisal Devji has noted, Jinnah's reform in 1937 created a system whereby wealth could be accumulated within the family, similar to an HUF, thereby avoiding division according to Sharia laws of inheritance. Muslims need to move a step further and reform the family waqf into a family trust, one that aligns with modernity in that it does not tie up property indefinitely. These are some pointers for a future which otherwise looks uniformly dismal.

However, absent a political voice in a political system driven by majoritarian thinking, Muslims have little or no political recourse, as India is fast ceasing to be a political society and is increasingly becoming an authoritarian one. Let us go back to ancient Greece: when in 416 BCE Athens had attacked Melos, its inhabitants had sued for peace. To that, Thucydides had famously remarked 'the strong do what they can and the weak suffer what they must.'[13] This, regrettably, is the plight of the minorities in the matrix of the new nationalism.

EPILOGUE

The controversies raised by the majoritarian agenda and its effects and consequences are not limited to the minorities; of course, the terminology is fluid, and what is majority and what is minority changes as per context. But if we examine the impact of this nationalism and the skewed political discourse on 90 per cent of the Indian population, it offers little beyond a temporary palliative of false pride, with little or no improvement to their lives. In fact, it operates and is intended to operate, as a distraction from the realities of living in India. The present government itself has coined the term 'ease of living' and perhaps to understand what citizenship means we need to look at it through that prism. Ease of living would necessarily involve institutional recognition of the citizen's time, health, safety and dignity. This is the bare minimum that the government can do to make citizenship tangible. Yet, for most, if not all the 90 per cent, there is little recognition by the state of the value of these fundamental aspects of everyday life.

For instance, let's look at safety. Maintenance of law and order is one of the most basic tasks of the government. We have a judicial system that is overburdened and under the heavy influence of the executive. Internationally, India ranks just above Gabon in contract enforcement of contracts. We have one of the largest populations of undertrials in our prison system (around 75 per cent of all prisoners are undertrials). The Indian police are highly politicised and corrupt, often giving scant regard to the travails of ordinary citizens.

Transportation is unsafe and chaotic. India has the highest number of deaths in road traffic accidents in the world, while incidents arising from bridge collapses and other substandard infrastructure keep recurring. Cleanliness of air and water is a serious issue in urban India. Most of the highly polluted cities in the world fall in the Indian subcontinent, with New Delhi taking the lead. Cases of death linked to contaminated water continue to rise, even as access to safe drinking water remains uneven and often inadequate. This unease of living has become the new 'normal' and does not evince much mention in the public discourse.

In fact, the government often diverts attention from these serious issues to matters which are peripheral to its remit, heralding India as the fastest growing world economy based on dubious GDP numbers which, in turn, are based on the size of the population, consumption patterns and production terms—matters independent of government policy, which, at the highest, only have a limited facilitating role. However, under this nationalist carapace, the Indian government has essentially freed itself from its responsibilities. It no longer sees its role as one that requires the securing of basic citizenship rights for Indians as adumbrated above. What it seeks to do now is to facilitate cash transfers to people rather than to build capacities, which only governments can do, in terms of urban planning, infrastructure, education, health, law and order. The Sixteenth Finance Commission, in a study of twenty-one states, showed a sharp increase in subsidies in the form of cash transfers from INR 3.86 trillion in 2018-19 to INR 9.73 trillion in 2024-25. This is quite plainly a dereliction of duty and responsibility. It is also oddly Marxian in that it represents the withering away of the state, but not in the way Marx intended.

Devesh Kapur and Arvind Subramaniam in their magisterial book *A Sixth of Humanity: Independent India's Development Odyssey* comment on India being a 'precocious' democracy where public accountability is defined by the trifecta of promising 'subsidy, concession and quota' rather than the provision of public goods, law and order and good infrastructure. To address the plight of the non-Brahmin/non-Baniya castes, primarily the OBCs, this policy confection of subsidies, concession and quotas has become normal. Also, state elections increasingly involve cash handouts to the electors are made to win elections, irrespective of the attendant fiscal strain to the public exchequer. However, even these handouts must be funded from somewhere, leading ineluctably to a high tax economy.

Many of the beneficiaries of the status quo, who remain tolerably ensconced in their gilded, gated communities, are subject to these taxes. Yet, even they have to breathe the foul air and put up with the escalating urban pollution and chaos. Even these, otherwise stalwarts of nationalism, have now started looking for greener pastures in cities abroad such as Dubai or Singapore. As we have seen in Pakistan and Bangladesh, where sections of the elite have long migrated outward, there are indications that we are witnessing a similar exodus from India, evident from the alacrity shown in purchasing foreign citizenship, displaying an ominous portend of what is still to come.

With delimitation looming and a census projected to happen in 2027, Hindutva politics will inevitably become even more charged, particularly given its tendency to consider any form of public accountability as grossly impertinent, even bordering on anti-national. The stage is set for the evacuation of the upper middle class, the rich already having a foothold abroad in some shape or form. But this migration of the best and the brightest will not assist India in its aspirations to become a superpower and 'Vishwa Guru' any time soon.

This, unfortunately, is the telos of the India/Bharat dichotomy: the BJP's insistence that Bharat triumph over India, which means expanding the footprint of the cow belt ideology, and poisoning the already putrid air with the toxicity of pseudo nationalism that thrives on hate and division.

Javed Gaya
12 January 2026

NOTES

1. Raman, A.S.; 'A Meeting with C.N. Annadurai'; *Illustrated Weekly of India*; 26 September 1965.

INTRODUCTION

1. Benda, Julien; *The Treason of Intellectuals*: 2006; New York; Routledge.
2. Habib, S. Irfan; *Indian Nationalism; The Essential Writings;* New Delhi; 2017; Aleph Book Company.
3. Ibid.
4. Seneca, Lucius Annaeus; *De Otio: Édition Accompagnée de Notes Critiques Et d'un Commentaire Explicatif (French Edition)*; London; 2018; Forgotten Books.
5. Devji, Faisal; *Muslim Zion; Pakistan as a Political Idea*; Cambridge, MA; 2013; HUP.
6. Devji, Faisal; 'An Impossible Founding'; *Global Intellectual History*; 8 (1); 2023; https://www.tandfonline.com/doi/full/10.1080/23801883.2021.1962584
7. Kirpal, Saurabh; *Who is Equal?*; India, 2024; Penguin Random House; p. 7.
8. Berlin, Isaiah; *Two Concepts of Liberty*; *Four Essays on Liberty;* India; 1958; Clarendon Press.
9. Fukuyama, Francis; 'In an age of identity politics, inclusive national identity matters more than ever.'; *ABC*; 27 November 2018; https://www.abc.net.au/religion/why-national-identity-matters/10559382
10. Ibid.
11. Fukuyama, Francis; *Liberalism and its Discontents;* London; 2022; Hachette; p. 8.
12. Basu, Amrita; *Violent Conjunctures in Democratic India*; Cambridge, U.K.; 2015; CUP.
13. Raghavan, Pallavi; *Animosity at Bay;* India; 2020; Harper Collins; p. 159.

NOTES

1. THE MYTH OF ETERNAL INDIA

1. Chatterjee, Partha; *Empire and Nation*; New York; 2010; Columbia University Press.
2. Menon, V. P.*; Integration of the Indian States;* India; 2014; Orient Black Swan.
3. Ambedkar, B.R; *Pakistan or the Partition of India;* Chapter 2; India; 2017; Kalpaz Publications.
4. Subrahmanyam, Sanjay; *Is Indian Civilization a Myth?;* India; 2013; Orient Black Swan; p. 3.
5. Nehru, Jawaharlal; *Discovery of India:* India; 2008; Penguin.
6. Chattopadhyaya, B.D.; *The Concept of Bharatvarsha and Other Essays*; India; 2017; Permanent Black; p. 23.
7. Devji, Faisal; *The Impossible Indian*; Cambridge, MA; 2012; HUP; p. 22.
8. Ibid., p. 40.
9. Ibid., p. 46.
10. Menon, Dilip & Srinivasan, T.N. [Ed]; *The Future of Secularism*; U.K.; 2007; OUP; p. 75.
11. Savarkar, V.D.; *Hindu Rashtra Darshan;* India; 1949; Laxman Ganesh Khare; p. 38.

2. THE COLONIAL STATE AND THE SACRED SPACE

1. Eaton, Richard; *India in the Persianate Age; 1,000-1,765;* California; 2020; University of California Press; p. 16.
2. Edney, Matthew; *Mapping an Empire: The Geographical Construction of British India*; Chicago; 1997; University of Chicago.
3. Mishra, Atul; *The Sovereign Lives of India and Pakistan;* Oxford, U.K.; 2021; OUP; p. 20.
4. Ibid., p. 175.
5. Ayoob, Mohammed; 'Muslim, Islamic, Indian or all of the above'; *The Hindu*; 17 January 2019; https://www.thehindu.com/opinion/op-ed/muslim-islamic-indian-or-all-of-the-above/article26007019.ece.
6. Jaffrelot, Christophe & Joshi, Kalrav; 'Hindutva and Zionism'; *The Indian Express*; 7 December 2023; https://indianexpress.com/article/opinion/columns/from-savarkar-to-golwankar-why-hindutva-admires-zionism-9057486/
7. Ghosh, Amitav; Lecture on his book *The Sea of Poppies;* Mumbai.
8. Menon, Shivshankar; *India and Asian Geopolitics*; Washington, D.C.; 2021; Brookings Institution Press; p. 94.
9. Ayoob, Mohammed; 'In Defence of Nehru'; *The Hindu*; 17 April 2018; https://www.thehindu.com/opinion/op-ed/in-defence-of-nehru/article23563560.ece

10 Giridharadas, Akshobh, 'Nehru's Legacy, 51 Years After his Death,' *The*

Diplomat, 11 June 2015: https://thediplomat.com/2015/06/nehrus-legacy-51-years-after-his-death/

11. Kaplan, Robert; *The Revenge of Geography*; New York; 2017; Random House; p. 254.

3. THE COLONIAL STATE AND MINORITY RIGHTS

1. Chandrachud, Abhinav; *Republic of Religion:* India; 2020; Viking; p. 58.
2. Ibid.
3. Seervai, H.M.; *Partition of India-Legend and Reality*; India; 1989; Emmenem; p. 10.
4. Chopra, P.N. [Ed]; *The Collected Works by Sardar Vallabhbhai Patel;* India; 2015; Konark Publishers; p. 196.
5. Ambedkar, B.R.; 'Article II Section IV Part I, Clause 1(2)(A)(a)-(b); Ambedkar's memorandum and draft articles on the rights of states and minorities (24 March 1947), Rao. *The Framing of India's Constitution*; Vol. 2; p. 108.
6. Ibid., p. 110.
7. Chatterji, Joya; *Shadows at Noon*; U.K.; 2023; Penguin Viking; p. 76.
8. Dobbin, Christine E.; *Basic Documents in the Development of Modern India and Pakistan;* 1835-1947; London & New York; 1970; Van Nostrand Reinhold.
9. Saiyid, M.H.; *Quaid-I-Azam Muhammad Ali Jinnah*; Lahore, India; 1945; Ashraf; pp. 432–435.
10. Gould, William; *Hindu Nationalism and the Language of Politics in Late Colonial India*; U.K.; 2024; CUP.
11. Chandrachud, Abhinav; *These Seats Are Reserved;* India; 2023; Penguin Random House; p. 32.
12. Copland, Ian; *India 1885-1947 The Unmaking of an Empire*; U.K.; 2001, Longman; p. 62.
13. Nanda, B. R.; *Three Statesmen: Gokhale, Gandhi and Nehru*; India; 1974; George Allen & Unwin; p. 174.
14. Gould, William; *Hindu Nationalism and the Language of Politics in Late Colonial India*; U.K.; CUP; p. 174.
15. Ibid., p. 153.
16. Hodson, H.V.; *The Great Divide: Britain, India, Pakistan*; Pakistan; 1969; OUP.
17. Moon, Sir Penderel; *Divide and Quit*; India; 1961; Chatto & Windus.
18. Purushotham, Sunil; *From Raj to Republic: Sovereignty, Violence and Democracy in India*; California; 2021; Stanford University Press; p. 119.
19. Nehru to Provincial Congress Committee Presidents; 5 August 1954.
20. Ambedkar, B.R.; *States and Minorities*; India; 2008; Siddharth Books; Chapter 10.
21. Setalvad, M.C.; *Builders of Modern India;* India; 1968; Ministry of Information and Broadcasting, Government of India.
22. Ibid., p. 37.

23. Khosla, Madhav; *India's Founding Moment;* Cambridge, MA; 2020; HUP; p. 9.
24. Chandhoke, Neera*; Rethinking Pluralism, Secularism and Tolerance*; 2019; SAGE; p. 141.
25. Devji, Faisal; 'An Impossible Founding'; pp. 97-104.
26. Ignatieff, Michael; *Isaiah Berlin: A Life;* U.K.; 2000; Random House; p. 227.
27. Tudor, Maya; *The Promise of Power*; New York; 2017; Columbia University Press; p. 65.

4. THE PARTITION

1. Mansergh, Nicholas [Ed]; *Transfer of Power in India, Volume VII*; 1982; Her Majesty's Stationery Office.
2. Kearney, Richard & Fitzpatrick, Melissa; *Radical Hospitality: From Thought to Action*; New York; 2021; Fordham University Press.
3. Khan, Yasmin; *The Great Partition*; New Haven and London; 2017; Yale University Press; p. 10.
4. Masani, Zareer; 'The Ideal Against the Political'; *Open*; 16 July 2021; https://openthemagazine.com/essay/the-ideal-against-the-political/.
5. Mansergh, Nicholas [Ed]; *Transfer of Power in India, Volume X*; India; 1982; Her Majesty's Stationery Office; (Sardar Patel stated that 'Congress would not accept any suggestion for a further degree of parity in the present Central Government); p. 507.
6. Seervai, H.M., *Partition of India: Legend and Reality*, Emmenem Publications, Bombay, 1990 at p. 124.
7. Hodson, H.V: *The Great Divide: Britain-India-Pakistan*; p. 162.
8. Anderson, Perry; *The Indian Ideology*; London; 2021; Verso; p. 43.
9. Smith, Donald; *India as a Secular State;* New Jersey, 1963; Princeton; p. 144.
10. Malik, Professor Hafeez; 'Abdul Kalam Azad's Theory of Nationalism'; *Association of Asian Studies;* 3 April 1962.
11. Ibid., p. 121.
12. Butterfield, Herbert; *The Whig Interpretation of History*; U.K.; 1931; University of Cambridge.
13. Kaviraj, Sudipta; *The Enchantment of Democracy in India*: India; 2011; Permanent Black; p. 188.
14. Purushotham, Sunil; *From Raj to Republic: Sovereignty, Violence and Democracy in India*; California; 2021; Stanford University Press; p. 119.
15. Ibid., p. 67.
16. Clarke, Peter; *Nation's Voice* (cited in *The Last Thousand Days of the British Empire);* 2007; London; Penguin; p 687.
17. Nair, Neeti; *Changing Homelands, Hindu Politics and the Partition of India*: India; 2011; Permanent Black; p.1.
18. Patel, Aakar; *Our Hindu Rashtra:* India; 2020; Westland Publications; p. 31.
19. Ambedkar, B.R; *Thoughts on Pakistan*; India; 1941; Thacker and Co.

20. Shruti Kapila; *Violent Fraternity;* New Jersey; 2021; Princeton University Press; p. 165.
21. Ibid., p. 109.
22. Mosley, Leonard; *The Last Days of the British Raj;* U.K.; 1961; Weidenfeld & Nicolson.
23. Ibid., p. 250.
24. Noorani, A.G.; *Jinnah and Tilak;* Pakistan; 2010; OUP; p. 244.
25. Mehra, Girish N.; *Nearer Heaven Than Earth*; New Delhi, India; 2007; Rupa Publications.
26. Basu, Narayani; *VP Menon: The Unsung Architect of Modern India;* India; 2020; Simon & Schuster.
27. Ibid., p. 413.
28. Raghavan, S; *Letter Neru to Patel;* India; 2020; The Print.
29. Pandey, Gyanendra; *Remembering Partition—Violence Partition & History*; 2001; India; CUP; p. 41.
30. Chatterji, Joya; *Bengal Divided;* India; 1994; CUP.
31. Raghavan, Pallavi; *Animosity at Bay;* India; 2020; Harper Collins; p. 64.
32. Harun-ur-Rashid; *Inside Bengal Politics 1936-1947*; Dhaka, Bangladesh; 2003; University Press; p. 452.
33. Harun-ur-Rashid; *The Foreshadowing of Bangladesh* 1987; Bangladesh; Asiatic Society of Bangladesh.
34. Chatterji, Joya; *Bengal Divided; Hindu Communalism & Partition 1932-1947;* India; 1994; CUP; pp. 260–61.
35. Moorehouse, Geoffrey; *Calcutta: The City Revealed;* India; 2000; Penguin.
36. Ibid., p. 119.
37. Tripathi, Amales; *The Fourth Phase (1943-1947);* India; 2014; Oxford Academic.
38. 'A Tale of Two Ethnic Cleansings In Kashmir'; The Times of India/ Swaminomics; 18 January 2015; https://swaminomics.org/a-tale-of-two-ethnic-cleansings-in-kashmir/
39. Gandi, M.K.; *The Collected Works of Mahatma Gandhi, Volume 90*; India; 2017; BJP Library; p. 241.
40. Noorani, A.G.; *The Destruction of Hyderabad:* India; 2014, Tulika Books; p. 293.
41. Ibid.
42 The Razakars were the paramilitary wing of the Majlis-e-Ittehadul Muslimeen headed by Qasim Razvi, who were determined to prevent the accession of Hyderabad to India and terrorised the largely Hindu hinterland to serve that end. See Purushottam, Sunil, From *Raj to Republic* at p. 84.
43. Ibid.
44. Patel, Sardar Vallabhbhai; *For a United India: Speeches of Sardar Patel, 1947–1950*; 1967; India; Publications Division of the Ministry of Information and Broadcasting; p. 128.
45. Speech at Island Grounds, Madras; 23 February 1949.

46 Mani Shankar Iyer, *Pakistan Papers*, UBS Publishers, 1994 at p. 60.
47. Nandurkar, G.M.; [Ed.]; *Sardar's Letters Mostly Unknown;Volume II*; 1982; India; Sardar Vallabhbhai Patel Smarak Bhavan; p. 209.
48. Devji, Faisal; *The Impossible Indian;* London, 2012; C Hurst & Co Publishers; pp. 68–71.
49. Nussbaum, Martha C.; *The Cosmopolitan Tradition*; Cambridge, MA., and London; 2019; HUP; p. 3.
50. Gandhi; M. K.; *Hind Swaraj or Indian Home Rule*; India; 2009; Createspace.
51. Ibid.
52. Nandy, Ashish & Bhargava, Rajeev [Ed]; *Secularism and its Critics: The Politics of Secularism and the Recovery of Religious Tolerance;* 1998 OUP; p. 321.
53. 'Why Bapu Matters'; The Indian Express; 28 January 2008; https://cprindia.org/opinions/why-bapu-matters/
54. Ibid., p. 42.
55. Ibid., p. 43.
56. Iqbal, Mohammad; *The Reconstruction of Religious Thought in Islam*; California; 1930; Stanford University Press.
57. Iqbal, Javed; *Zinda Rood*; Pakistan; 2019; Sang-e-Meel Publications.
58. Ibid.
59. Dhulipala, Venkat; *Creating a New Medina*; U.K. 2014, CUP (This narrative draws its impetus from the supposed existential struggle between the West and Jihadi Islam which reached its apogee in the 9/11 attacks on New York in 2001.)
60. Mani Shankar Iyer, *Pakistan Papers*, UBS Publishers, 1994 at p. 94.
61. Jalal, Ayesha; *The Sole Spokesman: Jinnah the Muslim League and the Demand for Pakistan*; Pakistan; 1995; CUP; p. 14.
62. White-Spunner, Barney; *Partition;* U.K.; 2018; Simon & Schuster; p. 117.
63. Ibid., pp. 112–14.
64. Khosla, Madhav; *India's Founding Movement;* London and Cambridge, MA, 2020; HUP.
65. Devji, Faisal; *The Impossible Indian: Gandhi and the Temptation of Violence*; Cambridge, MA & London; 2012; HUP; p. 171.
66. Ahmed, Ishtiaq; *Jinnah: His Successes, Failures and Role in History*; 2020; Pakistan; 2020; Vanguard.
67. Ibid., pp. 8–9.
68. Roberts, Andrew; *Eminent Churchillians*; U.K.; 1994; Weidenfeld & Nicolson; p. 82.
69. Ibid., p. 80.
70. Ibid., p. 87.
71. Andrew Roberts remarks on this as does Richard Hough, although Philip Zeigler, Mountbatten's biographer, disagrees.
72. Hough, Richard; *Mountbatten: Hero of Our Time;* 1980; U.K.; Weidenfeld & Nicolson.

73. Roberts, Andrew; *Eminent Churchillians*; U.K.; 1994; Weidenfeld & Nicolson; p. 88.
74. Khan, Yasmin; *The Great Partition;* New Haven and London; 2017; Yale University Press; p. 202.
75. Ibid., p. 536.
76. Ibid., p. 103.
77. von Tunzelmann, Alex; *Indian Summer -The Secret History of the End of an Empire*; U.K.; 2007; Simon & Schuster.
78. Ibid., p. 256.
79 The Punjab Award was announced on 9 August 1947 with no Indian being present. This award was quietly announced just before Independence so that it would be the new government that would have to face the consequences and not the British. See Seervai, H.M., *Legend and Reality* at p. 149.
80. Ibid., p. 293.
81. Setalvad, Sir Chimanlal Harilal; *The Times of India*; 15 June 1947.

5. THE RISE OF THE COW BELT

1. Gould, William; *Hindu Nationalism and the Language of Politics in Late Colonial India*; U.K.; CUP; 2004.
2. Masselos, Jim; *Indian Nationalism, A History;* India; 2010; Sterling Paperbacks; p. 120.
3. Singh, Pritam & Thandi, Shinder S.; *Punjabi Identity in a Global Context*; India; 1999; OUP; p. 9.
4. Talbot, Ian; *Khizr Tiwana, the Punjab Unionist Party and the Partition of India*; India; 2013; Routledge.
5. 'UP Governance Model Needs to Be Challenged'; *Indian Express*; 21 May 2021; https://indianexpress.com/article/opinion/columns/for-the-sake-of-indian-democracy-the-up-governance-model-needs-to-be-challenged-7323588/
6. Robinson, Francis; *Separatism Among Indian Muslims: The Politics of the United Provinces' Muslims 1860-1923*: Cambridge, U.K.; 1975; Cambridge University Press; p. 10.
7. Pai, Sudha Pai & Kumar, Sajjan; *Maya Modi, Azad: Dalit Politics in the time of Hindutva;* India; 2023; Harper Collins; p. 174.
8. Ibid., p. 56.
9. Pandey, Gyanendra; *The Construction of Communalism in Colonial North India*; India; 1990; OUP; p. 103.
10. Ibid.
11. Anil, Pratinav; *Another India*; London; 2023; C Hurst & Co Publishers; p. 53.
12. Panikkar, K.M.; 'Note on Uttar Pradesh'; *Report of the States Reorganisation Commission*; 1955.
13. Ambedkar, Dr. B. R.; 'Thoughts on Linguistic States'; Delhi; 1955; https://

www.mha.gov.in/sites/default/files/State%20Reorganisation%20Commisison%20Report%20of%201955_270614.pdf

14. Prakash, Abhigyan; *From Lucknow to Lutyens: The Power and Plight of Uttar Pradesh*; India; 2022; Harper Collins; p. 124.
15. Chandhoke, Neera; *Rethinking Pluralism, Secularism and Tolerance: Anxieties of Coexistence*; India; 2019; Sage Publication; p. 106.
16. Khilnani, Sunil; *The Idea of India;* India; Penguin; 2012; p. 185.
17. Christophe Jaffrelot; *India's Silent Revolution;* New York; Columbia University Press; 2003; pp. 85–6.
18. Chatterji, Joya; *Shadows at Noon*; U.K.; 2024; Vintage, Penguin Random House; p. 107.
19. Mody, Ashoka; *India is Broken: A People Betrayed, 1947 to Today*; California; 2023; Stanford University Press; p. 57.
20. 'India becoming most populous nation: Is it a bane or a boon?'; *Indian Express*; 28 April 2023; https://indianexpress.com/article/opinion/columns/sanjaya-baru-writes-india-becoming-most-populous-nation-is-it-a-bane-or-boon-8580002/
21. Banfield, Edward C.; *The Moral Basis of a Backward Society;* India; Free Press; 1967.
22. Acemoglu, Daron & Robinson, James A.; *Why Nations Fail: The Origins of Power, Prosperity and Poverty;* U.K.; 2012; Crown Publishers; p. 68.
23. Ibid.
24. 'SC directs UP to refund recovered damages'; *Times of India*; 18 February 2022; https://timesofindia.indiatimes.com/india/sc-directs-up-to-refund-recovered-damages-restoration-of-properties-of-anti-caa-protesters/articleshow/89668640.cms
25. '179 killed in over 10,000 encounters in UP in 6 years'; *Economic Times*; 16 March 2023; https://economictimes.indiatimes.com/news/india/179-killed-in-over-10000-encounters-in-up-in-6-years/articleshow/98711064.cms?from=mdr
26. Ibid.
27. 'Income tax exemption for activist Harsh Mander's NGO cancelled'; *Scroll*; 26 September 2024; https://scroll.in/latest/1073777/income-tax-exemption-for-activist-harsh-manders-ngo-cancelled
28. 'BSP risks losing national party status'; *The Indian Express*; 1 July 2024; https://indianexpress.com/article/political-pulse/bsp-risks-losing-national-party-status-rout-lok-sabha-polls-9424414/
29. Deshpande, Ashwini; *Affirmative Action in India*; India; 2013; OUP; p. 70.
30. Srinivas, M.S.; *Social Change in Modern India*; California; 1971; Berkeley University of California Press; p. 6.
31. Jaffrelot, Christophe; *India's Silent Revolution: The Rise of Low Castes in North Indian Politics*; 2003; Columbia University Press; p. 146.

32. Chandrachud, Abhinav; *These Seats Are Reserved—Caste, Quotas and the Constitution of India*; 2023; India; Penguin Books; p. 120.
33. 'Mirage of Social Justice'; *Indian Express*; 22 April 2023; https://indianexpress.com/article/opinion/columns/pratap-bhanu-mehta-opposition-social-justice-8569145/
34. Deshpande, Ashwini & Weisskopf, Thomas E Weisskopf; *Does Affirmative Action Reduce Productivity*; Cambridge, MA; 2014; Harvard Education.
35 Gupta, Shekhar, 'Sub-African India: Much of Africa is richer than us, has better indicators, while we diminish,' *Print*, 5 June 2021: https://theprint.in/national-interest/sub-african-india-much-of-africa-is-richer-than-us-has-better-indicators-while-we-diminish/672235/
36. 'India in Figures'; Government of India; 2018; https://mospi.gov.in/sites/default/files/publication_reports/India_in_figures-2018_rev.pdf
37. 'How census-based delimitation for Lok Sabha seats could shake up politics & disadvantage south'; *The Print*; 29 December 2022; https://theprint.in/india/governance/how-census-based-delimitation-for-lok-sabha-seats-could-shake-up-politics-disadvantage-south/1287536/
38. 'Delimitation fallout needs no political forecasting'; *The Hindu*; 19 May 2022; https://www.thehindu.com/opinion/lead/delimitation-fallout-needs-no-political-forecasting/article65426751.ece
39. Nilakantan R.S.; *South vs. North: India's Great Divide*; India; 2022; Juggernaut; pp. 187–98.
40. Surya, Saket, 'Report of the 15th Finance Commission for 2021-26,' *PRS Legislative Research*, 3 February 2021: https://prsindia.org/files/policy/policy_committee_reports/Report%20Summary_15th%20FC_2021-26.pdf
41. Ibid., p. 194.
42. 'ASER's 2023 survey results show gaps in learning'; *The Indian Express*; 19 January 2024; https://indianexpress.com/article/explained/expert-explains-gaps-in-learning-persist-but-access-to-tech-offers-avenues-beyond-physical-school-9114524/
43. 'A holy push by Uttar Pradesh religious affairs department'; *India Today*; 7 October 2022; https://www.indiatoday.in/magazine/up-front/story/ 20221017-a-holy-push-by-uttar-pradesh-religious-affairs-department-2009455-2022-10-07
44. '51,000 Government schools shut down in 2018'; *The Telegraph*, India; 9 May 2022; https://www.telegraphindia.com/india/51000-government-schools-closed-with-a-year-says-report/cid/1864203; 21 April 2025; These are All India figures but UP figures as the State which witnessed the highest decline in number of Government schools by 26,074 and these have disproportionately affected primary education.
45. 'Internet usage index across India in 2022, by category; *Statista*; 1 March 2024;

https://www.statista.com/statistics/1232337/internet-usage-index-by-category-india/

46. Jennings, Ivor; *Problems of the New Commonwealth*; North Carolina; 1958; Duke University Press; 1958; cited in *India's Founding Moment;* p. 8.
47. Jonathan Sumption, *Law and the Decline of Politics*; Profile Books; 21 May 2019, p. 25.
48. Menon, Nivedita; *Secularism as Misdirection*; India; 2023; Permanent Black; p. 110
49. Ambedkar, B.R.; *What Congress and Gandhi have done to untouchables, BAWS, Vol 9*; India; 2014; Dr. Ambedkar Foundation

6. LANGUAGE AND CULTURE

1. Steiner, George; *Errata an Examined Life;* London; 1997, Weidenfeld & Nicolson; p. 87.
2. Bajpai, Rochana; *Debating Difference: Group Rights and Liberal Democracy in India*; India; 2011; OUP; p. 145.
3. Orsini, Francesca; *Before the Divide*; India; 2011; Orient Blackswan.
4. Daniyal, Shoaib; 'From love songs to kurta ads, Urdu is popular with Indians'; *Scroll*; 24 October 2021; https://scroll.in/article/1008421/from-love-songs-to-kurta-ads-urdu-is-popular-with-indians-why-do-hindutva-backers-hate-it-so-much
5. Khare, Santosh Kumar; 'Truth about Language'; *Economic and Policy Weekly*; 14 December 2002; https://www.epw.in/journal/2002/50/commentary/truth-about-language-india.html
6. Chatterji, Joya; *Bengal Divided; Hindu Communalism and Partition: 1932-1947*; U.K.; 1994; CUP; p. 27.
7. Hasan, Mushirul; *Legacy of a Divided Nation: India's Muslims since Independence*; U.K., 1997; OUP; p. 158.
8. Nehru, Jawaharial; *Selected Works of Jawaharial Nehru; Vol.* 7; India; 1948, Jawaharlal Nehru Memorial Fund; p. 512.
9. Paz, Octavio; *In Light of India*; India; 1998; Rupa & Co; p. 70.
10. Bilal, Maaz Bin; 'Shamsur Rahman Faruqi (1935-2020): Why this death leaves a permanent patch of darkness in literature'; *Scroll*; 26 December 2020; https://scroll.in/article/982332/shamsur-rahman-faruqi-1935-2020-why-this-death-leaves-a-permanent-patch-of-darkness-in-literature
11. Dr. Sampurnanand; *Hindustan Times*; 18 April 1949.
12. Kudaisya, Gyanesh; *A Republic in the Making: India in the 1950s*; U.K.; 2017; OUP.
13. Ibid., p. 141.
14. Ibid., p. 142
15. Daniyal, Shoaib; 'From love songs to kurta ads, Urdu is popular with Indians'.

16. Madhusudan Harsh & Mantri, Rajeev; *A New Idea of India*; India; 2020; Westland Publishers.
17. Mehta, Pratap Bhanu; 'The current talk of decolonisation is about an exclusionary political agenda'; *Indian Express*; 31 August 2023; https://indianexpress.com/article/opinion/columns/current-talk-of-decolonisation-is-about-an-exclusionary-political-agenda-8918137/
18. Savarkar, Damodar Vinayak; *Essentials of Hindutva;* India; 1923; Hindi Sahitya Sadan.
19. Treanor, Tom; 'When Veer Savarkar told me Muslims in India should be treated as "Negroes"; *Daily O*; 24 October 2017; https://www.dailyo.in/politics/tom-treanor-vd-savarkar-mahatma-gandhi-hitler-nationalist-hindu-mahasabha-20207
20. Ambedkar, B.R.; *Writings and Speeches Vol. 10*; BAWS; India; 2014; Dr. Ambedkar Foundation; p. 145.
21. Puchner, Martin; *Culture: A New World History*; U.K.; 2023; Bonnier Books; p. 298.
22. Appiah, Kwame Anthony; *Cosmopolitanism: Ethics in a World of Strangers*; U.K.; 2006; Penguin; p. 112.
23. Ibid., pp. 119-20.
24. Puchner, Martin; *Culture: A New World History;* Introduction p. xxiii.
25. Ibid., p. 197.

7. THE WEAPONISATION OF HISTORY TO UNDERPIN NATIONALISM

1. Stanley, Professor Jason; *Erasing History: How Fascists Rewrite the Past to Control the Future*; 2024; Footnote Press; p. xi
2. Lannoy, Richard; *The Speaking Tree;* India; 1999; OUP; p. 292.
3. Ibid., p. 293.
4. 'There's a tendency in Indian history to have everyone as either a demon or an angel'; *Indian Express*; 12 January 2023; https://indianexpress.com/article/india/historian-william-dalrymple-theres-a-tendency-in-indian-history-to-have-everyone-as-either-a-demon-or-an-angel-8369230/
5. 'Debates not Deletions'; *India-Seminar*; 743, July 2021; https://www.india-seminar.com/2021/743.htm
6. Asif, Manan Ahmed; *The Loss of Hindustan, Invention of India*; Cambridge, MA; 2020; HUP; p. 13.
7. Golwalkar, M.S.; *Bunch of Thoughts;* India; 2020; Sahitya Sindhu Prakashan.
8. Joseph, Tony; *Early Indians: The Story of Our Ancestors and Where We Came From*; India; 2020; Juggernaut; p. 221.
9. Hardy, Peter; *Historians of Medieval India: Studies in India-Muslim Historical Writing*; London; 1960; Luzac; p. 3.
10. Ibid., p. 3.

11. Brzezinski, Zbigniew; *The Grand Chessboard: American Primacy and Its Geostrategic Imperatives;* New York; 1997; Basic Books; p. 37.
12. Mill, James; *History of British India*; U.K.; 1817; Baldwin, Cradock and Joy.
13. Ibid., p. 8.
14. Ibid, p. 18.
15. Marrewa-Karwoski, Christine; 'By Attacking the Mughals, Adityanath Is Erasing the History of His Own Nath Sampraday'; *The Wire*; 8 October 2020; https://thewire.in/communalism/by-attacking-the-mughals-adityanath-is-erasing-the-history-of-his-own-nath-sampraday
16. Ibid.
17. Chakravarthy, Pradeep & Sathyanathan, Vikram; *Thanjavur A Cultural History;* India; 2010; Niyogi Books.
18. Singh, Upinder; *The Idea of Ancient India*; India; 2023; Penguin; Introduction p. XXXIV.
19. Shahane, Girish; 'Rani Padmini and four other Hindutva history myths'; *Scroll*; 31 December 2014; https://scroll.in/article/698006/rani-padmini-and-four-other-hindutva-history-myths-exploded
20. Wendy, Doniger; *The Hindus: An Alternative History;* India; 2009; Speaking Tiger Books; p. 10.
21. Singh, Upinder; *Political Violence in Ancient India*; Cambridge, MA; 2017 HUP; p. 6.
22. Pollock, Sheldon; *The Language of the Gods in the World of Men: Sanskrit Culture and Power*; California; 2009; University of California Press. (Pollock's notion of a 'Sanskrit cosmopolis' referred to the enormous geographic sweep of Indic culture that stretched from Afghanistan through Vietnam and the East Indies and which spanned a millennium from the fourth to the fourteenth century.)
23. Tharoor, Shashi; 'Musings on 'Indic civilization' and Indianness'; *The Hindu*; 13 June 2022; https://www.thehindu.com/opinion/lead/musings-on-indic-civilization-and-indianness/article65521179.ece
24. Chakrabarty, Dipesh; *The Calling of History: Sir Jadunath Sarkar and His Empire of Truth;* India; 2015; Permanent Black; p. 19.
25. Sarkar, Sir Jadunath; *Fall of the Moghul Empire Vol. IV;* India; 1950; Orient Longman; p. 338.
26. Richards, John F.; *The Mughal Empire;* Cambridge, MA; 1993; CUP; p. 2.
27. Sharma, Parvathi; *Jahangir an Intimate Portrait of a Great Mughal;* India; 2020; Juggernaut; p. 263.
28. Frankopan, Peter; *The Silk Roads: A New History of the World;* London; 2015; Bloomsbury; p. 235.
29. Tharoor, Shashi; *An Era of Darkness the British Empire in India*; India; 2016; Aleph; p. 22.
30. Ibid., p. 371.
31. Subramanian, Lakshmi; *India Before Ambanis;* India; 2025; Penguin; p. 9.

32. Maddison, Angus; *The World Economy-A Millennial Perspective*; Paris; 2001; OECD.
33. Smith, Adam; *The Wealth of Nations;* India; 2021; OM Books International.
34. Sreevatsan, Ajai; 'British Raj siphoned out $45 trillion from India'; Mint: 21 November 2018; https://www.livemint.com/Companies/HNZA71LNVNNVXQ1eaIKu6M/British-Raj-siphoned-out-45-trillion-from-India-Utsa-Patna.html
35. Nehru, B. K.; *Nice Guys Finish Second*; India; 1997; Penguin Books; pp. 238-39.
36 D. Clark, 'Life expectancy in India 1800-2020', *Statista*, 28 November 2025; https://www.statista.com/statistics/1041383/life-expectancy-india-all-time/?srsltid=AfmBOoqd92VbSxqW-12WAWEsuseVCoJlTKzRdkPrXO3D8VI1N1OcVNTe
37. Vivekananda, Swami; *Swami Vivekananda's Speeches & Writings (in Bengali); Volume 5; 'Bharater Mahapurushgan' ('The Great Men of India')*; India; 1968; Udbodhan Karyalaya; p. 158.
38. Ibid., p. 29.
39. YouTube interview; Medieval Indian Rulers and Temple Destruction; 2021; Aligarh Society of History.
40. *Shree Adi Vishweshwar vs. State of UP 4 SCC 1997*; p. 606; Indian Kanoon; 14 March 1997; https://indiankanoon.org/doc/923604/
41. Mavad, Asra; 'ASI is Criminally Underfunded'; *Deccan Herald*; 11 January 2025; https://www.deccanherald.com/features/books/asi-is-criminally-underfunded-3349558

8. THE INDIAN VERSION OF SECULARISM

1. 'Indian Society and the Secular'; *Sage/Indian Journal of Public Administration*; Volume 64 Issue 1, March 2018; https://journals.sagepub.com/toc/ipaa/64/1
2. Bose, Sumantra; *Secular States, Religious Politics: India, Turkey and the Future of Secularism*; 2018; Cambridge, MA; CUP 2018; p. 359.
3. Ibid., p. 94.
4. Ibid., pp. 359–60.
5. Baer, Marc David; *The Ottomans Khans, Caesars and Caliphs*; Basic Books; London, New York; 2021; p. 10.
6. Bajpai, Rochana*; Debating Difference Group Rights and Liberal Democracy in India;* U.K.; 2016; OUP; p. 24.
7. *Anjum Kadari vs Union of India*; India Kannon; 5 November 2024; https://indiankanoon.org/doc/67107476/
8. Srinivas, M.N.; *Social Change in Modern India*; India; 1966; Allied Publishers.
9. Pai, Nitin; 'NCERT's curriculum for science needs to be 'rationalized' again'; *Mint*; 5 June 2023; https://www.livemint.com/opinion/columns/science-education-in-india-a-national-priority-for-economic-growth-and-societal-progress-11685901570435.html

10. Mudur, G.S.; 'India facing 'a systematic threat' to its scientific and educational foundations' *The Telegraph*, India; 27 February 2024; https://www.telegraphindia.com/india/india-facing-a-systematic-threat-to-its-scientific-and-educational-foundations-scientists/cid/2003179
11. Mehta, Pratap Bhanu; 'The religious life of Indians, according to a recent survey; *Indian Express*; 2 July 2021; https://indianexpress.com/article/opinion/columns/the-religious-life-of-indians-according-to-a-recent-survey-7385080/
12. Ibid., p. 203.
13. Jaffrelot, Christophe & Laliwala, Sharik; 'The segregated city'; *Indian Express*; 26 May 2018; https://indianexpress.com/article/opinion/columns/muslims-in-india-hindus-jains-gujarat-love-jihad-5191304/
14. Bhargava, Rajeev; *Secularism and its Critics*; U.K.; 2000; OUP; p. 487.
15. Ibid., p. 487.
16. Mehta, Uday & Puniyani, Ram [Eds]; *Secularism in India, Concept and Practice*; India; Kalpaz Publications; 2017; p. 73.
17. Ibid., p. 73.
18. French, Patrick; *India a Portrait*; U.K.; 2011; Penguin Book; p. 27.
19. Ibid.
20. Vidal, Gore; *The Selected Essays of Gore Vidal;* New York; 2008; Doubleday.
21. Subrahmanyam, Sanjay; *Is Indian Civilisation a Myth?*; India; 2013; Permanent Black, p. 22.
22. 'Secularism in the Constituent Assembly Debates, 1946-1950'; India; 22 July 2002; *Economic & Political Weekly Vol. 37.*
23. Ibid.
24. Hingorani, Anand [Ed]; *To Hindu and Muslims;* India; 1942; Law Journal Press.
25. Anthony Appiah, Kwame; *Cosmopolitanism: Ethics in a World of Strangers;* India; 2007; Penguin.
26. Ibid., p. 94.
27. Mookerji, Radhakumud; *Nationalism in Hindu Culture*; London; 1921; Theosophical Publishing House.
28 Figures taken from article: Jeelani, Gulam; 'Mahakumbh 2025: From ₹7,500 cr budget to ₹2 lakh cr expected revenue – mega mela economy's multiplier effect revealed,' *Mint*, 14 January 2025: https://www.livemint.com/news/mahakumbh-2025-from-7-500-cr-budget-to-2-lakh-cr-expected-revenue-the-mela-economy-s-multiplier-effect-11736835828399.html
29. Tumbe, Chinmay; *The Age of Pandemics 1817-1920: How they Shaped India and the World;* India; 2020; Harper Collins; p. 61.
30. 'Maa Ganga's Blessings in Flow, There Should Be No Corona'; *The Wire* Science; 12 April 2021; https://science.thewire.in/health/maa-gangas-blessings-in-flow-there-should-be-no-corona-uttarakhand-cm-on-kumbh-vs-markaz/

31. Biswas, Soutik; 'Why India's real COVID toll may never be known'; *BBC News*; 5 May 2022; https://www.bbc.co.uk/news/world-asia-india-60981318
32. Ahmed, Hilal; *A Brief history of the Present: Muslims in the New India*; 2024; Penguin;; p. 164.
33. Munshi, K.M.; *Constituent Assembly Debates VII*; 6 December 1948; https://indiankanoon.org/doc/1933556/
34. 'Why Hindu Rastra?'; Archives of the RSS; 1 May 1977; https://www.archivesofrss.org/Why-Hindu-Rashtra.aspx
35 See *DAV College v. State of Punjab* reported as (1971)2 SCC 558.
36. 'Sachar Committee Report'; Minority Affairs Government of India; 8 May 2023; https://www.minorityaffairs.gov.in/show_content.php?lang=1&level=0&ls_id=14&lid=14
37. Ahmed, Hilal; *Siyasi Muslims: A Story of Political Islams in India*; India; 2019; Viking; p 186

9. SECULARISM AND CASTE

1. Ibid.
2. *State of Madras v. Champakam Dorairajan (AIR 1951 SC 226)*; Indian Kanoon; 9 April 1951; https://indiankanoon.org/doc/149321/
3. S. Muralidhar, *Incomplete Justice? The Supreme Court at 75*, Juggernaut, India, 2025 at p. 304.
4. Smith, Donald; *India as a Secular State*; New Jersey; 2019; Princeton University Press refers to a Circular to Pradesh Congress Committees, New Delhi, All India Congress Committee 1954.
5. *Ashoka Kumar Thakur vs Union of India And Ors*; India Kantoon; 10 April 2008; https://indiankanoon.org/doc/1219385/
6. Yap, Po Jen & Chandrachud, Chintan; 'Unstable Constitutionalism—Law and Politics in South Asia'; *International Journal of Constitutional Law*; 2 April 2018; https://academic.oup.com/icon/article/16/2/690/5036465; p. 40.
7. *Indra Sawhney Etc. Etc vs Union of India and Others*; India Kanoon; 16 November 1992; https://indiankanoon.org/doc/1363234/

10. SECULARISM, PERSONAL LAWS AND THE UNIFORM CIVIL CODE

1. Abhinav Chandrachud, *Republic of Religion: The Rise and Fall of Colonial Secularism in India*, Penguin Viking, 2020 at p. 125.
2. Derrett, J Duncan; *Introduction to Modern Hindu Law*; U.K. 1963; OUP.
3. Pillai, Manu S.; *Gods Guns and Missionaries*; London; 2024; Penguin Random House; p. 108.
4. Ambedkar, B. R. & Bhagwan, Das [Compiled Essays]; *Dr. B R Ambedkar selected Speeches by 1963 Vol I;* India; 1963; Bheem Patrika Publications.

5. Ambedkar, B. R.; *B R Ambedkar Writings and Speeches, Volume 14*; India; 1995; Bombay Educational Dept. Govt. of Maharashtra.
6. Ibid., p. 156.
7. Sarkar, Tanika; *Hindu Wife, Hindu Nation: Community, Religion and Cultural Nationalism*; India; 2001; Ashoka University; pp. 18-19.
8. *Naveen Kohli v. Neelu Kohli*; India Kanoon; 21 March 2006, 4 SCC 558; https://indiankanoon.org/doc/1643829/
9. Misra, Maria; *Vishnu's Crowded Temple, India since the Great Rebellion*; Penguin 2008; pp. 296–7.
10. *Joseph Shine v. Union of India*; 27 September 2018; India Kanoon; https://indiankanoon.org/doc/42184625/
11 *Supriyo v. Union of India* reported as (2018)5 SCC 1.
12. Ambedkar, Dr. B.R.; *Report of the Select Committee on the Hindu Code*; 12 August 1948; India; Government of India.
13. Kakar, Katharina & Kakar, Sudhir; *The Indians, The Portrait of a People*; India; 2007; Penguin; p. 11.
14. Dwyer, Rachel; *Picture Abhi Baaki Hai: Bollywood as a Guide to Modern India*; India; 2014; Hachette; p. 207.
15. Newbigin, Eleanor; *The Hindu Family and the Emergence of Modern India*; U.K.; 2013; Cambridge Studies in Indian History and Society.
16. 'Hindu Succession Bill, 1954', *Rajya Sabha Debates*, 22 March 1955: https://rsdebate.nic.in/bitstream/123456789/583599/1/PD_09_22031955_1_p2711_p2806_2.pdf
17. Birla, Ritu; *Stages of Capital*; North Carolina; 2009; Duke University Press; p. 223.
18. Datta, Kanika; 'Why India is struggling to produce CEOs like Nadella, Pichai at home'; *Business Standard*; 9 January 2025; https://www.business-standard.com/opinion/columns/why-india-is-struggling-to-produce-ceos-like-nadella-pichai-at-home-125010801413_1.html
19. Wanchoo, K. N; *Direct Taxes Enquiry Committee; Final Report;* 1971; New Delhi Ministry of Finance
20. Joshi, Deepak; 'Uniform Civil Code: Why it can impact Hindu Undivided Family's tax benefits'; *Indian Express*; 18 July 2024; https://indianexpress.com/article/explained/explained-law/expert-explains-hindu-undivided-family-ucc-8823492/
21. Ibid.
22. Venkataramakrishnan, Rohan; 'Muslim women and the surprising facts about polygamy in India'; *Scroll*; 8 July 2014; https://scroll.in/article/669083/muslim-women-and-the-surprising-facts-about-polygamy-in-india
23. Madhusudan, Harsh & Mantri, Rajeev; *A New Idea of India; The Civilizational Republic*; India; 2023; Penguin.
24. 'National Family Health Survey-5 (2019-2021)'; Ministry of Health and

Family Welfare; [Document Undated]; https://mohfw.gov.in/sites/default/files/NFHS-5_Phase-II_0.pdf
25. Quraishi, S.Y.; *Population Myth: Islam, Family Planning & Politics in India*; India; 2021; Harper Collins.
26. Ibid.
27. National Family Health Survey.
28. *Shayara Bano v. Union of India* reported as (2017)9 SCC 1.
29. Ahmed, Hilal; *Siyasi Muslims: A Story of Political Islams in India*; India; 2019; Viking; p 140.
30. *Mohd. Ahmed Khan v. Shah Bano Begum* reported as (1985)2 SCC 556.
31. Ibid.
32. *Noor Saba Khatoon vs Mohd. Quasim*; India Kanoon; 29 July 1997; https://indiankanoon.org/doc/1512218/
33. Mustafa, Faizan; 'Explained: Uniform Civil code: the debate, the status'; *Indian Express*; 18 September 2019; https://indianexpress.com/article/explained/explained-uniform-civil-code-the-debate-the-status-6004396/
34. Dasgupta, Swapan; *Awakening Bharat Mata: The Political Beliefs of the Indian Right*; India; 2018; Penguin Random House; p. 109.
35. Galanter, Marc & Krishnan Jayant & Gerald James Larson [Ed]; *Personal Law Systems and Religious Conflicts in Religion and Personal Law in Secular India;* India; 2001; Indiana University Press.
36. Bhatia, Gautam; 'Code that is neither uniform nor lawful'; *Hindustan Times*; 25 February 2024; https://www.hindustantimes.com/opinion/code-that-is-neither-uniform-nor-lawful-101708847351711.html

11. FEDERALISM, HISTORY AND THE ORIGINAL SIN

1 'Speech of B.R. Ambedkar introducing the Draft Constitution,' Constituent Assembly Debates, 4 November 1948: https://www.constitutionofindia.net/debates/04-nov-1948/
2. Anand, Prof. C.L.; *Parliamentary Debates, Indian Affairs, House of Commons*, Vol I, 1934-35, Col. 43: Constitutional Law and History of Government of India; India; 2009; Universal Law Publishing Company.
3. Hodson, H.V: *The Great Divide: Britain-India-Pakistan*; p. 48.
4. Ibid., p. 17.
5. Tomlinson, B.R.: *The Indian National Congress and the Raj*; London; 1976; Macmillan; pp. 32–48, 71–2.
6. Bhatia, Udit [Ed]; *The Indian Constituent Assembly: Deliberations on Democracy*; India; 2017 Routledge; p. 32.
7. Mansergh, Nicholas [Ed]; *Transfer of Power in India, Volume VII*; India; 1982; Her Majesty's Stationery Office.
8. Tillin, Louise; *Indian Federalism*; U.K.; 2019; OUP; p. 23.
9. Letter from Jawaharlal Nehru, Chairman of the Union Powers Committee,

to President, Constituent Assembly of India: 5 July 1947, in CAD, 5:58-59; p. 181.

10. Ackerman, Bruce; *Revolutionary Constitutions: Charismatic Leadership and the Rule of Law*; Cambridge, MA; 2019; HUP 2019; p. 11.
11. 'Constituent Assembly Debates'; Publications Division, Government of India: Vol. VII: pp. 42–43.
12. CAD V: p. 218.
13. Rao, Shiva; 1968: *The Framing of India's Constitution*; India; 1968; Indian Institute of Public Administration; p. 770.
14. CAD VII: p. 299.
15. CAD VII: 1017, 1157.8.
16. Teltumbde, Anand and Yengde,Suraj [Eds]; *The Radical in Ambedkar: Critical Reflections*; India; 2018; Allen Lane.
17. CAD Vol. VII: p. 299.
18. Bajpai, Rochana; *Debating Difference Group Rights and Liberal Democracy in India*; U.K.; 2011; OUP; p. 53.
19. CAD VIII: p. 270.
20. Schneider, Suzanne; *The Apocalypse and the End of History;* Verso; 2021; p. 95.
21. Ibid., p. 52.
22. *Babulal Parate v. State of Bombay* reported as (1960) 1 SCR 605.
23. Ibid.
24. Menon, N. R, Madhava [Ed]: *Nehru and Indian Constitutionalism:* India; 2015; Indus Source Books; p. 83.
25. *ML Sharma & Others vs Union of India*; 2023; INSC 1058.
26. Mehta, Pratap Bhanu; 'Pratap Bhanu Mehta writes on abrogation of Article 370 being upheld: Has SC established a dangerous precedent for federalism?'; *Indian Express*; 14 December 2023; https://indianexpress.com/article/opinion/columns/pratap-bhanu-mehta-abrogation-article-370-supreme-court-kashmir-9063575/
27. McGarry, John & O'Leary, Brendon [authors], Cordell, Karl & Wolff, Stefan [Eds]; *The Routledge Handbook of Ethnic Conflict;* chapter *Territorial Approaches to Ethnic Conflict;* London; 2016; Routledge; pp. 249–65.
28. Ibid.
29. Bhatia, Gautam; *Unsealed Covers;* India; 2023; Harper Collins; p. 267.
30. Ibid., p. 24.
31. AIR 1994 SC 1980.
32. Unstable Constitutionalism, Constitutional Federalism in the Indian Supreme Court: p. 373.
33. Vishwanath, Apurva; 'Key aspects of the Article 370 verdict'; *Indian Express*; 13 December 2023; https://indianexpress.com/article/explained/key-aspects-of-article-370-verdict-unpacked-9064079/
34. 'No-confidence motion: NCP's Supriya Sule castigates Modi govt's track record; says BJP toppled 9 state govt's in as many years'; *Mid-Day*; 8

August 2023; https://www.mid-day.com/news/india-news/article/no-confidence-motion-ncps-supriya-sule-castigates-modi-govts-track-record-says-bjp-toppled-9-state-govts-in-as-many-years-23302533

35. Ibid., p. 24.
36. *State of Tamil Nadu v. Governor of Tamil Nadu* reported as (2025)8 SCC 1 [2JB].
37. *In re: Assent, Withholding or Reservation of Bills by the Governor and the President of India* reported as (2026)1 SCC 1 [5JB].
38. Morris-Jones, W.H.; *Parliament in India*; London; 1957; Longmans, Green and Co; and other works.
39. Ibid. pp. 37–8.
40. *Kuldip Nayar & Ors. vs. Union of India & Ors. (2006) 7 SCC 1.*
41 *Justice K.S. Puttuswamy v. Union of India* reported as AIR 2017 SC 4161.
42. Seminar Magazine 358.
43. Sridevan, Srinath & Pattabhiraman, Ananya; 'A case for a more federal judiciary'; *The Hindu*; 17 February 2022; https://www.thehindu.com/opinion/lead/a-case-for-a-more-federal-judiciary/article65055822.ece
44. Chagla, M.C.; *Roses in December—An Autobiography*; India; 1973; Bharatiya Vidya Bhavan.
45. Sridevan, Srinath & Pattabhiraman, Ananya; 'A case for a more federal judiciary'.
46. Mishra, Pallavi; 'NCLT Mumbai Approves Resolution Plan for Reliance Communications Infrastructure'; *Live Law*; 22 December; https://www.livelaw.in/ibc-cases/nclt-mumbai-approves-resolution-plan-for-reliance-communications-infrastructure-ltd-245182
47. *Hemant S. Hathi v. Central Bureau of Investigation*; Writ Petition (Crl.) 37/2020; Order dated passed by Justice J.K. Maheshwari and Justice Vijay Bishnoi.
48. Sridevan, Srinath & Pattabhiraman, Ananya; 'A case for a more federal judiciary'.
49. Cited in Govt. of India 1988: Clause 8.7.06.
50. Muralidharan, Karthik; *Accelerating India's Development*; 2024; Penguin Viking; p. 82.
51. De, Rohit & Shani, Ornit; *Assembling India's Constitution: A New Democratic History*; Cambridge; Cambridge University Press; 2025; p. 196.
52. Ibid., p. 99.
53. Ibid., p. 72.
54. Mounk, Yascha T.; *The People vs Democracy*; London; 2018; HUP; p. 200.
55. Dave, Dushyant; 'State must remember its obligations and duties to Constitution'; *Indian Express*; 18.September 2021; https://indianexpress.com/article/opinion/columns/indian-government-judiciary-constitution-7516254/
56. Jha, Prem Shankar, *The Dismantling of India's Democracy: 1947–2025*; Speaking Tiger; 2025; p. 293.

12. RECENT PROBLEMS WITH FEDERALISM

1. Pande, Amitabha; 'Mediating Centre-State Relations'; *Seminar*; May 2019; https://www.india-seminar.com/2019/717/717_amitabha_pande.htm.
2. Seminar Magazine 358.
3. World Economic Forum; *The Global Risks Report 2022*; 17th ed; Geneva; World Economic Forum; 2022; p. 101.
4. Seminar Magazine 358.
5. Thapar, Romila; *On Citizenship;* India; 2021; Aleph Book Company; p. 20.
6. Nilakantan, R.S.; *South vs North: India's Great Divide*; India; 2022; Juggernaut; p. 191.
7. Government of India, Ministry of Finance; *Terms of Reference of the Fifteenth Finance Commission*; New Delhi; Department of Economic Affairs; 2017 (as amended in 2019).
8. Sharma, Shailendra; 'The Delhi model of education'; *The Hindu*; 25 May 2021; https://www.thehindu.com/opinion/op-ed/the-delhi-model-of-education/article30796187.ece#:~:text=Its%20approach%20stems%20from%20the,the%20next%20set%20of%20reforms.
9. 'Subsidy for 5,000 Jobs'; *The Mint*; 15 June 2024; https://www.livemint.com/politics/news/rs-16-000-subsidy-for-5-000-jobs-hd-kumaraswamy-questions-us-firm-in-gujarat-getting-incentives-clarifies-later-11718435245675.html
10. 'Banks write off bad loans worth Rs 16.35 lakh crore in last 10 years'; *Economic Times*; 20 December 2022; https://economictimes.indiatimes.com/industry/banking/finance/banking/banks-write-off-bad-loans-worth-rs-16-35-lakh-crore-in-last-10-years/articleshow/119110675.cms?from=mdr
11. Sharma, Mihir; 'The Crisis of Federalism'; *India Seminar*; https://www.india-seminar.com/2020/725/725_mihir_s_sharma.htm
12. 'MPA Act 2021 benefits only corporate houses: dock workers'; *The Hindu*; 10 February 2023; https;//www.thehindu.com/news/cities/Madurai/mpa-act-2021-benefits-only-corporate-houses-dock-workers/article66493636.ece
13. PTI; 'Tamil Nadu Chief Minister writes to PM over concerns against Electricity (Amendment) Bill, 2021; *NDTV*; 8 December 2021; https://www.ndtv.com/india-news/tn-cm-voices-concern-against-electricity-amendment-bill-2021-2642074
14. 'Ethnicity and Nationalism Theory and Comparison'; *Paul Brass Blog* [1991; Undated]; https://www.paulbrass.com/ethnicity_and_nationalism__theory_and_comparison_20230.htm
15. Wolf, Martin; *The Crisis of Democratic Capitalism*; New York; 2023; Penguin Press; p. 266.
16. 'Tax Divide: Why are Southern States upset?'; *The Mint*; 4 April 2024;

https://www.pressreader.com/india/mint-hyderabad/20240405/282295325221713?srsltid=AfmBOoo1cUEMa2ClcH_SinoYlDCHwnwD3Gc4_NIJmhpDPYYNGN8tOfZo

17. Sharma, Mihir; 'The world's biggest country is showing signs of data anxiety'; *Mint*; 24 April 2023; https://www.livemint.com/opinion/online-views/indias-delayed-census-what-it-means-for-politics-demographics-and-economic-data-11682269444044.html
18. 'Supreme Court sets aside HC order staying 75% quota for Haryana locals in private jobs'; *Indian Express*; 18 February 2022; https://indianexpress.com/article/india/supreme-court-haryana-75-per-cent-locals-job-quota-7777873/
19. Ibid., p. 213.
20. Ibid., p. 118.
21. Mihir Sharma; 'The Crisis of Federalism'.
22. Ibid., p. 185.
23. Nilakantan, R.S.; *South vs North: India's Great Divide*; India; 2022; Juggernaut; p. 85.
24. 'Kerala, Tamil Nadu, West Bengal have received no funds under Samagra Shiksha for FY2024-25'; *The Hindu*; 4 April 2025; https://www.thehindu.com/news/national/kerala-tamil-nadu-west-bengal-have-received-no-funds-under-samagra-shiksha-for-fy2024-25/article69409044.ece
25. Piketty, Thomas; *Capital in the Twenty-First Century*; 2014; Cambridge, MA; HUP.
26. Bharti, Nitin Kumar, et al; 'Economic Inequality in India: The "Billionaire Raj" Is Now More Unequal than the British Colonial Raj'; *World Inequality Database*; 19 March 2024; https://wid.world/news-article/inequality-in-india-the-billionaire-raj-is-now-more-unequal-than-the-british-colonial-raj/
27. Ibid.
28. Mehta, Pratap Bhanu; 'MNREGA was the ground beneath our feet. It's slipping away.'; *The Indian Express*; 19 December 2025; https://indianexpress.com/article/opinion/columns/p-b-mehta-writes-mnrega-was-the-ground-beneath-our-feet-its-slipping-away-10427710/
29. Naqushbandi, Ubeer; 'VB-G RAM G Bill repeals job guarantee, warns economist Jean Drèze.'; The Federal; 18 December 2025; https://thefederal.com/category/news/vb-g-ram-g-bill-mgnrega-jean-dreze-100-days-work-221356
30. Drèze, Jean; 'With MGNREGA, India set an example for the world. VB-G RAM G destroys that legacy.'; *The Indian Express*; 17 December 2025; https://indianexpress.com/article/opinion/columns/mgnrega-vb-g-ram-g-rural-employment-viksit-bharat-10424877/>
31. Ibid., pp. 104–115.
32. 'Labour participation rates dwindle'; https://www.cmie.com/kommon/

bin/sr.php?kall=warticle&dt=20230627171423&msec=676 and 'Bangladesh BD: Labour Force: Female: % of Total Labour Force'; https://www.ceicdata.com/en/bangladesh/labour-force/bd-labour-force-female--of-total-labour-force .

33. Narayan, Swati; *Unequal: Why India Lags Behind Its Neighbours*; India; 2023; Context.
34. Roy, Anna & Panda, Shaifalika; 'The empowerment of women is a reliable formula for prosperity'; *Mint*; 7 September 2023; http://livemint.com/opinion/online-views/the-empowerment-of-women-is-a-reliable-formula-for-prosperity-11694017244162.html
35. Ibid., p. 6.
36. Mody, Ashoka; *India Is Broken: And Why It's Hard to Fix*; India; 2023; Juggernaut; p. 11.
37. Sircar, Nilanjan; 'The centralisation of Politics and Business;' *Hindustan Times*; 13 November 2021; https://www.hindustantimes.com/opinion/the-centralisation-of-politics-and-business-101636822490146.html
38. Aristotle; *Politics*; London; 1981; Penguin Classics.
39. Ibid., p. 378.
40. Mohan, Archis; 'Modi, BJP and the Presidential form of Government;' *Deccan Herald*; 20 December 2022; https://www.deccanherald.com/india/modi-bjp-and-the-presidential-form-of-government-1164182.html; (Where reference is given to Modi's recent statement while campaigning for Himachal Pradesh and Gujarat that India needs to adopt a Presidential system of Government, there are a number of statements that show the need in his words for 'one nation, one election.')
41. 'Representative Democracy Remains a Popular Ideal, but People Around the World Are Critical of How It's Working'; *Pew Research Centre*; 28 February 2024; https://www.pewresearch.org/global/2024/02/28/representative-democracy-remains-a-popular-ideal-but-people-around-the-world-are-critical-of-how-its-working/
42. Raman, Anuradha; 'Is Modi the best communicator of them all?'; *The Hindu*; 29 March 2019; https://www.thehindu.com/opinion/op-ed/is-modi-the-best-communicator-of-them-all/article62110032.ece
43. Aiyar, Yamini; 'Simultaneous polls may hurt federalism'; *Hindustan Times*; 6 September,2023; https://www.hindustantimes.com/opinion/simultaneous-polls-may-hurt-federalism-101693922913079.html
44. 'CAG flags gaps in DBT system, says crores flow without proper checks'; *The Economic Times*; 18 December 2025; https://economictimes.indiatimes.com/news/india/cag-flags-gaps-in-dbt-system-says-crores-flow-without-proper-checks/articleshow/126054446.cms
45. Raghavan, T.C.A. Sharad; 'IMF gives India a "C" on its GDP and other national accounts data, the second-lowest grade'; *The Hindu*; 27 November

2025; https://www.thehindu.com/business/Economy/imf-gives-india-a-c-on-its-gdp-and-other-national-accounts-data-the-second-lowest-grade/article70330780.ece

46. Datta, Devangshu; 'The Ease of doing Politics'; *Business Standard*; 12 February 2022; https://www.business-standard.com/article/opinion/the-ease-of-doing-politics-122021101817_1.html
47. Crabtree, James; *The Billionaire Raj;* Harper Collins; India; 2018; p. 136.
48. *Association for Democratic Reforms & Ors. vs. Union of India, 2024 INSC 113.*
49. Radhakrishnan, Vignesh; 'Companies under ED, I-T scanner donated poll bonds to BJP, BRS, Congress'; *The Hindu*; 21 March 2024; https://www.thehindu.com/data/electoral-bonds-data-companies-under-ed-i-t-scanner-donated-poll-bonds-to-bjp-brs-congress/article67977729.ece
50. Mishra, Lalatendu; 'Acharya urges detariffing, breakup of conglomerates'; *The Hindu*; 02 September 2024; https://www.thehindu.com/business/Economy/acharya- urges-detariffing-break-up-of-conglomerates/article68598073.ece
51. Singhal, Rajrishi; 'There's scant oversight of India's oligopolistic markets'; *Mint*; 24 April 2023; https://www.livemint.com/opinion/online-views/nyu-academics-acharya-and-roubini-unite-against-india-s-oligopolistic-trend-warning-of-hampered-competition-growth-stagnation-and-abuse-of-pricing-power-11682269688848.html
52. D'Souza, Faye, Sainath, P.; 'Why farmers are refusing to back down'; *YouTube*; 20 December 2018.
53. Scott J Shapiro; The Federalist Number 51 cited in 'Legality'; HUP; p. 324.

13. ASYMMETRICAL FEDERALISM

1. 'India a case of Asymmetrical Federalis'; *Economic & Political Weekly*; 14 January 2012; https://www.epw.in/journal/2012/02/notes/india-case-asymmetrical-federalism.html
2. Gellner, Ernest, *Nations and Nationalism*; New Jersey; 1983; Cornell University Press.
3. *R.C. Poudyal v. Union of India* reported as *AIR 1993 SC 1804*.
4. Tushnet Mark & Khosla, Madhav [Eds]; *Unstable Constitutionalism: Law and Politics in South Asia*; Cambridge, U.K.; 2015; CUP; p. 366.
5. Ibid., p. 367.
6. *In Re: Article 370 of the Constitution* reported as (2023)16 SCC 1.
7. Roy, Ishita; 'The Conjuring'; *Indian Express*; 12 December 2023; https://www.newindianexpress.com/cities/delhi/2023/Dec/12/the-conjuring-2640719.html
8. Arghya Sengupta, Jinaly Dani, Kevin James & Pranay Modi; *Hamīñ Ast? A Biography of Article 370;* India; 2022; Navi Books.
9. Bhasin, Anuradha; *A Dismantled State: The Untold Story of Kashmir After Article 370*; India; 2023; Harper Collins 2023; p. 94.

10. Ibid., p. 38.
11. Mehta, Pratap Bhanu; 'The story of Indian democracy written in blood and betrayal'; *Indian Express*; 6 August 2019; http://indianexpress.com/article/opinion/columns/jammu-kashmir-article-370-scrapped-special-status-amit-shah-narendra-modi-bjp-5880797/
12. Anderson, Perry; *The Indian Ideology*; London; 2021; Verso.

14. CITIZENSHIP AND THE CITIZENSHIP AMENDMENT ACT

1. Jayal, Niraja Gopal: Citizenship and its discontents; Cambridge, MA; 2013; HUP.
2. Citizenship and Social Class: Lectures delivered in Cambridge; February 1949; Marshall 1950; pp 28–9.
3. Roy, Anupama; *Citizenship in India;* U.K. 2016; OUP; p. 117.
4. Malviya, Amit & Khurshid, Salman; *The Citizenship Debate CAA & NRC*; 2020; Rupa; p. 162.
5. Hasan, Mushirul; *Legacy of a Divided Nation: India's Muslims since Independence*; p. 180.
6. Ibid., p 185.
7. Ibid., p. 56.
8. Roy, Anupama; *Citizenship in India*; U.K. 2016; OUP;
9. Karmakar, Rahul; 'Chakmas and Hajongs: The peoples without a state'; *The Hindu*; 30 January 2022; https://www.thehindu.com/news/national/chakmas-and-hajongs-the-peoples-without-a-state/article38346684.ece
10. Chatterjee, Chhanda [Ed]; *The Partition of the Indian Subcontinent (1947) and Beyond*; India; 2023; Routledge p. 73.
11. The original section 2(1)(b) of the Citizenship Act of 1955 gives the definition of an 'illegal migrant'. Through the amendment act of 2019, a proviso was added to the section stating Provided that any person belonging to Hindu, Sikh, Buddhist, Jain, Parsi or Christian community from Afghanistan, Bangladesh or Pakistan, who entered into India on or before the 31st day of December, 2014 and who has been exempted by the Central Government by or under clause (c) of sub-section (2) of section 3 of the Passport (Entry into India) Act, 1920 or from the application of the provisions of the Foreigners Act, 1946 or any rule or order made thereunder, shall not be treated as illegal migrant for the purposes of this Act.
12. Bhatia, Gautam; 'CAA Is a Matter of Constitutional Concern'; *NewsClick*; 4 January 2020; https://www.newsclick.in/caa-matter-constitutional-concern-gautam-bhatia
13. 'CAA is necessary, not meant to send Muslims out of India, says top lawyer Harish Salve,' *The New India Express*, 5 March 2020: https://www.newindianexpress.com/nation/2020/Mar/05/caa-is-necessary-

not-meant-to-send-muslims-out-of-india-says-top-lawyer-harish-salve-2112705.html

14. Malviya, Amit & Khurshid, Salman; *The Citizenship Debate CAA & NRC*; India; 2020; Rupa Publications.
15. 'CAA is necessary, not meant to send Muslims out of India, says top lawyer Harish Salve,' *The New India Express.*
16. Ibid.
17. Hindustan Times, 9 February 2023; these figures came from a written reply from the Ministry of External Affairs to a question in the Rajya Sabha.
18. *Trump vs. Hawaii, 585 U.S. (2018)* (Sotomayor J Dissent).
19. *Sarbananda Sonowal vs Union of India & Anr. 5 SCC 665* (see discussion of this Judgement in an Unconscionable Judgement in Outlook by Prashant Bhushan on 5 February 2022.
20. Roy, Anupama; *Citizenship in India;* U.K. 2016; OUP 2016; p.38
21. Tharoor, Shashi; 'India needs a refugee and asylum law'; *The Hindu*; 20 February 2022; https://www.thehindu.com/opinion/lead/india-needs-a-refugee-and-asylum-law/article65063388.ece

15. THE INDIAN DIASPORA

1. 'Making it as migrants'; *The Economist*; 17 June 2023; UN Estimate from 2020 cited in the article.
2. 'India's diaspora is bigger and more influential than any in history,' *The Economist*, 12 June 2023: https://www.economist.com/international/2023/06/12/indias-diaspora-is-bigger-and-more-influential-than-any-in-history
3. Pai, Nitin; 'We can expect more turbulence ahead in Indian diaspora politics'; *The Mint*; 15 July 2023; https://www.livemint.com/opinion/online-views/we-can-expect-more-turbulence-ahead-in-indian-diaspora-politics-11689495209780.html
4. Menon, Nivedita; *Secularism as Misdirection*; India; 2023; Permanent Black; p. 123.

16. THE HISTORICAL ROLE OF THE JUDICIARY POST-INDEPENDENCE

1. Dworkin, Ronald; *Freedom's Law: The Moral Reading of the American Constitution*; Cambridge, MA; 1997; HUP: pp. 1-38.
2. Sengupta, Arghya; *The Colonial Constitution; 2023;* U.K. Harper Collins; p. 66.
3. Chandra, Aparna & Kalantry, Sital & Hubbard, William H.J.; *Court on Trial: A Data-Driven Account of the Supreme Court of India:* India; 2023; Penguin Random House.

4. Pratap Bhanu Mehta, 'The Rise of Judicial Sovereignty,' *The Oxford Companion to Politics in India*, ed. Niraja Gopal Jayal and Pratap Bhanu Mehta, Oxford University Press, New Delhi, 2010, p. 381.
5. Bhatia, Gautam; 'The Citizenship (Amendment) Act Challenge: Three Ideas'; *Constitutional Law and Philosophy;* 21 January 2020; https://indconlawphil.wordpress.com/2020/01/21/the-citizenship- amendment-act-challenge-three-ideas/
6. Tharoor, Shashi: *Ambedkar: A Life*; India; 2023; Aleph Books; p. 147.
7. Saxena, Namit; 'Disproportionate representation at the Supreme Court'; *Bar & Bench*; 23 May 2021; https://www.barandbench.com/columns/disproportionate-representation-supreme-court-caste-and-religion-of-judges
8. Sharma, Padmakshi; 'Theocratic Judges who finds source of law in religion than Constitution'; *Live Law*; 18 February 2023; https://www.livelaw.in/top-stories/theocratic-judges-who-find-source-of-law-in-religion-than-constitution-have-sharply-increased-dr-mohan-gopal-221925
9. Reference to *Aishat Shifa vs. State of Karnataka: (2022)* Livelaw (SC); p. 842.
10. *Golaknath v. State of Punjab*: AIR 1967 SC; p. 1643.
11. *Kesavananda Bharati Sripadagalvaru v. State of Kerala*: AIR 1973 SC 1461: 1973.
12. Prasad, Dr. Rajendra: Letter dated 7 August 1947 in Valmiki Choudhary New Delhi: Allied Publishers Pvt. Ltd: 1987.

17. THE ELEVATION OF THE COW

1. According to the Indian National Family Health Survey 2005-06 and 2015-16 NFHS Survey, the number is 78% for women and 70% for men.
2. *Mohammed Salil vs. Ramkumar Singh (1928);* July 2024; https://www.allahabadhighcourt.in/ILR/ilr-2024/Jul2024.pdf; Online Allahabad; p. 176
3. Naqvi, Saeed; *Being the Other: The Muslim in India*; India; 2016; Aleph Book Company; p. 54.
4. Gandhi, Mahatma; *Hindu–Muslim Tensions, Vol 28; Collected Works of Mahatma Gandhi*; 1869-1948; India; 1924; Young India Publisher.
5. Singer, Peter; *Animal Liberation Now*; London; 2023; Bodley Head.
6. Constituent Assembly debates (24 November 1948).
7. AIR 1958 SC 731.
8. Smith, Donald Eugene; *India as a Secular State*; New Jersey; 1963; Princeton University Press; p. 444.
9. Baxi, Dr. Upendra; *The Little Done, the Vast Undone: Some Reflections on Reading Granville Austin's 'The Indian Constitution';* India; 1967; Journal of the Indian Law Institute, Vol. 9, pp. 323–430, 349.
10. Jha, D.N.; *The Myth of the Holy Cow;* India; 2002; Verso.
11. Nath, Damini; 'Cattle, buffalo meat residue found in Indus Valley vessels'; *The Hindu*; 9 December 2020; https://www.thehindu.com/news/national/

study-of-lipid-residue-reveals-cattle-buffalo-meat-in-indus-valley-vessels/article33292289.ece

12. Doniger, Wendy; *The Hindus: An Alternative History*; India; 2010; Penguin Books.
13. Ibid; p. 658.
14. De Rohit; *A People's Constitution*; New Jersey; 2012; Princeton University Press; p. 155.
15. Ibid., p. 157.
16. (2005) 8 SCC 534.
17. Gandhi, M. K.; *Save the Cow*; India; 8 June 1921; Young India.
18. De, Rohit; *A People's Constitution*; p. 131.
19. Appiah, Kwame Anthony; *Cosmopolitanism: Ethics in a World of Strangers*; U.K.; 2006; Penguin; p. 52.
20 Reuters; 'Cattle slaughter crackdown ripples through India's leather industry'; *Firstpost*; 14 June 2017; https://www.firstpost.com/india/cattle-slaughter-crackdown-ripples-through-indias-leather-industry-reuters-3645013.html
21. 'Report of the Gosamvardhan Inquiry Committee'; India; 1955; Superintendent, Printing and Stationery, U.P. Allahabad; pp. 74–6.
22. Rawal, Vikas; 'On Economic Implications of the Restrictions on Cow Slaughter'; *Statistics on Indian Economy and Society*; 19 July 2017; https://indianstatistics.org/2017/07/19/economic-implications-of-cow-slaughter.html
23. Shukla, Avay; 'Kanpur Diary: No More Waiting Till the Cows Come Home'; *The Wire*; 18 December 2018; https://thewire.in/caste/cows-coming-home
24. Narain, Sunita; 'Why I don't advocate vegetarianism; *Scroll*; 28 March 2017; https://scroll.in/article/832980/why-i-dont-advocate-vegetarianism-indian-environmentalist-sunita-narain-explains-her-position
25. 'UP's Anti-Cow Slaughter is being misused'; *The Hindu*; 26 October 2020; https://www.thehindu.com/news/national/anti-cow-slaughter-law-in-up-being-misused-says-high-court/article32946857.ece
26. 'As UP Government invokes NSA on Frivolous Grounds, Allahabad High Court quashes 94 of 120 Orders'; *The Wire*; 6 April 2021; https://thewire.in/law/as-up-govt-invokes-nsa-on-frivolous-grounds-allahabad-hc-quashes-94-of-120-orders-report.
27. Ibid., pp. 299–300.

18. THE ESSENTIAL RELIGIOUS PRACTICES TEST

1. *The Commissioner, Hindu Religious Endowments, Madras v. Sri Lakshmindra Thirtha Swamiar of Sri Shirur Mutt* reported as AIR 1954 SC 282.
2. The Supreme Court eventually dismissed the State's argument stating that 'under Article 26(d), it is the fundamental right of a religious denomination

or its representative to administer its properties in accordance with law; and the law, therefore, must leave the right of administration to the religious denomination itself subject to such restrictions and regulations as it might choose to impose.'

3. *Sardar Syedna Saifuddin Saheb v. State of Bombay* reported as AIR 1962 SC 853.
4. *Dr. Noorjahan Safia Niaz v. State of Maharashtra* reported as AIR 2017 (NOC) 45 (Bom).
5. *Resham v. State of Karnataka* reported as 2022 SCC OnLine Kar 315.
6. *Aishat Shifa v. State of Karnataka* reported as (2023)2 SCC 1.
7. Faizan Mustafa, 'The Problem with Karnataka's HC's Hijab ruling,' *Indian Express*, 19 March 2022; https://indianexpress.com/article/opinion/columns/the-problem-with-the-hijab-ruling-karnataka-high-court-muslim-women-religious-practice-7821512/
8. *Jeeja Ghosh v. Union of India* reported as (2016)7 SCC 761.
9. *Bijoe Emmanuel v. State of Kerala* reported as AIR 1987 SC 748.
10. Sanjay Hegde, 'The Kamalesan case and its simple lesson,' *The Hindu*, 28 November 2025; https://www.thehindu.com/opinion/lead/the-kamalesan-case-and-its-simple-lesson/article70331102.ece
11. Gautam Bhatia, 'The Essential Religious Practices Test and the Inversion of Agency: Notes from the Hijab Hearing,' *Constitutional Law and Philosophy*, 9 February 2022: https://indconlawphil.wordpress.com/2022/02/09/the-essential-religious-practices-test-and-the-inversion-of-agency-notes-from-the-hijab-hearing/

19. CONVERSIONS BECOME CRIMINAL

1. Ibid., p. 182.
2. Constituent Assembly debate 1947 (Volume 3, Page 484).
3. National Christian Council Review 1947: Volume 67.
4. Arora, Tehmina; 'For 70 years, Dalits have been denied freedom of religion—through a presidential order'; *Scroll*; 21 August 2020; https://scroll.in/article/970613/for-70-years-dalits-have-been-denied-freedom-of-religion-through-a-presidential-order
5. Natarajan:, S.; *A Century of Social Reform in India*; India, 1959; Asia Publishing House; p. 194.
6. Galanter, Marc; *Law and Society in Modern India*; U.K.; 1989; OUP; p. 119.
7. Niyogi Committee Report 1956; published by Government of Madhya Pradesh.
8. (1977) I SCC 677.
9. Ibid., p. 44.
10. Ibid., pp. 174–5.
11. Ibid., p. 175.
12. DNA; 8 January 2016.

13. Bhattacharya, Abhik; 'Why Adivasis Are Claiming Sarna as Their Religion'; *Outlook*; 24 November 2022; https://www.outlookindia.com/national/why-adivasis-are-claiming-sarna-as-their-religion-magazine-239655
14. Ibid., p. 204.
15. Gopal [Ed]; *Selected Works of Jawaharlal Nehru,* Second Series, Vol. 23, pp. 246–47; Reference in *Republic of Religion* to Rajendra Prasad being reprimanded by Nehru for attending an event where Christian missionaries were criticised for converting tribals by offering inducements. Nehru to Prasad Letter dated 10 August 1953.
16. Ministry of Home Affairs 2021–22 Annual Report referring to NGOs spending on unproductive items such as inflated staff salaries, posh buildings and office and luxurious vehicles.
17. *Noel Harper v. Union of India*; reported as 2022 SCC OnLine SC 434.
18. Kotecha, Sima; 'India Covid: How law stops NGOs distributing essential aid'; *BBC*; 14 May 2021; https://www.bbc.com/news/world-asia-india-57095591
19. Pande, Aparna; *Making India Great;* India; 2020; Harper Collins; p. 33.

20. RELIGION, ELECTORAL POLITICS AND THE DISAPPEARANCE OF MINORITIES FROM THE PUBLIC SPACE

1. Rawls, John; *The Law of Peoples: With the Idea of Public Reason Revisited*; Cambridge, MA; 2001; HUP.
2. Perry, Michael John: *Law and Power: The Role of Religion and Morality in American Politics*; U.K,; 1991; OUP.
3. Ibid.
4. *S.R. Bommai v. Union of India (AIR 1994 SC 1918).*
5. *Dr. Ramesh Prabhoo v. Prabhakar Kashinath Kunte AIR 1996 1113.*
6. *S.R. Bommai v. Union of India.*
7. *Dr. Ramesh Prabhoo vs Prabhakar Kashinath Kunte.*
8. *Manohar Joshi v. Nitin Bhaurao Patil &Anr.: AIR 1996 SC*; p. 796.
9. Ibid., p. 230.
10. *Abhiram Singh, Narayan Singh v. Sundarlal Patwa: 2017 2 SCC* 629.
11. Uttar Pradesh Religion Population Data 2011.
12. Ibid., p. 237.

21. THE AFTERMATH OF PARTITION

1. 1951 Census of Displaced Persons.
2. Ibid.
3. Mehta, Pratap Bhanu; 'Single Garment of Destiny'; *Indian Express*; 20 October 2021; https://indianexpress.com/article/opinion/columns/violence-and-communalism-south-asias-disturbing-commonality-7580597/
4. Ibid.

5. Shivshankar, Menon; *India and Asian Geopolitics: The Past, Present*; India; 2021; Penguin Random House; (General Cariappa, then Chief of Army Staff, told Nehru in October 1950 that India could only spare one battalion of troops for Tibet (around 1,000 men) as the rest were engaged in Kashmir cited in India and Asian Geopolitics; p. 57.
6. Lieven, Anatol; *Pakistan: A Hard Country*; India; 2011; Allan Lane; p. 58.
7. Ibid., p. 58.
8. Ibid., p. 58.
9. Rushdie, Salman; *Shame*; London; 1983; Jonathan Cape.
10. Ibid., p. 172.

22. KASHMIR

1. Zutshi, Chitralekha; *Kashmir;* U.K.; 2019; OUP; p. 110.
2. Sneddon, Christopher; *Kashmir, the Unwritten History*; London; 2011; Harper Collins; pp. 39–45.
3. Bajwa, Farooq; *From Kutch to Tashkent: The Indo-Pakistan War of 1965*; London; C Hurst & Co Publishers; 2013; p. 10.
4. Zubrzycki, John; *Dethroned: The Downfall of India's Princely States*; London; C Hurst & Co Publishers; 2023.
5. Nayyar, Kuldip; *Beyond the Lines—An Autobiography*; U.K.; Lotus; 2012.
6. Ziegler, Philip; *Mountbatten:Viceroy's Personal Report No.15: 1.8.1947; Transfer of Power. Vol. XII*; U.K. 1985; Harper & Row Publishers.
7. Wolpert, Stanley; *Nehru: A Tryst with Destiny*; Cambridge, MA; CUP; 1996.
8. Dutta, Anisha; 'Kashmir letters cast doubt on claims Nehru blundered by agreeing'; *The Guardian*; 8 March 2023; https://www.theguardian.com/world/2023/mar/08/kashmir-letters-cast-doubt-claims-nehru-blundered-agreeing-ceasefire
9. Bikhchandani, Raghav; 'Who was Roy Bucher India's last British Army Chief whose J&K insights remain under wraps?; *The Print*; 17 October 2021; https://theprint.in/theprint-essential/who-was-roy-bucher-indias-last-british-army-chief-whose-jk-insights-remain-under-wraps/750959/
10. Ibid., pp. 24–8.
11. Bhattacharjee, Malini & and Venkatraman, P.C.; 'Sylhet Referendum Anniversary: A Time to Remember Partition Wasn't Only About a Hindu–Muslim Binary'; *The Wire*; 6 July 2023; https://thewire.in/history/sylhet-referendum-is-a-reminder-that-partition-wasnt-only-about-a-Hindu–Muslim-binary
12. Das, Durga [Ed]; *Sardar Patel's Correspondence, 1945-50, Volume 10*; India; 1974; Navajivan Publishing House.
13. Mustafa, Faizan; 'Article 370 and Territorial Pluralism;' *Indian Express*; 5 August 2020; https://indianexpress.com/article/opinion/jammu-and-kashmir-article-370-and-territorial-pluralism-faizan-mustafa-6541101/

14. Shankar, V.; *Selected Correspondence of Sardar Patel, 1945-50, Vol. 1*; Ahmedabad; Navajivan Publishing House; 2011; pp. 373-375.
15. Joshi, Manoj; *Understanding the India China Border*; India; 2022; Harper Collins; pp. 249–51.
16. 'Foreign Ministry Spokesperson Wang Wenbin's Press Conference' in China; 29 September 2020; http://mo.ocmfa.gov.cn/eng/zxxw/fyrth_1/202009/t20200929_7934876.htmhttp://mo.ocmfa.gov.cn/eng/zxxw/fyrth_1/202009/t20200929_7934876.htm
17. Ibid.
18. Anil, Pratinav; *Another India*; London; 2023; C Hurst & Co Publishers; p. 204.
19. Kumar, Radha; *Making Peace with Partition*; London; 2005; Penguin Random House; p. 49.

23. PAKISTAN

1. Ibid., p. 39.
2. Hasan, Mushirul; *Legacy of Divided Nation*; London; 1997; C Hurst & Co; p. 120.
3. Tan, Tai Yong & Kudaisya, Gyanesh; *The Aftermath of Partition in South Asia;* India; 2000; Routledge; p. 217.
4. Ibid., p. 189.
5. An apocryphal story quote is ascribed to General Zia when he introduced Nizam-e-Mustafa (the rule of the Prophet) to Islamicise Pakistan. When asked why, he is believed to have said, 'If an Egyptian stops being a Muslim he remains an Egyptian, if a Turk stops being a Muslim he remains a Turk but if a Pakistani stops being a Muslim he becomes an Indian. See Menon, Shivshankar; *India and Asian Geopolitics: The Past, Present*; Penguin; 2021; p. 53.

24. THE PLIGHT OF INDIAN MUSLIMS

1. 'Gandhi, Nehru strove for inclusive polity'; *The Hindu*; 24 March 2016; https://www.thehindu.com/news/cities/Vijayawada/gandhi-nehru-strove-for-inclusive-polity-bilgrami/article8044409.ece
2. Piscatori, James & Eickelman, Dale; *Muslim Politics*; 1996; New Jersey; Princeton University Press.
3. Ignatieff, Michael; *Isaiah Berlin: A Life;* p. 184.
4. Devji; Faisal; 'After the Talaq'; *Open Magazine*; 7 September 2017; https://openthemagazine.com/essay/after-the-talaq/
5. Chaudhuri, Nirad C; *The Heart of India*; India; 1966; Jaico Publishing; p. 264.
6. Ibid., p. 200.
7. Hasan, Waquar; 'India: Data show Muslims disproportionately in jail relative to their population'; *Maktoob Media*; 11 January 2022; https://

maktoobmedia.com/india/india-data-show-muslims-disproportionately-in-jail-relative-to-their-population/

8. Jaffrelot, Christophe & Kalaiyarasan, A; 'Muslims in Higher Education: A Sobering Tale'; *The Indian Express*; 9 May 2023; https://indianexpress.com/article/opinion/columns/lower-in-higher-education-8598739/
9. Jaffrelot, Christophe & Kalaiyarasan, A; 'Muslims in higher education: A sobering tale'.
10. Mahmudabad, Ali Khan; 'Manufacturing Conflict: Indian Muslims and the Shift from Marginalisation to Exclusion; *Observation Research Foundation*; 22 August 2020, https://www.orfonline.org/expert-speak/manufacturing-conflict
11. Devji, Faisal; *Terrorist in Search of Humanity*; U.K.; 2019; OUP; p. 4.
12. Ibid., p. 4.
13. Thucydides; *History of the Peloponnesian War;* London; 2000; Penguin Classics.

BIBLIOGRAPHY

Acemoglu, Daron, and James A. Robinson. *Why Nations Fail: The Origins of Power, Prosperity and Poverty*. London: Crown Publishers, 2012.

Ackerman, Bruce. *Revolutionary Constitutions: Charismatic Leadership and the Rule of Law*. Cambridge, MA: Harvard University Press, 2019.

Ahmed, Hilal. *Siyasi Muslims: A Story of Political Islams in India*. New Delhi: Viking, 2019.

Ahmed, Hilal. *A Brief History of the Present: Muslims in the New India*. New Delhi: Penguin, 2024.

Ahmed, Ishtiaq. *Jinnah: His Successes, Failures and Role in History*. Lahore: Vanguard, 2020.

Ambedkar, B. R. 'Memorandum and Draft Articles on the Rights of States and Minorities (24 March 1947)'. In *The Framing of India's Constitution*, vol. 2, edited by B. Shiva Rao. New Delhi: Indian Institute of Public Administration, 1967.

Ambedkar, B. R. *Dr. Babasaheb Ambedkar: Writings and Speeches*. Vol. 10. New Delhi: Dr. Ambedkar Foundation, 2014.

Ambedkar, B. R. 'What Congress and Gandhi Have Done to the Untouchables'. In *Dr. Babasaheb Ambedkar: Writings and Speeches*, vol. 9. New Delhi: Dr. Ambedkar Foundation, 2014.

Ambedkar, B. R., and Bhagwan Das, comp. *Dr. Babasaheb Ambedkar: Selected Speeches*. Vol. 1. Jalandhar: Bheem Patrika Publications, 1963.

Ambedkar, B.R. *Thoughts on Pakistan*. Bombay: Thacker, 1941.

Ambedkar, B.R. *Dr. Babasaheb Ambedkar: Writings and Speeches*. New Delhi: Dr. Ambedkar Foundation, various volumes.

Ambedkar, B.R. *Pakistan or the Partition of India*. New Delhi: Kalpaz Publications, 2017.

Ambedkar, B.R. *States and Minorities*. New Delhi: Siddharth Books, 2008.

Anand, C. L. *Parliamentary Debates, Indian Affairs, House of Commons, 1934–35*. New Delhi: Universal Law Publishing, 2009.

Anderson, Perry. *The Indian Ideology*. London: Verso, 2021.

Anil, Pratinav. *Another India: The Making of the World's Largest Muslim Minority, 1947–77*. London: Hurst, 2023.

Appiah, Kwame Anthony. *Cosmopolitanism: Ethics in a World of Strangers*. New Delhi: Penguin, 2007.

Aristotle. *The Politics*. London: Penguin Classics, 1981.

Asif, Manan Ahmed. *The Loss of Hindustan: The Invention of India*. Cambridge, MA: Harvard University Press, 2020.

Baer, Marc David. *The Ottomans: Khans, Caesars and Caliphs*. New York: Basic Books, 2021.

Bajpai, Rochana. *Debating Difference: Group Rights and Liberal Democracy in India*. Oxford: Oxford University Press, 2011.

Bajwa, Farooq. *From Kutch to Tashkent: The Indo-Pakistan War of 1965*. London: Hurst, 2013.

Banfield, Edward C. *The Moral Basis of a Backward Society*. New York: Free Press, 1967.

Basu, Amrita. *Violent Conjunctures in Democratic India*. Cambridge: Cambridge University Press, 2015.

Basu, Narayani. *V. P. Menon: The Unsung Architect of Modern India*. New Delhi: Simon & Schuster India, 2020.

Benda, Julien. *The Treason of the Intellectuals*. New York: Routledge, 2006.

Berlin, Isaiah. "Two Concepts of Liberty." In *Four Essays on Liberty*. Oxford: Clarendon Press, 1969.

Bhargava, Rajeev, ed. *Secularism and Its Critics*. New Delhi: Oxford University Press, 2000.

Bhasin, Anuradha. *A Dismantled State*. New Delhi: HarperCollins India, 2022.

Bhatia, Gautam. *Unsealed Covers*. New Delhi: HarperCollins India, 2023.

Bhatia, Udit, ed. *The Indian Constituent Assembly*. London: Routledge, 2017.

Birla, Ritu. *Stages of Capital*. Durham, NC: Duke University Press, 2009.

Bose, Sumantra. *Secular States, Religious Politics*. Cambridge: Cambridge University Press, 2018.

Brzezinski, Zbigniew. *The Grand Chessboard*. New York: Basic Books, 1997.

Butterfield, Herbert. *The Whig Interpretation of History*. Cambridge: Cambridge University Press, 1931.

Chagla, M. C. *Roses in December*. Mumbai: Bharatiya Vidya Bhavan, 1973.

Chakrabarty, Dipesh. *The Calling of History*. Ranikhet: Permanent Black, 2015.

Chakravarthy, Pradeep. *Thanjavur: A Cultural History*. New Delhi: Niyogi, 2010.

Chandhoke, Neera. *Rethinking Pluralism*. New Delhi: Sage, 2019.

Chandra, Aparna, Sital Kalantry, and William H. J. Hubbard. *Court on Trial*. New Delhi: Penguin Random House India, 2023.

Chandrachud, Abhinav. *Republic of Religion*. New Delhi: Penguin Viking, 2020.

Chandrachud, Abhinav. *These Seats Are Reserved*. New Delhi: Penguin, 2023.

Chatterjee, Chhanda. *The Partition of the Indian Subcontinent (1947) and Beyond: Uneasy Borders*. India: Routledge, 2023.

Chatterjee, Partha. *Empire and Nation*. New York: Columbia University Press, 2010.

Chatterji, Joya. *Bengal Divided*. Cambridge: Cambridge University Press, 1994.

Chatterji, Joya. *Shadows at Noon*. London: Penguin Viking, 2023.

Chattopadhyaya, B.D. *The Concept of Bharatvarsha and Other Essays*. India: Permanent Black, 2017.

Chaudhuri, Nirad C. *The Heart of India*. Mumbai: Jaico, 1966.

Chopra, P.N. [Ed]. *The Collected Works by Sardar Vallabhbhai Patel*. India: Konark Publishers, 2015.

Choudhary, Valmiki [Ed.]. *Dr. Rajendra Prasad: Correspondence and Select Documents, Volume 7*. India: Allied Publishers, 1987.

Clarke, Peter. *The Last Thousand Days of the British Empire*. London: Penguin, 2007.

Constituent Assembly of India. *Debates*. New Delhi: Government of India, 1946–50.

Copland, Ian. *India 1885–1947*. London: Longman, 2001.

Cordell, Karl & Wolff, Stefan [Eds]. *Routledge Handbook of Ethnic Conflict*. London: Routledge, 2016.

Crabtree, James. *The Billionaire Raj: A Journey through India's New Gilded Age*. India: Harper Collins, 2018.

Das, Durga, ed. *Sardar Patel's Correspondence*. Ahmedabad: Navajivan, 1974.

Dasgupta, Swapan. *Awakening Bharat Mata*. New Delhi: Penguin Random House India, 2018.

De, Rohit and Ornit Shani. *Assembling India's Constitution: A New Democratic History*. Cambridge: Cambridge University Press, 2025.

De, Rohit. *A People's Constitution*. Princeton, NJ: Princeton University Press, 2018.

Derrett, J. Duncan M. *Introduction to Modern Hindu Law*. UK: Oxford University Press, 1963.

Deshpande, Ashwini. *Affirmative Action in India*. India: Oxford University Press, 2013.

Devji, Faisal. *Muslim Zion*. Cambridge, MA: Harvard University Press, 2013.

Devji, Faisal. *The Impossible Indian*. Cambridge, MA: Harvard University Press, 2012.

Devji, Faisal. *Terrorist in Search of Humanity*. London: Hurst, 2019.

Dhulipala, Venkat. *Creating a New Medina*. Cambridge: Cambridge University Press, 2015.

Dobbin, Christine. *Basic Documents in the Development of Modern India and Pakistan, 1835-1947*. London & New York: Van Nostrand Reinhold, 1970.

Doniger, Wendy. *The Hindus: An Alternative History*. New Delhi: Penguin, 2010.

Dworkin, Ronald. *Freedom's Law*. Cambridge, MA: Harvard University Press, 1997.

Dwyer, Rachel. *Picture Abhi Baaki Hai: Bollywood as a Guide to Modern India*. India: Hachette, 2014.

Eaton, Richard M. *India in the Persianate Age*. Oakland: University of California Press, 2019.

Edney, Matthew H. *Mapping an Empire*. Chicago: University of Chicago Press, 1997.

Eickelman, Dale F., and James Piscatori. *Muslim Politics*. Princeton, NJ: Princeton University Press, 1996.

Frankopan, Peter. *The Silk Roads*. London: Bloomsbury, 2015.

French, Patrick. *India: A Portrait*. London: Penguin, 2011.

Fukuyama, Francis. *Liberalism and Its Discontents*. London: Profile Books, 2022.

Nandurkar, G.M. [Ed.]. *Sardar's Letters. Mostly Unknown*. India: Sardar Vallabh Bhai Patel Smarak Bhavan, 1982.

Galanter, Marc, Jayanth Krishnan and G. Larson [Ed]. *Religion and Personal Law in Secular India*. Indianna: Indiana University Press, 2001.

Galanter, Marc. *Law and Society in Modern India*. UK: Oxford University Press, 1989.

Gandhi, M.K. *Hind Swaraj*. Ahmedabad: Navajivan, 2009.

Gandhi, M.K. *The Collected Works of Mahatma Gandhi*. India: BJP Library, 2017.

Gellner, Ernest. *Nations and Nationalism*. Ithaca, NY: Cornell University Press, 1983.

Golwalkar, M.S. *Bunch of Thoughts*. India: Sahitya Sindhu Prakashan, 2020.

Gould, William. *Hindu Nationalism and the Language of Politics*. Cambridge: Cambridge University Press, 2004.

Habib, S. Irfan. *Indian Nationalism*. New Delhi: Aleph, 2017.

Hardy, Peter. *Historians of Medieval India*. London: Luzac, 1960.

Harun-or-Rashid. *Inside Bengal Politics 1936-1947*. Dhaka: The University Press Ltd., 2003.

Harun-or-Rashid. *The Foreshadowing of Bangladesh: Bengal Muslim League and Muslim Politics, 1906-1947*. Bangladesh: Asiatic Society of Bangladesh.

Hasan, Mushirul. *Legacy of a Divided Nation*. London: Hurst, 1997.

Hingorani, Anand [Ed]. *To the Hindu and Muslims*. India: Allahabad Law Journal Press, 1942.

Hodson, H.V. *The Great Divide*. Karachi: Oxford University Press, 1969.

Hough, Richard. *Mountbatten: Hero of Our Time*. UK: Weidenfeld & Nicolson, 1980.

Ignatieff, Michael. *Isaiah Berlin: A Life*. London: Vintage, 2000.

Iqbal, Javed. *Zinda Rood*. Lahore: Sang-e-Meel Publications, 2019.

Iqbal, Muhammad. *The Reconstruction of Religious Thought in Islam*. Stanford, CA: Stanford University Press, 1930.

Iyer, Mani Shankar. *Pakistan Papers*. New Delhi: UBS Publishers, 1994.

Jaffrelot, Christophe. *India's Silent Revolution*. New York: Columbia University Press, 2003.

Jalal, Ayesha. *The Sole Spokesman*. Cambridge: Cambridge University Press, 1985.

Jayal, Niraja Gopal. *Citizenship and Its Discontents*. Cambridge, MA: Harvard University Press, 2013.

Jennings, Ivor. *Problems of the New Commonwealth*. Durham, NC: Duke University Press, 1958.

Jha, D. N. *The Myth of the Holy Cow*. London: Verso, 2002.

Jha, Prem Shankar. *The Dismantling of India's Democracy: 1947–2025*. New Delhi: Speaking Tiger, 2025.

Joseph, Tony. *Early Indians*. New Delhi: Juggernaut, 2018.

Kakar, Katharina, and Sudhir Kakar. *The Indians: Portrait of a People*. New Delhi: Penguin, 2007.

Kapila, Shruti. *Violent Fraternity*. Princeton, NJ: Princeton University Press, 2021.

Kaplan, Robert D. *The Revenge of Geography: What the Map Tells Us About Coming Conflicts and the Battle Against Fate*. New York: Random House, 2017.

Kaviraj, Sudipta. *The Enchantment of Democracy and India*. Ranikhet: Permanent Black, 2011.

Kearney, Richard, and Melissa Fitzpatrick. *Radical Hospitality: From Thought to Action*. New York: Fordham University Press, 2021.

Khan, Yasmin. *The Great Partition*. New Haven: Yale University Press, 2007.

Khilnani, Sunil. *The Idea of India*. London: Penguin, 1997.

Khosla, Madhav. *India's Founding Moment*. Cambridge, MA: Harvard University Press, 2020.

Kirpal, Saurabh. *Who Is Equal: The Equality Code of the Constitution*. New Delhi: Penguin Random House India, 2024.

Kudaisya, Gyanesh. *A Republic in the Making: India in the 1950s*. Cambridge: Cambridge University Press, 2017.

Kumar, Radha. *Making Peace with Partition*. New Delhi: Penguin Random House India, 2005.

Lannoy, Richard. *The Speaking Tree: A Study of Indian Culture and Society*. New Delhi: Oxford University Press, 1999.

Lieven, Anatol. *Pakistan: A Hard Country*. London: Penguin, 2011.

Maddison, Angus. *The World Economy: A Millennial Perspective*. Paris: Organisation for Economic Co-operation and Development (OECD), 2001.

Madhusudan, Harsh, and Rajeev Mantri. *A New Idea of India: The Civilizational Republic*. New Delhi: Westland Publications, 2020.

Malviya, Amit, and Salman Khurshid. *The Citizenship Debate: CAA and NRC*. New Delhi: Rupa Publications, 2020.

Joshi, Manoj. *Understanding the India–China Border*. New Delhi: HarperCollins India, 2022.

Mansergh, Nicholas, ed. *The Transfer of Power 1942–47*. London: HMSO, 1970–83.

Marshall, T. H. *Citizenship and Social Class and Other Essays.* Cambridge: Cambridge University Press, 1950.

Masselos, Jim. *Indian Nationalism: A History*. New Delhi: Sterling Publishers, 2010.

Mehra, Girish N. *Nearer Heaven Than Earth*. New Delhi: Rupa Publications, 2007.

Mehta, Pratap Bhanu. "The Rise of Judicial Sovereignty." In *The Oxford Companion to Politics in India*, edited by Niraja Gopal Jayal and Pratap Bhanu Mehta. New Delhi: Oxford University Press, 2010.

Mehta, Uday, and Ram Puniyani, eds. *Secularism in India: Concept and Practice*. New Delhi: Kalpaz Publications, 2017.

Menon, N. R. Madhava, ed. *Nehru and Indian Constitutionalism*. New Delhi: Indus Source Books, 2015.

Menon, Nivedita. *Secularism as Misdirection: Critical Thought from the Global South*. Ranikhet: Permanent Black, 2023.

Menon, Shivshankar. *India and Asian Geopolitics: The Past, Present*. New Delhi: Penguin, 2021.

Menon, V. P. *The Integration of the Indian States*. Hyderabad: Orient BlackSwan, 2014.

Mill, James. *The History of British India*. London: Baldwin, Cradock and Joy, 1817.

Mishra, Atul. *The Sovereign Lives of India and Pakistan: Post-Partition Statehood in South Asia*. Oxford: Oxford University Press, 2021.

Misra, Maria. *Vishnu's Crowded Temple: India since the Great Rebellion*. London: Penguin, 2008.

Mody, Ashoka. *India Is Broken*. Stanford, CA: Stanford University Press, 2023.

Mookerji, Radhakumud. *Nationalism in Hindu Culture*. London: Theosophical Publishing House, 1921.

Moon, Penderel. *Divide and Quit*. London: Chatto & Windus, 1961.

Moorhouse, Geoffrey. *Calcutta: The City Revealed*. London: Penguin, 2000.

Morris-Jones, W. H. *Parliament in India*. London: Longmans, Green and Co., 1957.

Mosley, Leonard. *The Last Days of the British Raj*. London: Weidenfeld & Nicolson, 1961.

Mounk, Yascha. *The People vs. Democracy*. Cambridge, MA: Harvard University Press, 2018.

Muralidharan, Karthik. *Accelerating India's Development*. New Delhi: Penguin Viking, 2024.

Nair, Neeti. *Changing Homelands: Hindu Politics and the Partition of India*. Ranikhet: Permanent Black, 2011.

Nanda, B. R. *Three Statesmen: Gokhale, Gandhi and Nehru*. London: George Allen & Unwin, 1974.

Nandurkar, G. M., ed. *Sardar's Letters: Mostly Unknown*. Ahmedabad: Sardar Vallabhbhai Patel Smarak Bhavan, 1982.

Nandy, Ashis, and Rajeev Bhargava, eds. *Secularism and Its Critics: The Politics of Secularism and the Recovery of Religious Tolerance*. Delhi: Oxford University Press, 1998.

Naqvi, Saeed. *Being the Other: The Muslim in India*. New Delhi: Aleph Book Company, 2016.

Narayan, Swati. *Unequal: Why India Lags Behind Its Neighbours*. New Delhi: Context (Westland), 2023.

Natarajan, S. *A Century of Social Reform in India*. Bombay: Asia Publishing House, 1959.

Nayar, Kuldip. *Beyond the Lines: An Autobiography*. New Delhi: Lotus Collection, 2012.

Nehru, B.K. *Nice Guys Finish Second*. New Delhi: Penguin Books, 1997.

Nehru, Jawaharlal. *Selected Works of Jawaharlal Nehru*. Vol. 7. New Delhi: Jawaharlal Nehru Memorial Fund, 1948.

Nehru, Jawaharlal. *The Discovery of India*. New Delhi: Penguin, 2004.

Newbigin, Eleanor. *The Hindu Family and the Emergence of Modern India*. Cambridge: Cambridge University Press, 2013.

Nilakantan, R.S. *South vs North: India's Great Divide*. New Delhi: Juggernaut, 2022.

Noorani, A. G. *Jinnah and Tilak: Comrades in the Freedom Struggle*. Karachi: Oxford University Press, 2010.

Noorani, A. G. *The Destruction of Hyderabad*. New Delhi: Tulika Books, 2014.

Nussbaum, Martha C. *The Cosmopolitan Tradition*. Cambridge, MA: Harvard University Press, 2019.

Orsini, Francesca. *Before the Divide: Hindi and Urdu Literary Culture*. New Delhi: Orient BlackSwan, 2011.

Pai, Sudha, and Sajjan Kumar. *Maya, Modi, Azad: Dalit Politics in the Time of Hindutva*. New Delhi: HarperCollins India, 2023.

Pandey, Gyanendra. *Remembering Partition*. Cambridge: Cambridge University Press, 2001.

Pandey, Gyanendra. *The Construction of Communalism in Colonial North India*. Delhi: Oxford University Press, 1990.

Parliament of the United Kingdom. *House of Commons Debates (Indian Affairs)*. London, various years.

Patel, Aakar. *Our Hindu Rashtra*. New Delhi: Westland, 2020.

Patel, Vallabhbhai. *For a United India: Speeches of Sardar Patel, 1947–1950*. New Delhi: Publications Division, Ministry of Information and Broadcasting, 1967.

Paz, Octavio. *In Light of India*. New Delhi: Rupa & Co., 1998.

Piketty, Thomas. *Capital in the Twenty-First Century*. Cambridge, MA: Harvard University Press, 2014.

Pillai, Manu S. *Gods, Guns and Missionaries*. London: Penguin Random House, 2024.

Pollock, Sheldon. *The Language of the Gods in the World of Men*. Berkeley: University of California Press, 2006.

Prakash, Abhigyan. *From Lucknow to Lutyens: The Power and Plight of Uttar Pradesh*. New Delhi: HarperCollins India, 2022.

Puchner, Martin. *Culture: A New World History*. London: Bonnier Books, 2023.

Purushotham, Sunil. *From Raj to Republic*. Stanford, CA: Stanford University Press, 2021.

Quraishi, S.Y. *The Population Myth*. New Delhi: HarperCollins India, 2021.

Raghavan, Pallavi. *Animosity at Bay*. New Delhi: HarperCollins India, 2020.
Rao, B. Shiva. *The Framing of India's Constitution*. New Delhi: IIPA, 1968.
Richards, John F. *The Mughal Empire*. Cambridge: Cambridge University Press, 1993.
Roberts, Andrew. *Eminent Churchillians*. London: Weidenfeld & Nicolson, 1994.
Robinson, Francis. *Separatism among Indian Muslims*. Cambridge: Cambridge University Press, 1974.
Roy, Anupama. *Citizenship in India*. Oxford: Oxford University Press, 2016.
Rushdie, Salman. *Shame*. London: Jonathan Cape, 1983.
Muralidhar, S. *Incomplete Justice? The Supreme Court at 75*. New Delhi: Juggernaut, 2025.
Saiyid, M.H. *Quaid-i-Azam Muhammad Ali Jinnah: A Political Study*. Lahore: Ashraf, 1945.
Sarkar, Jadunath. *The Fall of the Mughal Empire*. Vol. 4. Calcutta: Orient Longman, 1950.
Sarkar, Tanika. *Hindu Wife, Hindu Nation*. Bloomington: Indiana University Press, 2001.
Savarkar, Vinayak Damodar. *Essentials of Hindutva*. Nagpur: Hindi Sahitya Sadan, 1923.
Savarkar, V. D. *Hindu Rashtra Darshan*. Pune: Laxman Ganesh Khare, 1949.
Schneider, Suzanne. *The Apocalypse and the End of History: Modern Jihad and the Crisis of Liberalism*. London: Verso, 2021.
Seervai, H. M. *Partition of India*. Bombay: Emmenem, 1990.
Seneca, Lucius Annaeus. *De Otio: Édition accompagnée de notes critiques et d'un commentaire explicatif*. London: Forgotten Books, 2018.
Sengupta, Arghya, Jinaly Dani, Kevin James, and Pranay Modi. *Hamīñ Ast? A Biography of Article 370*. New Delhi: Navi Books, 2022.
Sengupta, Arghya. *The Colonial Constitution*. London: HarperCollins, 2023.
Setalvad, M. C. *Builders of Modern India*. New Delhi: Publications Division, Ministry of Information and Broadcasting, 1968.
Shankar, V. *Selected Correspondence of Sardar Patel, 1945–50*. Vol. 1. Ahmedabad: Navajivan Publishing House, 2011.
Shapiro, Scott J. "The Federalist No. 51." In *Legality*. Cambridge, MA: Harvard University Press, 2013.
Sharma, Parvati. *Jahangir: An Intimate Portrait of a Great Mughal*. New Delhi: Juggernaut, 2020.
Singer, Peter. *Animal Liberation Now*. London: Bodley Head, 2023.
Singh, Pritam, and Shinder S. Thandi. *Punjabi Identity in a Global Context*. New Delhi: Oxford University Press, 1999.

Singh, Upinder. *Political Violence in Ancient India*. Cambridge, MA: Harvard University Press, 2017.

Singh, Upinder. *The Idea of Ancient India: Essays on Religion, Politics, and Archaeology*. New Delhi: Penguin, 2023.

Smith, Adam. *An Inquiry into the Nature and Causes of the Wealth of Nations*. New Delhi: OM Books International, 2021.

Smith, Donald Eugene. *India as a Secular State*. Princeton, NJ: Princeton University Press, 1963.

Sneddon, Christopher. *Kashmir: The Unwritten History*. London: HarperCollins, 2011.

Srinivas, M. N. *Social Change in Modern India*. New Delhi: Allied Publishers, 1966.

Srinivasan, T. N., ed. *The Future of Secularism*. Oxford: Oxford University Press, 2007.

Stanley, Jason. *Erasing History: How Fascists Rewrite the Past to Control the Future*. London: Footnote Press, 2024.

Steiner, George. *Errata: An Examined Life*. London: Weidenfeld & Nicolson, 1997.

Subrahmanyam, Sanjay. *Is Indian Civilisation a Myth?*. Ranikhet: Permanent Black, 2013.

Subramanian, Lakshmi. *India Before Ambanis*. New Delhi: Penguin, 2025.

Sumption, Jonathan. *Trials of the State: Law and the Decline of Politics*. London: Profile Books, 2019.

Talbot, Ian. *Khizr Tiwana, the Punjab Unionist Party and the Partition of India*. New Delhi: Routledge, 2013.

Tan, Tai Yong, and Gyanesh Kudaisya. *The Aftermath of Partition in South Asia*. New Delhi: Routledge, 2000.

Teltumbde, Anand, and Suraj Yengde, eds. *The Radical in Ambedkar: Critical Reflections*. New Delhi: Allen Lane, 2018.

Thapar, Romila. *On Citizenship*. New Delhi: Aleph, 2021.

Tharoor, Shashi. *Ambedkar: A Life*. New Delhi: Aleph Book Company, 2023.

Tharoor, Shashi. *An Era of Darkness: The British Empire in India*. New Delhi: Aleph Book Company, 2016.

Thucydides. *History of the Peloponnesian War*. London: Penguin Classics, 2003.

Tillin, Louise. *Indian Federalism*. Oxford: Oxford University Press, 2019.

Tomlinson, B. R. *The Indian National Congress and the Raj*. London: Macmillan, 1976.

Tripathi, Amales. *The Fourth Phase (1943–1947)*. New Delhi: Oxford University Press, 2014.

Tudor, Maya. *The Promise of Power*. Cambridge: Cambridge University Press, 2013.

Tumbe, Chinmay. The Age of Pandemics, 1817–1920: How They Shaped India and the World. New Delhi: HarperCollins India, 2020.

Tushnet, Mark, and Madhav Khosla, eds. Unstable Constitutionalism: Law and Politics in South Asia. Cambridge: Cambridge University Press, 2015.

Vidal, Gore. The Selected Essays of Gore Vidal. New York: Doubleday, 2008.

Vivekananda, Swami. Swami Vivekananda's Speeches and Writings. Vol. 5. Kolkata: Udbodhan Karyalaya, 1968.

von Tunzelmann, Alex. Indian Summer: The Secret History of the End of an Empire. London: Simon & Schuster, 2007.

White-Spunner, Barney. Partition: The Story of Indian Independence and the Creation of Pakistan in 1947. London: Simon & Schuster, 2018.

Wolf, Martin. The Crisis of Democratic Capitalism. New York: Penguin Press, 2023.

Wolpert, Stanley. *Nehru: A Tryst with Destiny*. Oxford: Oxford University Press, 1996.

Zubrzycki, John. *Dethroned*. London: Hurst, 2023.

Zutshi, Chitralekha. *Kashmir*. Cambridge: Cambridge University Press, 2019.

INDEX